AF580860

Digital Media and Democratic Futures

DEMOCRACY, CITIZENSHIP, AND CONSTITUTIONALISM

Rogers M. Smith and Mary L. Dudziak, Series Editors

Digital Media and Democratic Futures

Edited by

Michael X. Delli Carpini

UNIVERSITY OF PENNSYLVANIA PRESS

PHILADELPHIA

Published by
University of Pennsylvania Press
Philadelphia, Pennsylvania 19104-4112
www.upenn.edu/pennpress

Printed in the United States of America on acid-free paper

10 9 8 7 6 5 4 3 2 1

Library of Congress Cataloging-in-Publication Data

Names: Delli Carpini, Michael X., editor.
Title: Digital media and democratic futures / edited by Michael X. Delli Carpini. Other titles: Democracy, citizenship, and constitutionalism.
Description: 1st edition. | Philadelphia : University of Pennsylvania Press, [2019] | Series: Democracy, Citizenship, and Constitutionalism | Includes bibliographical references and index.
Identifiers: LCCN 2018034564 | ISBN 978-0-8122-5116-6 (hardcover : alk. paper)
Subjects: LCSH: Communication in politics—United States—21st century. | Digital media—Political aspects—United States—21st century. | Communication—Political aspects—United States—21st century. | Democracy—United States—21st century.
Classification: LCC P95.82.U6 D54 2019 | DDC 320.973—dc23
LC record available at https://lccn.loc.gov/2018034564

CONTENTS

Introduction: Digital Media and the Future(s) of Democracy

Michael X. Delli Carpini

On January 27, 2017 newly elected U.S. president Donald Trump signed Executive Order 13769, placing limits on the number of refugees admitted into the United States, suspending entry of aliens from seven predominantly Muslim nations, and indefinitely barring Syrian refugees from entering the country. Within minutes of its announcement, individuals and groups opposed to what was being called a "Muslim ban" took to social media, resulting in large and spontaneous demonstrations at airports and in cities around the globe. In the days that followed, President Trump defended his decision and criticized those challenging it through a series of late-night tweets, while White House representatives scrambled to explain the chaotically implemented policy on more traditional news outlets. Numerous legal challenges resulted in a federal district judge issuing a temporary restraining order on major parts of the executive order, a ruling unanimously upheld two days later by a three-judge panel of the United States Court of Appeals for the Ninth Circuit.

The furor over immigration was only one of numerous conflicts during the first several weeks of Trump's presidency. Some involved seemingly trivial matters such as the size of the crowd and the weather at his inauguration, the decision by the Nordstrom department store chain to drop the clothing line produced by his daughter Ivanka's company, and his biting reactions to the poor ratings of his *Celebrity Apprentice* replacement (Arnold Schwarzenegger). There were also more substantive issues such as unsubstantiated claims by the president that he lost the popular vote due to voter fraud; ethical and substantive concerns about his nominees to cabinet posts (which prompted the eventual resignation of his national security advisor); executive orders and actions regarding financial, environmental, ethics, health care, and immigration regulations; dueling accusations between the current and former presidents regarding campaign fraud related to Russian interference in the presidential election; and a drumbeat of attacks on the news media, which Trump and his chief strategist (Steve Bannon) labeled "fake news" and "the enemy of the people." All were hotly debated and contested in the news, on talk shows, on the streets, and, most relevant to this volume, through social media.

Ideological and partisan disagreements are not new, and the more heightened and divisive variant that characterizes our current era predates the Trump presidency. Nonetheless, the extent to which the state of contemporary politics represents an existential threat to the theory and practice of constitutional democracy is more palpable than at any point since the Watergate era. Adding to this unease is the sense that verifiable facts and logical reasoning as the basis for political discourse and decision making are being replaced by an acceptance of "alternative facts" and a reliance on unfettered emotions. Equally concerning is that similar populist unravelings of democratic institutions and norms appear to be occurring across the globe.

The reasons for this unease and the events behind them are complex. Clearly, substantive issues such as growing economic inequality and insecurity, globalization, destabilization in the Middle East and the resulting European refugee crisis, and ongoing concerns over terrorism are playing a role. So too is the culmination of a steady increase in public distrust of the elite institutions of government, big business, and the media. But if real-world issues are the firewood of our current state, and public mistrust the kindling, the radically changed information environment brought about by social media and other forms of digital information and communications technologies (ICTs) are increasingly identified as the match that set fire to this combustible mix.

There is another side to this story, however. The digital revolution has also been seen as a potential boon to the practice of democracy in various, evolving forms. Examples abound: the 2008 Obama campaign's use of ICTs to energize and mobilize new voters; the important role of social media in the early days of the Arab Spring, and as a catalyst for the Occupy Wall Street movement, both in 2011; the 2013 online campaign that led to the Black Lives Matter movement; the growing and more impactful role of citizen journalists as well as more "random acts of journalism"; the use of computational science methods, large data sets, and visualization technologies to create new forms of investigative journalism; the improvement of government services through the use of more interactive and responsive websites; and experiments in crowdsourcing to discuss and sometimes develop public policy. Indeed, even as critics raised concerns about the role of digital technologies in the 2016 presidential campaign and the early days of the Trump presidency, one must also note the democratic elements of not only Trump's campaign (which gave voice to large swaths of the American public) but also that of Bernie Sanders, the unlikely challenger to Hillary Clinton. Digital technologies have been involved in spreading "fake news" and "alternative facts" but also in aiding efforts to counter them; in fueling concerns about the loss of privacy but also in providing citizens with more targeted, useful, and useable information precisely because of this loss; in creating echo chambers in which like-minded people talk only to themselves but also in allowing people to engage each other across temporal, geographic, political, and cultural boundaries (Delli Carpini 2018).

This tension between the democratic and undemocratic potentials of the digital media environment is not new, and interest in it is not limited to pundits and practitioners. The role of social media and other forms of digital ICTs in political development and disruption has been the subject of scholarly speculation and empirical research for decades. The authors of this body of work can be seen as initially falling into one of three camps: those who argued or found that the digital information environment had the potential to democratize politics in new and encouraging ways (e.g., Benkler 2006); those who argued or found that it represented a threat to well-functioning democracies (e.g., Sunstein 2001); and those who argued or found that it was essentially "old wine in new bottles," with little chance of playing a significant new role in how politics fundamentally operated (e.g., Bimber and Davis 2003). As the new information environment evolved, as new examples emerged, and as our theorizing, data, and research methods expanded and improved, these initial camps have blurred; the central question has shifted (perhaps inevitably) from whether the digital information environment is good or bad for democratic politics to how and in what contexts *specific* attributes of this environment are having an influence on *specific* theories and practices of democracy, citizenship, and constitutionalism (Williams and Delli Carpini 2011). It is only through the careful analysis of specific, contextualized examples that we can begin to build a more comprehensive understanding of digital media's still evolving role in democratic theory and practice.

Emerging out of a yearlong set of workshops and a closing conference held at the University of Pennsylvania during the 2015–2016 academic year, this volume is an effort to provide some of these building blocks. Part I, "Designing Digital Democracies," explores the crucial importance—for both scholars and practitioners—of understanding how the structure of digital ICTs can enhance or inhibit their effectiveness in achieving desired sociopolitical outcomes. In Chapter 1 Rena Bivens examines the ways in which nonprofit organizations (NPOs) use social media as a tool for achieving their goals. At the core of her argument is that the potential impact of social media is not simply or centrally in its use, but rather in "the design of the social media platforms themselves," and that ultimately, "Design decisions made by platform owners and computer programmers impact the everyday work of NPOs, and the values that motivate those design decisions become embedded in the technology itself." Focusing on "antiviolence" NPOs and their use of Facebook, Bivens unpacks these often invisible design decisions and how they, along with constraints introduced by what she calls the "nonprofit industrial complex," shape the NPOs' rules of engagement with their publics. She concludes that this combination severely limits the potential of social media to serve as a critical tool for social change. But she also notes that the embedded logics of mainstream social media platforms and of the mainstream nonprofit system are not immutable, but rather the result of "design politics." This opens the door to the possibility of making more visible the politics underlying design decisions, of designing platforms that are more effectively "oriented toward social justice," and thus of moving "toward a material-discursive construction of social change work that refuses to be co-opted."

In Chapter 2 Daniel Kreiss provides what might be thought of as an example of how collective action can be designed with the very attributes Bivens points to in her conclusion. Focusing on Bernie Sanders's surprising though ultimately unsuccessful bid for the U.S. Democratic Party's nomination for president, Kreiss shows how his campaign was able to combine "symbolic resources from the civil *sphere*," Sanders's unique "position in a *field* of democratic candidates," and "*networks* of campaign staffers with particular sets of skills, and technologies with particular affordances" to digitally mobilize large numbers of (typically disengaged) supporters. This combination of spheres, fields, and networks, Kreiss argues, constitutes the "digital opportunity structure" that must be understood and exploited by any contemporary effort at collective political action. Further, he uses this case study "to advance the sociological concept of 'political opportunity structure' more broadly," and to "more systematically theorize and integrate" what he argues are "the foundational elements of social life: spheres of cultural meaning that are institutionally regulated, fields of relational symbolic and social activity, and networks of social and technological relations that cross, shape, and change both spheres and fields over time."

While using different language and focusing on yet a different dimension of democratic engagement, Chapter 3, authored by Thomas Elliott and Jennifer Earl, can be seen as a synthesis of Biven's focus on platform design and Kreiss's on digital opportunity structures. In this chapter Elliott and Earl examine both the "supply" and "demand" sides for young people's online civic engagement. Their starting points are the "general sense among many scholars and activists that today's young people are not as engaged in or as integral to movements as they once were," and their own working premise that the reasons for this problem start not with young people themselves, but with the failure of social movements to reach out effectively to them. In short, the relative dearth of youth engagement in social movements is driven not by the demand side but by the supply side of the equation. To examine the supply side, Elliott and Earl use a unique and original database of systematically coded content from 363 carefully selected and arguably representative social movement "web spaces" that, combined, address twenty core sociopolitical issues and refer to over 1,400 specific protest actions. They then analyze this data by focusing on the presence or absence of three "youth-facing" design elements: content relevant to youth; efforts to specifically target or address young people; and describing, hosting, or linking to specific protest actions that explicitly encourage youth to participate. To examine the demand side, they draw on data from "a nationally representative survey of 2,920 youth in which respondents were asked questions about their engagement with politics, online digital media, and civic and volunteer programs." The results of these analyses lead to several important conclusions: that "youth are not as disengaged as some have worried"; that this engagement is occurring "despite a lack of significant targeting and tailoring" by social movements in their online presences; that disengagement from particular types of protest activity "may be due to a lack of opportunity for youth to participate"; and that ultimately, young people's levels of engagement could be even greater "if movements more directly attempt to recruit and involve youth" through the design of their web spaces.

While issues of "design" remain important to the three chapters in Part II, "Rethinking Expertise in Digital Democracies," what ties them together is the ways in which the digital media environment can influence power relationships between political institutions, political elites, and citizens, altering our notions of knowledge producers and consumers. In Chapter 4 Beth Noveck makes the case for "tapping into the collective intelligence of our communities," and "drawing power from the participation of the many rather than the participation of the few" through the development of "participatory bureaucracy." Her reasons for this call are threefold. First, while the tension between democracy and professional expertise is not new, global public trust in the traditional institutions of government is at an all-time low, and responsible in part for the populist turns evidenced in events such as Brexit and the unexpected U.S. presidential election victory of Donald Trump. This mistrust, while often misplaced and exploited, is due at least in part to legitimate concerns about the limits of professional expertise and of the opaque, exclusionary, and often self-interested nature of the policy-making process. Second, Noveck argues that collectively, the public "possesses extraordinary know-how, skills, experience, and passions . . . to participate in solving problems," and that this citizen expertise "is widely distributed in society" and if tapped, can be of great value to the policy-making process. And third, she argues that the current digital environment provides new opportunities for increasing public expertise, identifying these public experts, and allowing "more members of the public to participate actively in problem solving and governing" through various forms of "smarter crowdsourcing." Bolstering her arguments with a range of case studies, Noveck both demonstrates the democratic potential of technology in the service of tapping public expertise and provides a roadmap for how this potential might be better integrated into democratic institutions in the future.

Crowdsourcing also plays a prominent role in Kelly Gates's Chapter 5, though in this case it is used not by government institutions but by journalistic ones. The backdrop for Gates's analysis is the emergence of police killings of unarmed black men as a political issue, sparked in part by the killings of Eric Garner and Michael Brown in the summer of 2014. Gates notes the importance of mobile cameras (used by both citizens and police forces) in this debate, but her central focus is on the "absence of official data on police killings," the resulting difficulty in comparing the visual record with "hard data" on the prevalence of such shootings, and the attempt on the part of "journalists and other concerned actors" to resolve the problem of missing data through online crowdsourcing initiatives. She then provides a detailed analysis and critique of one such initiative: "a two-year effort by a team at the *Guardian* newspaper to make the absent data present, leveraging what they called 'verified crowdsourcing' to get 'undone science done.'" Her analysis highlights how both the promise and the limitations of such projects are determined by the way news organizations conceptualize the role of citizens in the production of data and/or news, and how these conceptualizations are implemented through the specific design and implementation of crowdsourcing platforms. She concludes that, while flawed in several ways, crowdsourcing efforts such as the *Guardian*'s represent "one important model for the future of journalism as a form of public knowledge that is especially critical as modern states move away from democratic ideals and functions."

In Chapter 6 Lisa Poggiali explores the "politics of expertise" as they play out through the lens of the Muhimu Mapping Project (MMP), a nongovernmental organization's effort to produce "the first publicly circulating map of any kind to acknowledge" the existence of an invisible and illegal settlement in Nairobi, Kenya. On the "digital peripheries" of Kenya's growing technology sector known as "Silicon Savannah," Poggiali explores the limitations inherent in ICT4D (information and communication technologies for development) efforts that pitted "Kenya's ethnically divisive history against its future modernity, fashioning 'digital citizenship' as an expression of the latter." Through extensive ethnographic research, she documents that while "MMP helped to produce Nairobi's urban poor as technical experts" through their digital mapping project, "the mapmakers' sociopolitical status as slum dwellers colored the production and reception of the information they produced." As a result, the initiative ultimately "undermined the mappers' ability to utilize this expertise, thus reinforcing the social and political exclusion the mappers were attempting to overcome." She concludes that "future scholarship on technologies in postcolonial contexts should focus not only on how new media technologies generate novel social relations or economic opportunities 'at the margins' . . . but also how they produce new explanatory models that both precipitate and conceal relations of inequality," and that "we must analyze new media technologies as both potential vectors of sociopolitical recognition and battlegrounds on which the urban poor's claims to inclusion are affirmed or ignored, heeded or disregarded."

Part III, "Digital Media and Public Voices," continues Part II's focus on the changing power relationships between political institutions, political elites, and citizens, though here the emphasis shifts from "expertise" to other ways in which citizens can collectively wield influence. In Chapter 7, Daniela Stockmann and Ting Luo address "the growing importance of online political discussion in nondemocratic contexts" and the questions it raises "about the nature and political consequences of authoritarian deliberation"—deliberation that occurs in nations where censorship and/or surveillance is common. Drawing on data from 92 in-depth interviews as well as survey results from a random sample of 1,005 Chinese Internet users, Stockmann and Luo find that "lurkers," who greatly outnumber those who actually participate in online discussions, "are more concerned about privacy, not necessarily out of concern about censorship but more out of concern about how their close social networks may perceive them." Lurkers also tend to "follow online discourse closely as they use social media to learn about politics. Therefore, this group of people tends to be composed of people who are already engaged in politics." Contrasted to this are "discussants," who "voice their views—not because of the information they gather from the discussion, but because of their need for recognition." As a result, "they may not always present their views honestly, as they are more sensitive to response bias, but they are also less concerned about privacy and therefore likely to express opinions." To the extent that they do have privacy concerns, "discussants seem to find ways to hide in cyberspace other than lurking—for example, by using fake accounts online." Several implications emerge from these findings. Even in totalitarian regimes, social media plays a role in allowing "people who were otherwise likely to be excluded from public discourse to voice their opinions," providing a platform for "people who are politically less engaged, thus fostering political engagement." But this somewhat promising finding is countered by the fact that biases in who express opinions online and who do not, coupled with Chinese officials' and journalists' use of the Internet "as a means to learn about citizen preferences," can mean that while social media is likely to have a strong impact on setting the agenda for public discourse in China, it is "unlikely to reflect public opinion on the issues it raises." In addition, this biased understanding of public opinion "may become more pronounced as the state intervenes more directly in online discussion by actively censoring content."

The theme of the democratic utility of digital media in authoritarian regimes continues in the contribution by Jennifer Pan (Chapter 8), albeit in ways that challenge rather than simply inform political elites. In this chapter Pan examines the potential for the Internet and online social media platforms to "disrupt the ability of authoritarian regimes to censor, and ultimately, to maintain political power" by improving "coordination in collective action against authoritarian regimes and increas[ing] the reliability of information, especially information that is not accommodating toward the regime." She does so by assessing whether or not the largely successful "technical strategies of censoring social media employed by China are likely to be replicated by other countries," including but not limited to ostensibly "authoritarian regimes." Through a mix of quantitative and qualitative analyses, she shows that "China's success in social media censorship is inexorably tied to the dominance of domestic companies" that allows the government to "quickly and reliably eliminate content deemed to be inappropriate, which in turn decreases the coordination potential of social media and covertly diminishes the reliability of information." Replicating these conditions in other authoritarian (as well as democratic) regimes would be difficult, since most are "dominated by multinational firms (e.g., Facebook, YouTube, Twitter), which prevents these regimes from engaging effectively in censorship through content removal" and forces them to depend on less effective methods such as content blocking. Pan further argues that the ability of domestic firms to dominate China's social media market was the result of timing, in that their market penetration predated that of foreign companies. There is little evidence that once U.S. companies have established a strong foothold in other authoritarian regimes this dominance can be reversed through either the development of domestic social media platforms or the importing of Chinese ones. This is true even when these regimes engage in long-term content blocking (i.e., "de facto protectionism"). Taken as a whole, Pan's findings suggest that China's success at controlling content and thus limiting the democratic potential of digital media may be an outlier. And even in China, the negative impact of content control on domestic social media companies' profits may lead to pressure to ease such control. But not unlike the conclusions reached by Stockmann and Luo, these more cautiously optimistic possibilities are tempered by the fact that regimes "may choose to use other strategies, such as real-world repression, to impose control over social media," as appears to be the case in Russia.

The utility of digital media in efforts to challenge the state is an issue that goes beyond authoritarian regimes. In Chapter 9, Deen Freelon explores how the use of digital tools and technologies can, in the right context, influence the power of social movements in the United States. Central to Freelon's approach is the argument that to understand the impact of social media, researchers must go beyond the use of ICTs by movements themselves, to include the "broader set of actors that interact with one another on the issue." "Most popular social media platforms," he notes, "are open enough that movement actors cannot isolate themselves from commentary and criticism from individuals outside the movement. Such outside actors and interests can provide insight into a social movement's capacity to achieve its goals. This capacity is an important type of power." Using Black Lives Matter as his case study, Charles Tilly's concept of WUNC (worthiness, unity, numbers, commitment) as his measure of a social movement's strength, and tweets about police shootings of unarmed black people as his data, Freelon demonstrates that "the digital manifestations of three of WUNC's four elements can be measured quantitatively" and "that these measures constitute consequential forms of social media power." He also finds that—at least in the case of Black Lives Matter—social movements have the power to dominate the larger social media conversations on the issue of relevance, though this "dominance is not consistent in magnitude across metrics or across time." These shifts in the circulation of online power appear to be driven by major events of relevance, and by responses to these events by the movement, its critics, and other political actors.

"Regulating Digital Democracies," the fourth and final part of this volume, returns to issues of structure and design, albeit as it relates to the state more than to technology. In Chapter 10 Helen Nissenbaum addresses the issue of privacy and privacy regulation in the era of data science. She dissects an argument that is "gathering momentum in the academy, information industries, and public policy"—that in an era in which policy designed to restrict information collection is increasingly untenable, "attention should focus instead on how information is used." Nissenbaum unpacks the numerous "conceptual ambiguities" found in key terms such as *privacy*, *collection*, and *use*, demonstrating how greater definitional clarity reshapes debates over what she labels *big data exceptionalism* (BDE). She then interrogates and challenges the descriptive and the normative arguments underpinning the very notion of BDE—that is, its assumptions that regulating data collection is technically, institutionally, or ethically "impossible," and/or that the benefits derived from BDEs would be lost by regulating collection and its potential harms can be controlled by regulating use. The conclusion Nissenbaum arrives at from this careful analysis is that "the push to regulate use instead of collection is problematic and possibly even dangerous." What is needed, at a minimum, is to "strengthen efforts to regulate both collection and use," and "regulate collection and use along contextual lines, not lines of data ownership," in the hope of increasing the chances that data will "serve the public interest, not merely at the discretion of the data holder (i.e., not as "data philanthropy") but at the determination of the people's will."

Central to Nissenbaum's argument is her notion of "conceptual integrity"—that is, that "privacy is about the appropriate flow of personal information, not control or secrecy." In Chapter 11, Philip Howard picks up this notion of information flow by exploring the democratic peril and promise of the "Internet of Things" (IoT), provocatively suggesting how it might come to "rival a constitution as the primary structure of political life." Underlying Howard's argument is a simple but important observation—that "governance systems involve not just governments; they appear whenever a powerful actor can set rules and restrictions on people's behavior"—and an assumption—that the IoT, "made up of billions of devices with small sensors . . . will generate perfect behavioral data without giving citizens the right to opt out of data collection." The behavioral data produced by this ubiquitous and invisible "sensory network" will, Howard argues, replace the traditional means of political representation and public voice in democratic societies. In short, the IoT will come to "encapsulate our political lives, communicate our political values, and constitute our political identities." But will this new form of representation threaten or enhance democratic politics and the public will? The answer lies in part with "the algorithms, terms of service, and interoperability protocols" that make the IoT operate. These "scripts" are akin to political constitutions, which are, after all, "collections of codified traditions and conventions that provide structure for political life." Given that the IoT "will be the greatest surveillance network ever established," it is incumbent on us "to settle on some basic forms of representation for the coming world of networked devices"—that is, to establish a "new constitution, one written for the public life and information infrastructure we are developing."

> Good constitutions offer the terms under which we citizens agree to submit to an authority that is legitimate and not abusive. We need to *consent* to the IoT, because we will be surrendering our privacy for good. We will be submitting ourselves to data mining and behavioral analysis orders of magnitude more invasive, comprehensive, and valuable than we live with now. If we surrender our privacy to the IoT, we should get some protections and rights in exchange. Thus, if data is valuable and the primary value of the IoT, we need a social contract

> that turns on the notion that if we give up data, it must generate some public good. Data that flows from the IoT must concurrently generate value for innovative entrepreneurs and support civic values.

Individually, each of the chapters in this volume provides a nuanced, theoretically rich, empirically grounded, and substantively informative example of the complex relationships between digital media and democracy. Collectively, they provide a number of important insights: that there is no one way for scholars to study these relationships; that digital information and communication technologies have the potential to either enhance or encumber democratic practice; that their impact is context dependent, with multiple contingencies; that these contexts and contingencies can vary not only by technology or regime, but by the specific social, cultural, economic, and political rules and norms that can inhibit or encourage democratic forms of engagement.

Finally, these chapters collectively remind us that just as the question "What is the impact of digital media on democracy?" cannot be answered with a simple "good" or "bad," "promising" or "perilous," neither can the question, "What is the future of democracy in the digital age?" Democracy is not an either-or proposition. "More" or "less" hits closer to the mark, but even this misses the numerous ways in which models of democracy can vary (across polities and within them); the myriad acts that can constitute smaller but crucial democratic moments (even in otherwise nondemocratic or less democratic systems); and the numerous actors (from the private, public, and governmental sectors) that play a role in these micro-, meso-, and meta-level processes (see, e.g., Pateman 1970; Mansbridge 1983; Held 2006; Dahl 2015).

The thread connecting these democratic moments and models—to each other and to digital media—is that they individually and collectively influence citizens' potential to have an authoritative voice in the allocation of a community's goods, services, and values (Easton 1965). This voice can be codified in constitutions and laws, but also in codes and algorithms, as made clear in the chapters by Howard, Nissenbaum, and Bivens. It can be facilitated by the state and its actors (as the chapters by Kreiss and Noveck point out), but it also can be inhibited (as in the case presented by Gates), misrepresented (e.g., Stockmann and Luo), or purposively stifled (e.g., Pan) by the state. It can emerge, albeit often imperfectly, from the targeted efforts of nongovernmental organizations (e.g., Elliott and Earl), private-public partnerships (e.g., Poggiali; Gates), and grassroots movements (e.g., Freelon), as well as from the appropriation of technologies intended for other purposes (e.g., as in Stockmann and Luo; Poggiali; Pan). It can involve behaviors as diverse as campaigning (e.g., Kreiss), data gathering (e.g., Gates), protesting (e.g., Freelon; Elliott and Earl), and even map making (Poggiali), and people as diverse as young adults in the United States (Elliott and Earl), programmers in Nairobi (Poggiali), and Internet "lurkers" in China (Stockmann and Luo). And it can be limited—intentionally or not—in ostensibly democratic regimes (e.g., Elliott and Earl; Gates; Nissenbaum) and at least partially nourished—again, intentionally or not—in nondemocratic ones (e.g., Stockmann and Luo; Pan).

In short, the chapters in this volume show us that just as there are multiple, inconsistent, and path-dependent ways in which digital information and communication technologies can influence democratic norms, behaviors, and institutions, *how* they do so, and the democratic norms, behaviors, and institutions that are enhanced, constructed, or imperiled by them, are equally multiple, inconsistent, and path-dependent. Like that of information and communication technologies of the past (though perhaps more dramatically so), the democratic potential of digital media is matched only by its equally present potential to do harm. Ultimately, how digital media is used, what roles it plays in reconceptualizing twenty-first-century democratic practice and democratic systems, depends on context-specific political choices and political will. In short, the chapters in this volume tell us that there is no single future of democracy in the digital information environment—there are only futures.

References

Benkler, Yochai. 2006. *The Wealth of Networks: How Social Production Transforms Markets and Freedom*. New Haven, Conn.: Yale University Press.

Bimber, Bruce, and Richard Davis. 2003. *Campaigning Online: The Internet in US Elections*. New York: Oxford University Press.

Dahl, Robert. 2015. *On Democracy*. 2nd ed. New Haven, Conn.: Yale University Press.

Delli Carpini, Michael X. 2018. "Alternative Facts: Donald Trump and the Emergence of a New U.S. Media Regime." In *Trump and the Media*, edited by Pablo Boczkowski and Zizi Papacharissi, 17–24. Cambridge, Mass.: MIT Press.

Easton, David. 1965. *A Framework for Political Analysis*. Englewood Cliffs, N.J.: Prentice-Hall.

Held, David. 2006. *Models of Democracy*. 3rd ed. Cambridge, U.K.: Polity Press.

Mansbridge, Jane. 1983. *Beyond Adversary Democracy.* New York: Basic Books.

Pateman, Carole. 1970. *Participation and Democratic Theory.* Cambridge, U.K.: Cambridge University Press.

Sunstein, Cass R. 2001. *Republic.com.* Princeton, N.J.: Princeton University Press.

Williams, Bruce, and Michael X. Delli Carpini. 2011. *After Broadcast News: Media Regimes, Democracy, and the New Information Environment.* Cambridge, U.K.: Cambridge University Press.

PART I

Designing Digital Democracies

CHAPTER 1

Programming the Rules of Engagement: Social Media Design and the Nonprofit System

Rena Bivens

Social Media for Social Change?

A rising crop of social media managers, coaches, and self-proclaimed gurus enthusiastically point to social media as a vital platform for a wide range of marketing and public relations activities. These voices add another layer on top of advocates who once focused on the promise of printing technologies, radio, television, online discussion groups, email, and websites. In many ways, then, social media offers another tool in the contemporary marketing toolbox. Social media may recycle the logics of "old" media in their design (van Dijck and Poell 2013), but it also appears to offer new affordances, such as the ability to reach publics old and new—including journalists, politicians, and previously unknown stakeholders (Sedereviciute and Valentini 2011). Perhaps unsurprisingly, given their personal investment in the debate, social media managers and coaches regularly place social media on a pedestal, imbuing these platforms with extraordinary powers. Many have set their sights on the nonprofit sector in particular, arguing that social media is a critical tool for social change (Mansfield 2012; Kanter and Fine 2010; Diaz-Ortiz 2011).

Of course there are also open critics of nonprofit social media use. For instance: "It's time to step away from the belief that charities have to be on social media and need to invest in it. It's not the best marketing tool we have" (Collins 2016). Instead, the advice is to activate dormant email lists, build effective website content, advertise on search results, and focus on search engine optimization. Social media managers are quick to defend their territory, typically arguing that critics are simply not using it effectively and that, regardless, social media cannot be ignored since it is "the status quo" and has "revolutionized the very way in which humans interact with each other" (Campbell 2016). Yet, as Feenberg (2016, 25) notes, "We have had enough experience with [the Internet] by now to realize that it is a mixed phenomenon unlikely to fulfil the promise of democratic transformation it inspired in the early years." And according to Lim (2013, 638), "Social media should not be perceived as a causal agent having a pivotal role in promoting social change or advancing democracy." Instead, "societal contexts and arrangements around technology are key to its impact on politics" (638).

To investigate the potential for nonprofit organizations (NPOs) to use social media for social change, I argue that we must interrogate the design of the social media platforms themselves—not simply the ways in which NPOs use the platforms. Design decisions made by platform owners and computer programmers impact the everyday work of NPOs, and the values that motivate those design decisions become embedded in the technology itself. Platforms mediate communication and, as such, the design of their technological architecture matters in a very material sense. Yet, much of the scholarly literature on nonprofit communication begins with an unexamined assumption that online platforms hold great potential for the work of nonprofit organizations, and often concludes that NPOs should do better (Lovejoy et al. 2012; Waters et al. 2009; Muralidharan et al. 2011; Briones et al. 2011; Curtis et al. 2010; Echenberg 2010; Waters and Jones 2011; Zorn et al. 2012). NPOs are repeatedly criticized for either underutilizing social media or missing opportunities while attempting to engage with online networks of stakeholders (Bortree and Seltzer 2009; Waters et al. 2009; Lovejoy et al. 2012).

These critiques stem from a user-centric approach that positions the potential of social media as an a priori benchmark against which the actual use of social media is judged. As a consequence, the affordances (or opportunities) ascribed to social media are not directly assessed. Instead, social media merely offers affordances that ought to be capitalized on. For example, if NPOs were to follow Bortree and Seltzer's conclusions that "advocacy organizations should post frequently to their own profile [in ways that] will serve to stimulate discussion" (2009, 318–19), they would do so without contending with the programmed limits of these platforms. The potential for stimulating discussion is tied to algorithms that determine how content propagates through the network. These algorithms are programmed into social media software and directly impact how many users and which users will see posted content.

It is these sorts of design decisions and the material rules of engagement they engender that I investigate when considering whether social media is a critical tool for social change. The analysis presented in this chapter draws from a larger project that explores the design of Facebook and Twitter (the two most popular social media platforms used by NPOs) and how and why antiviolence NPOs use these spaces. While many of the issues discussed will relate to NPOs broadly, bear in mind that the research underpinning this chapter is specific to the antiviolence sector (including shelters, rape crisis and domestic violence centers, and other gender justice organizations, many of which specifically highlight the needs and experiences of marginalized populations like LGBTQ and racialized groups). The methods for this project include platform analysis, using historical screenshots alongside the current user interface, help and information pages (especially the "Facebook for Nonprofits" online guide), news stories about updates to the software, newsletters, blog posts and opinion pieces written by social media managers that discuss software changes, interviews with antiviolence nonprofit social media workers, and many years of participation in antiviolence NPO communities.

Antiviolence Nonprofits Navigate Both Software Design and the Nonprofit System

There are two sets of material rules of engagement that I am interested in, and my work here reads one set of rules through the other. The nonprofit system has its own set of rules, while social media software have been programmed with another set. These rules are material in that they refer to infrastructures, interfaces, resources, arrangements, conditions, and relations that are productive in so much as they enable and disable, encourage, reward, and obscure. Ultimately, the notion that designed artifacts "reflexively design us" (Bardzell 2010, 1307) structures my broader analysis of how social media design shapes and bounds nonprofit work. This section briefly sketches the issues that inform this analysis, beginning with materiality and software design before turning to criticisms of the nonprofit system. I draw from two sets of disparate yet loosely connected fields of scholarly inquiry: science and technology studies, human-computer interaction, and critical communication studies on one hand and feminist, queer, and trans theories on the other.

Materiality and Software Design

To analyze the material rules of engagement embedded in social media platform design, I draw from work that offers a complex understanding of the relationship between technology and society. From this perspective, technology and society are never separate, "never merely technical or social" (Wajcman 2010, 149). Mainstream science and technology studies (STS) analyses unpack the processes of technological innovation and design, considering the projected users and uses that designers embed within their technical artifacts (Wajcman 2004; Oudshoorn and Pinch 2003). From the perspective of human-computer interaction research, assumptions about users are inseparable from design processes. While users can help make these assumptions more reasonable by participating in design processes, it is impossible to conceive of every potential future user (van der Velden and Mörtberg 2012). Instead, "every design projects its own 'ideal user'" and "the closer actual users conform to this ideal, the easier, or more powerfully, or more pleasurably they will interact with the design" (Bardzell 2010, 1307). During the design process, "ideal users" and expected uses are anticipated. Certain uses are deemed more valid than others, and design decisions are oriented toward encouraging or rewarding them.

By centering the technical artifact itself, the values that are embedded in it can be made visible. This does not mean that people and social practices are overlooked in the process. It is always a sociotechnical artifact that is built by people and used by people. However, when we bracket software design by choosing to target surface discourse alone (e.g., profiles, posts, and "likes"), any problems lying underneath can become further entrenched (Bivens 2015). Deeper software levels—including database structures, algorithms, and code—function as another structural arena through which social life is regulated (Bivens 2015, 2017). Barad (2007) suggests that the apparatuses that we assemble to investigate our research interests always make ethical cuts by determining what is included and what is bracketed off to the side. Including software design in our apparatus has become an increasingly important choice that we can make. Alongside those working at the intersection of critical communication studies and science and technology studies, I am concerned that materiality has been "consistently overlooked" in favor of constructivism and representation (Gillespie et al. 2014). As a result, I draw again from Barad (2007) when I emphasize the material dimensions of power. As Mayer and Simon (2013, n.p.) explain, power ought to be considered "in terms of who/what matters and who/what is excluded from mattering." In the context of this chapter, then, I explore which elements of social change work by nonprofits materialize and come to matter, as an outcome of the rules of engagement embedded through software design, and how these elements relate to the rules of engagement that nonprofits are already contending with in the nonprofit system.

While making an early feminist intervention into the field of human-computer interaction, Bardzell (2010, 1307) emphasizes that we must "attend to the ways that design artifacts in-the-world reflexively design us." From this perspective, we can begin to imagine how social media software can pressure certain types of users into existence, evoking, for example, programmatically inspired forms of sociality. As Bardzell explains, "we can also see that using software *constitutes* users as subjects; that is, it makes us become the kind of user the software is for, bracketing aside the rest of ourselves that is not relevant to the software" (2010, 1307, original italics). This aligns well with Barad's (2007) emphasis on the material dimensions of power. What NPOs bracket aside in their social change work—because of the material rules of engagement they face when using social media software—can influence what they come to understand as relevant and useful for their social change work. The dimensions of social change work that come to matter are the dimensions that are programmatically possible through social media, anticipated by design, and rewarded through visibility and favorable analytics.

Criticisms of the Nonprofit System

The material rules of engagement stemming from the nonprofit system take on a different form than those embedded in software design, yet they often have similar effects. Feminist, queer, and trans theories have been instrumental in naming and critiquing the "nonprofit industrial complex" by exploring the origins of the nonprofit system, particularly in the U.S. context, and the ways in which the state and funders have bounded social movements to work within their systems and adhere to their logics (Incite! 2007; Spade 2015). Three specific rules of engagement are worthy of note here. Encouragement and rewards are bestowed upon NPOs who (1) maintain policy-focused strategies that work within current systems; (2) target permissible forms of violence; and (3) advance professionalization of the industry.

Working Within Current Systems

First, encouraging and funding policy-focused strategies has the effect of curbing advocacy work. In the United States, 501(c)(3) nonprofit organizations were established and accompanied by support from foundations, which helped secure the wealth of the elite who set up the foundations by permitting them to contribute to NPOs through tax-deductible donations (Smith 2007). Yet these funds often came with strings attached, as did nonprofit status, prohibiting "direct involvement in political advocacy" (Smith 2007, 7). Government restrictions on the nonprofit sector have broadly led to "a climate of advocacy restriction"[1] (Bonisteel and Green 2005, 1). In this climate, social media use can be risky since content added by NPOs is easily replicated and may remain cached or accessible through search engines even after it has been deleted (boyd 2010).

Rewarding policy-focused strategies also encourages NPOs to work within current institutions and systems, such as the legal and prison system. Yet, as marginalized actors in the antiviolence movement (including trans and gender nonconforming folks, racialized groups, people with disabilities, and those dealing with fraught immigration policies) will attest, historical and ongoing violence is not merely something to be *dealt with* by the state. This violence also *originates* from the state and its institutions. As Razack (2015) explains, structured by the legacy of colonialism and its ongoing effects, Indigenous peoples are overrepresented in the prison population, receive harsher penalties, and die in custody in disproportionate numbers. Meanwhile, the state obstructs trans people from obtaining ID and accessing social services and health care, measures that effectively shorten their lives (Spade 2015).

Despite these and other examples of state-inflicted violence, many antiviolence NPOs have worked to strengthen elements of the state—like the criminal justice system—as a means of reducing sexual and domestic violence (Smith 2005). Yet, advocating for increased criminalization (in the form of mandatory arrest laws, for instance) exacerbates the problem since "racial bias permeates legal and other state systems, with disproportionately devastating effects on communities of color, poor, and immigrant peoples" (Dasgupta 2003, 12). As Spade (2015, 208) puts it, "expand[ing] the punishing power of the criminal system that targets us" is an impossible option. While the nonprofit system as a whole may be a worthy target of critique, it is important to acknowledge that some nonprofit workers would argue that it is possible, and often preferable, to avoid carceral responses to violence altogether. That is, NPOs can choose to work within current systems while actively avoiding strategies that strengthen or otherwise endorse the criminal justice system.

Permissible Forms of Violence

The material rules of engagement that have sought to reward NPOs for abiding by political advocacy restrictions and working within current systems bleed into the next rule. The scope of violence that NPOs can target has also been bounded. As Durazo explains, funding calls and policies have influenced what has come to matter for NPOs: "The movement was literally split in two when funding came in to work discretely on *either* domestic violence *or* sexual assault, but not both . . . [and] certain state-based forms of sexual assault were kept out of the discourse of violence against women (for example, militarized and prison sexual assaults, militarized border rapes, and sterilization and other population control practices)" (2007, 117–18, original italics). While nonprofits are not confined to these definitions, their funding can hang in the balance. For example, when the Department of Justice offered the National Coalition of Anti-Violence Programs $600,000, the coalition rejected the funds because the federal agency had "refused the group's references to lesbian battering, racism, and commitment to organizing" (Durazo 2007, 125).

Professionalization

Professionalization can appear in the form of "leadership training" that seeks to redirect potential organizers toward policymaking. For instance, funders express "their preference for degree-bearing professionals instead of community organizers; [and] organizations [are] expected to have hierarchical structures" (Durazo 2007, 117). The promise of a career and an income has also led many into the nonprofit sector and away from community organizing. Meanwhile, work that seeks to challenge root causes of violence (social change work) has been systemically diminished in favor of social service work, which is more therapeutic in nature and addresses "the needs of individuals reeling from the personal and devastating impact of institutional systems of exploitation and violence" (Kivel 2007, 129).

Together, these material rules of engagement produced by the nonprofit system function as nudges, encouragement, and rewards. While they may be prescriptive, they are not mandatory. For an underfunded, struggling nonprofit, modulating their work and efforts to fit the system can be attractive, but any recursive impacts influencing the organization long-term may be subtle and indiscernible. The next section of this chapter draws out the patterns that surface when examining the material rules of engagement embedded in software design alongside these rules emerging from the nonprofit system.

Materially Constructing Social Change Work Through Facebook's Design

From the perspective of antiviolence nonprofit organizations, this section considers how their social media work is prescribed, bounded, and shaped by Facebook's software design. The following pages identify three analytical themes that surfaced while reading the material rules of engagement stemming from the nonprofit system through an analysis of Facebook's software: (1) the reproduction of violence through policies and programming practices; (2) the monetization of visibility; and (3) the fetishizing of analytics. Again, Bardzell's (2010) notion that software has recursive consequences for its users is instrumental in framing the impact of the themes explored here.

Violent Systems

This analytical theme resonates with the issues raised earlier about the paradox nonprofits face when working within systems that reproduce violence. As Smith (2005, 257) argues, "there is an inherent contradiction in relying upon the state to solve those problems that it is responsible for creating." By participating in "building and growing [these] systems of control" (Spade 2015, 209), harmful conditions are exacerbated. The concern here is that antiviolence nonprofits are under pressure to work with tools and within systems that reify some of the very problems they seek to resolve. To consider Facebook's role in reproducing violence, this section briefly explores two examples: "real name" policies and transphobic programming practices.

"Real Name" Policies

The first example is more widely known given that the popular press covered it extensively in late 2014. Facebook's "real name" or "authentic" name policy led to many individuals losing access to their accounts because the system determined the names listed on their profiles were inappropriate or inadequate (Holpuch 2015). Despite the company's suggestions that the policy had been improved, evidence continued to mount. Vulnerable and marginalized users have been disproportionately targeted by the policy, including, for example, domestic violence survivors who use alternate names to avoid being found by abusers. Exposed as "a ridiculous form of linguistic colonialism," "patriarchal," and a "massive cultural misunderstanding," Facebook's practices endanger the lives of users by unilaterally altering accounts to list legal names without consent or notice and collecting legal documents without using encryption from people already at risk of increased surveillance (Nameless Coalition 2015a, 2015b).

Facebook claims to be "committed to looking after the most vulnerable people using [their] product" (Ray 2015). The company speaks of trying to find "a balance" that "minimizes bullying but maximizes the potential for people to be their authentic selves" (Ray 2015). As their user base has grown, the company has sought increasingly sophisticated "tools for understanding who's real and who's not" (Cox 2014). Ultimately, they have designed software and governance practices that police users by requiring compliance with their own set of norms, regardless of the violence that it inflicts (Haimson and Hoffmann 2016).

Transphobic Programming Practices

The second example also exposes Facebook's software as violent, but does so by exploring a deeper level—the database. In 2014 Facebook revealed fifty-six additional options for people to use to identify outside of the traditional gender binary of male and female (Goldman 2014). While this was seen as a progressive move by many, my own investigation demonstrated that it was merely a superficial change to the surface of the software—a modification to the familiar blue and white user interface (Bivens 2017). Through my database queries, I found that a user's gender registered only as "male" or "female." If a user selected "gender questioning" and the pronoun "she," for instance, the database would store "female" as that user's gender despite their identification as "gender questioning" (or "genderqueer," "two spirit," or any other nonbinary option). This reclassification system is invisible to the trans and gender nonconforming users who now identify under the "custom" option. In situations where the pronoun "they" was selected, no information about gender appeared at all, as though these users have no gender at all. This is because the gender stored for each user in the database is not based on the gender they select; it is based on the *pronoun* they select. To complete the selection of a "custom" gender on Facebook, users are required to select a preferred pronoun (he, she, or they).

This programming practice actively misgenders trans and gender nonconforming users. Given that misgendering can lead to increased stigma and negative affect (McLemore, 2015), this practice is problematic in and of itself. Yet the capacity for programmers to bury this violent practice in a deep layer of the software that is inaccessible to the general public while maintaining a "progressive" surface heightens concern. It is a capitalist logic that motivated this design decision, since advertising, marketing, and other third-party clients depend on access to a data set that is regulated by a binary logic (Bivens 2017). Nonprofits working within this system may not be aware that their efforts toward dismantling hegemonic regimes of gender control—that rely on traditional ideas like the gender binary—are taking place on a platform that is itself calcifying a binary logic within the software's core. In fact, social media platforms have been granted increasing authority over the definition of identity categories, making programming decisions as they see fit, with repercussions for both users and advertisers (Bivens and Haimson 2016).

Monetization of Visibility

A different concern shared by many who seek to effect change through social media is how to achieve visibility in an age of information abundance.

Since visibility is also a design feature, programming decisions have the capacity to regulate visibility for different content and different users. Nonprofits with limited time and resources, but that feel pressured to use social media, must contend with systems that intentionally conceal the material rules of engagement determining visibility. Obfuscating code is an increasingly normalized programming practice for social media companies, along with proprietary algorithms that aim to protect companies from competitors. Three examples support this analytical theme: (1) classifying NPOs and restricting their reach; (2) permissible audiences; and (3) professionalization without support.

Classifying NPOs and Restricting Their Reach

When Facebook first launched in 2004, the anticipated "ideal" users were university students. Profiles to be completed and updated were designed specifically for students. Nonprofit organizations were not on Facebook's radar. Three years later, a new feature was designed, mainly to accommodate the businesses, brands, and public figures that had become viable users. This feature—pages (in contrast to profiles)[2]—continues to exist today and constitutes the space cordoned off for nonprofit organizations to use. Yet this is a shared space that merges business users with nonprofit users. Both sets of users are strongly encouraged to set up pages instead of profiles, particularly since it is only page owners who have access to analytics (called "Page Insights"). There are no visible design strategies that differentiate between the types of users; each have access to an identical set of programmed affordances. In the midst of this strategy, however, NPOs are nudged to adapt their practices to marketing logics.

Steering NPOs into specialized software spaces ultimately designed for business-related endeavors parallels the rules of engagement materialized within the nonprofit industrial complex that request NPOs to "run [their] resistance organizations like businesses" (Spade 2015, 209). If, as Dean (2010) argues, participation on social media drives capitalism as opposed to challenging it, we might consider whether social media work by NPOs has been co-opted through material rules of engagement that bound social change work by filtering it through the logics of consumer capitalism.

What is obscured when NPOs enter these separate spaces are the specialized material rules of engagement reserved for page users. While many NPOs assume that each post they create appears in the news feed of everyone in their social network, programmed restrictions severely limit this reach. As soon as a nonprofit creates a page instead of a profile, any posts they make automatically decrease in value because they do not appear in the news feed as frequently as posts from individual profiles. This is because "organic reach" (or unpaid distribution of posts to one's network) has been programmatically reduced since the introduction of pages in 2007. In 2012, organic reach had been restricted to 12 percent (Oldham 2014). By 2014 reports suggested reductions closer to 6 percent, and some are now reporting that organic reach is algorithmically capped at 2 percent for many popular pages, with further indications that organic reach will soon disappear altogether (Manson 2014). To translate, if one hundred people "like" your page, only two of them will see your posts under the 2 percent cap. It is important to note, however, that this information does not appear in Facebook's extensive online guide specifically designed for nonprofits. NPOs learn, for instance, that "people who like your Page *may* see your posts in News Feed when they visit Facebook" (Facebook 2016f, italics added). Yet there is no explicit mention of the reach restrictions.

Restricting organic reach is a design strategy that actively stifles the flow of information. Businesses understood this development to be a move toward monetizing visibility for Facebook while curbing their free advertising opportunities. For NPOs, however, this move situates social media platforms on the same plane as any other mass communication venue where free dissemination of information is possible but infrequent and guaranteed messaging is only accessible with adequate funding (or strategic planning and luck). Restricting organic reach presents a sociotechnical obstacle for nonprofits—one that could be abated if social media were designed differently.

Permissible Audiences

Another effect of the monetization of visibility (i.e., severe reach restrictions) through social media design is the programmatic elimination of NPOs' capacity to effectively reach the "unconverted"; in other words, people who are not already supporters of an NPO's work are designed out of organic reach. The only effective way to reach this group is through paid reach (boosting a post) or creating a paid ad campaign. As the online guide for nonprofits notes, "Ads are effective ways to reach new people whom you might not be able to find otherwise" (Facebook 2016a). "Preaching to the choir," as it is known colloquially, is futile in the context of public education and advocacy work. Reaching those who continue to hold traditional, hegemonic understandings of gender, for instance, is desirable since NPOs see them as complacent in reproducing the status quo. Yet, Facebook's design logic restricts these efforts and actively prescribes NPOs to reach out to audiences who will already be amenable to their message. For instance, the guide advises that "on Facebook, people share interests and opinions, and they're more likely to like, comment on and share posts that reflect their own perspective" (Facebook 2016b). Tips for creating relevant content include ideas such as: "Think about what kind of content supporters probably want to see in News Feed before you post" (Facebook 2016b). However, this logic is antithetical to the work that many NPOs are trying to achieve. Over time, these material rules of engagement may curb advocacy work, as we have already seen in the nonprofit system more broadly. At the very least, this design strategy discourages advocacy and public education work.

Facebook's advice to nonprofits is ultimately geared toward the material rules of engagement and assumptions about users it has programmed into its software. Here is another example from Facebook's nonprofit guide: "The Facebook News Feed is designed to show people content they're interested in. Our system uses engagement as a way to determine whether a post is relevant to people. For example, posts that people like, comment on and share are considered more relevant, so creating posts that people engage with is key to raising awareness" (Facebook 2016b).

Now we can more clearly identify the link between advising NPOs to create content that people will be interested in and the design of the news feed algorithm. The algorithm is programmed to achieve the company's objectives: it is designed to collect enough data about users to permit proficient assumptions about users' preferences in order to display content that will keep them engaged and on the platform. It is the company's underlying ideology that drives its instructions to NPOs to regulate their content in this way. For NPOs, the effect is a demarcation of what social change work ought to be, which is further reinforced by visibility in the news feed. The ultimate reward is a higher probability of demonstrable user engagement within the NPO's analytics. These material rules of engagement also drive the objective of reaching the "unconverted" further and further out of the bounds of "measurably effective" social change work. It is crucial that we question the assumptions and broader objectives embedded in these logics, particularly when social media could be designed differently. For example, social media could actively expose users to information they may not otherwise see.

Professionalization Without Support

Many nonprofit social media workers noted the increasing necessity of having a marketing or public relations background to be able to understand how the platforms work and decipher the analytics they are encouraged to pay attention to and report on. Social media design thus contributes to the demand for skill sets that are amenable to the logics of consumer capitalism. As a result, the professionalization norm embedded in the rules of engagement that feeds the nonprofit system emerges here. These logics become further entrenched when the rules of engagement encourage NPOs to set aside time and resources once they have set up a page to ensure it remains active. First, to gain visibility, Facebook advises NPOs to completely fill out each of the seven page sections since "Facebook News Feed prioritizes showing people Pages that are more complete to help them find the highest quality Pages" (Facebook 2016c). Then, Facebook advises nonprofit social media workers to post regularly to "help maintain supporter confidence": "If you're new to creating content for social media, aim for a post 2–3 times per week. Eventually, you'll want to post daily to maintain a presence in your followers' News Feeds" (Facebook 2016d).

While maintaining an active presence on social media is encouraged, these instructions elide other pertinent information. Again, there is no mention of the severely restricted reach that the system imposes, which prevents NPOs from achieving visibility in their followers' news feeds. Further, NPOs are advised to "reply to posts and comments quickly" (Facebook 2016d). This action is translated into another metric that is displayed for page owners, nudging them to track their performance. However, the cost of spending so much time in spaces that are also home to a great deal of misogynistic, transphobic, and racist content, among others, is overlooked. Roberts's (2016) work on commercial content moderation has shed light on the precarious workers who deal with reported content in an environment that her informants have described as a "digital cesspool." Apart from advising NPOs to "respond to post comments in a positive and timely manner" (Facebook 2016d), which is a questionable practice in the face of trolls, Facebook's extensive guide for nonprofits remains completely silent about a problem that the company pays to push off its own plate. The valid concerns that antiviolence NPOs have about safety within spaces fraught with privacy, surveillance (Mason and Magnet 2012), and complex dialogic issues that have consequences for their work, staff, supporters, and clients are also ignored.

Fetishizing Analytics

Analytics are positioned as a perk granted exclusively to page owners. Facebook's material rules of engagement seek to cultivate a dependency on this data. While the objective may be to improve the effectiveness of NPOs' social change work, recursive implications include shaping the future strategies and actions of NPOs and immersing them in a marketing ethos. While Facebook's analytics are presented as neutral data, they are always already baked with norms, values, and assumptions. Analytics are regulated first by Facebook's programmed set of possible user actions and then by those particular actions culled by the system and translated into data that becomes visible—and thus comes to matter—within the analytics page. Three final issues are relevant to explore here: (1) designing for "ideal users"; (2) superior analytics; and (3) system-favored metrics.

Designing for "Ideal" Users

Courtesy of Facebook's nonprofit guide, we learn that "engagement" has been imbued with tremendous value by the system and is defined, tracked, and measured in specific ways. Perhaps ideal users anticipated by Facebook's designers (or users the company hopes to produce) *are* prone to "engage" by liking, commenting on, and sharing posts they find relevant. However, not all users are ideal. Some are lurkers (reading but not leaving digital traces of "engagement"), while others may avoid "engagement" because of the imagined audience they conjure up when considering whether to react. Despite this diversity, Facebook's design strategy is driven by the idealized user (whose actions are likely to be idealized by advertisers, marketers, and third-party developers as well).

Consider what this ideal user might look like from a design perspective. An ideal (profile) user has cultivated a wide network of "friends" and has "liked" many pages. As a result, an ideal user requires an algorithm to sort through the copious amount of potential news feed content to determine which items are worthy of visibility. Spending a lot of time on Facebook, the ideal user demonstrates "engagement" by clicking, liking, commenting on, sharing, and viewing photos and videos. These are the primary user actions that have been programmed. This bounded set of possibilities leaves digital traces that are translated into data and programmatically move through the system to appear within different spaces, such as the analytics offerings that page owners can access. As van Dijck (2013, 12) argues in her critical history of social media, it is not socializing but the generation of data that "has become a primary objective" for social media platforms. Design decisions determine the set of possible user actions that can become data and, as a result, come to matter within this sociomaterial arrangement.

Superior Analytics

Exploring Page Insights[3] is depicted as a normal, inevitable, and desirable activity. As the nonprofit guide explains, "Your Facebook Page presents a natural opportunity to test and measure the results of various messaging strategies and techniques" (Facebook 2016e). NPOs are also advised to use these analytics to find out more about their supporters. Noting that this feature is exclusive to Facebook, which positions Facebook as a superior platform, NPOs are encouraged to explore supporters' demographic information and location. Page Insights, along with Audience Insights (the ad portal equivalent), encourage NPOs to understand their social change work as measurable, which coincides with the material rules of engagement embedded within the nonprofit system: "Antiviolence programs often feel required to demonstrate that their programs are successful (whether or not they are) to ensure continued funding" (Ptaceck 2010, 274). This compulsion also has direct implications for their future work: "After being forced to frame everything we do as a "success," we become stuck in having to repeat the same strategies because we insisted to funders they were successful, even if they were not" (Smith 2007, 10). Similarly, Facebook encourages NPOs to learn from their analytics in order to engage in more effective social change work: "By understanding your activity and performance, fan response, trends and comparisons, you are better equipped to improve your presence on Facebook and elsewhere" (Nonprofits on Facebook 2009). The suggestion here is that Facebook's metrics are valuable enough to improve the work of a nonprofit in spaces external to Facebook, which imbues the company with even more value.

In the context of paid advertisements, NPOs are again sharing the space with businesses. An enhanced suite of analytics and audience-targeting variables are available. The additional data that becomes accessible through Audience Insights includes data gathered from third-party partners, such as "US demographic and interest data based on purchase behavior, brand affinity and other activities" (Rosales 2014). Data brokers collect data from sources like loyalty cards and are used by social media companies eager to complement their own data sets to gain a competitive edge. This practice is not yet common knowledge. The types of data on offer are more amenable to businesses, yet NPOs may end up cultivating a desire to test out these enhanced targeting capabilities.

System-Favored Metrics

Facebook consistently encourages NPOs to determine "what is resonating with [their] audience" (Facebook 2016b). Yet, even the "post quality score," which calculates the degree of "engagement" per supporter for each post, is divorced from the other material rules of engagement designed into the system. Under these sociomaterial conditions, NPOs are not simply learning what may resonate. Instead, NPOs' social change work is modulated by logics embedded in the software's design. This is because they are encouraged to use the post quality score as an indicator of success to gauge whether the post should inform future posts. Yet these logics may have no direct relation to the information the NPO is trying to gather. A low post quality score may indicate that the post's reach was stunted by the restrictions placed upon unpaid, organic distribution. The low score could also be a consequence of the opaque algorithmic distribution to news feeds that is dependent on over 100,000 factors (Constine 2014). Yet Facebook encourages NPOs to seriously evaluate this metric—citing it as "one of the most important new metrics to pay attention to" (Nonprofits on Facebook 2009)—while eliding the underlying and opaque material structures that determine it. In the end, what is certain is that NPOs who pay close attention to metrics such as this without any critical evaluation will gradually produce more and more content that Facebook's system favors.

NPOs are also encouraged to model their advertisements on former page posts that have performed well, which further entrenches the material rules of engagement discussed above. Once again, a feedback loop is created. Along with reach and "engagement," conversion is another metric on offer, calculating "how many people took a specific action in response to a post, such as taking a pledge, signing up for an email list or purchasing a t-shirt" (Facebook 2016e). Yet all metrics are infused with assumptions. For example: "Our system measures click-through rates as well as time spent at the external link and the ratio of likes and comments to clicks. This helps us determine whether people find a post relevant. For example, if many people click a link but few like, comment on or share the post, it suggests that people didn't find the link interesting and the post may receive less reach" (Facebook 2016b).

Here we see that Facebook's relevance calculation involves link clicks, time spent at the link, and a combination of likes, comments, and shares. While all of these programmed possibilities are visible and come to matter to the system, and possibly to NPOs as well, it is important to consider what is invisible. A user who encounters a link may click, think about it over the course of the week, and discuss it with friends and colleagues. How much time the user spent thinking about it, and how often they discussed it, while certainly relevant, are digitally invisible actions. All of these activities may still be taking place, but only activities amenable to digital traces, only activities that can be translated into data (and only those that Facebook has deemed valuable enough to program) come to matter to the NPO analyzing analytics. To be clear, the implication here is not that Facebook ought to develop ways to track *more* human behavior. Instead, by highlighting which activities come to matter to Facebook's system and which activities are unaccounted for, nonprofits will have a better opportunity to make their own judgements about the relevance or effectiveness of their messaging strategies.

Conclusion

Instead of criticizing nonprofits' use of social media, this chapter has explored the material rules of engagement installed in the systems in which they operate. On Facebook, they are thrust onto pages that offer metrics they can use to report back to boards, the state, and various funders. Yet pages are also programmed spaces that offer severely restricted access, even to those who already support the page. Reaching people beyond this is extremely difficult, unless posts are promoted financially or NPOs finance advertising campaigns. Ultimately, the "unconverted" have been programmed out of reach, reducing the effectiveness and likelihood of advocacy and public education work. While business owners nostalgically look to the past when they could freely advertise on Facebook, NPOs' activities have been equally restricted despite seeking social change as opposed to profit because reach restrictions are concealed. Instead, nonprofits are encouraged to interpret their work on social media at face value, as though the invisible software processes are not operating underneath. The effect of this obfuscation is that nonprofits are not privy to the material rules of engagement that deeply influence their work. For instance, design decisions are oriented toward an "idealized" user who actively "engages" in permissible, visible, and measurable ways, consuming content deemed favorable by the system's algorithm.

Working within a system that is perpetually iterative may be akin to the nonprofit system (with ongoing changes to permissible terminology, restrictions, and funding opportunities, etc.), but in the social media world, programming decisions are proprietary and therefore inaccessible, which causes further obstacles for NPOs. Some social media managers have called for greater transparency: "Last year [Facebook] began publicizing major News Feed algorithm changes, but it needs to break open the black box of how feed sorting fundamentally works and why it does it" (Constine 2014). The material realities that bound and define social change work *for* nonprofits are largely invisible, and as such, any recursive effects on how NPOs understand their work and carry it out in the future are also obscured. While many NPOs are aware of the contradiction of working within a system that is itself violent, and some actively resist strategies that increase criminalization, the violent consequences of Facebook's "real name" policy and the transphobic programming practices that remain embedded in Facebook's database are also difficult realities that NPOs contend with.

The material rules of engagement that structure the nonprofit system produce similar patterns. NPOs are expected to professionalize and adopt logics from business while squeezing their work into funding schemas that too often come with strings attached, curbing advocacy and public education work. At times, the scope of permissible violence has been dictated by the state and funders, and NPOs are encouraged to work within current systems—as opposed to radically challenging them—and to overlook the violence that they continue to exact. Arguably, NPOs are more aware of and familiar with the rules of engagement they navigate within the nonprofit system than the rules set out for them by social media corporations. Perhaps the capacity for software to be programmed in such a way as to obfuscate these rules sets social media design apart.

Ultimately, though, can social media be understood as a critical tool for social change? And if not, under current material conditions and their embedded logics, could it become an effective tool in the future? Research investigating how design can be oriented toward social justice (Dombrowski et al. 2016) and how speculative design can be used to uncover design politics (DiSalvo 2014) is encouraging. Following Barad's (2007) logic, we can also make more ethical cuts by reconfiguring possibilities for action while broadening user assumptions and values to ensure that they too matter. By reading the material rules of engagement from one system through another, social change work has come into view as a material-discursive construct. Perhaps we could begin to understand it as a tool in and of itself that can be transformed, outside of the nonprofit and social media systems. Indeed, social change work is not fixed, but perpetually open to new possibilities and configurations. Perhaps the elements of the construct that is "social change work" might leverage other activities to come to matter in big data, analytics, and software. Ultimately, the aim is to move toward a material-discursive construction of social change work that refuses to be co-opted.

Notes

1. The government of Canada recently overturned a decade-long restriction that deemed advocacy work ineligible for funding from projects submitted to Status of Women Canada, an organization of the federal government (Status of Women Canada 2016).

2. Profiles are designed explicitly for individual people seeking noncommercial use of the platform, whereas pages look very similar but are designed for businesses, brands, and organizations. A user requires a personal profile in order to manage a page.

3. This data becomes available once a page has amassed thirty supporters.

References

Barad, K. M. 2007. *Meeting the Universe Halfway: Quantum Physics and the Entanglement of Matter and Meaning.* Durham, N.C.: Duke University Press.

Bardzell, S. 2010. "Feminist HCI: Taking Stock and Outlining an Agenda for Design." In *Proceedings of the SIGCHI Conference on Human Factors in Computing Systems*, 1301–10. New York: ACM. https://doi.org/10.1145/1753326.1753521.

Bivens, R. 2015. "Under the Hood: The Software in Your Feminist Approach." *Feminist Media Studies* 15 (4): 714–17. https://doi.org/10.1080/14680777.2015.1053717.

———. 2017. "The Gender Binary Will Not Be Deprogrammed: Ten Years of Coding Gender on Facebook." *New Media and Society* 19 (6): 880–98. https://doi.org/10.1177/1461444815621527.

Bivens, R., and O. L. Haimson. 2016. "Baking Gender into Social Media Design: How Platforms Shape Categories for Users and Advertisers." *Social Media + Society* (July–September): 1–12. https://doi.org/10.1177/2056305116672486.

Bonisteel, M., and L. Green. 2005. "Implications of the Shrinking Space for Feminist Anti-violence Advocacy." Paper presented at the Canadian Social Welfare Policy Conference, Forging Social Futures, Fredericton, New Brunswick.

Bortree, D. S., and T. Seltzer. 2009. "Dialogic Strategies and Outcomes: An Analysis of Environmental Advocacy Groups' Facebook Profiles." *Public Relations Review* 35 (3): 317–19. https://doi.org/10.1016/j.pubrev.2009.05.002.

boyd, danah. 2010. "Social Network Sites as Networked Publics: Affordances, Dynamics, and Implications." In *A Networked Self: Identity, Community and Culture on Social Network Sites*, edited by Zizi Papacharissi, 39–58. New York: Routledge.

Briones, R. L., B. Kuch, B. F. Liu, and Y. Jin. 2011. "Keeping Up with the Digital Age: How the American Red Cross Uses Social Media to Build Relationships." *Public Relations Review* 37 (1): 37–43. https://doi.org/10.1016/j.pubrev.2010.12.006.

Campbell, J. C. 2016. "Is Nonprofit Social Media a Waste of Time?" Julia Campbell Social Marketing, March 22. http://jcsocialmarketing.com/2016/03/nonprofit-social-media-waste-time.

Collins, M. 2016. "It's Time for Charities to Stop Wasting Money on Social Media: Businesses Have Found That Tweets and Facebook Posts Don't Boost Sales—Voluntary Groups Must Realise This Is True for Donations." *Guardian*, March 11. http://www.theguardian.com/voluntary-sector-network/2016/mar/11/charities-wasting-money-social-media.

Constine, J. 2014. "Why Is Facebook Page Reach Decreasing? More Competition and Limited Attention." *TechCrunch*, April 3. http://social.techcrunch.com/2014/04/03/the-filtered-feed-problem/.

Cox, C. 2014. "I want to apologize to the affected community. . . ." Facebook, October 1. https://www.facebook.com/chris.cox/posts/10101301777354543.

Curtis, L., C. Edwards, K. L. Fraser, S. Gudelsky, J. Holmquist, K. Thornton, K., and K. D. Sweetser. 2010. "Adoption of Social Media for Public Relations by Nonprofit Organizations." *Public Relations Review* 36 (1): 90–92. https://doi.org/10.1016/j.pubrev.2009.10.003.

Dasgupta, S. D. 2003. *Safety and Justice for All: Examining the Relationship Between the Women's Anti-Violence Movement and the Criminal Legal System*. New York: Ms. Foundation for Women. http://www.ncdsv.org/images/Ms_SafetyJusticeForAll_2003.pdf.

Dean, J. 2010. *Blog Theory: Feedback and Capture in the Circuits of Drive*. Cambridge, U.K.: Polity Press.

Diaz-Ortiz, C. 2011. *Twitter for Good: Change the World One Tweet at a Time*. San Francisco: Jossey-Bass.

DiSalvo, C. 2014. "Critical Making as Materializing the Politics of Design." *The Information Society* 30 (2): 96–105. https://doi.org/10.1080/01972243.2014.875770.

Dombrowski, L., E. Harmon, and S. Fox. 2016. "Social Justice-Oriented Interaction Design: Outlining Key Design Strategies and Commitments." In *Proceedings of the 2016 ACM Conference on Designing Interactive Systems*, 656–71. New York: ACM. https://doi.org/10.1145/2901790.2901861.

Durazo, A. C. R. 2007. "'We Were Never Meant to Survive': Fighting Violence Against Women and the Fourth World War." In *The Revolution Will Not Be Funded: Beyond the Non-Profit Industrial Complex*, edited by Incite!, 113–28. Cambridge, Mass.: South End Press.

Echenberg, H. 2010. "Facebook for Non-Profits." *The Philanthropist* 23 (1): 83–84.

Facebook. 2016a. "Attract Your First Non-Profit Page Followers." https://nonprofits.fb.com/topic/get-people-to-like-your-page.

———. 2016b. "Create Good Content That Catches Attention." https://nonprofits.fb.com/topic/grab-peoples-attention.

———. 2016c. "Enhance Your Non-Profit Organization's Page." from https://nonprofits.fb.com/topic/enhance-your-page.

———. 2016d. "Interact with Your Non-Profit Supporters." https://nonprofits.fb.com/topic/strengthen-relationships.

———. 2016e. "Measurement and Tracking for Non-Profits." https://nonprofits.fb.com/topic/measurement-tracking.

———. 2016f. "Set up a Facebook Page for Your Non-Profit." https://nonprofits.fb.com/topic/set-up-a-page.

Feenberg, A. 2016. "The Internet in Question." In *The Digital Nexus: Identity, Agency, and Political Engagement*, edited by Raphael Foshay, 25–48. Edmonton, Canada: Athabasca University Press. http://www.aupress.ca/books/120253/ebook/99Z_Foshay_2016-The_Digital_Nexus.pdf.

Gillespie, T., P. J. Boczkowski, and K. A. Foot, eds. 2014. *Media Technologies: Essays on Communication, Materiality, and Society*. Cambridge, Mass.: MIT Press.

Goldman, R. 2014. "Here's a List of 58 Gender Options for Facebook Users." ABC News, February 13. http://abcnews.go.com/blogs/headlines/2014/02/heres-a-list-of-58-gender-options-for-facebook-users/.

Haimson, O. L. and A. L. Hoffmann. 2016. "Constructing and Enforcing 'Authentic' Identity Online: Facebook, Real Names, and Non-Normative Identities." *First Monday* 21 (6). http://dx.doi.org/10.5210/fm.v21i6.6791.

Holpuch, A. 2014. "Victory for Drag Queens as Facebook Apologises for 'Real-Name' Policy." *Guardian*, October 1. https://www.theguardian.com/technology/2014/oct/01/victory-drag-queens-facebook-apologises-real-name-policy.

———. 2015. "Native American Activist to Sue Facebook over Site's 'Real Name' Policy." *Guardian*, February 19. https://www.theguardian.com/technology/2015/feb/19/native-american-activist-facebook-lawsuit-real-name.

Incite!, ed. 2007. *The Revolution Will Not Be Funded: Beyond the Non-Profit Industrial Complex*. Cambridge, Mass.: South End Press.

Kanter, B., and A. Fine. 2010. *The Networked Nonprofit: Connecting with Social Media to Drive Change*. Chichester, U.K.: John Wiley.

Kivel, P. 2007. "Social Service or Social Change?" In *The Revolution Will Not Be Funded: Beyond the Non-Profit Industrial Complex*, edited by Incite!, 129–50. Cambridge, Mass.: South End Press.

Lim, M. 2013. "Many Clicks but Little Sticks: Social Media Activism in Indonesia." *Journal of Contemporary Asia* 43 (4): 636–57. https://doi.org/10.1080/00472336.2013.769386.

Lovejoy, K., R. D. Waters, and G. D. Saxton. 2012. "Engaging Stakeholders Through Twitter: How Nonprofit Organizations Are Getting More Out of 140 Characters or Less." *Public Relations Review* 38 (2): 313–18. https://doi.org/10.1016/j.pubrev.2012.01.005.

Mansfield, H. 2012. *Social Media for Social Good: A How-to Guide for Nonprofits*. New York: McGraw-Hill.

Manson, M. 2014. "Facebook Zero: Considering Life After the Demise of Organic Reach." Social@Ogilvy, March 6. https://social.ogilvy.com/facebook-zero-considering-life-after-the-demise-of-organic-reach/.

Mason, C. L., and S. Magnet. 2012. "Surveillance Studies and Violence Against Women." *Surveillance and Society* 10 (2): 105–18.

Mayer, K., and J. Simon. 2013. "Desired Becomings." *Journal of Peer Production* 3. http://peerproduction.net/issues/issue-3-free-software-epistemics/debate/desired-becomings/.

McLemore, K. A. 2015. "Experiences with Misgendering: Identity Misclassification of Transgender Spectrum Individuals." *Self and Identity* 14 (1): 51–74. https://doi.org/10.1080/15298868.2014.950691.

Muralidharan, S., L. Rasmussen, D. Patterson, and J.-H. Shin. 2011. "Hope for Haiti: An Analysis of Facebook and Twitter Usage During the Earthquake Relief Efforts." *Public Relations Review* 37 (2): 175–77. https://doi.org/10.1016/j.pubrev.2011.01.010.

Nameless Coalition. 2015a. "Appendix to October 5, 2015 Letter to Facebook." Electronic Frontier Foundation. https://www.eff.org/files/2015/10/05/10052015_appendix.pdf.

———. 2015b. "Open Letter to Facebook About Its Real Names Policy." Electronic Frontier Foundation. https://www.eff.org/document/open-letter-facebook-about-its-real-names-policy.

National Coalition of Anti-Violence Programs (NCAVP). 2015. *Lesbian, Gay, Bisexual, Transgender, Queer and HIV-Affected Hate Violence in 2014*. New York: Author. https://avp.org/wp-content/uploads/2017/04/2014_HV_Report-Final.pdf.

Nonprofits on Facebook. 2009. "We've Upgraded the Insights Tools for Your Facebook Page!" Facebook, May 11. https://www.facebook.com/notes/nonprofits-on-facebook/weve-upgraded-the-insights-tools-for-your-facebook-page/86841291636/.

Oldham, J. 2014. "Say Goodbye to Facebook Organic Reach." SuperDrive. https://www.superdrive.io/2015/01/say-goodbye-to-facebook-organic-reach/.

Oudshoorn, N., and T. J. Pinch. 2003. "Introduction: How Users and Non-Users Matter." In *How Users Matter: The Co-Construction of Users and Technologies*, edited by N. Oudshoorn and T. J. Pinch, 1–25. Cambridge, Mass.: MIT Press.

Ptacek, J. 2010. "Resisting Co-Optation: Three Feminist Challenges to Antiviolence Work." In *Restorative Justice and Violence Against Women*, edited by J. Ptacek, 5–36. New York: Oxford University Press.

Ray, B. 2015. "Facebook's Reply to Open Letter on 'Real name' Policy." *Gadgets Now*, October 31. http://www.gadgetsnow.com/social/Facebooks-reply-to-open-letter-on-real-name-policy/articleshow/49608159.cms.

Razack, S. 2015. *Dying from Improvement: Inquests and Inquiries into Indigenous Deaths in Custody.* Toronto: University of Toronto Press.

Roberts, S. 2016. "Commercial Content Moderation: Digital Laborers' Dirty Work." In *The Intersectional Internet: Race, Sex, Class and Culture Online*, edited by Safiya Umoja Noble and Brendesha Tynes, 147–60. New York: Peter Lang.

Rosales, F. 2014. "How to Use Facebook Audience Insights: What Marketers Need to Know." *Social Media Examiner*, June 23. http://www.socialmediaexaminer.com/facebook-audience-insights-for-marketers/.

Sedereviciute, K., and C. Valentini. 2011. "Towards a More Holistic Stakeholder Analysis Approach. Mapping Known and Undiscovered Stakeholders from Social Media." *International Journal of Strategic Communication* 5 (4): 221–39. https://doi.org/10.1080/1553118X.2011.592170.

Smith, A. 2005. *Conquest: Sexual Violence and American Indian Genocide.* Cambridge, Mass.: South End Press.

———. 2007. "Introduction: The Revolution Will Not Be Funded." In *The Revolution Will Not Be Funded: Beyond the Non-Profit Industrial Complex*, edited by Incite!, 1–18. Cambridge, Mass.: South End Press.

Spade, D. 2015. *Normal Life: Administrative Violence, Critical Trans Politics, and the Limits of Law.* Durham, N.C.: Duke University Press.

Status of Women Canada. 2016. "Government of Canada Restores Advocacy to Scope of Status of Women Canada Projects." Government of Canada, July 18. https://www.canada.ca/en/status-women/news/2016/07/government-of-canada-restores-advocacy-to-scope-of-status-of-women-canada-projects.html.

Van der Velden, M., and C. Mörtberg. 2012. "Between Need and Desire: Exploring Strategies for Gendering Design." *Science, Technology and Human Values* 37 (6): 663–83. https://doi.org/10.1177/0162243911401632.

Van Dijck, J. 2013. *The Culture of Connectivity: A Critical History of Social Media.* New York: Oxford University Press.

Van Dijck, J., and T. Poell. 2013. "Understanding Social Media Logic." *Media and Communication* 1 (1): 2–14. https://doi.org/10.17645/mac.v1i1.70.

Wajcman, J. 2004. *Technofeminism.* Cambridge: Polity Press.

———. 2010. "Feminist Theories of Technology." *Cambridge Journal of Economics* 34 (1): 143–52. https://doi.org/10.1093/cje/ben057.

Waters, R. D., E. Burnett, A. Lamm, and J. Lucas. 2009. "Engaging Stakeholders Through Social Networking: How Nonprofit Organizations Are Using Facebook." *Public Relations Review* 35 (2): 102–6. https://doi.org/10.1016/j.pubrev.2009.01.006.

Waters, R. D., and P. M. Jones. 2011. "Using Video to Build an Organization's Identity and Brand: A Content Analysis of Nonprofit Organizations' YouTube Videos." *Journal of Nonprofit and Public Sector Marketing* 23(3): 248–68. https://doi.org/10.1080/10495142.2011.594779

Zorn, T. E., S. Grant, and A. Henderson. 2012. "Strengthening Resource Mobilization Chains: Developing the Social Media Competencies of Community and Voluntary Organizations in New Zealand." *VOLUNTAS: International Journal of Voluntary and Nonprofit Organizations* 24 (3): 666–87. https://doi.org/10.1007/s11266-012-9265-1.

CHAPTER 2

Digital Opportunity Structures: Explaining Variation in Digital Mobilization During the 2016 Democratic Primaries

Daniel Kreiss

In early 2016, the Bernie Sanders campaign for president released a campaign ad titled, simply, "America." The ad consisted of troubadours Simon and Garfunkel's classic 1960s song of the same name played over a video of people from all walks of life—old and young, heterosexual and LGBTQ, farmers and young creatives, moms and dads—carrying out their daily lives of work and care and participation in the political process. The implicit message was that the Sanders campaign was made up of ordinary Americans, and the candidate, his policies, and, ultimately, his presidency would represent them. Perhaps because these images are so easily associated with deep-seated ideals many Americans hold about democracy being about "the people" (Alexander 2010; Morone 1998), it is easy to forget that the vision of America contained in the ad is a particularistic, not universalistic, representation of what the country is, and ultimately *should* be. There was, for instance, nary a banker to be found in Sanders's particular version of America.

Critiques aside, it was clear that this ad resonated with a lot of people, and I suspect among Democrats, both Sanders and Clinton supporters alike. "America" was viewed over 3.5 million times on YouTube and 1.6 million times on Facebook through early May 2016. It received widespread acclaim in the political press, with laudatory headlines such as *Esquire*'s declaration that "This Bernie Ad May Be the Best Political Commercial

I've Ever Seen" (Pierce 2016). The digital resonance of the Sanders campaign's communications extended beyond this one ad, however. The campaign set nearly every record for digital fundraising during the 2016 cycle, including raising $54 million in donations of $200 or less in 2015 and $8 million in the forty-eight hours after the candidate's New Hampshire primary victory.

"America" and the digital resonance and mobilization that it, the candidate, and the campaign inspired raises a set of issues that are at the heart of this chapter, which broadly asks, what shapes the opportunities for, and ultimately the success of, digital mobilization? I argue that despite the candidate's ultimate faltering in the primaries, the Sanders campaign was successful at digital mobilization precisely because the candidate's rhetoric and the campaign's symbolism encoded a set of moral claims deeply attuned with normative understandings of democracy. Meanwhile, the candidate espoused policy narratives and performances of identity that resonated with particular subsets of voters in the Democratic Party and those ideologically aligned with it, which were powerful because of Sanders's position in a field of candidates and because of their amplification by the legacy press. This rhetoric and these symbols, narratives, and performances were given force and presence by being artfully incorporated into media forms such as digital ads by Sanders's campaign staffers, who perceived the opportunity and had the skills to both mobilize existing supporters and cultivate new ones through digital and social media communications.

In the theoretical terms of this chapter, Sanders successfully drew symbolic resources from the civil *sphere*, a culturally defined and institutionally regulated domain of democratic solidarity (Alexander 2006, 31), capitalized on his position in a *field* of democratic candidates, and took strategic symbolic and social action through *networks* of campaign staffers with particular sets of skills and technologies with particular affordances. This chapter argues that taken together, features of the political environment shaped by spheres, fields, and networks constitute the "digital opportunity structure" that a candidate faces, and must navigate, in order to realize digital mobilization in the service of her electoral goals.[1] The theorization of digital opportunity structures offered here is not limited to electoral politics. This concept offers a framework for understanding collective action more generally, but I apply it here in the context of digital mobilization during an electoral campaign as a case study. My argument is also intended to advance the sociological concept of "political opportunity structure" more broadly. I hope to more systematically theorize and integrate what I take to be the foundational elements of social life: spheres of cultural meaning that are institutionally regulated, fields of relational symbolic and social activity, and networks of social and technological relations that cross, shape, and change both spheres and fields over time.

In the pages that follow, first I turn to the concepts of spheres, fields, and networks and integrate the vast bodies of work around them. I bring these ideas together in the concept of "digital opportunity structures." Finally, through an interview with the Sanders campaign's social media director and interpretive analysis of the campaign's digital content, I show how the concept of digital opportunity structures helps explain the Sanders campaign's digital organizing success. I conclude with an argument about how this conceptualization can be more broadly applied to explain the elements of collective action more generally.

Literature Review

Spheres, Fields, and Networks as the Conceptual Building Blocks of the Social

Before developing the concept of "digital opportunity structures," I want to sketch a broader conceptual framework that integrates a number of different analytical perspectives on social life. In the context of electoral politics, candidates are embedded in spheres, fields, and networks that shape their capacities for, and the outcomes of, strategic social and symbolic action. The building blocks of the idea of digital opportunity structures are these three levels of analysis—spheres, fields, and networks—that theorists and empirical researchers in different literatures have extensively elaborated but generally failed to integrate (see Figure 2.1). And the concepts of spheres, fields, and networks have cultural, social, and technological dimensions, which all need to be accounted for.

First, in defining spheres, I start from Alexander's (2006, 4; 2010) conceptualization of the "civil sphere" as "a world of values and institutions that generates the capacity for social criticism and democratic integration at the same time." There are many spheres in social life, such as religious and market spheres, all of which exist within broader landscapes of meaning that are "arrangements of signification and representation" and give rise to the mo-

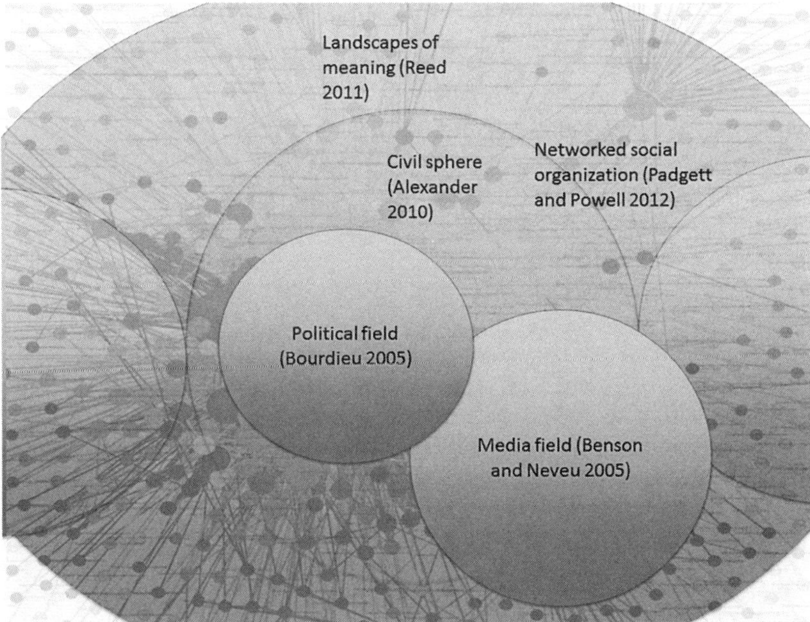

Figure 2.1. Spheres, fields, and networks

tivations and mechanisms for social action (Reed 2011, 143). Spheres consist of durable structures of cultural and moral meaning that give shape to distinct domains of social life, as well as the institutions that organize and regulate them.

It is the "civil sphere" that is the most germane for the discussion here. Alexander argues that "civil society is not merely an institutional realm. It is also a realm of structured, socially established consciousness, a network of understandings creating structures of feeling that permeate social life and run just below the surface of strategic institutions and self-conscious elites" (2006, 54). The democratic values of the civil sphere consist of equality, liberty, and justice, which its communicative institutions (such as mass media and technologies of public opinion) and regulative institutions (such as political parties, electoral rules, offices, and the law) both give shape to and protect. There are binary codes that structure the moral understandings of the civil sphere, where the motives and relationships of actors and institutions are categorized in civil and anticivil terms. For example, persons considered to be civil have motives that are autonomous, rational, and self-controlled, not dependent, irrational, or wild-passionate. Civil social relationships are open, altruistic, and truthful, not secretive, greedy, or deceitful. Civil institutions are rule regulated, premised on equality, and impersonal, as opposed to arbitrary, hierarchical, and personal. Actors, whether individuals, movements, groups, or organizations, strive to pollute opponents or define who is outside of the civil sphere by deploying anticivil categories against them (2006, 57–59).

The civil sphere is made up of durable, yet ultimately changeable, cultural repertoires, codes, and institutions of democratic meaning and practice that have more or less legitimacy to political actors and citizens at moments in time, are subject to contestation, and change over the course of history (not always through intentional action). Michael Schudson's (1998) *The Good Citizen*, for instance, revealed how the cultural meanings of "good" citizenship and its practices are subject to change. Similarly, Jonathan Israel's body of work (e.g., 2014) shows how the ideas of "equality" and "freedom" were not universal features of the Enlightenment, but values that had to be contested against other normative understandings of democracy that resisted radical egalitarianism.

Taken together, from these various works comes the important idea that cultural frameworks underpin and shape the possibilities for social and symbolic action, through orienting the discourse and action of political actors and providing the criteria of evaluation for what citizens consider legitimate and inspiring to work toward. The idea of spheres offers, at root, a way of understanding meaning as both central to the democratic process and bounded (i.e., not endlessly interpretively flexible or free to be remade). For example, Smith (2003) argues that "stories of peoplehood" are a key way that political identity is crafted. While these stories of peoplehood can be particularistic in many domains of social life that do not require universalistic democratic solidarity, in the civil sphere these stories of peoplehood must be articulated from, and kept in accordance with, the democratic values and cultural meanings of the civil sphere in order to be considered legitimate by regulative institutions and the broader populace. The LGBTQ movement, for instance, crafted a distinct identity in domains outside the civil sphere, which then had to be articulated within the civil sphere as a claim for *equality* amid difference. For Alexander, the historical development of the civil sphere comes in part through the work of movements to ground their particularistic identities in terms of democratic universality:

> Political struggles over the status of lower-class groups, or racial, ethnic, and religious minorities, of women, children, and homosexuals, of those who are constructed as criminals and as mentally, emotionally, and physically handicapped—these conflicts have always involved discursive struggles over whether and how the discourse of liberty can be extended and applied. Insofar as the founding cultural myths and constitutional documents of democratic societies are universalistic, they implicitly stipulated that the discourse can always be further extended, and that it eventually must be. (2006, 61)

In sum, spheres provide a historically developed, overarching framework for a recognizable cultural and institutional domain of "civic" life. The civil sphere is the realm that gives form to our debates over what is "political" and what values such as liberty and equality mean and how they should be enacted in democracy. At the same time, there are meso-level "fields" embedded within, and sometimes traversing, spheres. As my colleagues and I have previously argued, "fields texture the civil sphere" (Kreiss, Meadows, and Remensperger 2014, 16). There are sprawling literatures about "fields," a concept originally formulated by Pierre Bourdieu (e.g., 2005). While I cannot address the different strains of the literature here, I follow Fligstein and McAdam (2012) in conceptualizing fields as arenas of contestation populated by individuals, groups, or organizations that are nested within one another in ways that span micro- and macro-levels of social action. The idea of nesting offers an important advance over previous theory in conceptualizing hierarchical and vertical relations within, between, and among fields.

That said, Fligstein and McAdam's conceptualization of fields lacks an explanation of what culturally or institutionally *bounds* or *organizes* multiple fields into coherent, higher-order domains (such as those characterizing civil democratic processes). To this end, fields should be conceptualized as being embedded within spheres, more or less fully and alone or in combinations with other fields, and fields can also spill across the boundaries of spheres. For example, a strategic action field defined by conflict between regulators and the biotechnology industry crosses both the civil sphere (regulators are part of the state bureaucracy and bound by its cultural logics and regulatory institutions that require equality under the law) and the economic sphere (in terms of commercial and marketplace logics and regulatory institutions such as the Federal Trade Commission)—not unlike Boltanski and Thévenot's (2006) work on "justification," which posits multiple orders of worth that may come into conflict or around which actors may create temporary compromises.

Most relevant for this essay are the meso-level political and media fields that are largely contained within the civil sphere and made up of heterogeneous organizational and individual actors that generally see themselves, and actors in other related fields, engaging in similar sets of activities. The organizational fields of politics and media (Cook 1998) feature coherent groups of actors whose relations are organized through the cultural logics of *both* the civil sphere and their respective fields. Internal and external field actors (such as citizens and regulative institutions) can hold these actors accountable for their actions vis-à-vis the cultural logics of the civil sphere and the regulative logics of their fields (there is also hybridity among organizations that bridge the fields of politics and media, such as the movement media organization of Fox News; see, e.g., Skocpol and Williamson 2011).

The workings of the field of politics are highly consequential for actors in the media field, and vice versa. As Tim Cook (1998) demonstrated, political actors seek out, work through, and are constrained by media actors. For their part, media actors need political actors to hold accountable, to provide them with and organize their access to political power, and ultimately to legitimate them as a part of governance and electoral processes. Put simply, these two fields are entwined in their workings but organized according to different logics. Following Fligstein and McAdam, there are also nested fields within the political and media fields. In the context of electoral politics, for instance, there are fields of candidates within the Republican and Democratic primaries who vie for electoral resources, party-network endorsements, media attention from the adjacent field, and ultimately citizen support at the ballot box. During general elections, there is a field of struggle between the two parties' nominees and their extended networks of actors. In other words, nested within the political field are smaller domains of strategic contested action, where candidates vie for votes (or activists such as the Koch brothers organize against, and for, the Republican establishment).

Finally, networks cross both spheres and fields. Networks are historically conditioned patterns of relations that encompass ties between and among individuals, organizations, and technologies (Latour 2005; Padgett and Powell 2012). Networks serve as conduits of things such as cultural meaning (DiMaggio 1997), resources, knowledge, skills, practice, information, and opinion (e.g., Christakis and Fowler 2009). We can also posit the existence of symbolic networks of cultural associations and meanings that transcend specific ties between humans and nonhumans and are embedded in and constituted through durable institutions, laws, media forms, practices, and so on (see, e.g., Sewell 1980; Wuthnow 2009).

Extending the work of Padgett and Powell (2012), I posit that the folding of networks (social, technological, or cultural) across domains works to transform fields and spheres over time. Boundary crossing and domain switching can give rise to innovations that ultimately spur the emergence of new organizational, cultural, social, or technological forms. I conceptualize "organizations" here as comparatively stabilized networks, which are held in place by institutions, fields, and spheres. Organizations stabilize people and their multiple ties and associations through both formal means (such as employment obligations, roles, contractual labor, boards of directors, etc.) and informal means (such as repeated patterns of exchange between organizations), subject to the regulations of institutions, fields, and spheres.

Digital Opportunity Structures

Spheres, fields, and networks give rise to what I have called "digital opportunity structures."[2] The social movement scholar Sidney Tarrow (2011, 32) defined "political opportunity structure" as the "consistent—but not necessarily formal or permanent—dimensions of the political environment that provide incentives for people to undertake collective action by affecting their expectations for success or failure." Elizabeth Clemens (1997, 72) has used the concept in her historical work to detail how institutional rules, elite divisions, and broader political environments provided opportunities for and constraints on challenges to the party system by women, workers, and farmers movements, which in turn gave rise to the organizational innovation of the contemporary interest group.

Building from this line of work, but more explicitly adding considerations of culture and technology, I conceptualize digital opportunity structures as features of the political environment and candidates' and campaigns' symbolic, material, and relational position in it that shape the possibilities for using digital media for strategic ends. These opportunities are only realized, however, when a candidate and her staffers perceive them, and have the skills to navigate the networked, hybrid media environment. Every candidate faces a different digital opportunity structure. Digital opportunity structures are the hands campaigns are dealt by the electoral context, the candidate, and the fields of politics and media that shape the possibility for specifically *digital* mobilization. And, staffers have to perceive the salient features of their environment and candidate so as to be able to act within this structure more or less well for competitive advantage, even as structures change over time as the result of the actions that campaigns and parties take and shifting electoral contexts (such as the outcome of primary contests).

The elements of digital opportunity structures map onto the concepts of spheres, fields, and networks. As Alexander (2010) argues, candidates vie to become a collective representation of the body politic, which entails aligning themselves with the civil side of the democratic moral binary while symbolically polluting their opponents. These binaries, as well as the broader cultural context that shapes what narratives democratic citizens believe are desirable and legitimate, are structural in the sense that they bound candidates' attempts to narrate themselves and shape what will resonate with democratic citizens. Alexander (2010), for instance, furnishes the example of the war hero John McCain attempting to narrate himself as a civil hero in 2008, a moment in time when the public was resolutely focused on domestic issues. The candidate's biography interacted with the cultural structure of the civil sphere to bound the script that McCain was able to perform and the possibilities that his life story would resonate with the public. Broadly speaking, apart from the more enduring moral binaries in the civil sphere that all candidates must speak to, there are some issues favored by the political context, and a candidate's biography shapes her ability to credibly and legitimately speak to them.

At the level of the field, candidates are bound relationally within the fields they occupy and by the logics of the adjacent fields that shape them (and these fields, detailed above in the discussion of the work of Fligstein and McAdam, need not be as formally structured as in models such as Bourdieu's). For instance, during the 2016 cycle, Republican candidates vied against one another to occupy different cultural spaces that would connect with, mobilize, and ultimately represent different categories of Republican voters. What is important about the idea of "fields" is that it is a fundamentally relational concept; candidates have to vie against one another to occupy or create new cultural spaces for electoral gain. For example, as Bart Bonikowski and Noam Gidron's (2016) work has revealed, rhetoric such as populist claims can be understood through the lens of field theory: challengers to incumbents or elites generally rely on more populist claims during primaries, and then mitigate this rhetoric as they move toward general elections. There are other dynamics at play that relate to candidates' relational positions in fields. A number of scholars have noted that insurgent candidates have greater incentives to use digital media in the attempt to inspire collective social and symbolic action among their supporters and to secure resources in the absence of institutional party support. In part, this is because challengers to establishment frontrunners can often inspire digital mobilization among passionate subgroups of party activists. Where a candidate is situated in a field of other candidates shapes the possibilities for digital mobilization.

In sum, the field of candidates, the composition of the electorate, the relative power of groups in the party network, which party holds office, the issues the candidate is running on vis-à-vis the field, the candidate's charisma (a candidate's public persona and the willingness of people to believe and follow her), the media habits of the candidate's supporters and the ideological and party activists she appeals to, all shape the field-level possibilities for digital mobilization (Kreiss 2016). At the same time, as Tim Cook (1998) pointed out two decades ago, the field of journalism is deeply intertwined with the field of politics. Structures and patterns of legacy media coverage and journalists' perceptions of candidates' viability shape how successful candidates are and can be (e.g., Williams and Delli Carpini 2011), and media coverage also attracts the "bystanders" that candidates can leverage to support their cause (e.g., Gamson 2004).

Networks are comparatively less structured and more flexibly organized than spheres and fields. Strategic gain is achieved through the mobilization of existing networks, constitution of new networks, and reconfiguring of networks across domains of social life. Existing patterns of relations, such as what Andrew Chadwick (2007) calls "sedimentary networks," are resources that candidates have the potential to mobilize. Candidates also can create new political networks, often based on who they are and the stories they craft to constitute peoplehood and bring identities into existence (Smith 2003). This includes knitting together networks of party actors for competitive electoral advantage, including through the symbolic work that articulates the identity of a party from the background of historical cultural associations.

Spheres, fields, and networks together constitute the features of the political environment that shape the possibilities for and constraints on digital mobilization, but a campaign's staffers need to perceive opportunities and take advantage of them. These are *learned perceptual and social and technological skills* that are, in part, the product of the historical workings of party *networks* in producing people conditioned to recognize and have the skills to capitalize on digital opportunities. A candidate's capacity to act is also conditioned by creative recombinations of ways of seeing, knowledge, and skills across domains through the networked biographies of the staffers they bring together in their campaign organizations (Kreiss 2016). Candidates and their campaign staffers or consultants need to have the perceptual ability to recognize digital opportunities and the skill to navigate these structures. Ways of seeing are produced by the networks of staffers that campaigns draw together. Staffers have biographies constituted by work in institutions and organizations that have produced their knowledge and skills, including those they learned and practiced in their work outside of politics. Following organizational sociologists de Vaan, Stark, and Vedres (2015), in campaign organizations what matters is "cognitive diversity" coupled with the "structural folding" that holds assemblages of disparate people together and makes their work recognizable to particular fields; in other words, recombinations of political field–based knowledge with knowledges from outsiders generates innovation in line with electoral goals.

For example, social skill and, in the context of digital opportunity structures, "technological skill" are the products of historically constituted networked social relations and individual experience in fields, organizations, and institutions. This historical work constitutes biographies that give rise to social and technological skills, which are then carried across disparate organizations and even social domains including the technology industry and electoral politics and contentious action. In my work with Christopher Jasinski (2016), for instance, we showed how "field crossers" were sources of innovation in electoral politics in bringing the insights of the technology and commercial data industries to bear on campaigns and party politics. The idea of networks is the right way to conceptualize this, because networks are an analytical tool that enables us to trace, over time, how *people* are constructed as they move through relations, organizations, fields, and institutions. In other words, following Padgett and Powell (2012), specific *biographies* are produced through relations over time, and those biographies command social and technological skills, knowledge, and ways of seeing at moments in time.

People emerge from networks of relations, and those relations should be conceptualized broadly enough to encompass ties with other people, organizations, institutions, and fields. And, following the insight of Bruno Latour and the actor-network theory framework more broadly, technologies are also embedded in networks and share relations with other nonhumans and humans. In the context of electoral politics, campaigns assemble technologies from party networks but also from commercial firms, open-source development projects, and nonprofit and advocacy organizations. The opportunities to assemble these technologies again relate to perception and skill, as well as to the range of available technologies and their affordances (which also affect the possibilities for digital mobilization). For example, with respect to affordances, the digital mobilization possibilities of the technologies of the mid-1990s were limited compared to today, given lengthy donation processing times, the comparatively constrained social affordances of the Internet, and lack of infrastructural political sites to facilitate digital engagement (such as ACT Blue for fundraising or NGP VAN for voter databases on the Democratic side of the aisle). Affordances matter, as do the specific ways that technologies can be assembled; for instance, the lack of integration on the data back end of campaign technologies limits the possibilities for digital mobilization (Kreiss 2016).

In sum, the idea of digital opportunity structures and the perceptual acuity and skills needed to navigate them pushes simultaneously against the ideas that candidates are interchangeable and that there are infinite opportunities for mobilization and agency if only technologies were wielded correctly (i.e., the campaign strategy view that tends to glamorize consultancies). Some candidates are better suited to navigate digital (or other) structures by virtue of their biographies, relational positions vis-à-vis opponents, and the electoral and cultural contexts that create the opportunities for successful outcomes. At the same time, candidates and their campaigns must act within the structure they face, and performance in the moment, rhetorical and cultural work based on the political context, the cultural stylings of candidate personas with respect to particular audiences, and the technologies campaigns take up, all matter as well.

I turn now to the case of the Bernie Sanders 2016 campaign for president as a way to show how this framework of digital opportunity structures helps us understand the possibilities for digital social and symbolic action. The following section reveals how structures such as spheres, fields, and networks interacted to shape the digital opportunities that the Sanders campaign could grasp. I draw on an interview with Hector Sigala, the social media director of the campaign, in addition to an analysis of some of Bernie Sanders's iconic digital communications, from his "America" ad to the graphics the campaign deployed, to demonstrate this.[3] First, I discuss networks of campaign technologies and staffers and the political opportunities offered by fields, before turning to the ways the candidates used rhetoric and symbols of the civil sphere to digitally mobilize members of the public.

Digital Mobilization and the 2016 Bernie Sanders Campaign

Infrastructural Networks and Political Opportunities Offered by Fields

Since opportunities are often not of a candidates' own making, it is important for campaigns to grasp them when they present themselves, even if they cannot necessarily predict them in advance. This is where the importance of technological infrastructure, composed of networks of artifacts, organizations, and staffers, is clear. Candidates who create an infrastructure by assembling technologies and staffers with the specialized expertise to maintain and expand them are positioned to grasp digital mobilization opportunities when they present themselves. For example, when Sanders announced, the campaign had the infrastructure in place to translate the enthusiasm around his candidacy into electoral resources. As Hector Sigala, the social media director for the campaign, described: "So within the first 24 hours, I don't exactly remember, but I'm 90% sure we were able to raise I think a million dollars those first 24 hours just because we had a good website that we set up and captured all the enthusiasm of Bernie just announcing his candidacy" (personal communication, July 13, 2016).

The outpouring of support for Sanders was not entirely unexpected. The candidate had long embraced social media for both practical and symbolic reasons. Sanders believed that the legacy press failed to cover serious issues and let commercial concerns interfere with the facts on issues such as climate change and economic inequality. As such, Sanders sought to use social media tools to speak directly to his supporters, which both enabled him to better get his message out and, symbolically, fashioned him into someone who spoke plainly and directly to the American people without the filter of the mass media. As a result of Sanders's uptake of these tools, Sigala reported that as a senator Sanders had amassed one of the largest social media followings before the campaign started, perceived the value of it, and was even in the practice of writing his own social media posts. Thus, the value of digital infrastructure was both readily apparent to the candidate and an area of initial investment for the fledgling campaign, and the senator had a dedicated and cultivated following that could be easily mobilized to give money at the commencement of the candidate's campaign.

The execution of the digital strategy fell to experienced staffers drawn together by the campaign who had biographies that provided them with the perceptual sensitivity and technological skills to both navigate and take advantage of the digital opportunity structure that the candidate faced. The Sanders campaign built an organization that assembled staffers with diverse professional biographies leveraging skills from the political and other fields in the service of its electoral bid. This is precisely the blend of domain shifting that Padgett and Powell (2012) argue has the potential to give rise to new technologies and practices, and the campaign likely featured the cognitive diversity and structural folding (de Vaan, Stark, and Vedres 2015) that helps ensure these new technologies and practices are relevant to innovation in the political field.

For example, Sigala himself joined the campaign with knowledge of digital organizing in the political field, having served as the communications director for the Congressional Hispanic Staff Association before spending more than three years working for the senator as a systems administrator and telecom legislative correspondent. This experience gave Sigala the ability to channel the senator's voice on the campaign's social media properties; as he put it: "My expertise here, being the social media guru or a campaign veteran, is knowing Bernie. I worked for him for a long time. He trusts me. I know his voice, and I'm able to kind of be pretty on top of it and posting for Bernie as Bernie, and that's really, I think, what my strength is" (personal communication, July 13, 2016). This was important because the campaign's key asset on social media, according to Sigala, was the senator's voice:

> We do take a lot more intimate approach and a more Bernie approach. We try to make it as much as if Bernie were posting himself. . . . People don't wanna follow a brand; they don't wanna follow a company; they wanna follow a person. If they wanted to learn more about your company or about what's on your website, then they would just go to your website, but they wanna have a conversation with you. And that really worked out really well . . . rather than what had been a staff-driven approach, this was Bernie-driven, his voice. Most of our stuff is in first-person.

Meanwhile, the Sanders campaign hired Revolution Messaging to handle its digital operations. Revolution Messaging was founded by the Obama 2008 campaign's external online director, Scott Goodstein. The firm itself employs a number of employees with extensive backgrounds in progressive political causes. Among them are Tim Tagaris, who served as the Internet communications director at the DNC under chairman Howard Dean, digital lead for Ned Lamont's insurgent 2006 campaign against Senator Joe Lieberman, digital director for the presidential campaign of Chris Dodd, and founder of the Service Employees International Union's new media department. Revolution Messaging also employed people such as Douglas Busk, who according to his bio joined the firm to support the development of its digital platform after working for a number of wireless technology firms such as Verizon Wireless and Cingular (and also leading mobile brand strategy for Coca-Cola). The campaign also hired Zack Exley as a senior advisor. Exley started his career as a labor organizer and subsequently became the organizing director of MoveOn.org, an advisor to the Dean campaign, director of online organizing for Kerry's presidential bid, and cofounder and president of the New Organizing Institute.

All of which meant that the candidate had made a rich investment in a digital-intensive strategy and infrastructure—comparable with Clinton (Associated Press 2015)—that positioned the campaign to capitalize on digital opportunities should they arise. And they clearly did, with Sanders's cultivated base of digitally engaged supporters. The value of this infrastructure is apparent in the contrast with the Trump campaign. The Trump campaign *lacked* digital infrastructure (and much else besides), which meant the candidate was not able to capitalize on digital opportunities until well into the general election, when Trump began raising millions of dollars in small-donor online donations. Had Trump done that throughout the primary, he would likely have been in a much stronger financial position for the general election and have had campaign staples such as field offices in place (regardless, Trump's lack of a conventional campaign seemed to not have an impact on the final result).

While the Sanders campaign had networks of talented staffers and technologies in place, there were aspects of digital mobilization that they did not anticipate, aptly demonstrating the fact that digital opportunities are not entirely known in advance and staffers need to be ready to act when the moment presents itself. The Sanders campaign *discovered* that millennials were interested in the candidate's message. Not ony did the campaign not anticipate millennial support, but it came as a complete surprise, and independent from anything the candidate actually did to inspire it. As Sigala stated:

> So, we didn't target millennials. That's one thing. We didn't get millennials because we targeted them and because we had a good digital program that was based around them. I think millennials are kind of—they liked Bernie for whatever other reason, and they stayed around because we had a good digital program. But it wasn't something that we targeted, and in fact, when we started this campaign—I've worked for Bernie for four years before this, and he would be one of the most boring senators, because he was the one who was always talking about Social Security, always talking about Medicare and Medicaid. . . . And so, I thought, when we got on this campaign, "Well, one thing we've got for sure is the senior citizen vote," and it turns out it was kind of the opposite, right? . . . So, really, the oldest candidate, a 74-year-old man who calls Snapchat "snapshot," ended up doing really well on social media and getting the votes of young people all across America. So, it wasn't something that was planned. It wasn't the grassroots strategy of the campaign. It was just something that worked. (personal communication, July 13, 2016)

This quote reveals not only that opportunities are sometimes completely unanticipated and candidates and campaigns need to be in a position to capitalize on them ("they stayed around because we had a good digital program"), but also, as importantly, that campaign events are contingent, depending on fields—it was not necessarily the *intrinsic* appeal of Sanders to millennials so much as a relational opportunity created by the field of candidates during the 2016 primaries. In this case, there was no progressive alternative to Hillary Clinton, and it was likely a mix of the senator's avowed democratic socialism, his presumed authenticity and purity as an outsider and insurgent candidate (perceived qualities that also offered a particularly compelling contrast with Senator Clinton), and appeals to progressive policies and transcendent American values that proved so appealing to younger voters. Indeed, while history does not enable us to go back in time and run a field experiment with a different primary contest, staffers themselves wondered whether Sanders's exceptional run was the product of the right candidate, at the right moment, in the right primary field. In response to a question asking him to assess whether it was the work that the Sanders digital team did or the features of the candidate during this particular race that enabled the campaign to mount such a strong challenge to Clinton, Sigala wondered: "We can A/B test everything, but at the end, you do have to ask yourself: does any of this matter—any of the digital work, any of the field work matter in a presidential race, or is it really just the candidate and the timing? Was it that we had the Occupy Wall Street movement a few years ago and Bernie's kind of the reverberation of that on a national, presidential scale?" (personal communication, July 13, 2016).

With millennials backing the senator, the campaign sought to use digital media to expand Sanders's base of support. This offers another illustration of the ways the structure of factions within parties interact with the field of candidates to shape the opportunities for appealing to groups of voters and provide, or limit, potential opportunities for digital mobilization. Despite all of the celebration of the Sanders campaign and its digital prowess, and targeted efforts to expand the senator's base to include African Americans, Latinos, and Native Americans in key primary states, the campaign made little headway among more diverse Democratic Party voters (Scheiber 2016).

Even if the campaign ultimately came up short, it was able to use digital media to knit supporters together into new networks and, ultimately, leverage them for resources. The Bernie Sanders campaign attracted a bevy of grassroots volunteers to work on technical projects by promoting a technologically enabled vision of electoral politics that included the volunteer development of a "Field the Bern" field canvassing application (Corasaniti 2015). Through the campaign's cultural work and its inspirational message that resonated with many young, technically skilled individuals—along with the campaign's decision as an organization to provide these individuals with the autonomy to develop and launch projects for the campaign—new networks were formed around the campaign and it was able to leverage them for electoral purposes.

Deriving Stories from the Cultural Background of the Civil Sphere

What did these staffers and consultants to the campaign produce and disseminate using digital and social media technologies? A different type of structure, and ultimately opportunity, came with respect to the democratic symbolic code that both provided the repertoire for, and bounded the cultural objects the Sanders campaign effectively could produce and deploy, as the candidate vied for the highest office in the United States. The idea of a symbolic code (Alexander 2006) broadly refers to the unwritten cultural rules that shape what symbols can legitimately be deployed in the civil sphere in accord with its moral binaries. In Alexander's theory, the civil sphere is structured by moral binaries, and candidates and campaigns must align their symbolic material (such as candidate rhetoric and the campaign's digital images, advertisements and videos, etc.) with the civil side of these binaries for their communication to be legitimate, effective, and resonant with members of the democratic public.

For example, the Sanders campaign narrated the candidate and campaign on the civil side of the moral binary of the civil sphere. While a systematic review of the Sanders campaign's communications is beyond the scope of this chapter, the "America" advertisement discussed above provides an illustrative example (see Figure 2.2).

The still from the ad clearly reveals its overarching theme of democratic inclusion, a graphic representation of "we the people." As the political philosopher Danielle Allen (2014) has argued, the Declaration of Independence offers a sophisticated argument for democratic inclusion, liberty, and equality. These cultural ideals at the root of America's democratic imagination are given contemporary media form in the Sanders video as a representation of the country, and by extension, the campaign, made up of ordinary, hardworking, and diverse citizens. It resonated among so many in the democratic public because its theme was about American democracy itself, given 2016 form in a video that draws on the cultural discourse of the Declaration of Independence. And the ad is powerful precisely for what it is also

Figure 2.2. Screenshot from Bernie Sanders's "America" ad
Source: https://www.youtube.com/watch?v=2nwRiuh1Cug

missing: the Wall Street bankers, for instance, who are a part of an empirical, not an ideal, America. Indeed, Sanders, through his rhetoric, often cast his Wall Street opponents as standing on the anticivil side of the democratic moral binary, castigating them as subverting and corrupting democracy through anticivil flows of money and influence.

Indeed, the Sanders campaign's symbolic framing not only appeals on a cultural structural level to deep-seated civil democratic morality, but also tells a particular story of peoplehood, in Smith's (2003) terms, that is rich with an identity-based appeal. The Sanders ad celebrates diversity (not demographic homogeneity), middle-class people (as opposed to economic elites or the destitute), and civil harmony (not partisan agonism). This portrayal of Sanders's supporters is designed to draw others in through their identification with these values and these proffered identities, as well as to narrate these identities on terms that are in accord with the structuring moral codes of the civil sphere (such as emphasizing civil solidarity, equality, and democratic inclusiveness.) Indeed, one tactic of the campaign was to encourage the digital social sharing of the candidate's message and campaign's symbolic content—in essence, urging supporters to make the campaign's message a part of their identity in ways that would radiate outward through social networks (Kreiss 2016). As the call to share tweets clearly reveals (see Figure 2.3), these messages were articulated from and in accord with normative cultural understandings about democracy, while conveying an identity narrative about Sanders supporters (i.e., they are not the "few on top").

What is poignant here is that the ad and the "Vote Together" effort say nothing about policy. They present normative visions of a democratic America. Indeed, Hillary Clinton criticized Sanders (and Obama before him in 2008) for his lack of specific policy details and empty, dreamlike promises. But as Alexander (2010) specifically argues, in the context of electoral politics, policy statements are less important than how candidates narrate themselves on the civil side of the moral binary of the civil sphere and create meaningful symbolic difference from their political opponents.

Much of the literature on collective action and mobilization is narrowly concerned with information instead of the cultural and identity narratives that give shape to democracy and social distinction. Sanders's "America" ad, after all, conveyed little in the way of information about policies or politics, and neither does the "Vote Together" social sharing effort. The "America" ad and the campaign's other digital symbolic content were meaningful precisely because of their conveyance of the candidate's values and morals and vision

It would help us greatly if you could retweet our posts from @BernieSanders, and then adopt the hashtag as your own! Share your stories. What does it mean to you? Why do you think it's important that we #VoteTogether? **Remember:** having many **unique** tweets in addition to all the retweets is necessary to get us trending – so please improvise! **And don't forget, we have a huge repository of amazing posters at the bottom of this page!**

EXAMPLE TWEETS (CLICK TO SHARE)

★ America becomes a greater nation when we stand together and say no to racism, hatred, and bigotry. #VoteTogether

★ When people come together, we can beat any amount of money thrown around by the Koch Brothers, Goldman Sachs executives. #VoteTogether

★ Our most important task is to revitalize American democracy. When we do that we change America. #VoteTogether

★ #VoteTogether so we can build a future that works for all of us, not just the few on top.

★ When people stand together, and are prepared to fight back, there's nothing we can't accomplish. #VoteTogether

★ We need a revolution in how healthcare is provided in this country. #VoteTogether

★ America should work for all of us, not just a handful of billionaires. Watch, share, and #VoteTogether

★ New Hampshire, every vote counts. Take back your Democracy on Tuesday and let's #VoteTogether

★ Let us understand that when we stand together, we will always win. #VoteTogether

Figure 2.3. VoteTogether social sharing
Source: https://berniesanders.com/vote-together/

of what America and democracy is and should be, in addition to their invitation to citizens to imagine themselves in these terms. And this fit between civic morality, Sanders's position in a field of Democratic candidates, and the audiences in the electorate helped the campaign's appeals resonate with a lot of people and subsequently resulted in the campaign's extraordinary digital mobilization.

In sum, the Sanders campaign's cultural appeals such as the "America" ad were successful in terms of resonating with members of the public and inspiring digital mobilization because of the alignment of the biography of the candidate, the cultural context and its favorability to populist, power-to-the-people democratic appeals, the field that the candidate existed within, and the composition of the electorate. Martin O'Malley's performances likely fell flat because the candidate was not a cultural outsider, nor could he claim the mantle of the progressive movement as Sanders could. Hillary Clinton's campaign certainly achieved digital mobilization during the primaries and general election but did not come close to the record-setting performance of the Sanders campaign. Clinton could not narrate herself as an outsider, a populist, or a purely civil candidate in relation to Sanders because she is a known insider with a long record in government (she could narrate her historic candidacy as the first woman nominee, however, and she did). And Clinton had less success articulating a

Figure 2.4. Sanders art
Source: https://berniesanders.com/vote-together/

narrative that created a movement behind her for similar reasons. Indeed, it is hard to imagine Clinton or O'Malley being able to wear the symbolic clothing that Sanders donned during the cycle (see Figure 2.4) without attracting charges of inauthenticity (although during the general election, Clinton did seek to wear the garb of civil hero in relation to Trump).

Discussion

This chapter has focused narrowly on electoral politics and digital mobilization, but the analytical framework is designed to be portable across domains of social life and applied to collective action in various settings more generally. Indeed, this chapter strives to integrate various strands of social theory to create a conceptual model for understanding opportunities for and constraints on symbolic and social action and conditions for agency more broadly.

An integrated framework of spheres, fields, and networks has significant analytical advantages over existing conceptual approaches to social life, which largely analyze these things in isolation (e.g., Alexander 2006; Fligstein and McAdam 2012; Padgett and Powell 2012). Thinking across different levels of analysis simultaneously (a) provides an opportunity to think about culture and meaning that is patterned and durable across time (although certainly not unchanging) and provides the background context for social and symbolic action; (b) enables us to think about the logic of fields as more or less coherent domains of activity and the relational positions of actors within them on cultural, technological, and resource levels; and (c) helps us analyze historical shifts in spheres through the dynamics of cultural articulation, field-level changes, and networks that are gathered together across social domains—changes at each level that affect the other two.

While a number of scholars have detailed the workings of cultural structures and the domain-specific meaning of spheres, adding field and network-level perspectives facilitates analysis of meso-level dynamics, networked processes including the connections that actors and meanings have across spheres, and mechanisms for cultural change. For scholars of fields, larger, more durable patterns of cultural meaning and institutional regulation that can give rise to fields, shape their routine workings, ground their legitimacy as organized domains of social life, and change their internal logics and workings are often left out of analyses, even as we often lack accounts of how fields change through the dynamics that scholars such as Padgett and Powell (2012) detail. The field perspective of Fligstein and McAdam and network perspective of Padgett and Powell, meanwhile, lack explicit considerations of meaning and culture that theories of spheres and landscapes (Reed 2011) provide, as well as considerations of the ways that changes in the cultural dynamics of spheres can broadly change the workings of fields and the structure of networks (by making certain forms of relations desirable or illegitimate, for instance.) For example, why do people cross fields to take jobs in electoral politics, if not because of some deep-seated belief in a candidate, her message and values, and democracy more broadly? Meanwhile, we need to understand how networks are shaped by power embedded in spheres and fields, including symbolic and economic power.

The concept of digital opportunity structures explicitly offers a way of bringing these disparate theoretical perspectives together (see Figure 2.5). In the context of electoral politics (but applicable more widely), the idea of digital opportunity structures and levels of sphere, field, and network analysis specifically accounts for deep-seated patterns of cultural meaning that shape the rhetoric that candidates can craft and the cultural scripts they can perform, in large part because in the civil sphere the audiences for these electoral performances, whether they are other field actors or citizens, use the moral logic of democracy as part of their criteria of evaluation of what they do. As detailed above, Alexander's framework does much to anticipate the specific rhetorical stylings of the Sanders campaign in terms of the framing of "we" and the populist appeals to "take back our country" (which are narrated on civil terms.)

At the same time, what Alexander's account does not address, but field perspectives (specifically, the Fligstein and McAdam version) do, is that quite apart from structural moral binaries, to understand the Sanders phenome-

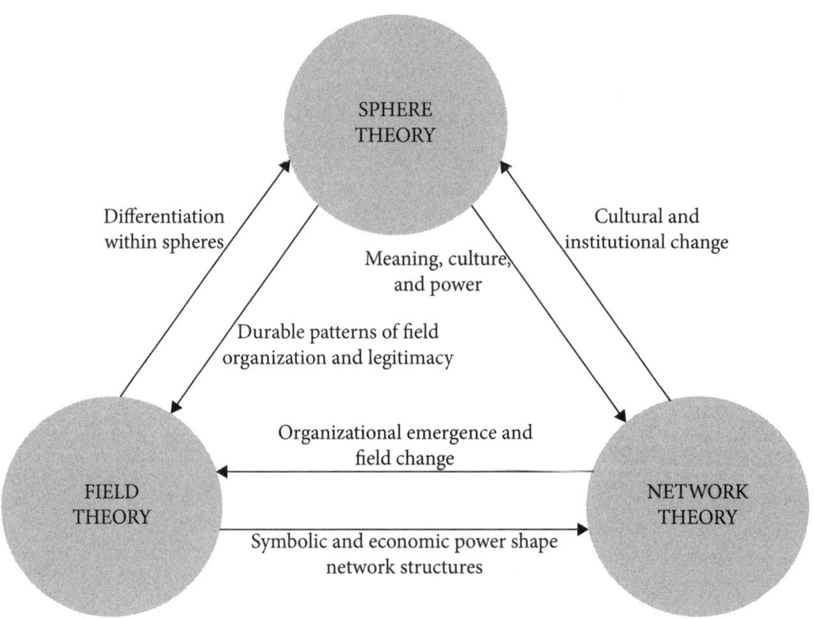

Figure 2.5. Integration of sphere, field, and network theories

non requires understanding how the candidate is positioned relationally within the Democratic Party's field of presidential candidates, and specifically, understanding the ideological, cultural, and policy appeals that he is able to make to certain factions within the electorate. Finally, understanding the phenomenon of the Sanders campaign also requires analysis of the networks, which gave rise to the campaign, in part, in terms of enabling the candidate to capitalize on digital opportunities, and which the campaign itself created through the appeals of the candidate. Sanders was able to capitalize on the cultural context and his position in the Democratic field, in part because he had the staffers with the perceptual knowledge and social skill in place to recognize these opportunities, build the necessary infrastructure, and grow the phenomenon through digital performance.

Conclusion

The integrated framework of spheres, fields, and networks in the context of digital opportunity structures offers much for the theory of "political opportunity structures" more generally. For one, explicitly thinking about spheres, fields, and networks provides more explicit levels of analysis to what are often undifferentiated features of the "environment" in scholarship. Second, it offers an integrated framework for thinking about the conceptual areas of spheres, fields, and networks that in the literature on collective action are too often kept separate: spheres of cultural meaning, fields of activity, and networks of relations. Thinking across all three helps explain their mutual imbrication.

Acknowledgment

The author thanks Victor Pickard for his extensive comments on an earlier draft of this chapter.

Notes

1. I first proposed the idea of "digital opportunity structures" in Kreiss 2016, without the express conceptualization of spheres, fields, and networks.

2. This section is adapted from Daniel Kreiss, *Prototype Politics: Technology-Intensive Campaigning and the Data of Democracy* (New York: Oxford University Press, 2016), 109–13.

3. This interview with Hector Sigala was conducted by Shannon McGregor in the context of another research project (Kreiss, Lawrence, and McGregor 2018).

References

Allen, Danielle. 2014. *Our Declaration: A Reading of the Declaration of Independence in Defense of Equality*. New York: W. W. Norton.

Alexander, Jeffrey C. 2006. *The Civil Sphere*. New York: Oxford University Press.

———. 2010. *The Performance of Politics: Obama's Victory and the Democratic Struggle for Power*. New York: Oxford University Press.

Associated Press. 2015. "How Bernie Standers and Hillary Clinton Differ in Campaign Spending." CBS News, October 16. http://www.cbsnews.com/news/how-bernie-sanders-and-hillary-clinton-differ-in-campaign-spending/.

Boltanski, Luc, and Laurent Thévenot. 2006. *On Justification: Economies of Worth*. Princeton, N.J.: Princeton University Press.

Bonikowski, Bart, and Noam Gidron. 2016. "The Populist Style in American Politics: Presidential Campaign Discourse, 1952–1996." *Social Forces* 94 (4): 1593–621.

Bourdieu, Pierre. 2005. "The Political Field, the Social Science Field, and the Journalistic Field." In *Bourdieu and the Journalistic Field*, edited by Rodney Benson and Erik Neveu, 29–47. Cambridge, U.K.: Polity.

Chadwick, A. 2007. "Digital Network Repertoires and Organizational Hybridity." *Political Communication* 24 (3): 283–301.

Christakis, Nicholas A., and James H. Fowler. 2009. *Connected: The Surprising Power of Our Social Networks and How They Shape Our Lives*. Boston: Little, Brown.

Clemens, Elisabeth S. 1997. *The People's Lobby: Organizational Innovation and the Rise of Interest Group Politics in the United States, 1890–1925*. Chicago: University of Chicago Press.

Cook, Timothy E. 1998. *Governing with the News: The News Media as a Political Institution*. Chicago: University of Chicago Press.

Corasaniti, Nick. 2015. "Legion of Tech Volunteers Lead a Charge for Bernie Sanders." *New York Times*, September 3. http://www.nytimes.com/2015/09/04/us/politics/bernie-sanders-presidential-campaign-tech- supporters.html?_ r=2.

De Vaan, Mathijs, David Stark, and Balázs Vedres. 2015. "Game Changer: The Topology of Creativity." *American Journal of Sociology* 120 (4): 1144–94.

DiMaggio, Paul. 1997. "Culture and Cognition." *Annual Review of Sociology* 23: 263–87.

Fligstein, Neil, and Doug McAdam. 2012. *A Theory of Fields*. New York: Oxford University Press.

Gamson, William A. 2004. "Bystanders, Public Opinion, and the Media." In *The Blackwell Companion to Social Movements*, edited by David Snow, Sarah A. Soule, and Hanspeter Kriesi, 242–61. Malden, Mass.: Blackwell.

Israel, Jonathan. 2014. *Revolutionary Ideas: An Intellectual History of the French Revolution from "The Rights of Man" to Robespierre.* Chicago: University of Chicago Press.

Kreiss, Daniel. 2016. *Prototype Politics: Technology-Intensive Campaigning and the Data of Democracy.* New York: Oxford University Press.

Kreiss, Daniel, and Christopher Jasinski. 2016. "The Tech Industry Meets Presidential Politics: Explaining the Democratic Party's Technological Advantage in Electoral Campaigning, 2004–2012." *Political Communication* 33 (4): 1–19.

Kreiss, Daniel, Regina G. Lawrence, and Shannon C. McGregor. 2018. "In Their Own Words: Political Practitioner Accounts of Candidates, Audiences, Affordances, Genres, and Timing in Strategic Social Media Use." *Political Communication* 35 (1): 8–31.

Kreiss, Daniel, Laura Meadows, and John Remensperger. 2014. "Political Performance, Boundary Spaces, and Active Spectatorship: Media Production at the 2012 Democratic National Convention." *Journalism* 16 (5): 577–95. doi. 1464884914525562.

Latour, Bruno. 2005. *Reassembling the Social: An Introduction to Actor-Network-Theory.* New York: Oxford University Press.

Morone, James A. 1998. *The Democratic Wish: Popular Participation and the Limits of American Government.* New Haven, Conn.: Yale University Press.

Padgett, John F., and Walter W. Powell. 2012. *The Emergence of Organizations and Markets.* Princeton, N.J.: Princeton University Press.

Pierce, Charles. 2016. "This Bernie Ad May Be the Best Political Commercial I've Ever Seen." *Esquire*, January 22. http://www.esquire.com/news-politics/politics/news/a41418/bernie-sanders-america-ad/.

Reed, Isaac. 2011. *Interpretation and Social Knowledge: On the Use of Theory in the Human Sciences.* Chicago: University of Chicago Press.

Scheiber, Noam. 2016. "Why Sanders Trails Clinton Among Minority Voters." *New York Times*, March 21. http://www.nytimes.com/2016/03/22/business/economy/why-sanders-trails-clinton-among-minority-voters.html?_r=0.

Schudson, Michael. 1998. *The Good Citizen: A History of American Civil Life.* New York: Free Press.

Sewell, William Hamilton. 1980. *Work and Revolution in France: The Language of Labor from the Old Regime to 1848.* New York: Cambridge University Press.

Skocpol, Theda, and Vanessa Williamson. 2011. *The Tea Party and the Remaking of Republican Conservatism.* New York: Oxford University Press.

Smith, Rogers M. 2003. *Stories of Peoplehood: The Politics and Morals of Political Membership.* New York: Cambridge University Press.

Tarrow, Sidney. 2011. *Power in Movement: Social Movements, Collective Action and Politics.* Cambridge, U.K.: Cambridge University Press.

Williams, Bruce A., and Michael X. Delli Carpini. 2011. *After Broadcast News: Media Regimes, Democracy, and the New Information Environment*. New York: Cambridge University Press.

Wuthnow, Robert. 2009. *Communities of Discourse: Ideology and Social Structure in the Reformation, the Enlightenment, and European Socialism*. Cambridge, Mass.: Harvard University Press.

CHAPTER 3

Kids These Days: Supply and Demand for Youth Online Political Engagement

Thomas Elliott and Jennifer Earl

It is hard to remember the heyday of the 1960s protest cycle without picturing young people, including high school and college-aged activists, as integral to that picture. Whether it was college students, young teachers, and clergy joining Freedom Summer (McAdam 1988), students from historically black colleges participating in sit-ins (Andrews and Biggs 2006; McAdam 1982; Morris 1981), the free speech movement at Berkeley (Klatch 1999), or key players in the radical antiwar movement and New Left (Gitlin 1980), young people were integral to the 1960s protest cycle. Theoretically, youth have also been important. For instance, the enduring attention to biographical availability in micro-mobilization processes owes to the hypothesis that young people participate more than other demographic groups because they have more discretionary time and fewer commitments that compete against activism (Caren, Ghoshal, and Ribas 2011; Schussman and Soule 2005; Snow, Zurcher, and Ekland-Olson 1980). Likewise, most of what we know about the long-term biographical consequences of activism comes from studying differences between people who participated when they were young in the 1960s protest cycle, or specific campaigns within it, versus those who did not (Giugni 2004, 2008; McAdam 1988, 1989).

While there are certainly young faces associated with activism today—whether that be young African American men and women participating in the Black Lives Matter movement, young women participating in anti–sexual assault/Title IX advocacy on college campuses, Dreamers as part of the immigration reform movement, young Occupy participants, or young Middle Eastern participants in the Arab Spring—as we discuss in more depth below, there is still a general sense among many scholars and activists that today's young people are not as engaged in or as integral to movements as they once were (Bennett 2008; Bennett and Segerberg 2013; Delli Carpini 2000; Gordon 2007; O'Donoghue and Strobel 2007; Putnam 2000; Zukin et al. 2006). This impression exists despite evidence suggesting that youth may have traded off some of their institutional political participation in favor of greater protest participation (Dalton 2009).

If, as these arguments imply, youth are in fact less integral to movements today, this should be terribly troubling for social movement scholars and activists alike. For movements to thrive across time, they need new participants joining their ranks as older members are pulled away by competing obligations or disengage for other reasons. Indeed, a marked decline in youth participation that owes to some irremediable lack of interest or motivation on the part of youth would have immense negative consequences for the future of activism. A decline in youth participation in traditional social movements due to changes in the way youth participate would likewise spell trouble, indicating that movements are not keeping up with the changing landscape of activism.

In this chapter, we address potential changes to the role youth are playing in contemporary movements by considering that the problem may start with the movements themselves, rather than with youth. Most pointedly, we turn the question of youth participation on its head, reminding readers that it is nonparticipation (not participation) that is the norm across all age groups. As the large literature on micro-mobilization suggests, nonparticipation is overdetermined; it is explaining *why people do* participate that is difficult.

Thus, we ask how movements are attempting to engage youth. Using a representative sample drawn in 2010 of online spaces from twenty different issue areas, we show that social movements themselves are not doing much to connect with youth, or to provide explicit invitations and entry points for youth to engage in movements (at least online). This suggests that to the extent young people are participating in contemporary movements, they are doing so despite a lack of entry points, and not because of ample welcome.

Skeptics, though, may downplay a lack of entry points, seeing this dearth as a result rather than a cause of youth disengagement. Therefore, we draw on survey data from a 2011 nationally representative sample of American youth to show that there is substantial demand for many different kinds of political engagement among youth. Attention to the opportunities offered to youth can forward our understanding of the relationship between youth and activism today and also contribute to the broader debate about youth political engagement.

Changing Youth Engagement?

Starting around the turn of the current century, scholars began expressing concern that youth have disengaged from politics, both institutional and extrainstitutional (Delli Carpini 2000; Putnam 2000). However, others countered that models of citizenship have changed and that concerns about declining involvement are exclusively measuring old-fashioned forms of engagement: younger citizens simply have been moving from a more traditional or "dutiful," model of citizenship to an "engaged" (Dalton 2009) or "actualized" (Bennett 2008) model of citizenship. These new models of citizenship place less stress on institutional forms of engagement such as voting and relatively more emphasis on noninstitutional engagement (e.g., protest; Dalton 2009), civic engagement (e.g., volunteering; Dalton 2009), and other forms of more personalized political expression (Bennett 2008). In a similar vein, Dahlgren has argued that contemporary youth engagement represents a new civic culture (Dahlgren 2000, 2005; Dahlgren and Olsson 2007). Bennett and Segerberg (2013) argue that the new forms of participation offered by new information and communication technologies (ICT) operate under qualitatively different logics than previous generations of political participation, ones that decenter the importance of organizational membership and collective action.

Scholars have also argued that to the extent to which there has been some decline in youth institutional political engagement, current political elites might be more to blame than youth. For instance, Bennett (2008), among others, argues that highly negative political campaigns and a seemingly unresponsive political system facing grand challenges that even the most functional of political systems may struggle to resolve have come together to drive declining trust and/or interest in traditional political institutions. Similarly, Zukin and colleagues (2006) document how the political climate that Gen-Xers and Millennials grew up in was riddled with scandal and intense partisanship, leading to a deep cynicism about the efficacy of institutional politics. In other words, it is not just that youth opted into new forms of citizenship, but also that the negative climate of institutional politics drove them out of more traditional forms of engagement.

Recent research on youth activism, however, finds similar forces at work in adult-dominated social movement organizations (SMOs) (Gordon 2007; O'Donoghue and Strobel 2007). Even though SMOs are the formal organizations (e.g., NAACP, ACLU, PETA) that have traditionally been the infrastructural backbone of social movements, research finds that youth today feel traditional SMOs marginalize their voices and are unresponsive to their issues.[1] Because disenchantment with institutional politics may have pushed youth away from that arena, social movement scholars should question whether social movements have been sufficiently welcoming to youth, working hard to both recruit and retain them.

Understanding the Supply Side of Social Movement Engagement

An important element in evaluating how social movements have worked (or failed to work) to recruit and retain young participants is understanding the extent to which youth specifically have been targeted for recruitment efforts. Understanding this begins with what Klandermans (2004) refers to as the "supply side" of participation, by which he means the structured opportunities presented to potential participants by social movements.

Klandersmans argues that social movement participation results from the nexus of demand for engagement by prospective participants and a supply of protest opportunities by social movements, often provided by specific SMOs. SMOs and movements more broadly also work to connect, as Klandermans (2004) puts it, supply and demand, by trying to pull willing individuals into supplied opportunities, often by targeting specific groups for participation. For instance, young men were targeted by the anti–Vietnam War movement, young women by second-wave feminism, and youth of color by the civil rights movement, Chicano rights movement, and American Indian movement, among others.

One can measure the importance of this targeting by observing it "in the breach"; historically, it is clear how problematic a lack of targeting and/or openness to specific subgroups can be. For instance, African American women have long argued that a predominately white, liberal feminist movement isn't welcoming to them or their needs and is thus likely to remain a predominately white women's movement. Likewise, young women made similar complaints about the male-centered formal leadership structure of the civil rights movement (McAdam 1988, but see Robnett 1996) and the antiwar movement (Mollin 2009) in the 1960s and 1970s.

Micro-level research also shows that it is important that prospective participants get connected to opportunities to participate, whether through invitations, informal networks, or formal organizational memberships. Indeed, invitations are the most obvious and critically important way to encourage participation according to research. Schussman and Soule's (2005) study of predictors of protest, demonstration, or march participation in the last twelve months finds that "being asked to protest is the strongest predictor of participating in protest" (1083). Passy and Giugni (2001) examine different data but also find being asked is one of the top two strongest predictors of participation. Classic research is similar: Klandermans and Oegema (1987) suggest a four-stage process that culminates in participation if completed successfully. Stage Two of their model requires that individuals are targeted for mobilization through recruitment networks. It is even possible that one of the reasons that network ties have been so influential in producing participation is that invitations to participate flow through them (Passy 2001).

One should infer from this research that if movements or SMOs are keen to include youth, they should make explicit overtures to youth. This might involve discussing issues that are important to youth, explicitly or implicitly targeting youth as prospective audience members, or explicitly asking for youth participation in the movement and/or specific events. Existing research implies that the more these kinds of invitations to participate exist, the more mobilized youth will be. Schussman and Soule (2005) found that when there are not invitations to participate, other factors such as political interest, political engagement, and civic skills should explain self-motivated engagement with a movement, meaning that movements are subject to the prevailing levels of these factors in building a mobilization base if they are not extending invitations or targeting potential participants.

Two other key predictors of individual participation in movement activities are network ties to the movement (see Diani 2004 for a review of this research) and organizational ties to specific SMOs. A number of studies have demonstrated the significance of networks and/or organizational ties to participation in such varied contexts as the French Revolution (Gould 1991, 1993) and the civil rights movement (McAdam 1988; McAdam and Paulsen 1993). Studies have consistently confirmed that both kinds of ties to a movement matter for explaining participation (e.g., Lim 2008; Passy and Giugni 2001; Schussman and Soule 2005).

This work suggests that movements and SMOs should be trying to build networks that include youth and establish organizational ties to specific youth. For instance, in online presences, one might expect that there would be specific sections of a SMO website or other digital presence targeted to youth. Digital materials might also either focus on issues of particular concern to youth or discuss the importance to youth of specific issues (e.g., younger generations will face far larger effects of climate change). Alternatively, movements might try to engage youth by using research about what has made websites successful at this in the past (Bachen et al. 2008; Montgomery 2001) and incorporating specific design features into their own digital spaces. For instance, websites might feature polls or games that give users an opportunity to interact with the content on the site. Websites might also feature online chat technologies, allowing users to interact with each other.

If movements take none of these steps, then this important gateway to recruitment would be stunted for youth. To the extent that youth participation is seen as being less prominent in contemporary protest than it was in the 1960s, the focus should be on asking how movements and SMOs are trying to bring youth into movements, instead of what is pulling young people away from movements and/or out of activism. We treat the extent to which movements try to engage youth as an empirical question. In the next section, we argue that studying online overtures to youth is important in light of both their high levels of screen time and the difficulties they have reported with regard to SMOs that are primarily focused on offline action.

Connecting with Youth Online

In this chapter, we focus on attempts to recruit youth through online media for several reasons. First, the research discussed above makes clear that youth often face dilemmas in being incorporated into traditional SMOs and even into youth-focused SMOs through face-to-face interactions (Gordon 2007;

O'Donoghue and Strobel 2007). But young people spend a great deal of time online (Hargittai 2010; Palfrey and Gasser 2008) and digital tools are deeply embedded in the pathways that shape young people's decisions to participate or not in social movement activities (Maher and Earl 2017), making it important to investigate how movements attempt to connect with youth online, too.

Second, because online activism can involve issues that are not traditionally political, such as fan activism (Earl and Kimport 2009), with many such sites focusing on issues and targets likely to appeal to youth (Earl and Schussman 2008), it is possible that young people get pulled into activism through their interests. Historically, once someone has been active in protest, they are more likely to act again later (e.g., McAdam 1988), suggesting these interest-based online efforts may pull youth into future engagements.

Third, online material could potentially be used to recruit youth through invitations to participate (which we examine in depth below) and through driving greater political interest in a topic (Boulianne 2011). As noted above, the best predictor of participation is having been invited (Schussman and Soule 2005), but for individuals who have not been invited, the best predictor is political interest. Since online spaces can direct invitations and drive interest, and do so within a sharable and potentially social context, these spaces hold great potential for attracting young people. Moreover, young people also share a great deal of information online (boyd 2007, 2014; Ito et al. 2009; Mishna et al. 2012), and social information referrals may reduce the effects of selective attention (Earl and Garrett 2017). This suggests that digital recruitment has the potential to have amplified effects as recruitment efforts flow through social networks and benefit from social filtering processes.

The question that we focus on is whether social movements make use of this ripe space for recruitment. In the next section, we introduce data on random samples of social movement–relevant web presences that we use to answer this question. Following that, we evaluate the possibility that lack of a supply is a consequence, not a cause, of youth disengagement, introducing and evaluating relevant survey data.

Data and Methods: Supply Side

In order to understand the supply side of activism, we need to know how and how often online social movement–relevant spaces engage youth. To address this empirically, we construct a database based on quantitatively content coding random samples of publicly available, web-addressable spaces related to twenty different common social movement issues. Previous studies of youth activism online have relied on convenience samples of websites, focusing on one or two websites chosen for their exemplar status. While this research has produced illuminating results, these samples are unlikely to be representative of the population of online movement–relevant content as a whole, or even of websites that engage youth in activism.

However, alternatives to studying convenience samples of websites have been difficult to identify, until now. For instance, randomly sampling online content has proven difficult in the past because there is no practical way to preidentify the population of web-addressable material engaged in advocacy from which to draw a random sample, nor was there a way to randomly guess at valid URLs, which disallows work-arounds to the lack of a population list (an approach analogous to random digit dialing).

We rely on an important simplifying assumption to make identifying a population from which to sample tractable: since we are interested in understanding public protest engagement, we assume that we need to identify only relevant online material that other users could reasonably identify and visit themselves. Thus, whether it is an organizational website, a blog, a public-facing Facebook or Twitter profile[2] (i.e., no log-in required), or any other online space reachable via a web address, if we can define the population of such spaces that potential users could also find, we can also randomly sample from it. Although this means we ignore the deep Web, our focus on the population of web-addressable spaces that we refer to as "reachable" (i.e., spaces we can locate without knowing the URL in advance) does allow us to map the public-facing supply side of online protest.

To do this, we use a process that mimics the way individuals typically find online material—either by searching for it through a major search engine or by navigating from links posted on other visited spaces. Specifically, we use repeated searches on Google (the leading search engine), which itself relies on Googlebot (which relies on link-crawling to identify new sites). To do this, we first identify twenty social movement issue areas, selected to represent issue areas traditionally studied by social movement scholars (e.g., abortion and civil rights), issue areas where mobilization has increased or decreased significantly over time (e.g., immigration and globalization), and issue areas tied to the Internet (e.g., open source). For each issue, we generate a list of pretested search terms to capture both the pro and con sides of the issue (e.g., the abortion issue area includes search terms to identify both pro-life and pro-choice spaces). We use two sources to identify search terms. First, we use common keywords in academic and popular literatures (e.g., "free speech" for the civil liberties issue) that passed a pretest threshold for identifying social movement content. Second, we investigate exemplar spaces for each issue area (e.g., NOW for the feminist issue area) and use high-frequency words found on these sites that also passed a pretest threshold for identifying social movement content. From both sources, we pair terms with an action word, such as *protest* or *stop*, and pretest each search term phrase for the quality of results returned from Google. Using this approach, we generated a total of 175 search terms across the twenty issue areas.

We then use a Google API to retrieve one thousand search results per query, each search term constituting a query to the Google API. Multiple queries for the same issue area are appended to generate twenty independent populations of reachable web-addressable spaces for each issue area. After removing duplicates, we are able to identify over one hundred thousand unique URLs (for more details on an earlier wave of data collection using the same method, see Earl et al. 2010).

Having identified a population of reachable, web-addressable spaces for each of the twenty issue areas in 2010, we drew a 1 percent random sample by movement issue area and downloaded a copy of each space in the sample to a local server to facilitate quantitative content coding. For sites identified in 2010, we code 1,084 web spaces across these twenty causes. Any protest linked to or hosted by one of these sites was also separately coded, yielding 3,659 protest actions (for a visual representation of this process, see Earl and Kimport 2009).[3]

In the analyses below, because we want to narrow our focus to what social movement spaces in particular were doing, we reduce this overall data set in two ways. First, we focus only on digital spaces that, when coded, contained content that appealed for change. In other words, if there was content relevant to social movements but the space did not engage in advocacy, it is dropped from our analyses below. Second, we analyzed only data from sites that advocated for change on the issue for which they were sampled (e.g., we drop from our analyses situations in which the space was sampled as an environmental site but contained peace advocacy when we archived the site).

This substantially reduces our data set: our final sample includes 363 web spaces and 1,402 protest actions.

Coding

Coding proceeded in two waves. The first wave of coding occurred in 2010–2011 and coded for ninety-three measures about the digital spaces themselves and another forty-six measures about every protest action hosted or linked to from those spaces (e.g., online petitions spaces that encouraged users to sign; in-person protest rallies the site invited users to attend). A second wave of coding occurred in 2013–2014 to code for youth-specific elements, coding an additional twenty-eight measures about the overall digital space and seven additional protest action measures. This second wave of coding used the same saved copies of the spaces as the first wave, so the content being coded was identical across both waves. Coders in the first wave of coding had a reliability of 98.2 percent for site-level measures and 97.7 percent for protest action measures. Coders in the second wave had a reliability of 96.9 percent for site-level measures and 99.1 percent for protest action measures.

To measure youth-facing elements of these digital spaces, we focus on three major measures of youth orientation. The first measure, youth issues, measures whether the site contains content relevant to youth, regardless of the intended audience. This could include sites that tell parents how to talk to their kids about drugs, or public Twitter feeds that educate youth directly about sexual health. The second, youth audience, measures whether the space specifically targets a youth audience or addresses a youth constituency. For instance, a site could do this by containing a separate section specifically for youth, or by including youth in the intended audience more broadly. The third measure, youth participation, measures whether the digital space describes, hosts, or links to any protest actions that explicitly encourage youth to participate. To count as a protest action, the action should be documented on the space and the space should endorse or encourage participation in the action. To count as encouraging youth participation, the action should be explicitly trying to recruit youth to participate, with a specific reference to youth. For all of the above, we define youth as college age (approximately twenty-two years old) or younger.

We also use coded data on the issues about which the spaces advocated. These were issues or causes the space took a position on or endorsed, reflecting the site's overall stance. There were almost four hundred detailed cause claims that could be applied; most were drawn from the Dynamics of Collective Action data set (McAdam et al. 2009), but some were added to capture more recent protest developments. Drawing on insights from Earl (2013), we also code for site features that increase their participatory nature. We code for whether the site allows users to get information about a cause, such as research reports or press accounts, and whether the space allows users to provide information to the site, such as by posting reports or press accounts or by using a tip line that allows them to provide information about companies with contested business practices. We also code for whether the space allows users to express their own opinions about a cause or to read other users' opinions. We also looked for design features that prior research associated with exemplary youth sites, such as hosting polls, quizzes, games, or crossword puzzles, and/or allowing live chats.

Finally, we code for whether endorsed protest actions took place offline, took place online and were hosted by the site itself, or took place online at a different space (i.e., the coded site linked to the action). Offline actions require a participant to be copresent with other participants. This could include attending rallies or meetings, participating in a strike or sit-in, lobbying, and so on. An internal online action did not require copresence with other participants, and all necessary requirements for participation could be found on the coded space. An external online action did not require copresence, and the user had to follow a link to an external online space in order to participate. Online activities could include letter writing and emailing political figures online, participating in boycotts organized online, signing online petitions, and even more disruptive actions like denial of service attacks.

Findings: The Supply Side for Youth Engagement

The central question animating this part of our study is how often and in what ways digital spaces demonstrably try to engage youth in activism. Figure 3.1 graphs the percentage of digital spaces that engage youth across our three measures of youth engagement: content geared to youth, youth as a clear site audience, and requests for youth participation in advocacy. Nearly 40 percent of sites contain content on youth-related issues, while only 15 percent of sites target a youth audience, and only 3 percent of sites encourage youth to

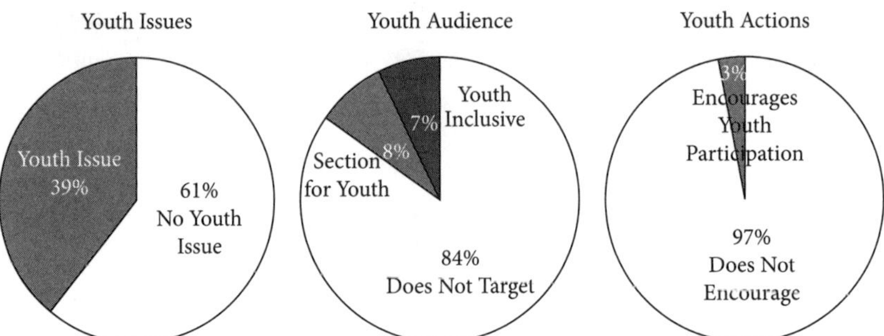

Figure 3.1. Percentage of sites that engage youth across three different measures

participate in protest actions. In other words, while sites very commonly discuss issues relevant to youth, they don't often include youth in the intended audience of that discussion, nor do they specifically invite youth to participate in protest actions.

Youth engagement does vary by cause, though, as shown in Figure 3.2. Labor, LGBTQ, and globalization spaces most often include youth issues. LGBTQ, green, and labor spaces top the list in terms of targeting a youth audience, and green, LGBTQ, and globalization spaces most frequently encourage youth participation in protest actions. Although these four causes—globalization, green, labor, and LGBTQ—are leaders across multiple measures of youth engagement, even these leaders rarely—11 percent or less of the time—encourage youth participation in protest.

Previous research has found a set of features that consistently promote youth engagement online, namely interactive elements such as polls, games, and live chat opportunities. Montgomery (2001) found that some of the most popular commercial sites for teens offered ways for their users to interact and express their identity and creativity through chat, message boards, polls, quizzes, and other forms of content creation. Bachen and colleagues (2008) similarly argue that effective engagement of youth requires higher levels of interactivity on civic sites, including features such as polls, games, and opportunities to chat with other users. They find, however, that civic sites do not often include these features when they try to target youth. Figure 3.3 graphs the percentage of sites in our study with these features and other opportunities for engagement for sites that do and don't target a youth audience. While nearly all sites allow users to get information about a cause, only about half allow users to express their opinions about a cause or to view other

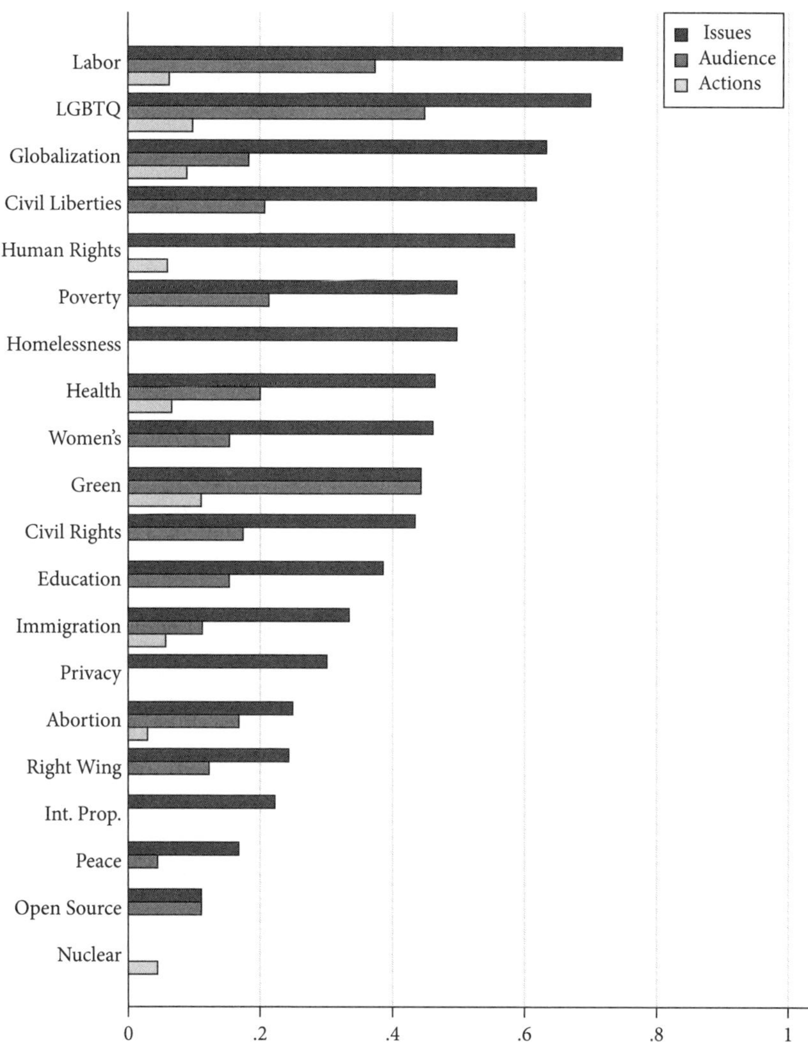

Figure 3.2. Percentage of sites engaging youth across causes

users' opinions; less than a quarter allow users to provide information about a cause, and few contain polls, games, or live chat features.

Not only are these features not common on sites in general, but they are also not much more common on sites that we could consider youth-facing based on the three primary indicators of youth engagement. That is, the

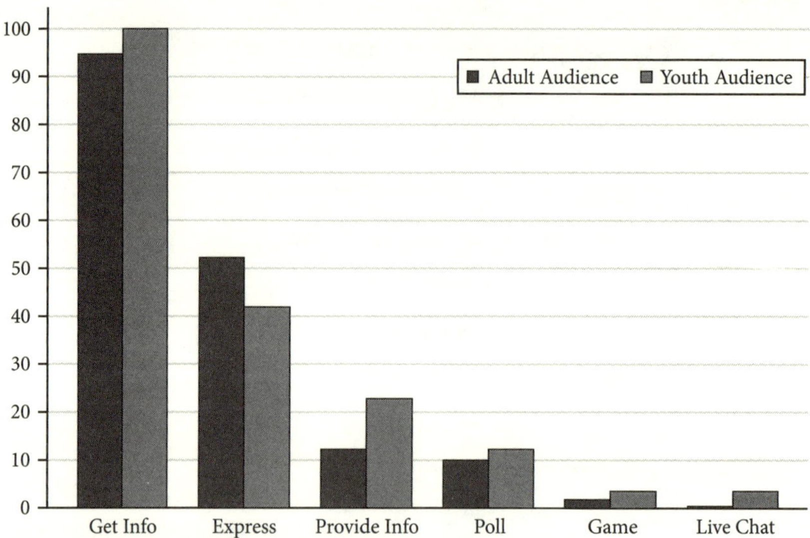

Figure 3.3. Percentage of sites with features by audience

difference between sites that target a youth audience and those that don't are largely negligible. Only live chat and the ability to provide information to a web space have statistically significant differences, with youth-targeting sites containing this feature more often. However, both features are relatively rare, even for youth-targeting sites.

It is also worthwhile to understand the kinds of actions that youth are targeted to engage in. In Figure 3.4, we display the percentage of sites that engaged youth across each type of action the space offered. For example, 46 percent of sites that promote offline protest actions include youth content, while only 15 percent of such sites target a youth audience or encourage youth participation in protest actions. Across all types of protest offerings, including youth issues is relatively common, but targeting a youth audience or encouraging youth participation is rarer, which should raise some concerns given the importance of targeting and invitations.

Thus far, we have established that despite having a great deal of content relevant to youth, only a small minority of sites explicitly target youth as a site audience, fewer still ask youth to participate in social movement advocacy, and few also include features that have been commonly associated with youth-oriented sites. This speaks directly to the larger issue we are raising: movement sites are not doing much to engage youth, so it should not sur-

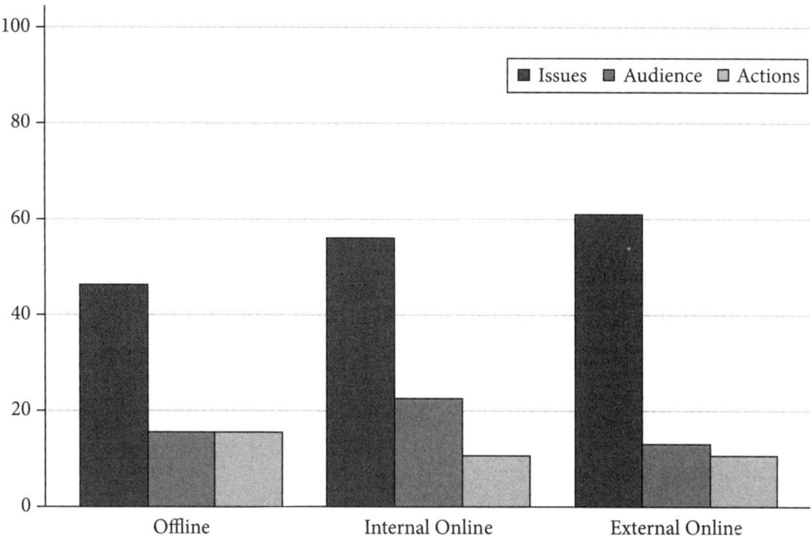

Figure 3.4. Percent of sites that engage youth through protest offerings

prise scholars that youth may not be as engaged as social movement activists would like. We take this as evidence that any potential participation gap owes more to the supply side of social movements than the demand side (which we discuss in the next several sections).

Do Some Kinds of Sites Support Youth Recruitment More?

It is also reasonable to ask whether specific kinds of sites attempt to engage youth more. We consider two kinds of sites. First, we expect that sites that are broader in terms of the range of causes they advocate on will be more likely to engage youth-related issues. We think of this in terms of cause-based specialization and divide sites into generalist versus specialist sites.[4]

Figure 3.5 graphs the percentage of generalist versus specialist sites that engaged youth across our three engagement measures. As expected, it shows that generalist sites are significantly more likely to have youth content on them, but there is no significant difference between generalist and specialist sites in terms of youth audience and youth participation. Generalist sites contained youth-related issues over half the time, while specialist sites included

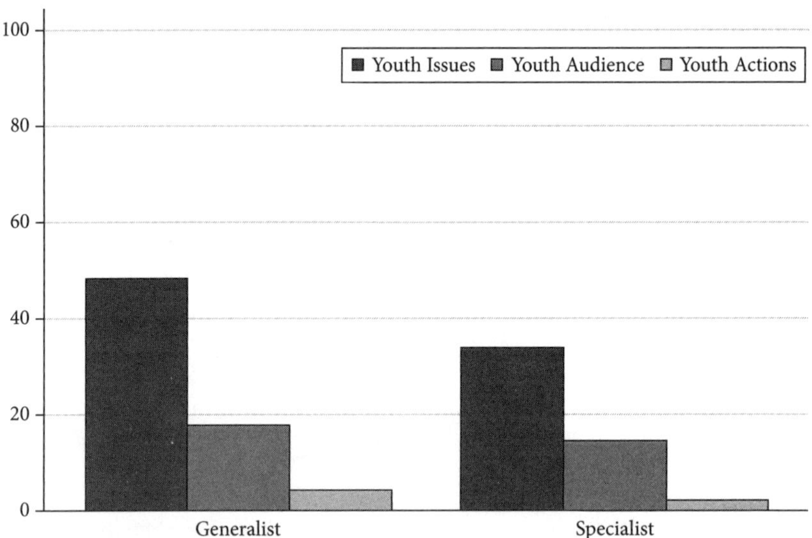

Figure 3.5. Youth engagement in generalist versus specialist sites

youth issues only a third of the time. Since generalist sites engage many different causes, they have more opportunities to engage youth in several particular causes.

Second, we have elsewhere shown that SMO-run sites are more likely than non-SMO sites to engage youth (Elliott and Earl 2018). Two of SMOs' primary responsibilities are recruitment and targeting, and so it makes sense that they would target youth. However, youth engagement is still low, even on SMO-run websites.

Is Supply Just Responding to Demand?

We are arguing that social movements have not done enough to build youth engagement. However, a critical reader might suggest that movements have not targeted youth because there is little demand on the part of youth for this engagement. That is, instead of "wasting" resources by trying to attract uninterested youth, these sites focus on older groups that are more likely to be interested, or do not specifically consider age in their outreach. To explore this, we conduct a secondary analysis of data from a 2011 nationally representative survey of youth, finding that there is substantial demand from youth for different kinds of engagement and that youth are actually managing to engage *despite* the lack of a robust supply side.

Data and Methods: Measuring Demand

The 2011 Youth Participatory Politics (YPP) Survey is a nationally representative survey of 2,920 youth in which respondents were asked questions about their engagement with politics, online digital media, and civic and volunteer programs. The survey was conducted both online and over the phone. In order to be eligible to complete the survey, the respondent had to be between the ages of fifteen and twenty-five (inclusive), which is a slightly different than the twenty-two or younger we used to gather our supply side data. The survey was commissioned by Mills College and conducted by Knowledge Networks (KN).

Three separate samples were surveyed to produce the overall dataset. First, KN administered KnowledgePanel, a probability-based online panel. Participants without a home computer and Internet were provided both. KnowledgePanel had approximately fifty-five thousand active participants, a sample of which was drawn for each study using KnowledgePanel, although they were asked to complete a survey no more than once a week to avoid burnout. The main sample was administered online to KnowledgePanel participants. In this sample 1,782 participants completed the survey, representing a completion rate of 94.7 percent.

A second sample of KnowledgePanel participants was drawn and the survey completed over the phone.[5] Participants were first contacted online to get consent to participate via telephone, and those consenting were then called at a later time to complete the survey. In this sample 284 respondents were included, with a completion rate of 42.4 percent.

To supplement the KnowledgePanel sample and ensure enough age by race respondents were included in the final study, an additional probability-based sample was included using the U.S. Postal Service Delivery Sequence File. Matching addresses to other information such as names, telephone numbers, ages of heads of households, and race/ethnicity of heads of households, this sample targeted households with Asian, Latino, and black members. In this third sample 854 respondents were included, with a completion rate of 46.8 percent. All three samples are combined into one data set.

We use this combined data set to address the demand side of activism, and in particular, what kinds of activities youth are currently engaging in. Specifically, we construct four measures of youth engagement from the survey data, including participation in institutional politics, protest, participatory politics, and/or volunteerism. These four measures create a richer understanding of youth political demand; all are based on answers to a series of questions about specific types of activities the respondent had engaged in within the last twelve months, as listed in the findings in Table 3.1.[6] Since these measures capture only activities that youth report having actually participated in, and do not capture what youth would have liked to have participated in, we regard this measure as a very conservative measure of demand.

Specifically, for institutional politics, a respondent scores 1 on this measure if they answer yes to working on a political campaign, wearing a campaign button, putting a campaign sticker on their car and/or placing a sign in their front yard, expressing support for a campaign on a social network, raising or donating money for a campaign, or signing up to receive information from a campaign. If the respondent voted in the last election, they are also coded as engaging in institutional politics.

Respondents were coded as having engaged in protest if they responded yes to taking part in a protest, demonstration, or sit-in; attending a meeting, rally, speech, or dinner related to politics;[7] starting or joining a political group on a social networking site; participating in a boycott or a "buycott" (where someone buys a product because they like the social or political values of the company that makes the product); or signing a petition either online or offline.

Participatory politics is a concept meant to capture how youth may more broadly and actively engage in politics through creating, investigating, and sharing (Soep 2014). It is an important form of involvement to study because while it may be facilitated by others, it doesn't require that a clear opportunity to engage be presented. Instead, youth are constantly choosing when and how to engage, respond to, and share political and civic information they find online. It is also important to study because "social filtering" of information can upset well-known information selection and consumption processes, perhaps leading otherwise uninterested or avoidant individuals to connect with political information or requests (see Earl and Garrett 2017). Respondents are coded as having engaged in participatory politics if they forward or post someone else's political commentary or news; contribute their own article, opinion piece, picture, or video about a political campaign or issue; forward or circulate a funny video, comic, or other artistic item about a political campaign or issue; comment on a news story or blog about a political campaign or issue, write an email or a blog post about a campaign or issue; or participate in an event where young people expressed their political views, such as a poetry slam or musical event.

Finally, the volunteering measure is coded as 1 if the respondent raises money for a charitable cause, participates in a community service or volunteer activity, or works or cooperates with others to try to solve a problem not "traditionally" political in nature that affects their city or neighborhood.

We note that our grouping of these questions varies slightly from other published work using the survey (e.g., Cohen et al. 2012). We construct a category of action not present in Cohen and colleagues (2012)—protest activity—and different categorizations accommodate this.[8]

Results: Measuring Youth Demand

Figure 3.6 shows that youth are engaged in institutional and noninstitutional political and civic activities at relatively high rates.[9] Roughly half report having participated in institutional politics and/or volunteered in the last year, and around one-third engage in protest and/or participatory politics. Three-quarters of respondents participate in at least one type of activity, and nearly half participate in more than one (see Figure 3.7), reinforcing Cohen and colleagues' (2012) findings that political and civic activities tend to be additive versus substitutions for one another. Together, the data show that claims that youth are disengaged, or prefer to be disengaged (as demand would have it), miss the mark.

In terms of activities traditionally associated with social movements, Table 3.1 shows that of the third of respondents who participate in protest activities, almost half of them signed an online petition, and an equal percentage signed a petition offline. Nearly a third of protesters participated in a buycott, and roughly the same percentage started or joined a political group online. Strikingly, a quarter of respondents who participate in protest did so by attending a rally, meeting, or speech, and a similar proportion participated in a boycott. Only 17 percent of respondents who engage in a protest activity engaged in a protest, demonstration, or sit-in, but this compares very favorably to overall population estimates, which sets the proportion of adults who have participated in a protest in the previous year at around 6 percent (Schussman and

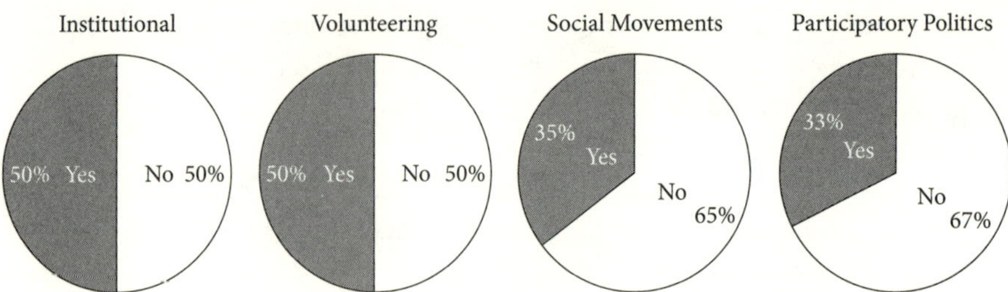

Figure 3.6. Youth participation in political and civic activities

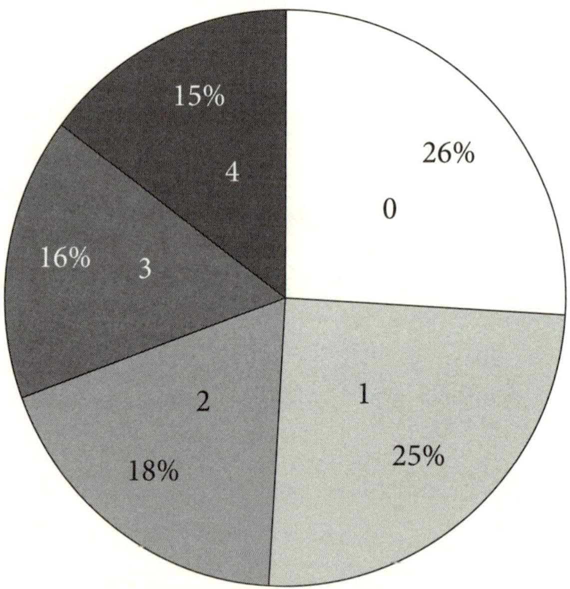

Figure 3.7. Percentage of youth involved in numbers of different activities

Soule 2005). Overall, then, even though activist sites reach out to youth at very low rates, youth are still finding ways to participate in protest activity.

Discussion, Conclusion, and Future Directions

We see a range of implications for our findings. First, there is well-worn debate surrounding youth institutional political engagement in the social sciences: following Putnam's (2000) warnings about declining social capital and

Table 3.1. Percent of Respondents Participating in Activities by Category of Activities

Question	*Percent of Category*	*Percent Overall*
Institutional		
Did you vote in the election last November?	76	42
Expressed support through a social network site such as Facebook, IM, or Twitter	56	28
Wore a campaign button, put a campaign sticker on your car, or placed a sign in your window or in front of your home	32	17
Signed up to receive information from candidates or campaigns via email or text	15	9
Worked on a campaign	9	4
Raised or donated money online (via website, Facebook, text)	7	4
Raised or donated money via offline methods (check, donations at an event)	6	3
Participatory Politics		
Forwarded or circulated funny videos or cartoons or circulated something artistic that related to a political candidate, campaign, or political issues	62	20
Forwarded or posted someone else's political commentary or news related to a political campaign, candidate, or issue	50	18
Commented on a news story or blog you read online about a political campaign, candidate, or issue	48	17
Wrote an email or wrote a blog about a political campaign, candidate, or issue	22	8
Participated in an event where young people express their political views (such as a poetry slam, musical event, etc.)	21	6
Contributed your own article, opinion piece, picture, or video about a political campaign, candidate, or issue to an online news site	17	6
Volunteering		
Participated in a community service or volunteer activity	88	40
Raised money for a charitable cause	54	25
Worked or cooperated with others to try to solve a (nonpolitical) problem affecting your city or neighborhood	34	16

(continued)

Table 3.1. (continued)

Question	*Percent of Category*	*Percent Overall*
Protest		
Signed a paper petition	44	17
Signed an email, Facebook, or other online petition	44	17
Engaged in buycott	32	12
Started or joined a political group on a social network site	31	12
Attended a meeting, rally, speech, or dinner	26	10
Participated in a boycott	26	10
Took part in a protest, demonstration, or sit-in	17	6

increasing political and civic disengagement, a number of commentators focused on the "disengagement" of youth, which led governments, funders, and civic organizations to wring their hands over what could be done to improve youth engagement. At the same time, other scholars contested Putnam's claims, and their implications, on a range of grounds (see Stolle and Hooghe 2005 for a brief review of critical replies).

We engage this well-known debate in a novel way. Scholars such as Dalton (2009) have argued that youth have shifted their involvement from institutional politics to civics/volunteering and activism. Instead of assuming that social movements and other forms of extrainstitutional engagement have received youth interest with open arms, our examination of the supply side of participation has shown that youth are engaging in activism *despite* a lack of significant targeting and tailoring. That is, youth engagement in activism could be even higher if movements more directly attempted to recruit and involve youth.

We also engage this debate in a more traditional way by showing that there is demand for activist engagement by youth. The survey data show that youth are not as disengaged as some have worried—three-quarters of youth, when asked, said they had engaged in volunteer, protest, institutional, or participatory political activities. Any disengagement from a particular activity may be due to a lack of opportunity for youth to participate. Researchers concerned about a potential decline in youth participation in political life should pay more attention to the ways in which youth are participating in political and civic life, and the opportunities available to youth within existing institutions and organizations.

This brings us to a second implication of our findings: it is important for social movements and SMOs to consider these findings and attempt to address the issues they raise. Replenishing the supply of activists is key to social movement survival and continuity across time. Moreover, a lifetime of activism often starts with engagement when one is young. Put simply, if movements want to survive into the future, they need to act *now*. We have pointed to two practical ways to do this: (1) attempt to directly engage youth and make them feel invited into movements; and (2) address issues that are of interest to youth. As we have shown, movements are already enjoying substantial youth engagement, but we believe that they could generate far more youth support and engagement if they do these two things; this is a hypothesis that future research should investigate.

Given that our "demand-side" data show that youth are already engaged, it is important to ask why social movements have been so limited in their attempts to connect further and more effectively with young people. The issue may be partly motivation: perhaps an aging and professionalized movement leadership cadre doesn't see youth engagement as vital. And it may be partly practical: perhaps projects that would build youth engagement are difficult to find support for within social movement fundraising circles. We lack data that would allow us to speak to why so few movements target youth, but future research on this topic is important for both scholars and, as importantly, practitioners.

Even if social movements were to connect with youth more, there are other important questions for social movement scholars to address. For instance, if youth are not invited to participate by existing movements and affiliated SMOs, but they want to participate nonetheless, they may find their way to participation through other means (but likely at lower rates than if recruitment was more targeted and focused). Could this dynamic help to explain the rise of movements like Black Lives Matter and Occupy Wall Street, and the novel tactics used by young women to protest the lack of appropriate action to address sexual assault on college campuses? That is, perhaps youth have begun to get active outside of traditional movements because they are eager to find ways to protest even though traditional SMOs are not providing opportunities for youth to participate.

Future research in allied areas could benefit from investigating whether these same dynamics are present. For instance, do our arguments apply to political campaigns like Bernie Sanders's presidential primary campaign in

2016? Do campaigns that are successful in engaging youth succeed because they attempt to connect with youth more than other campaigns? Do issuing specific invitations and building political interest also matter to institutional political participation, as they do in social movements?

More generally, researchers interested in youth engagement should also consider whether variation in the "supply" of opportunities, or the ability to participate without formal opportunities (as is true with participatory politics), can account for differences in youth participation across different types of engagement. For instance, it is possible that one of the reasons youth engage heavily in volunteering is that there are many opportunities for doing so. Opportunities to volunteer are often structured into high school and college curriculums through service learning, and the volunteer sector has a great deal of experience offering opportunities for youth engagement. Is there as much volunteering when such structured opportunities don't exist? When structured opportunities for other kinds of engagement exist on par with what exists for volunteering, do the levels of those forms of engagement rise to meet the opportunities, suggesting untapped demand? Is participatory politics popular in part because it is often a self-made opportunity? Future research should address all of these questions.

Acknowledgments

We would like to thank the National Science Foundation (Award SES-0547990) and the John D. and Catherine T. MacArthur Foundation (through a subaward from the Youth and Participatory Politics MacArthur Research Network) for critical funding that supported this research. We also thank the participants at the Democracy, Citizenship, and Constitutionalism series at the Annenberg School at the University of Pennsylvania for their feedback, and Michael X. Delli Carpini, who served as our thoughtful discussant.

Notes

1. SMOs are extrainstitutional organizations and thus do not include political parties or exclusively lobbying organizations.

2. Note that throughout the chapter, we use the term *site* to denote any publicly accessible URL on the web, including Facebook and Twitter profiles.

3. There were a few sites that had so many protest actions that random samples of tactics were taken from those sites because it was impossible to code so many actions.

4. We first grouped individual causes into cause families (e.g., black civil rights, LGBT rights, homelessness) and then calculated the number of different cause families a space engaged with. We chose a cut-off of engaging in three or more different cause families as defining a generalist, which represents the 50th percentile for number of cause families a space engaged. Engaging in fewer than three causes meant the space was coded as a specialist.

5. This study does not include an analysis of mode effects, but the responses from the phone survey are included in the present analysis.

6. We recognize that we are relying on what respondents *say* they did, which could be inflated through a social desirability effect. However, we believe this effect is mitigated at least somewhat by the fact that respondents were asked about what they did only in the last twelve months, and that we exclude the measure of intent to vote in the next election, which is likely to be inflated by social desirability effects.

7. This question could also potentially include rallies in support of a political candidate, for instance, and so by including it with protest we risk underestimating participation in institutional activities and overstating protest participation.

8. If we use the same categorization as the published survey results, 43 percent of youth have engaged in institutional political action and 41 percent have engaged in participatory political action.

9. We use survey weights to ensure the data in Figures 3.6 and 3.7, as well as Table 3.1, are as representative of the population overall as possible.

References

Andrews, Kenneth T., and Michael Biggs. 2006. “The Dynamics of Protest Diffusion: Movement Organizations, Social Networks, and News Media in the 1960 Sit-Ins.” *American Sociological Review* 71 (5): 752–77.

Bachen, Christine, Chad Raphael, Katherine-M. Lynn, Kristen McKee, and Jessica Philippi. 2008. “Civic Engagement, Pedagogy, and Information Technology on Web Sites for Youth.” *Political Communication* 25 (3): 290–310.

Bennett, W. Lance, ed. 2008. *Changing Citizenship in the Digital Age.* Cambridge, Mass.: MIT Press.

Bennett, W. Lance, and Alexandra Segerberg. 2013. *The Logic of Connective Action: Digital Media and the Personalization of Contentious Politics.* Cambridge, U.K.: Cambridge University Press.

Boulianne, Shelley. 2011. “Stimulating or Reinforcing Political Interest: Using Panel Data to Examine Reciprocal Effects between News Media and Political Interest.” *Political Communication* 28 (2): 147–62. doi:10.1080/10584609.2010.540305.

boyd, danah. 2007. "Why Youth (Heart) Social Network Sites: The Role of Networked Publics in Teenage Social Life." In *Youth, Identity, and Digital Media*, edited by D. Buckingham, 119–42. Cambridge, Mass.: MIT Press.

———. 2014. *It's Complicated: The Social Lives of Networked Teens.* New Haven, Conn.: Yale University Press.

Caren, Neal, Raj Andrew Ghoshal, and Vanesa Ribas. 2011. "A Social Movement Generation: Cohort and Period Trends in Protest Attendance and Petition Signing." *American Sociological Review* 76 (1): 125–51.

Cohen, Cathy J., Joseph Kahne, Benjamin Bowyer, Ellen Middaugh, and Jon Rogowski. 2012. "*Participatory Politics: New Media and Youth Political Action.* Oakland, Calif.: YPP Research Network. https://ypp.dmlcentral.net/sites/default/files/publications/Participatory_Politics_Report.pdf.

Dahlgren, Peter. 2000. "The Internet and the Democratization of Civic Culture." *Political Communication* 17 (4): 335–40.

———. 2005. "The Internet, Public Spheres, and Political Communication: Dispersion and Deliberation." *Political Communication* 22 (2): 147–62.

Dahlgren, Peter, and Tobias Olsson. 2007. "Young Activists, Political Horizons and the Internet: Adapting the Net to One's Purposes." In *Young Citizens in the Digital Age: Political Engagement, Young People and New Media*, edited by Brian Loader, 68–81. New York: Routledge.

Dalton, Russell J. 2009. *The Good Citizen: How a Younger Generation Is Reshaping American Politics.* Washington, D.C.: CQ Press.

Delli Carpini, Michael X. 2000. "Gen.Com: Youth, Civic Engagement, and the New Information Environment." *Political Communication* 17: 341–49.

Diani, Mario. 2004. "Networks and Participation." In *The Blackwell Companion to Social Movements*, edited by David A. Snow, Sarah A. Soule, and Hanspeter Kriesi, 339–59. Oxford, U.K.: Blackwell.

Earl, Jennifer. 2013. "Spreading the Word of Shaping the Conversation: 'Prosumption' in Protest Websites." *Research in Social Movements, Conflict, and Change* 36: 3–30.

Earl, Jennifer, and R. Kelly Garrett. 2017. "The New Information Frontier: Toward a More Nuanced View of Social Movement Communication." *Social Movement Studies* 16 (4): 479–93. http://dx.doi.org/10.1080/14742837.2016.1192028.

Earl, Jennifer, and Katrina Kimport. 2009. "Movement Societies and Digital Protest: Fan Activism and Other Nonpolitical Protest Online." *Sociological Theory* 27 (3): 220–43. doi:10.1111/j.1467-9558.2009.01346.x.

Earl, Jennifer, Katrina Kimport, Greg Prieto, Carly Rush, and Kimberly Reynoso. 2010. "Changing the World One Webpage at a Time: Conceptualizing and Explaining 'Internet Activism.'" *Mobilization* 15 (4): 425–46.

Earl, Jennifer, and Alan Schussman. 2008. "Contesting Cultural Control: Youth Culture and Online Petitioning." In *Civic Life Online: Learning How Digital Media*

Can Engage Youth, edited by W. Lance Bennet, 71–95. Cambridge, Mass.: MIT Press.

Elliott, Thomas, and Jennifer Earl. 2018. "Organizing the Next Generation: Youth Engagement with Activism Inside and Outside of Organizations." *Social Media + Society* 4 (1): 1–14.

Gitlin, Todd. 1980. *The Whole World Is Watching: Mass Media in the Making and Unmaking of the New Left*. Los Angeles: University of California Press.

Giugni, Marco. 2004. "Personal and Biographical Consequences." In *The Blackwell Companion to Social Movements*, edited by David A. Snow, Sarah A. Soule, and Hanspeter Kriesi, 489–507. Oxford, U.K.: Blackwell.

———. 2008. "Political, Biographical, and Cultural Consequences of Social Movements." *Sociology Compass* 2 (5): 1582–600.

Gordon, Hava Rachel. 2007. "Allies Within and Without: How Adolescent Activists Conceptualize Ageism and Navigate Adult Power in Youth Social Movements." *Journal of Contemporary Ethnography* 36 (6): 631–68. doi:10.1177/0891241606293608.

Gould, Roger V. 1991. "Multiple Networks and Mobilization in the Paris Commune, 1871." *American Sociological Review* 56 (6): 716–29. doi:10.2307/2096251.

———. 1993. "Collective Action and Network Structure." *American Sociological Review* 58 (2): 182–96.

Hargittai, Eszter. 2010. "Digital Na(T)ives? Variation in Internet Skills and Uses among Members of the 'Net Generation.'" *Sociological Inquiry* 80 (1): 92–113. doi:10.1111/j.1475-682X.2009.00317.x.

Ito, Mizuko, Sonja Baumer, Matteo Bittanti, danah boyd, Rachel Cody, Becky Herr Stephenson, Heather A. Horst, Patricia G. Lange, Dilan Mahendran, Katynka Z. Martínez, C. J. Pascoe, Dan Perkel, Laura Robinson, Christo Sims, and Lisa Tripp. 2009. *Hanging Out, Messing Around, and Geeking Out: Kids Living and Learning with New Media*. Cambridge, Mass.: MIT Press.

Klandermans, Bert. 2004. "The Demand and Supply of Participation: Social-Psychological Correlates of Participation in Social Movements." In *The Blackwell Companion to Social Movements*, edited by David A. Snow, Sarah A. Soule, and Hanspeter Kriesi, 360–79. Oxford, U.K.: Blackwell.

Klandermans, Bert, and Dirk Oegema. 1987. "Potentials, Networks, Motivations, and Barriers: Steps Towards Participation in Social Movements." *American Sociological Review* 52: 519–31.

Klatch, Rebecca E. 1999. *A Generation Divided: The New Left, the New Right, and the 1960s*. Berkeley: University of California Press.

Lim, Chaeyoon. 2008. "Social Networks and Political Participation: How Do Networks Matter?" *Social Forces* 87 (2): 961–82.

Maher, Thomas V., and Jennifer Earl. 2017. "Pathways to Contemporary Youth Protest: The Continuing Relevance of Family, Friends, and School for Youth Micromobilization." *Emerald Studies in Media and Communication* 14: 55–87.

McAdam, Doug. 1982. *Political Process and the Development of Black Insurgency, 1930–1970*. Chicago: University of Chicago Press.

———. 1988. *Freedom Summer*. New York: Oxford University Press.

———. 1989. "The Biographical Consequences of Activism." *American Sociological Review* 54: 744–60.

McAdam, Doug, John McCarthy, Susan Olzak, and Sarah A. Soule. 2009. Dynamics of Collective Action. http://web.stanford.edu/group/collectiveaction/cgi-bin/drupal/.

McAdam, Doug, and Ronnelle Paulsen. 1993. "Specifying the Relationship Between Social Ties and Activism." *American Journal of Sociology* 92: 54–90.

Mishna, Faye, Marion Bogo, Jennifer Root, Jami-Leigh Sawyer, and Mona Khoury-Kassabri. 2012. "'It Just Crept In': The Digital Age and Implications for Social Work Practice." *Clinical Social Work Journal* 40 (3): 277–86. doi:10.1007/s10615-012-0383-4.

Mollin, Marian. 2009. "Women's Struggles within the American Radical Pacifist Movement." *History Compass* 7 (3): 1064–90.

Montgomery, Kathryn. 2001. "*Teensites.Com: A Field Guide to the New Digital Landscape*. Washington, D.C.: Center for Media Education.

Morris, Aldon D. 1981. "Black Southern Student Sit-in Movement: An Analysis of Internal Organization." *American Sociological Review* 46: 744–67.

O'Donoghue, Jennifer L., and Karen R. Strobel. 2007. "Directivity and Freedom: Adult Support of Activism Among Urban Youth." *American Behavioral Scientist* 51 (3): 465–85. doi:10.1177/0002764207306071.

Palfrey, John, and Urs Gasser. 2008. *Born Digital: Understanding the First Generation of Digital Natives*. New York: Basic Books.

Passy, Florence. 2001. "Socialization, Connection, and the Structure/Agency Gap: A Specification of the Impact of Networks on Participation in Social Movements." *Mobilization* 6 (2): 173–92.

Passy, Florence, and Marco Giugni. 2001. "Social Networks and Individual Perceptions: Explaining Differential Participation in Social Movements." *Sociological Forum* 16 (1): 123–53.

Putnam, Robert. 2000. *Bowling Alone: The Collapse and Revival of American Community*. New York: Touchstone.

Robnett, Belinda. 1996. "African-American Women in the Civil Rights Movement, 1954–1965: Gender, Leadership, and Micromobilization." *American Journal of Sociology* 101 (6): 1661–93.

Schussman, Alan, and Sarah A. Soule. 2005. "Process and Protest: Accounting for Individual Protest Participation." *Social Forces* 84 (2): 1083–108.

Snow, David A., Louis A. Zurcher, and Sheldon Ekland-Olson. 1980. "Social Networks and Social Movements: A Microstructural Approach to Differential Recruitment." *American Sociological Review* 45: 787–801.

Soep, Elisabeth. 2014. *Participatory Politics: Next-Generation Tactics to Remake Public Spheres*. Boston: MIT Press.

Stolle, Dietlind, and Marc Hooghe. 2005. "Inaccurate, Exceptional, One-Sided or Irrelevant? The Debate About the Alleged Decline of Social Capital and Civic Engagement in Western Societies." *British Journal of Political Science* 35 (1): 149–67.

Zukin, Cliff, Scott Keeter, Molly Andolina, Krista Jenkins, and Michael X. Delli Carpini. 2006. *A New Engagement? Political Participation, Civic Life, and the Changing American Citizen*. Oxford, U.K.: Oxford University Press.

PART II

Rethinking Expertise in Digital Democracies

CHAPTER 4

Why Dewey Was Wrong

Beth Simone Noveck

The world faces daunting and complex challenges: poverty, hunger, epidemics, global warming. For society to succeed in tackling them, we must run our public institutions "smarter" by tapping into the collective intelligence of our communities and drawing power from the participation of the many rather than the participation of the few.

Dangerously, we lack open public institutions—a participatory bureaucracy and open parliamentary processes—in which we can participate as equals. The failure to create concrete, specific, and workable mental models for taking account of the views, voices, and know-how—the broad gamut of citizen expertise, not simply public opinion, of the many disaffected people who voted and the many who did not during the Brexit referendum and the U.S. presidential election in 2016—means that a vacuum arises that charismatic demagogues end up filling (Noveck 2016).

Whether because of or perhaps in spite of their xenophobic and racist overtones, the Brexit vote, the Trump presidential campaign, and the success of populist candidates around the world in the second decade of the millennium highlight a distrust of traditional government institutions manifesting itself as a dislike of credentialed expertise. "The people are right and the governing elite are wrong," declared President Donald Trump during a campaign known for its willingness to play fast and loose with the facts (Trump 2016). Despite his privileged background as the son of a real estate robber baron, Trump reinvented himself as the strong-man leader of a populist movement that will save Americans from the "ruinous rule by a handful of elites."

The United States is not alone in its pervasive contempt for expertise (Mallaby 2016). "We've had enough of experts," infamously declared Brexit campaigner Michael Gove (Mance 2016). The *Guardian* lamented that Prime Minister May reshuffled the British cabinet without any regard for whether her appointees knew much about their future portfolios (Walker 2016). The *Telegraph*, too, wrote about a "sinister and pervasive strain of anti-intellectualism" afoot (Wright 2016). Though there are profound differences between events in the United States, Hungary, Austria, France, and elsewhere during this period, there is a common thread of antielitist, antiestablishment sentiment—a rejection of the third-way postideological politics of Blair and Clinton. The pendulum has swung back, and there is now a political backlash against the supposed consensus that the most complex questions of governing should be managed by EU-centric, business-friendly, globalizing technocrats.

In 1997 Alan Blinder wrote, "Americans have decided, almost subconsciously, that we have drawn the line in the wrong place, leaving too many policy decisions in the realm of politics and too few in the realm of technocracy" (Blinder 1997). Nothing could seem further from the truth twenty years later. Rates of trust in government are at an all-time low. Pew Research reports that 74 percent of Americans feel that elected officials put their own interests ahead of the country's (Pew Research Center 2015). That translates into a 19 percent rate of trust in the federal government (Pew Research Center 2015) and according to Gallup, only a 9 percent rate of trust in Congress (Norman 2016). Fifty-five percent feel that ordinary Americans would do a better job of governing. In fact, over 43 percent of Americans name government as the number one problem we face (Norman 2015). Despite bipartisan consensus that the federal government should play a major role in dealing with terrorism, natural disasters, food and medicine safety, roads, infrastructure, and immigration, there is a disconnect between this desire for government that works and a faith that our institutions can deliver on that promise, or that they even want to (Pew Research Center 2015).

It is no wonder that expertise is a bad word. Expertise is fallible. The so-called experts got it wrong when they predicted a Clinton victory in the 2016 presidential election (Blanchflower 2016). The experts got it wrong when they failed to foresee the subprime mortgage crisis in which many economists were complicit (Blanchflower 2016). "In my experience," wrote Vikram Mansharamani in the *Harvard Business Review*, "experts are among the least successful predictors in times of massive uncertainty. This is not to suggest that experts don't have significant and valuable knowledge; quite the opposite, they likely do. Rather, it implies that they think they know more than they actually do and therefore exhibit more confidence than is warranted. The result: a significant number of very visible expert predictions have gone embarrassingly wrong" (Mansharamani 2012).

Expertise is also often unaccountable. Jürgen Habermas, Europe's most famous democratic theorist, has written trenchantly in *The Lure of Technocracy* against rule by elites and the dearth of mechanisms for "fulfilling the citizens' political will" in European institutions (Habermas 2015). The controversial and ultimately unsuccessful handling of the Greek debt crisis, says Habermas, was clear evidence of the need for more popular input into unaccountable technocratic decision-making. For Habermas, for too long, the chasm between citizen engagement and expert policy making has been excused with claims of incremental progress toward participation, but the crisis of democratic legitimacy is undermining the European project and becoming dangerous. His complaints about technocracy in Europe echo similar criticisms heard after the Dodd-Frank Wall Street Reform and Consumer Protection legislation enacted in the United States in 2010. To address the specter of another "too-big-to-fail" financial firm collapse like Lehman Brothers, the legislation created an elite Financial Stability Oversight Council comprised of the heads of the major financial regulatory agencies accountable only to Congress through the filing of an annual report (Rahman 2013, 9–11). Similarly, the Bank of England came under fire in 2016 for supposedly engaging in unaccountable and antidemocratic experiments that are accused of exacerbating inequality.

Despite shocking statements by the president of the United States that climate change is a Chinese hoax (Proctor 2016) and the willingness to appoint cabinet secretaries with little or no experience, this groundswell of antiexpert rhetoric is nothing new. Isaac Asimov wrote forty years ago about the cult of ignorance in the United States, "Anti-intellectualism has been a constant thread winding its way through our political and cultural life, nurtured by the false notion that democracy means that 'my ignorance is just as good as your knowledge'" (Asimov 1980). After all, Churchill said that "experts should be on tap but not on top."

There has long been a perception that expertise is not compatible with democracy. There is a conflict—one that has come to the fore again in the second decade of the twenty-first century—between governing by experts and democracy, which should be ruled by, for, and with the people. The concern with the lack of accountability on the part of unelected administrative agencies has been an inevitable reaction against the professionalization of the public service and the growth of the administrative state in the twentieth century.

Before the mid-nineteenth century (and even later in the United States), there was no formal professional civil service, with its system of merit-based exams and appointments. To be clear, even though the United States was late to the game, the absence of a professional public service and extensive constitutional provisions about the administrative state did not mean there was not already plenty of administration (Noveck 2015). The levying of taxes, collecting of duties on ships, and establishment of a private patent system, for example, were of vital importance, especially to generate revenue. The doling out of pensions to veterans and their widows and the provisioning of relief to those suffering from disasters were among the welfare state initiatives of the early nineteenth century. But administration was a patchwork of practices, mostly local in nature, and merit was not considered the key factor for employment.

In the new communities of the wide-open American Northwest, ordinary people participated actively in public affairs, as they had done in colonial times. Frederick Jackson Turner extolled the amateur governance of the American forest and frontier in his seminal book *The Significance of the Frontier in American History* (Elkins and McKitrick 1954, 336). The roster of offices to be filled and operated was blank, and men of no previous political experience had to do the job.

By the middle of the nineteenth century, however, the Age of the Founders had passed, and with it died the idea of gentleman lawmen and laissez-faire frontier democracy. It was replaced at the national and even local levels by professionals who decided and governed. Lost were both the informality of access and the robustness of informal participation that characterized life before industrialization, when everyone had to do his part in running things. As the nineteenth century progressed and technology advanced, progressive concerns about urban problems—labor and social welfare, municipal reform, and consumer protection—and agrarian interests in railroad, tariff, and trust regulation took shape in opposition to the excesses of the emerging capitalist economy. In turn, these fueled a demand for stronger government (Noveck 2016).

In contrast to the 780 government employees (excluding deputy postmasters) in the United States at the turn of the nineteenth century (Library of Congress 1976, pt. 1, ch. 1, 3), there are more than two million civilian "professional" public servants employed in the federal executive branch in the United States today (United States OPM 2013) and half a million members of the civil service in Britain (United Kingdom ONS 2016), supported by attendant think tanks and lobbyists who help to generate the information needed for governing.

This growth of professional public administration in the nineteenth and early twentieth centuries was designed to apply scientific principles to governing while reducing corruption, patronage, and inefficiency. As science gave rise to tools, from timekeeping to mechanized transportation and electric lighting, to enable the orderly management of society, there also emerged the utopian vision of the meritocratic society controlled, managed, ordered, and run by middle-class university graduates trained in the newly minted political and social sciences. In was in this same period in the late nineteenth century that political and other social sciences emerged as formal disciplines.

But this model of professionalized governance by credentialed elites excluded the public from meaningful participation by design. Although in small communities, people can master knowledge of their environment, in a large and complex society, opined both Walter Lippmann *and* John Dewey in the 1920s, individuals cannot be omnicompetent. "The citizen . . . lives in a world which he cannot see, does not understand, and is unable to direct" (Lippmann 1925, 13–14). Voters, because of their position outside the traditional political system, are unable to grasp matters beyond their everyday experience. Walter Lippmann argued that that the best way to organize intelligence was rule by expert elites. Lippmann's goal was to elevate the position of government experts—the professional public service as advisors to the best and brightest. He felt that "organization of intelligence will accomplish what no reform in electoral methods . . . can effect" (quoted in Dewey 1922, 286).

Although in his review of Walter Lippmann's *Public Opinion* in the *New Republic* magazine, Dewey suggested that "thoroughgoing education" of the masses by the media was of equal importance, according to Columbia University's Michael Schudson's detailed analysis, there was no debate between Lippmann and Dewey about the competence of the public to participate in democracy (Schudson 2008). The dispassionate professional public servant is the superior knowledge producer who can inform and "tutor" self-interested political insiders. At the same time, in Great Britain R. H. Tawney and in

France Émile Durkheim were writing about the importance of specialized and professional experts as the means to institutionalize ethics and "civic morals" and elevate governing above baser self-interest. They saw professionalization as reigning in the materialist excesses of industrialization (Haskell 1998, 78).

The history of the twentieth century is what sociologist Burton Bledstein described as the century of professionals (Bledstein 1978). As the Industrial Revolution broke down the dominance of aristocracies, replacing them with a professional class of technocrats trained in the new tools of measurement, social life became thoroughly professionalized. Merit selection, specialized education, and training became the norm (Cook 2007, 131–32). New professional titles, honorifics, and professional associations mushroomed. In the 1890s, for example, the titles tree surgeon, sanitation engineer, beauty doctor, and mortician first appeared. Uroscoper evolved into urologist, and bonesetter into orthopedist. By 1870, Americans had committed themselves to a culture of professionalism. This was how they were going to govern large, complex institutions and territories. It was also how they were going to fight corruption, crony capitalism, and big-city machine politics.

Nonetheless, we can appreciate that experts, far from being neutral mandarins who speak truth to power in the view of Tawney or Lippmann or Durkheim, often turn out to be on someone's side, and that side is not usually ours (Shapiro 1994, 140). Think of Nazi doctors or Lysenko's agricultural policies and it becomes manifest that Tawney's professionals have clay feet. But public participation is not necessarily a desirable antidote to expertise (Rose-Ackerman 2017). Cognitive incapacity, disinterest in government, and passivity in the face of usually closed and sometimes corrupt bureaucratic and political institutions prevent the public from participating productively.

Hence, we have lived with the "permanent embarrassment" of expertise that violates the equality among citizens that democracy presupposes. "It may be accepted as a fact, however unpleasant," lamented Theodore Roosevelt, "that if steady work and much attention to detail are required, ordinary citizens, to whom participation in politics is merely a disagreeable duty, will always be beaten by the organized army of politicians to whom it is both business, duty, and pleasure" (Roosevelt 1906, 145). Our political culture swings back and forth between celebration and denigration of experts. But our institutions have reified that notion that citizens are spectators and can play only a limited role in day-to-day governing. Citizen engagement is largely confined to elections, opinion polls, or jury service—asking people what they *feel*, not what they know and can do.

The Rise of the Citizen Expert

But Dewey and his contemporaries were wrong. Pitting technocracy against citizenship is a false dichotomy resulting from the mistaken yet long-held belief, even among reformers, that only professional public servants or credentialed elites possess the requite skills and abilities to govern in a complex society. It is true that most people know little and care less about politics. But it is also true that what Laski called the "plain man" possesses extraordinary know-how, skills, experience, and passions—the broader palette of human capacity—to participate in solving problems, if we can shake off the outdated assumption that only professionals possess the necessary expertise to govern well.

In fact, expertise rooted in lived experience and scientific fact is widely distributed in society. We have witnessed a shift away from credentialed experts to citizen experts in everything from restaurant reviews to medical advising, where patients routinely demonstrate greater mastery than doctors (Grundmann 2016). There are many more academic researchers than those who are lucky enough to advise government. But expertise is also not limited to academics nor synonymous exclusively with credentials and the universities of higher education that award them.

People have always possessed skills, experience, and know-how, but it has been difficult to search for and pinpoint that expertise at scale. We have not been able to take advantage of the expertise possessed by those outside of government. But now tools that make know-how more searchable, such as LinkedIn, are becoming increasingly prevalent and making it possible for public institutions systematically to get more help from more diverse sources and for more members of the public to participate actively in problem solving and governing.

Now digital badges can be earned for everything from taking courses off- or online to completing levels in a game to selling many items on eBay or answering questions on a question-and-answer platform like Stack Exchange. Because the badges are digital, unlike a diploma, they are information-rich, permanent, and verifiable sources of evidence about a person's achievements. Badges can be used to credential new forms of learning and, above all, they are searchable, making it possible to find expertise more quickly.

For example, TaskRabbit, the marketplace for twenty thousand task workers who run errands, unpack boxes, or design websites, awards badges to its "elite" Taskers. Not unlike the Power Seller on eBay or the Best Seller on Amazon, badges denote the highest rating for service and performance as evaluated by customers, not by the platform provider. Kaggle is the world's largest online community of data scientists, who compete to solve complex data science problems. Based on the skills that these scientists display when submitting answers to Kaggle client competitions, Kaggle awards a "Top 0.5%" badge. Kaggle uses these profiles to connect scientists directly with Kaggle clients who are seeking specific skills.

This phenomenon of digital badging reflects the three ways the Internet is changing our relationship to expertise. First, as we have seen, technology is making a broad range of expertise more visible, independent of traditional institutions and proliferating the number and type of expertise markers. For example, on Khan Academy, an exclusively online learning platform, students receive points for every video watched and exercise completed, as well as extra points for successfully finishing challenges that demonstrate mastery of earlier concepts through self-graded multiple-choice questions, whether or not they are in school.

Second, it is expanding the definition of expertise to include more forms of craft knowledge, including skills, experience, and interests as well as credentials. For example, in some contexts, interests, rather than credentials, may be a better, more inclusive proxy for expertise (Ipeirotis and Gabrilovich 2014). If a user loves sports, regardless of whether she has a degree in physiology or ever played for a baseball team, she may be more likely to know the ins and outs of the game. More precisely, although a baseball player can throw a curve ball, an ardent fan might do a better job of calling the plays. In fact, the fan (and surely the blogger) might be more expert on the stats than the player. Similarly, patients may have more expertise than highly credentialed doctors about certain aspects of disease care and treatment because they are much more interested in finding something that works. Certain kinds of expertise may require actual doing, but astute observers motivated by passion are often better positioned to communicate what they know. New technology is helping to strip "expertise" of its elite connotation and render it a more neutral—and actionable—description of talent and ability.

Third, the Internet is permitting expertise to be expressed by means of manual and automatic data collection based on work completed, milestones accomplished, tasks and challenges undertaken, and time spent on an activity, thus enabling an infinite diversity of expressions of expertise based on different traits and characteristics. A Klout score, for example, is a vanity indicator that translates a person's activity on social media into a single number. It is intended to measure influence in the world based on how many people retweet and quote from what a person says. Klout boasts over six hundred million scored profiles (Holt 2014; Leiderman 2014). If a policy maker, for example, wanted to encourage compliance with a new law, he might use Klout to identify and ask the most influential people to promote the initiative, in turn, to their own networks (Klout 2018).

The democratization of expertise is salient for how we govern because the Internet makes expertise—broadly understood—the basis for search.

Linking Citizen Expertise to Governing: Enter Crowdsourcing

So how do we link this distributed expertise to governing? How do we create more participatory institutions that are capable of using new technology to tap into this citizen know how?

To be clear, government is not without outside advisors today. Approximately sixty-five thousand people serve on federal advisory committees in the United States, but there is scarcely a public decision that could not benefit from an infusion of either greater or more diverse or faster expertise, both credentialed and experiential, from outside government. Designing social services better requires insights from the people who receive that service, who are traditionally absent when governing takes place behind closed doors. We could improve health policies designed to prevent a pandemic, for example, when we understand what people do and do not know about a disease. When we limit outside expertise to small groups convening face to face, we often lack the most diverse and innovative new thinking from the academy and from industry to inform how we craft policies about education or entrepreneurship. For still other forms of decision making, the problem is not an absence of credentialed or experiential expertise, but a lack of agility and an inability to get at these new ideas fast enough.

Enter crowdsourcing. As noted earlier, online tools are making it possible for members of the public to participate in institutional problem solving by sharing their knowledge and skills. And when the questions asked in these open innovation processes are relevant to people's lives and experience, they participate in ways that enhance the legitimacy and, perhaps surprisingly, also the effectiveness of governing.

A recent case in point is Mapaton CDMX, an effort on the part of thirty-five collaborators from twelve different organizations in Mexico City who created an app that allowed riders of Mexico City's system of twenty-nine thousand microbuses (*peseros*) to enter GPS data into a shared database and thereby map these fifteen hundred informal bus routes while riding. Participants who mapped the most *pesero* routes could earn points toward tablets and cash prizes. The software used an algorithm to assign undermapped routes higher point values. In two weeks in February 2016, riders mapped almost the entire system, and with this data in hand, innovators were then able to create an SMS-based service that allows a commuter to enter an origin and destination and get route information.

In another successful crowdsourcing example, the U.S. federal government's Challenge.gov platform hosts requests from government agencies to members of the public to tackle hard problems in exchange for cash prizes and other incentives. Since its inception in 2010, federal agencies have run over seven hundred challenges, turning to the public to help ameliorate problems such as decreasing the "word gap" between children from high- and low-income families, and increasing the speed at which salt water can be turned into fresh water for farming in developing economies.

Since the 1970s, when Eric von Hippel at MIT illuminated a new view of innovation where customers are as important sources of innovation as producers themselves, what was viewed as an oddity—community innovation (also known as open innovation)—has now become mainstream in every sector (von Hippel 1988). The whole concept of customer-driven innovation draws on Greek ideals of citizen engagement as its antecedent, but the practical experience gained in companies has, in turn, given new momentum to open innovation and crowdsourcing in public life.

As governments continue to seek solutions to big and complex problems, the concept of open innovation (often backed by the incentive of a prize and known as a prize-backed challenge) has widened the pool of potential problem solvers beyond the "usual suspects" and created a new way of working that brings together the talent, abilities, and expertise of government and governed on a wide variety of topics, from improving methods to find asteroids that could threaten the Earth to reducing the amount of time required for highway construction projects.

Crowdsourcing is more than brainstorming. It goes beyond asking people to come up with ideas or supply information and includes asking people to perform tasks. On Amnesty International's Decoders Network, more than 8,000 volunteers from 150 countries participate in projects to identify human rights violations, using satellite photographs.

But the challenge of transferring the success of examples like Mapaton or Decoders to transform how public institutions work is the limitation of the "open call." Although Mapaton did attract a small crowd, those with the greatest know-how and passion often do not hear about the opportunity to participate. Challenge.gov is neither well-known nor widely used, and it represents a one-off adjunct to government more than a regular part of institutional practice. We cannot govern based on happenstance and serendipity.

Beyond Crowdsourcing to Smarter Crowdsourcing

For all forms of engagement—whether driven top-down or bottom-up—to be more effective, we need to increase the likelihood that the opportunity to participate will be more widely distributed and made visible to those who are needed and most likely to want to participate. When institutions combine a more open communications process, such as crowdsourcing or open innovation, with the matching and targeting enabled by expert networks and other platforms, the result is more systematic ways of engaging with citizens, civil servants, and global experts.

As a move in this direction, the Inter-American Development Bank, in collaboration with four Latin American governments, partnered with the GovLab (the research lab at NYU that I run) on what we called a "smarter crowdsourcing" process, in which we *curated* and *matched* global experts to specific problems that needed solving in connection with the fight against mosquito-borne diseases. Communities from Redbridge to Russia have begun practicing some form of crowdsourcing and more than seventy countries are signatories to the Open Government Partnership, which has civic engagement as one of its pillars. But the combination of crowdsourcing with targeted curation, as of this writing, resulted in innovative and implementable alternative approaches that work. That curated smarter crowdsourcing process is resulting in real changes in how those countries are responding to the pandemic.

The Smarter Crowdsourcing for Zika project involved taking the larger problem of Zika and breaking it down into fifteen constituent issues, such as the accumulation of trash and standing water and the challenges of long-term care. Then we recruited and organized over a hundred participants from a dozen countries to share what they know. The GovLab translated those ideas into detailed memoranda laying out the how-tos for implementing the suggestions.

Building on these manual curation processes, in the future, organizations can employ the technologies of expertise—or what many in the private sector also call people analytics, namely big data tools for understanding one's audience and targeting those civil servants, citizens, and global experts most likely to want to participate—to identify and reach out to possible audiences, enabling citizen engagement to become a sustainable component of how government works at scale.

Already an accelerating practice in the private sector, where managers want to increase the likelihood of finding employees with the right skills, (something they cannot do easily from transcripts alone), public institutions are beginning to follow suit in using technology to create more targeted crowdsourcing efforts. For example, the World Bank created its own expert network called SkillFinder to index the talents of its 27,000 employees, consultants and alumni to be able to better organize its human capital to achieve the bank's mission of eradicating poverty (Noveck 2015). In the United States, there are early efforts to help civil servants better target expertise among their colleagues at the rank-and-file level. HHS Profiles is a project designed to help the Department of Health and Human Services more quickly find employees based on their know-how, for example, to staff medical device safety review panels with the right expertise more quickly (Hernandez and Rosamilia 2015). And the Environmental Protection Agency's Project Marketplace enables the posting of project descriptions together with requests for help with specific assignments. The skills marketplace helps to match talent to those opportunities to use it. The marketplace encourages teams focused on outcomes rather than affiliation and helps to find the talent hiding in plain sight.

The use of big data tools to curate processes of engagement is not limited to civil servants. In an early (and now defunct) experiment, the small community of Torfaen, Wales, built a matching system to connect local citizens with experience in managing diabetes and Alzheimer's to other citizens newly diagnosed and needing help.

In an era of online dating in which it is commonplace for companies to use technology to target employees and customers to promote and improve their products, the idea of matching might sound obvious. But in public life, it represents a radical departure from entrenched but anemic conception of citizenship as something associated only with the act of voting.

With today's technologies for pinpointing and targeting of people based on what they know, people need not be able to name an MP or a congressman to participate in governing. Rather, the technologies of expertise make it possible to tap into one another's skills for public benefit so that patients with a common disease can help another or people with a demand can get matched to those with a supply of relevant skill or passion.

Institutional Readiness for Citizen Expertise: Achieving Smarter Crowdsourcing in Practice

To take advantage of the opportunity the technologies of expertise provide to enable the creation of more participatory governing practices, our governing institutions need, first, to overcome the assumption that the purpose of engagement is purely about legitimacy building. It is not. If the goal of participation is simply communication between government, citizens, and interest groups, then participation becomes focused almost exclusively on discourse, and we miss the epistemic and knowledge-building aspects of crowdsourcing that enable us to find missing information, generate alternate hypotheses, gather facts in support of a plan, undertake tasks, and get more eyeballs on a problem or more boots on the ground.

Second, we need to move past the assumption that participation must be mass-based and instead construct a multiplicity of different practices that speak to people's knowledge, experience, and passions, whether to spot problems, to design policies and services, to work on drafts, or to participate in implementation, and that tap citizens, civil servants, and global participation.

Third, in an era of networks, we must move past the assumption that engagement is limited to interest group representation (churches, unions, women's groups)—so-called multistakeholderism—and instead look to broader networks of people with innovative ideas to contribute. In the Smarter Crowdsourcing for Zika project, although we invited the World Health

Organization, we also invited the technologist from MIT who knows how to build trash-spotting drones, the researchers from Pakistan who are using predictive analytics to spot dengue, and the social entrepreneur from Brooklyn who has designed an app to coordinate school children to pick up trash.

Fourth, there is still too little high-quality empirical research about citizen engagement practices.[1] For example, there are questions of:

- Design: Do more time-intensive models of participation decrease diversity? How does asking people to undertake tasks versus generate ideas change the outcomes? What are the conditions necessary to recruit diverse and, especially, vulnerable groups and individuals?
- Incentives: What kinds of participation and engagement are most likely to lead to desired outcomes? What incentives are most likely to attract "unusual suspects" and deliver desirable outcomes?
- Targeting: How does the use of the technologies of expertise to match people to opportunities to participate impact engagement? Does matching work better based on credentials or experiences?
- Legitimacy: What is the influence of these kinds of exercises in the perception of government? How well represented are the interests of the most vulnerable communities?

Such research would draw upon and be informed by research on open innovation in companies and in online communities but, of necessity, would need to be adapted to take account of what it means to do research "in the wild" with real communities where the goal is to improve people's lives.

The absence of research stems from historic resistance to experimentation in how public institutions make decisions, but also from the practices of academic researchers themselves, many of whom are loath to label as "research" or "experiment" anything that deviates from the large sample sizes and neat conditions found in the lab. Elinor Ostrom felt that because we can never fully understand all the possible rule choices faced by a policy maker, let alone all their potential outcomes, analysis divorced from practice is essential (Ostrom 2005, 97). Computational social scientists like Duncan Watts work in "virtual labs," which are controlled environments where the scientific method can be adhered to when conducting macro-sociology experiments, including crowdsourcing experiments (Watts 2013). To them, online communities have the potential to provide larger sample sizes than they can typically access through offline research with human subjects. Also, computational social scientists tend to focus on individual behavior and motivations (or groups and their proclivities), but not on the design or redesign of organizations and institutions (Lazer et al. 2009).

As MIT professor Kurt Lewin famously said, research that produces nothing but books will not suffice, and there is a gradual move toward more research in the wild. Increasingly, "experimentalism is no longer confined to formal scientific labs," writes Charles Leadbeater. "It has become an organising method for social policy, startup businesses, venture capitalists, tech companies and the creative arts. Everyone it seems wants to experiment their way into the future and to do so they want labs, which are proliferating well beyond their traditional habitat in the natural sciences" (Leadbeater 2014). There is now a burgeoning movement of so-called public labs—explicitly experimental organizations with ties to government institutions. Though quite diverse in their approaches, these innovation labs engage in participatory and ethnographic processes of engaging citizens through observation and interviews in the design of public services (Ehn, Nilsson, and Topgaard 2014; Hassan 2014; Puttick, Baeck, and Colligan 2014).

In live experiments in administrative institutions, creating control groups with large enough sample sizes and running multiple, parallel trials can be challenging, especially when not enough participants show up. When studying institutions, there are myriad moving parts that are shaped by variables like power and money and influence that cannot be treated as simple abstractions if the goal is to understand what works in the real world and to develop "an epistemology based on practice as the fundamental unit of analysis" (Raelin 2009), where action research complements rather than replaces research in the lab.

By conducting systematic inquiries into group and organizational phenomena such as how institutions make decisions and solve problems, action research offers a pathway for solving social problems. Instead of a virtual lab in which real-world conditions are simulated on an instrumented platform where behavior is observed and measured, we need real-world "empirical and agile" action research laboratories where we can try "crowdsourcing smartly" in multiple contexts and across multiple countries, states, and cities to gain insight into what works. Many such pockets of such large-scale experimentation "in the wild" already exist in the business arena, where Internet-based businesses easily undertake randomized controlled trials (RCTs) by manipulating their customers' experience. Citizen research lags behind.

Countless PhDs are devoting time and attention to the question of how to match eyeballs to ads and get consumers to engage with retailers. How valuable it would be if only a fraction of that attention were diverted to focusing on citizens rather than consumers, on opportunities to engage in the life of our democracy rather than in buying toothpaste.

In order to transition from closed to open ways of governing, we want to be able to connect citizens to opportunities to participate at least as well as we can match consumers to advertisements. That requires testing to understand what works. Closed public institutions are in need of upgrade and improvement, and that means accelerating the pace of research in order to understand when and how we can know who knows what, who participates well, and what incentives they respond to. It will be impossible to convince politicians and policy makers, let alone the public, that the transformation of institutions is imperative without research and experimentation to prove the positive impact of such changes on real people's lives.

Around the world, governments are faced with a challenge: deliver services, make policies, and solve problems in ways that are more effective and transparent. Doing so requires going beyond thrusting the occasional reformer into an open government role or recruiting the Silicon Valley techie to do a tour of duty. Improving the level of expertise in government while at the same time democratizing participating requires more than tweeting a question or implementing a one-time open-call crowdsourcing project. Instead, we need to train today's public servants to know how and to want to use new tools to unlock talent and systematically connect motivated innovators both inside and outside of government to solve problems.

The Internet is radically decreasing the costs of identifying diverse forms of expertise. New platforms like expert networks are multiplying the number and types of expertise, including skills and experiences, that can be systematically searched. Because expertise can now be identified and collected both manually and automatically, it becomes possible to demand experience over credentials, certified skills over mere certifications, and practical ability over status hierarchy. When we can see with precision who knows what, we can harness that know-how for the public good—it is possible finally to realize what philosopher Danielle Allen describes as the "egalitarianism of co-creation and co-ownership of a shared world, an expectation for inclusive participation that fosters in each citizen the self-understanding that she, too, he, too, helps to make, and is responsible for, this world in which we live together" (Allen 2014, 258).

There is no more important public issue today than how to develop our governing organizations to make them smarter and better able to tackle the myriad and complex challenges we face. Over the next fifty years, we will face challenges that no previous generation of humanity has ever had to deal with. To overcome them, we must run our communities and our institutions differently. Centralized government based on bureaucratic control enforced by law and reinforced by closed-door tradition and hierarchy is out of date. The open and networked governance institutions of the future will work more effectively *and* more legitimately. They have to.

Notes

Portions of this chapter are drawn from Beth Simone Noveck, "Could Crowdsourcing Expertise Be the Future of Government?" *Guardian*, November 30, 2016, and Beth Simone Noveck, *Smart Citizens, Smarter State: The Technologies of Expertise and the Future of Governing* (Cambridge, Mass.: Harvard University Press, 2015), especially chapter 2.

1. One of the rare exceptions is Tiago Peixoto et al.'s *Civic Tech in the Global South* (2017). Using both qualitative and quantitative analysis, they confirm a lack of clear evidence that citizen participation produces institutional response. Whether the focus is technology to support aggregated individual assessments, such as complaint hotlines, or tools for collective action and mobilization, Peixoto et al.'s book has rigorously lain bare the fact that so-called "civic tech" is no better than old-fashioned dialogues in the church basement at producing changes in governing outcomes.

References

Allen, Danielle. 2014. *Our Declaration: A Reading of the Declaration of Independence in Defense of Equality*. New York: Liveright.

Allen, Will. 2018. "Participatory Action Research." Learning for Sustainability. http://www.learningforsustainability.net/research/action_research.php.

Amnesty International. 2018. "Amnesty Decoders." Accessed April 15. https://decoders.amnesty.org/.

Asimov, Isaac. 1980. "A Cult of Ignorance." *Newsweek*, January 21.

Blanchflower, David. 2016. "Experts Get It Wrong Again by Failing to Predict Trump Victory." *Guardian*, November 9. https://www.theguardian.com/business/2016/nov/09/experts-trump-victory-economic-political-forecasters-recession.

Bledstein, Burton. 1978. *The Culture of Professionalism: The Middle Class and the Development of Higher Education in America.* New York: W. W. Norton.

Blinder, Alan S. 1997. "Is Government Too Political?" *Foreign Affairs* 76 (6): 115–26.

Cook, Brian J. 2007. *Democracy and Administration: Woodrow Wilson's Ideas and the Challenges of Public Management.* Baltimore: Johns Hopkins University Press.

Dewey, John. 1922. Review of Walter Lippmann's *Public Opinion. New Republic,* May 3, 286–88.

Ehn, Pelle, Elisabet M. Nilsson, and Richard Topgaard. 2014. *Making Futures: Marginal Notes on Innovation, Design, and Democracy.* Cambridge, Mass.: MIT Press.

Elkins, Stanley, and Eric McKitrick. 1954. "A Meaning for Turner's Frontier: Democracy in the Old Northwest." *Political Science Quarterly* 69 (3): 321–53.

Grundmann, Reiner. 2016. "Who Are 'Experts,' Anyway?" *Guardian,* November 12. https://www.theguardian.com/science/political-science/2016/nov/12/who-are-experts-anyway.

GovLab. 2018. "Open Innovation for Solving Public Problems." Accessed June 18. http://www.thegovlab.org/project-open-innovation-for-solving-public-problems.html.

Habermas, Jürgen. 2015. *The Lure of Technocracy.* Cambridge, U.K.: Polity Press.

Haskell, Thomas. 1998. "Professionalism vs. Capitalism: R. H. Tawney, Émile Durkheim, and C. S. Pierce on the Disinterestedness of Professional Communities." In *Objectivity Is Not Neutrality,* edited by Thomas Haskell, 180–225. Baltimore: Johns Hopkins University Press.

Hassan, Zaid. 2014. *The Social Labs Revolution: A New Approach to Solving Our Most Complex Challenges.* San Francisco: Berrett-Koehler Publishers.

Hernandez, Jessica, and Nichole Rosamilia. 2015. "Developing a Model for Expert Networking Across Federal Government: The HHS Profiles Pilot." Paper presented at VIVO 2015 Annual Conference, Boston, August 11–14.

Holt, Jack. 2014. "Don't Count Klout Out: 4 Reasons It's the Platform to Watch in 2014." *Adotas,* March 26. http://www.adotas.com/2014/03/don%E2%80%99t-count-klout-out-4-reasons-it%E2%80%99s-the-platform-to-watch-in-2014/.

Ipeirotis, Panagiotis G., and Evgeniy Gabrilovich. 2014. "Quizz: Targeted Crowdsourcing with a Billion (Potential) Users." In *Proceedings of the 23rd International Conference on World Wide Web.* Geneva, Switzerland: International World Wide Web Conferences Steering Committee.

Klout. 2018. "About Klout." Accessed April 15. http://blog.klout.com/.

Lazer, David, Alex Pentland, Lada Adamic, Sinan Aral, Albert-László Barabási, Devon Brewer, Nicholas Christakis, Noshir Contractor, James Fowler, Myron Gutmann, Tony Jebara, Gary King, Michael Macy, Deb Roy, and Marshall Van Alstyne. 2009. "Computational Social Science." *Science* 323 (5915): 721–23.

Leadbeater, Charles. 2014. "Hooked on Labs." *The Long + Short,* November 27. https://thelongandshort.org/spaces/experimental-innovation-labs.

Leiderman, Lucy. 2014. "Understanding Klout as a Brokerage Business." The Next Web, April 4. https://thenextweb.com/socialmedia/2014/04/06/understanding-klout-brokerage-business/.

Library of Congress Congressional Research Service. 1976. *History of Civil Service Merit Systems of the United States and Selected Foreign Countries, Together with Executive Reorganization Studies and Personnel Recommendations*. Washington, D.C.: Government Printing Office. http://ufdc.ufl.edu/AA00024784/00001.

Lippmann, Walter. 1925. *The Phantom Public*. New York: Harcourt, Brace.

Mallaby, Sebastian. 2016. "The Cult of the Expert—and How It Collapsed." *Guardian*, October 20. https://www.theguardian.com/business/2016/oct/20/alan-greenspan-cult-of-expert-and-how-it-collapsed.

Mance, Henry. 2016. "Britain Has Had Enough of Experts, Says Gove." *Financial Times*, June 3. https://www.ft.com/content/3be49734-29cb-11e6-83e4-abc22d5d108c.

Mansharamani, Vikram. 2012. "Keep Experts on Tap, Not on Top." *Harvard Business Review*, July 23. https://hbr.org/2012/07/keep-experts-on-tap-not-on-top.

Norman, Jim. 2016. "Americans' Confidence in Institutions Stays Low." Gallup, June 13. http://news.gallup.com/poll/192581/americans-confidence-institutions-stays-low.aspx.

Noveck, Beth Simone. 2015a. "Hacking SkillFinder: How the World Bank's Talent Network Can Reduce Poverty." *Forbes*, October. https://www.forbes.com/sites/bethsimonenoveck/2015/10/01/hacking-skillfinder-using-the-world-banks-talent-network-to-reduce-poverty/#4254258e22a7.

———. 2015b. "The Rise of Professional Government." In *Smart Citizens, Smarter State: The Technologies of Expertise and the Future of Governing*, 44–74. Cambridge, Mass.: Harvard University Press.

———.2016. "Could Crowdsourcing Expertise Be the Future of Government?" *Guardian*, November 30. https://www.theguardian.com/science/political-science/2016/nov/30/could-crowdsourcing-expertise-be-the-future-of-government.

Ostrom, Elinor. 2005. *Understanding Institutional Diversity*. Princeton, N.J.: Princeton University Press.

Pew Research Center. 2015. "Beyond Distrust: How Americans View Their Government." November 23. http://www.people-press.org/2015/11/23/beyond-distrust-how-americans-view-their-government/.

Peixoto, Tiago C., Micah L. Sifry, Andrew J. Mellon, and Fredrik M. Sjoberg. 2017. *Civic Tech in the Global South: Assessing Technology for the Public Good*. Washington, D.C.: World Bank and Personal Democracy Press.

Proctor, Robert N. 2016. "Climate Change in Trump's Age of Ignorance." *New York Times*, November 19. https://www.nytimes.com/2016/11/20/opinion/climate-change-in-trumps-age-of-ignorance.html.

Puttick, Ruth, Peter Baeck, and Philip Colligan. 2014. *i-Teams: The Teams and Funds Making Innovation Happen in Governments Around the World*. London: NESTA. http://www.nesta.org.uk/sites/default/files/i-teams_june_2014.pdf.

Raelin, Joe. 2009. "Seeking Conceptual Clarity in the Action Modalities." *Action Learning: Research and Practice* 6 (1): 17–24.

Rahman, K. Sabeel. 2013. "Governing the Economy: Markets, Experts, and Citizens." PhD diss., Harvard University.

Roosevelt, Theodore. 1906. *The Works of Theodore Roosevelt: American Ideals and Other Essays*. New York: Scribner.

Rose-Ackerman, Susan. 2017. "Citizens and Technocrats: An Essay on Trust, Public Participation, and Government Legitimacy." In *Comparative Administrative Law*, 2nd ed., edited by Susan Rose-Ackerman, Peter L. Lindseth, and Blake Emerson, 251–67. Cheltenham, U.K.: Edward Elgar.

Schudson, Michael. 2008. "The 'Lippmann-Dewey Debate' and the Invention of Walter Lippmann as an Anti-Democrat 1986–1996." *International Journal of Communication* 2: 1031–42.

Shapiro, Ian. 1994. "Three Ways to Be a Democrat." *Political Theory* 22 (February): 124–51.

Trump, Donald J. 2016. "Let Me Ask America a Question." *Wall Street Journal*, April 14. https://www.wsj.com/articles/let-me-ask-america-a-question-1460675882.

United Kingdom Office for National Statistics (ONS). 2016. *Civil Service Statistics: 2016*. London: Author. https://www.ons.gov.uk/employmentandlabourmarket/peopleinwork/publicsectorpersonnel/bulletins/civilservicestatistics/2016.

United States Office of Personnel Management (OPM). 2013. *Employment and Trends—September 2013*. Washington, D.C.: Government Printing Office. https://www.opm.gov/policy-data-oversight/data-analysis-documentation/federal-employment-reports/employment-trends-data/2013/september/.

Von Hippel, Erik. 1988. *The Sources of Innovation*. New York: Oxford University Press.

Walker, David. 2016. "May's Whitehall Reshuffle Shows Disregard for Evidence and Expertise." *Guardian*, July 18. https://www.theguardian.com/public-leaders-network/2016/jul/18/theresa-may-whitehall-reshuffle-disregard-evidence-expertise-sajid-javid.

Watts, Duncan. 2013. "Computational Social Sciences: Exciting Progress and Future Directions." *The Bridge* (Winter).

Wright, Ben. 2016. "There's a Sinister Strain of Anti-intellectualism to Gove's Dismissal of 'Experts.'" *Telegraph*, June 21. https://www.telegraph.co.uk/business/2016/06/21/in-defence-of-experts-whether-they-support-leave-or-remain/.

CHAPTER 5

Counting the Uncounted: What the Absence of Data on Police Killings Reveals

Kelly Gates

In the wake of the stranglehold killing of Eric Garner in New York City in July 2014 and shooting death of Michael Brown in Ferguson, Missouri, that August, an issue emerged as a newly apparent matter of concern: the alarming number of unarmed black men being killed by the police, for sure, but also the glaring *absence of data* on those killings. When activists, journalists, and others concerned about police violence went looking for official statistics on the number of people killed by the police in the United States, they came up empty. While the killings seemed to be happening with more frequency and disproportionately to black men, there was no official data or centralized database that could serve as a resource for assessing the problem. This was not the first time that journalists reported on the missing data, but its glaring absence seemed to appear as a startling new discovery. From August 2014 through the first few months of 2015, news stories and commentary specifically addressing the absence of an official accounting of police killings appeared in born-digital media like *Gawker* (Burghart 2014) and *Deadspin* (Wagner 2014), in left-leaning press outlets like *Mother Jones* (Lee 2014), and in the conventional elite press, including the *New York Times* (Wines 2014), the *Washington Post* (Lowery 2014), the *Wall Street Journal* (Barry and Jones 2014), and the *Guardian* (McCarthy 2015).

If the absence of an official and thorough accounting of police killings was unsurprising on some level, it also seemed strange, given the extensive documentation involved in modern police work. Conventionally referred to as the "paper burden" of policing, the work of filing incident reports is an activity that rank-and-file police spend a great deal of time doing. This "knowledge work" of policing (Ericson and Haggerty 1997) is the stuff of *crime statistics*, and through a long and complex process of transition it is morphing increasingly into forms of digital labor. Given the veritable deluge of data produced by police workers in the service of crime tracking and analysis, *how could there be no ready answer to how many people are killed by the police in the United States?* How could there not be data available to determine who gets killed and who does the killing, year by year and place by place? If the lack of data on police killings clearly supported the assertion that "raw data is an oxymoron" (Bowker 2008; Gitelman 2015), the absence itself seemed both raw and revealing.

The absence of official data on police killings also stood in stark contrast to what appeared to be a proliferation of visual documentation of police actions, including plenty of use-of-force incidents and a number of actual killings recorded on both bystander and police cameras. In fact, the desire or demand to compare these visual records with hard data is partly what elevated the *absence* of data on police killings as a matter of concern. There tends to be some suspicion across public, legal, and scientific domains about the deceptive potential of images—a general sense that *visual* media can deceive, whereas *data* establishes objective realities. Of course, there is also the reverse belief that images capture *truth*, whereas data can be manipulated. And in polarized political debates, one stance or the other can be leveraged to dismiss any evidence, visual or statistical, that challenges firmly held beliefs. Nonetheless, on the question of whether there was an upsurge in police killings—and additional questions about whether certain groups have been disproportionately targeted and whether certain officers or agencies are using lethal force more frequently—the proliferating visual evidence demanded a comparison with good hard data, which was nowhere to be found.

In this chapter, I argue that the missing data on people killed by the police in the United States is a special case and a stark example of the way moral economies underpin and produce absent knowledge. That moral economies shape knowledge production is not a novel argument, yet the ways that *absent* knowledge is actively produced are rarely examined and so remain poorly understood. At present, many forms of absent knowledge face newly intensified obscurity thanks to the political assault on science, most obviously from climate-change deniers. But there are also other, more counterintuitive sources of the problem, and here I have in mind the bold claims of "big data" and what I have elsewhere identified as an emerging "epistemic virtue" (Daston and Galison 2007) of "computational objectivity." Computational objectivity is the belief that computational systems can overcome, once and for all, the limitations of expert forms of trained judgment, eliminating all the bias and error associated with human decisions and interpretation (Gates 2016). The absent data on police violence, and the resulting inability to analyze its scale and distribution, challenges the computationalist view that sees all the world as data and answers to all important questions in data analytics, revealing instead the way value systems define what data does and does not get produced in the first place.

The study of absence is an emerging area of inquiry in science and technologies studies (STS). In order to understand how absent knowledge gets produced in the case of police use of lethal force, I draw on concepts from STS, along with the evidence presented in journalistic accounts and a small number of existing criminological studies of this issue. I then consider "The Counted," a two-year effort by a team at the *Guardian* newspaper to make the absent data present, leveraging what they called "verified crowdsourcing" to get "undone science done" (Frickel et al. 2010; Frickel 2014; Hess 2009). "The Counted" represents one important model for the future of journalism as a form of public knowledge that is especially critical as modern states move away from democratic ideals and functions.[1] More specifically, it shows the potential of networked, data journalism to serve as what Eyal Weizman (2015) calls "forensis"—"an alternative to contemporary forensics, embodying the desire to invert the forensic gaze and turn forensics into a civil practice aimed at exposing the violence of states and holding them accountable" (232).

Absent Data and Invisible Deaths

Although absence and invisibility are rarely studied, they are not entirely new objects of inquiry in communication and the social sciences. In the 1970s, for example, communication scholars introduced the concept of "symbolic annihilation" to theorize the absence or underrepresentation of women and minorities in the media—a lack of visibility and voice tied up with systemic racism, sexism, and other forms of structural inequality (Gerbner 1972; Tuchman 1978). The concept has since fallen into disuse but it seems like a fitting term to describe the absence of official data on police use of lethal force in the United States, or for that matter, state failures to produce official accountings of other types of deaths, such as those from wars, genocides, migrations, disease, environmental disasters, and other causes.[2] The absence of an official accounting of deaths suggests a double annihilation, the first physical and the second symbolic. Yet a simple transition from material to symbolic annihilation does not hold up. In their edited collection on the anthropology of absence, Bille, Hastrup, and Flohr Sørensen (2010) discuss the "corporeality of absence," using the metaphor of the phantom pains that people with amputations experience in their missing limbs, "a sensuous experience of something which is materially absent" (3). The metaphor of phantom pains suggests that "what may be materially absent still influences people's experience of the material world" (4). "In the social realm, too," they explain, "people experience 'phantom pains' in the form of sensing the presence of people, places, and things that have been obliterated, lost, missing or missed, or that have not yet materialized" (3). Far more important than absent data or representations are absent *people*, and their disappearance has lasting meaning and material qualities.

The study of absent knowledge, or ignorance, has found a home in STS where the research has shown that absences are not empty; there is something to be found in absences themselves—specific actions, conditions, and assumptions that produce them. Most work that focuses on absence does so more theoretically than empirically, at a high level of abstraction; "efforts to pin down absences empirically remain in comparatively short supply" (Frickel 2014, 87). The relative absence of empirical data on absence no doubt stems from the obvious—it is difficult to study things that aren't there (Croissant 2014). Environmental sociologist Scott Frickel (2014) has identified three points of convergence among a collection of STS works on absence: (1) absences are inherent in technoscientific practice, (2) "absences are relational constructs complexly intertwined with presences," and (3) "absences are bound up in the moral economies of societies" (86). Each of these characteristics applies to the absence of data on police use of lethal force.

For example, one of the ways that absence is complexly intertwined with presence in this case is in the stark contrast between the absent data and the volumes of data made present by the administrative practices of policing, especially the production of *crime statistics*. In the United States, the federal government has seen fit to develop an extensive system for producing data about crime, mining the knowledge work of policing with the voluntary yet cooperative participation of the country's roughly "18,000 city, university/college, county, state, tribal, and federal law enforcement agencies" (FBI 2018).

This system, called the Uniform Crime Reporting (UCR) program, was "conceived in 1929 by the International Association of Chiefs of Police to meet the need for reliable uniform crime statistics for the nation" (FBI 2018). The UCR system is run by the U.S. Federal Bureau of Investigation (FBI), and UCR data is now used for new technoscientific practices of policing like crime-mapping systems and experiments in "predictive policing," including the development of algorithms for criminal sentencing (taking the form of proprietary software products produced by IT companies, with a primary interest in monetization). The latest technoscientific practices of policing rely on what is counted and not counted by the UCR system, reproducing its inherent tendencies and absences while also generating new ones.

Even without evidence of an intentional suppression of knowledge, it would hard to deny that what we know and do not know about crime, and about police use of lethal force, is bound up in the moral economy of U.S. society. The contrast between what is absent and present—the lack of data on people killed by the police and the more systematic collection of UCR data—itself is a measure of this moral economy. The absence of an official form of police accountability in the form of data on these deaths is consistent with the absence of criminal convictions (or even charges) against officers who kill, despite the obvious injustice of so many killings such as those of Michael Brown, Eric Garner, twelve-year-old Tamir Rice, Walter Scott, Freddie Gray, Samuel DuBose, and the list goes on. To rehearse an obvious but critical point, particular social groups have more agency relative to others in shaping this moral economy; there are hierarchies of agency determining what is valued and not valued in the production of life and death statistics, including the relative *valuation* of social groups themselves—"the distribution of the living in the domain of value and utility" (Foucault 1977, 144). In fact, it is no stretch to suggest that this moral economy is bound up with and dependent on the absence of an official accounting of police use of lethal force. Given the long brutal history of policing in the service of property and privilege that has shaped visuality itself (Mirzoeff 2011), the state would be expected to systematically produce such an absence, and even be required to do so, rendering invisible the deaths of those killed by police by its refusal to document the mortalities.

As the sociologist Jennifer Croissant (2014) has suggested, the *intentionality* of absent knowledge is complicated by the sometimes clear and other times blurry distinctions between willful ignorance, active suppression of knowledge, intentional falsehoods or distortions, strategic avoidances of uncomfortable or inconvenient matters, and other versions of purposeful not-knowing. Intentionality is one of five dimensions of absent knowledge that Croissant suggests in her taxonomy for the study of absent knowledge and ignorance, or "agnotology." She discusses four others: ontology, chronicity, granularity, and scale. To speak of the *ontology* of absent knowledge is much like Frickel's point that the "absences are relational constructs complexly intertwined with presences." For Croissant, the ontology of ignorance "refers to questions about the presence or absence of knowledge," both relatively speaking, as when one person or group has knowledge that another person or group is ignorant of, and in terms of the multiple meanings and uses of "uncertainty" (Croissant 2014, 6).[3] Ontologically, relative ignorance can also mean partial knowledge, especially when it is not recognized or acknowledged as such—knowing some things and not knowing others, without awareness of the limits of one's knowledge. Ontology suggests that absences have essences or identifiable forms, like the (Rumsfeldian) distinction between known unknowns and unknown unknowns, where the latter are doubly invisible—entirely unconscious blind spots. *Chronicity* of absent knowledge points to the temporalities of knowledge production or lack thereof, as in things that are not yet known versus things that are "forgotten or obliterated" (Croissant 2014, 7). *Granularity* as a dimension of absent knowledge is perhaps best understood in relation to censorship; there is high granularity in the censorship of specific words or statements, for example, and lower granularity in the censorship of entire documents, books, or schools of thought. To consider the *scale* of epistemological ignorance means to consider how widespread it is, or at what level of social formations absences are found, as well as the size and complexity of knowledge gaps. Some absences are produced at an organizational level by departmental compartmentalization or secrecy, while epistemological ignorances produced by conditions of subjugation and oppression (e.g., colonialism) have implications for absent knowledge on a much broader scale.

These dimensions of ignorance are tightly interconnected. Questions of intentionality implicate questions of scale and chronicity, for example—where and when intentional absences are produced. STS scholars have shown that intentional absences of knowledge are often produced on a large scale in the aftermath of major environmental catastrophes like oil spills and nuclear reactor meltdowns. In her study of the Chernobyl disaster and its long-term health effects in Belarus, Olga Kuchinskaya (2014) found "the production of invisibility"—an absence of knowledge resulting from the invisibility of radiation and the diverse health effects of exposure, to be sure, but further compounded by "the systematic disruption of the infrastructural conditions necessary for knowledge production" about levels of radiation contamination and their variable long-term effects on bodies (with varying types of susceptibility) (9). Infrastructures are scalar technologies, and their absence or systematic disruption produces other absences of varying magnitudes at different times and places. In such cases, intentionality is difficult to pin down. Systematic disruptions of knowledge production are elusive, and even intentionally hidden from view and dissimulated. The absences breed more absences.

We can use the dimensions of Croissant's taxonomy and other STS scholarship, along with the evidence about this absence produced by professional journalists and a small number of relevant criminological studies, to better understand how the absence of data on people killed by the police gets produced. This approach also helps shed light on why this particular absent data and knowledge presents a special challenge to facile notions of "raw data" and a corresponding belief in computational objectivity.

I have already begun to consider *intentionality*, which does not reduce to the simple question of whether the absence of data was or was not intentional, but instead asks what form intentionality took and at what level or *scale* it could be found. Journalists reporting on the lack of official data addressed a number of factors that spoke to the question of intentionality of the absence, including the challenge of finding evidence of explicit intentions (i.e., an absence of evidence about intentionality). In an August 2014 *Gawker* article titled "What I've Learned from Two Years Collecting Data on Police Killings," D. Brian Burghart explained that something he felt certain of but "would never be able to prove" was that the "lack of such a database is *intentional*." In his personal account, Burghart cited being lied to and delayed by the FBI, as well as by state, county, and local law enforcement agencies, in his efforts to make public records requests, suggesting intentional disruption at multiple levels. Other news coverage of the missing data suggested less of a systematic disruption or intentional suppression of knowledge production and more of a dearth of political will, resources, and sustained effort at federal and local levels to create the infrastructural conditions necessary to produce the data. An FBI spokesperson quoted in a 2011 article noted that the FBI does not "have a mandate" from Congress to make such an accounting, and that "budgetary concerns would likely preclude" the FBI from doing so (Maimon 2011). An ACLU spokesperson quoted in the same article noted that the NYPD has fought disclosure of information regarding officer-involved shootings, arguing that "it would violate the privacy of the officers and reveal investigative techniques" (Maimon 2011)—a statement that points to a more *granular* degree of secrecy or obfuscation, at the level of individual police officers and investigatory practices. Another article, published post-Ferguson, explained the problem in terms of the *scale* and decentralized nature of the police infrastructure—there are over 17,000 law enforcement agencies in the United States and thus researchers "aren't even sure how you'd go about" setting up a system (Wagner 2014). Yet another article cited "18,000-plus local law enforcement agencies in the US" (McCarthy 2015)—in short, a very large number of separately functioning police organizations, making systematic data generation a challenging problem of scale.

Assessing *intentionality* with regard to the missing data is complicated by its *relative* absence—there are, in fact, official sources of data on people killed by police, but their data is flawed and incomplete, minimizing the scope and distribution of the problem. This incompleteness also points to the *scale, granularity*, and *ontology* of absent knowledge. Two main sources of incomplete data are compiled by departments within the FBI and the U.S. Centers for Disease Control and Prevention (CDC) (McCarthy 2015). The FBI's UCR system includes a category called "justifiable homicide by weapon, law enforcement," which relies on police reports from state and local agencies. The CDC's National Center for Health Statistics collects national mortality data through its National Vital Statistics System (NVSS), which includes a "cause of death" category of "legal intervention." While some criminologists have used these partial sources of data to analyze and make problematic knowledge claims about deaths at the hands of police in the United States, others have shown the extent to which these official data collection systems have grossly underreported killings by police (Sherman and Langworthy 1979; Loftin et al. 2003; Klinger 2012). One study from the 1970s showed that the FBI's stats undercounted the number of people killed by at least 51% (Sherman and Langworthy 1979). A report from the FBI's own Bureau of Justice Statistics (BJS) found a similar percentage of undercount in a more recent assessment (Planty et al. 2015). In their study of both the FBI and CDC data published in 2003, Loftin and colleagues found that both underreported the deaths, but for different reasons—the FBI's UCR data was incomplete largely because of "agency nonresponse" and "incomplete information on the filed reports"; the CDC's NVSS data was incomplete largely because the death certificates that the system relies on usually fail to indicate that "the death was caused by a police officer" (1120).

To speak of the relative absences of data produced by official sources is to speak of the *ontology* of this absence, and its ontology is inseparable from other dimensions, not least its *granularity*. The FBI's UCR data on people killed by police is incomplete for a variety of identifiable reasons. Not all police agencies participate in reporting, which points to questions of *intentionality* and *scale*, and the count includes only deaths that involved police use of a weapon ("weapon" usually refers to a firearm; a stranglehold killing would not count, for example). Then of course there is the matter of "justifiability." "Justifiability" is in one sense a question of *granularity*, what Croissant describes as the "texture" of the absent knowledge, from concrete facts to broad knowledge statements. The UCR system includes "justifiable" killings in this category and presumably excludes "unjustifiable" ones. But "justifiability" is also a profoundly *ontological* matter; the nature of the absence here rides on the very fraught questions of which killings are deemed "justified," who determines "justifiability," and based on what criteria (what moral economy). And it is not clear where "unjustified homicides" would appear in this granular schematic—conceivably, in other UCR homicide data, although there is no explicit category in the UCR system for "unjustified homicides by law enforcement." The NVSS "death by legal intervention category," which possibly includes "unjustified" homicides by law enforcement personnel, bypasses the question of "justifiability" altogether but nonetheless raises similar questions about ontology and granularity. The NVSS data is drawn from medical records and death certificates, and not all these documents contain data of enough granularity to provide an accurate count of people killed by police (McCarthy 2015).[4]

The *chronicity* of absence is evident in the appearance and disappearance of official efforts to produce the data over time, and in variations in methodologies for counting deaths that result in incomplete data sets, producing relative absences of differing scale and granularity over time. Beginning in 2003, the U.S. Justice Department initiated a third federal effort to develop a system for assembling a more complete and accurate database of people killed by police in the United States. The BJS Arrest-Related Deaths (ARD) program was established as "an annual national census of persons who die either during the process of arrest or while in the custody of state or local law enforcement personnel" (Planty et al. 2015, 1). According to the *Guardian*, the ARD program was quietly shuttered in March 2014, five months before the shooting death of Michael Brown, after a decade of trying and failing to produce accurate numbers (McCarthy 2015). The BJS issued a report on the ARD program in March 2015 indicating that it captured only about half of law enforcement homicides from 2003 to 2009. The report also indicated that while there was some improvement in the quality of the census over time ("partially due to the use of open source searches"), the ARD was still failing to capture 31% to 41% of the homicides committed by law enforcement personnel (Planty et al. 2015, 1). While the BJS team was not able to produce adequate data, they were able to show the flawed nature of the existing numbers and to identify some of the granularity in the absent data. For example, the 2015 BJS report includes a table showing "states or jurisdictions that did not report to the Arrest-Related Deaths Program, 2003–2011," broken down by state and year (Planty et al. 2015, 6).[5]

My own effort to analyze the absence of official data on people killed by police suffers from a similar relative absence of empirical data, stemming from a lack of time, resources, and access to relevant primary sources. It is the nature of knowledge production that it can never be complete, and typically leads to a new set of known unknowns (as in, "suggestions for future research"). Unfortunately, a large-scale empirical study of the failure to produce official data on police use of lethal force may never happen. A study of this sort, with federal government agencies and state and local police departments as primary sources and objects of analysis, is likely to remain absent knowledge of the known unknown variety. The problem is compounded by the reality that while certain actors view the absent data as a matter of concern, others would prefer that this sort of absent knowledge remain unknown, seeing it as *not worth being known, not needing to be known,* or *needing to remain unknown.*

For the remainder of this chapter, I want to shift the focus from the absent data itself to efforts on the part of nonstate actors to make the absent data present using a combination of crowdsourcing, networked journalism, and professional news production work. Croissant's dimensions of absent knowledge come into sharper view when we consider the ways that "absences are complexly intertwined with presences" (Frickel 2014; Hess 2009). The absence of data on police use of lethal force is a form of what Frickel and others have called "undone science"—it is a known unknown thanks to concerned actors who have made the absence of data *public* or *visible,* bringing it to the attention of audiences, at least for a period of time (Frickel et al. 2010; Hess

2009). It is sometimes possible to study "undone science," as Frickel explains, thanks to "efforts by social movements and other civil society actors to identify and draw attention to areas of research that are ignored by the scientific and regulatory communities" (Frickel 2014, 88). The empirical basis for studying undone science draws from descriptions of the missing science by individuals and groups who are concerned about it and in turn, advocate "to get undone science done" (88). In the case of the missing data on people killed by police, the nature of the absence and its ontology, granularity, chronicity, scale, and intentionality become even more apparent when considering efforts to make the absent data present.

Crowdsourcing the Data?

One approach that journalists and other concerned actors envisioned for producing the missing data on people killed by police was to *crowdsource* it, designing platforms to appeal to and enable motivated Internet users to help assemble information about incidents of police use of lethal force. Crowdsourcing seemed to offer a promising corrective for assembling the data, one way of addressing the problem of *scale* and providing the digital labor needed to aggregate dispersed information and generate an alternative infrastructure for police accountability. It also seemed like a particularly democratic solution—in principle, anyone could contribute, ideally including those who had firsthand knowledge of incidents, mitigating the tendency in conventional news reporting to over-rely on the police themselves for information, especially at the local level (Chibnall 1975). Crowdsourcing seemed to align well with the *intentions* of grassroots organizers to elevate police killings as a matter of concern; for example, the Black Lives Matter movement was mobilized by the spate of highly visible police killings of unarmed black men, beginning with the killing of teenager Michael Brown. These efforts had the very explicit intention to do the work of knowledge production that the state had failed to do, to make the absent data present and make the extent of the killings more visible.

Several crowdsourcing projects were initiated by individuals—one or two people designing and promoting the platforms and doing the back-end digital labor of managing the database, including fact-checking and additional research. One project, called "Fatal Encounters," was developed by D. Brian Burghart, the editor of the *Reno News and Review*. In his August 2014 *Gawker* article, Burghart recounted how he had discovered the absence of a comprehensive data on police killings when he sought information in 2012 after driving past the aftermath of a police shooting, and then a few months later after reading about another incident. He described his effort to crowdsource the database, enlisting help from Internet users through a web-based platform that he designed and self-funded. He directed readers to the project's website and briefly explained how to perform the work of logging a policing killing incident. "After I fact-check and fill in the cracks," he explained, "your contribution will be added to the largest database about police violence in the country." Another initiative, called "Killed by Police," was established in May 2013 by an unnamed person.[6] Internet users could submit information by posting items to its Facebook Community page or emailing "submit@killedbypolice.net." A third effort was attempted after Ferguson, when a *Deadspin* blogger announced his own project in a post titled "We're Compiling Every Police-Involved Shooting in America. Help Us" (Wagner 2014). He and his colleagues would do it themselves, he explained, but "this is a time-intensive process, and our manpower is limited." He instructed readers to participate by conducting Google searches, isolating particular dates, and submitting relevant search results via the site's submission form.[7]

A unique effort relative to these individually initiated crowdsourcing experiments was "The Counted," an institutionally backed effort launched by the *Guardian* in June 2015.[8] The project resulted in a professionally produced, interactive piece of data journalism covering a two-year period (2015–2016). It consisted of a special feature website where users could submit "tips" and view the data in multiple ways, along with a Facebook page and Twitter profile providing other means of submitting information and following the project. According to the *Guardian*'s descriptions of the project, to help produce "The Counted" the *Guardian* team made use of what it called "verified crowdsourcing," a form that provided multiple means for Internet users to submit information, while also relying heavily on editorial and journalistic labor to do the work of vetting and fact-checking, assembling stories from other news sources, conducting additional research, formatting and standardizing the information, and plugging it into a professionally designed graphical web interface. "Verified crowdsourcing" was code for a great deal of invisible, back-end professional news-production labor.

For "The Counted," the *Guardian* used crowdsourcing as one of multiple methods for enabling many actors to collaborate and contribute to the project, with the web interface itself playing an important role in bringing actors together in the production of data and public knowledge.[9] If "networked journalism" represents "a synthesis of traditional news journalism and the emerging forms of participatory media" (Beckett 2010), the "networked" aspect of "The Counted" project involved not only the active participation of Internet users doing voluntary "public work" (Boyte 2014) but also the de facto participation of professional journalists and news organizations beyond the *Guardian* itself. "The Counted" assembled dispersed news production by aggregating the work of professional journalists from across the United States. Each record of a death included a short list of hyperlinks to news stories, most from sources other than the *Guardian*—that is, from the cities and towns where the killings occurred. In this way, local journalists became key nodes in a larger infrastructure for getting undone science done, producing pieces of data that could, in the aggregate, show the scale and distribution of people killed by police across the United States. However, it is important to recognize that the web interface of "The Counted" was more than an outcome or representation of a separate place where the real action happened; instead, the website itself was a vital site of activity—a network that assembled actors together to make visible both the problem of police killings and their systematic erasure.

Counting the Uncounted: Making Lost Lives Matter

If absences are "relational constructs complexly intertwined with presences," what does the *Guardian*'s effort to make the absent data present suggest about the *ontology* of this absence? The title of "The Counted" project itself speaks to the ontology of absence and presence, in a double entendre that refers to both the literal enumeration of deaths and the act of making those deaths *matter*. Similarly, the graphical interface of "The Counted" performs two functions at once, enumerating the deaths by presenting the numbers and aggregate data while also personalizing the deaths by visually displaying snapshot portraits of each lost life.[10]

"The Counted" interface begins with numbers. The total count for each year appears on the top left of the main page, under the title, displayed graphically so that the digits always appear as if rotating to the next number. So displayed, the numbers become "quantifacts" with "discursive currency," statistical representations for representing facts about the world typically associated with the official statistics of the state, especially crime statistics

(Comaroff and Comaroff 2006, 211). Next to the total count is a breakdown of the killings by race and ethnicity, which can be viewed "per million" or by total numbers in each category (white, black, Hispanic/Latino, Asian/Pacific Islander, and Native American). White was the racial category with the largest number of deaths in both years; the largest rates of people killed (deaths "per million") were black in 2015 and Native American in 2016. To the right of the racial and ethnic distribution is a breakdown by state, which can be sorted alphabetically by name of state, by total killings per capita per state, or by total number of killings per state, with the state with the largest number appearing first. In 2016, for example, Alaska had the largest number of killings per capita, while California was in the lead for total numbers of killings. (California is the most populous state by a wide margin, home to over thirty-nine million people; the state ranked eighteenth in per capita killings in 2016.)

There is of course an irony in seeking an accounting for state violence in something akin to crime statistics. This irony was captured in a blog post about the absence of data on police killings, published at *Cyborgology* in January 2015 by a PhD student named Candice Lanius. Lanius argued that the demand for statistical proof that police disproportionately target black men is itself racist. There is nothing neutral or objective about statistics, she argued, and insisting on statistical evidence that police are in fact killing alarming numbers of black men implies that the voices of black people on this matter are not credible. Lanius's critique of the demand for statistics speaks to the heart of the problem—the dismissal of the experiences and lives of African Americans and other oppressed groups. Yet it is not only the demand for statistical proof but also the absence of official statistics that is evidence of this dismissal. Can we identify the absence of data as evidence of a dismissal of black experience, while at the same time *not* insisting that the official data is *necessary* to confirm that experience?

As a piece of networked data journalism, "The Counted" tries to navigate precisely this double bind, at once representing both the personal tragedy of each killing and the collective tragedy of all the lost lives. The interface of "The Counted" displays not just numbers, but hundreds of images—found photographs of the faces of people killed by police. Below the graphical display of the total count and filters for sorting and searching the data, the interface displays rows of squares of these photographs representing each individual killed by police, grouped by month. Each square also contains textual data superimposed on the image, indicating the date, name, age, and cause of death ("gunshot" being the most common, followed by "taser"). The state in which the killing occurred appears at the bottom of each square. Squares with missing photos appear sporadically throughout the grid, and some of the names on these squares are listed as "unknown." Some of the photos look like mug shots, while others have a more candid and personal quality, showing the deceased smiling or posing. Clicking on an individual photo brings up a separate window containing additional information about the person and the circumstances of the killing, with cells for each of the following categories: demographics, location, armed (type of weapon, if any), classification (gunshot, etc.), name of police department, a brief narrative summary of the circumstances of the killing, and the status of the case (e.g., "under investigation"). The bottom of each file window then provides the list of links to news stories on the incident at other news outlets, along with three buttons to allow users to "Send us a tip," "Tweet," or "Link to this."

By graphically incorporating photographs of each individual so that they can be viewed both collectively and individually, "The Counted" interface design does *affective* work, conveying a visual impression of absence that feels less like "getting undone science done" and more like the phantom pain of amputated limbs—the intense, perceptible pain of corporeal absence (Bille, Hastrup, and Flohr Sørensen 2010). Viewing the many faces of the people displayed on "The Counted" web page as one scrolls down the screen gives the impression of the devastating loss of life. Even if one is not so moved, it would be hard to deny the humanity of the people depicted, some of them smiling and some of them very young (a six-year-old boy named Jeremy Mardis, killed in Louisiana when officers opened fire on his father's car; thirteen-year-old Tyre King killed in Ohio while running from police with a BB gun). Even images that have the appearance of mug shots of hardened criminals or men with severe expressions are humanized by their equal placement on the page with the other photos. Accessing any individual file, or any selection of files, provides an object lesson in tragedy, with a higher degree of granularity than the aggregated numbers. The absence of photos for some of the individuals killed, along with sporadic "unknown" names among the deceased, visually conveys the absences that still remain, giving those absences a distinct presence among the identified faces and files.

In April 2015, the *New York Times* published a piece of data journalism that revealed another, related absence, using census data to show that enormous numbers of black men are missing from their families and communities (Wolfers, Leonhardt, and Quealy 2015). Not all of these men have been killed by the police; many more of them are incarcerated, which is more appropriately understood as social death (Sexton 2011). The absence of these men matters not as an absence of data but in a more material sense, or in multiple material senses: economically and certainly affectively, including the absence of their physical presence in their homes and neighborhoods, the absence of their touch and the opportunity to touch them, to hear their voices and communicate with them, to receive and share their knowledge and experience. In this sense, their absence is also a partial loss of self for all those who would engage with them in such relations. For whole communities, the collective loss of all those who are missing is a devastating problem with far-reaching effects. While data may help to convey the scale and distribution of absent bodies, certainly the missing data does not matter as much as the missing people.

At the end of 2016 the *Guardian* stopped producing "The Counted." It continues to have an online presence, but now as an historical document of the two-year period it covers. (The individually produced crowdsourcing projects like "Fatal Encounters" carry on, but the lack of institutional support obviously poses challenges to those efforts.) The intention of the *Guardian* was not to institute a permanent system for assembling data on people killed by police, but instead to compel the state to act. During the two-year period of "The Counted," there were moments when it seemed possible that the *Guardian*'s effort would have this intended effect of prompting the U.S. federal government to establish a more comprehensive system for police accountability and to institute reforms with the aim of reducing police violence. James Comey, director of the FBI at the time, used the terms "ridiculous" and "embarrassing" to describe the fact that the *Guardian* had "better data" than the Justice Department on police use of lethal force (Davis and Lowery 2015). Yet, in the chronicity of absent and present knowledge on the matter of police violence, the period following the *Guardian's* two-year effort to produce the data has seen an alarming surge of willful ignorance at the federal level.

There are many reasons to feel less hopeful now about getting the undone science done in this case or prompting the federal government to act to curb police violence. It is important to acknowledge that visualizing the problem by making the absent data present does not automatically make it *concerning.* In other words, it cannot automatically make people care. Elevating the absent data and the killings themselves as a matter of concern—making them not just *present* and *visible*, but also *concerning*—requires an *audience who cares*, or a collection of subjects who can be enjoined to care. The question of care, or whether (enough) people can be enjoined to care about "undone science" on police use of lethal force, is tied up with a moral economy and the social valuation of lives; it is not exclusively a matter of rational argumentation or the presentation of evidence.

As noted at the outset, neither numbers nor images hold pride of place as evidence in fast-held belief systems; or, rather, often the same numbers and images are leveraged as authoritative evidence for one argument while being dismissed out of hand by another. Ultimately, as exhaustive as "The Counted" was, as rigorous as it was, as sophisticated a piece of data journalism as it was, with a well-designed interface and data visualization—all of this hit up against a highly polarized and fractured political culture. At another time and place, "The Counted" might matter in some more substantial way, by having an impact on sentiment and action. However, in its own time and place, entire publics simply disregard elite journalism of the kind adeptly produced by the *Guardian*. Unfortunately, we are confronted with yet another glaring absence—the disappearance of platforms for consensus formation, for reaching (even the appearance of) public agreement on matters of concern, including what should be counted, and in this case, whose lives and deaths should matter.

Conclusion: Journalism as Forensis

If "The Counted" reveals something about the ontology of absence in this case, it also suggests something about the ontology of journalism, or the changing form of journalism and its essential role in these challenging times, in the face of democratic ideals in grave crisis and decline. As both an active project and a historical document, "The Counted" represents one important case for querying the future of journalism. It appropriates and inverts crime statistics, weaving "quantifacts" together with found photos in a way that invokes what Eyal Weizman (2015) calls "forensis"—"something akin to a 'critical forensic practice'" (234). This critical forensic practice, or "counter-forensics," involves producing different evidence than the state produces—often, the evidence the state refuses to produce, or what it actively makes absent or invisible. It also involves "a querying of the practices of evidence making," whether one's own, in a self-reflexive move, or that of other actors, often with the aim of revealing the absences so produced (234). Although admittedly more concerned with producing evidence than with querying evidence making, "The Counted" performs a critical forensic practice, improvising the web interface as an alternative to the legal forum and mobilizing aesthetic practices "as investigative tools for the returning of the forensic gaze" (232). If forensics "is the art of the police," as Weizman has suggested (232), then a counterforensics is necessary in order to make visible what is made absent and invisible by the police, and by a moral economy that over-relies on the knowledge work of policing itself to determine what is knowable and what is not.[11]

Notes

1. Here I have in mind Jean Comaroff and John Comaroff's (2016) assessment of the morphing state form in *The Truth About Crime: Sovereignty, Knowledge, Social Order.* Their focus is South Africa but they see strong similarities with other states, including the United States. Modern states appear increasingly characterized by endemic corruption and fraud, owing "directly to the outsourcing of [state] functions"; outsourcing in particular "has transformed the state, in many respects, into something akin to a holding company, a metacorporation . . . [and] licensing authority . . . in the game of franchising out social, security, financial, carceral, administrative, military, and other services to profit-seeking firms" (32). They suggest that the late modern state is best understood as a form of "rentier government," with corruption and illicit economies laced seamlessly into its fabric, a "*systemic* feature of contemporary political economy" (32–33). Anyone still trying to make an argument for U.S. exceptionalism has been dealt a deadly blow with the 2016 election.

2. There are of course many contexts in which deaths are not counted, or not adequately counted, such as the number of Iraqis and Afghans killed in the U.S. wars in Iraq and Afghanistan, for example, or the number of people who die crossing the United States–Mexico border or the Mediterranean. All of these cases are worth considering individually and in relationship to one another, to understand differences and consistencies in cases of uncounted deaths. Whose deaths count in the official statistics of the state, and whose deaths are left uncounted in these official numbers? Are there explicit attempts at erasure, and what do the intentional and unintentional attempts at erasure look like? On the cultural politics at work in the disappearances and inclusions of physical bodies, see Casper and Moore's *Missing Bodies* (2009).

3. Croissant discusses ontological distinctions in the notion of "uncertainty," which have important implications for understanding the way climate change denial has operated, for example; conservative think tanks have produced ignorance on the issue of climate change by conflating the concept of uncertainty associated with scientific probability (which is inherent in all science) with "uncertainty meaning unknown or unreliable" (2014, 6).

4. Criminologist David Klinger (2012) maintains that a fundamental problem concerns the nature of what is being measured by the federal government systems, arguing that a better measure of police use of lethal force is not actual fatalities but *any* discharge of a firearm, whether someone dies or not—only then would a more complete picture of police behavior and use of lethal force become visible and knowable.

5. Another moment that promised to shed future light on what was not yet known was the 2013 renewal of the Deaths in Custody Reporting Act, which was created to monitor deaths in prisons but also mandated counting of arrest-related deaths.

6. The identity of the organizer of "Killed by Police" is nowhere identified, either on Facebook or on its website, but the author's use of first-person pronouns suggests that the project is managed by a single individual. I "liked," or opted to follow, the "Killed by Police" Community page on Facebook, so their posts, typically linking to stories in local news media, regularly appear in my Facebook feed. The page had a little over 43,000 followers at the time of writing.

7. Another example that could count as crowdsourcing broadly speaking is the Wikipedia entries titled "List of Killings by Law Enforcement Officers in the United States." There are separate pages for individual years, with a few entries going back as far as the nineteenth century. At the top of several of the Wikipedia pages there is a statement that reads: "*This list might be incomplete and may never be able to satisfy particular standards for completeness. You can help by expanding it with reliably sourced entries.*"

8. The feature was also the lead story on the front page of the *Guardian*'s print version the day it was launched, under the headline "Shoot to Kill: A U.S. Horror Story." The *Washington Post* also has an online web feature that presents compiled data, specifically on the number of people "shot dead" by police in 2015. It does not appear to rely on crowdsourcing, although there are certain features that resemble the *Guardian*'s interactive interface design. See https://www.washingtonpost.com/graphics/national/police-shootings/.

9. While the *Guardian* describes the project as employing "verified crowdsourcing," it is unclear exactly how much crowdsourcing was involved in the production of "The Counted." The project description explains that "The Counted" team relied on other crowdsourcing projects, specifically naming "Fatal Encounters" and "Killed by Police." Even if the *Guardian* received a large volume of "tips" through "The Counted" website, staff would have had to vet that information very carefully to make sure the information included in the database was not corrupted by misinformation submitted either unintentionally or maliciously. In an email response to my question about how much content originates from users/readers/the crowd as opposed to other sources, *Guardian* editor Ciara McCarthy explained: "We receive dozens of tips each week, all of which are passed on to our journalists for verification and/or additional reporting. I don't think we can give you an accurate breakdown of how many of our cases come from readers, because our readers each use the database and send us tips differently" (personal communication, September 23, 2016).

10. For the *Guardian*'s explanation of which deaths are included and not included in "The Counted," see the "About" page at https://www.theguardian.com/us-news/ng-interactive/2015/jun/01/about-the-counted.

11. In his cultural history of policing in the United States, Christopher Wilson (2000) observes "a startling paradox of modern American cultural life: the fact that much of our popular understanding of criminality and social *dis*order, particularly street disorder, comes from a knowledge economy that has the police—putatively agents of order—at its center" (5).

References

Barry, Rob, and Coulter Jones. 2014. "Hundreds of Police Killings Are Uncounted in Federal Stats." *Wall Street Journal*, December 3. http://www.wsj.com/articles/hundreds-of-police-killings-are-uncounted-in-federal-statistics-1417577504.

Beckett, Charlie. 2010. "*The Value of Networked Journalism*. London: Polis Journalism and Society. http://www.lse.ac.uk/media@lse/POLIS/Files/networkedjournalism.pdf.

Bille, Mikkel, Frida Hastrup, and Tim Flohr Sørensen. 2010. "Introduction: An Anthropology of Absence." In *An Anthropology of Absence: Materializations of Transcendence and Loss*, edited by Mikkel Bille, Frida Hastrup, and Tim Flohr Sørensen, 3–22. New York: Springer.

Bowker, Geoffrey. 2008. *Memory Practices in the Sciences*. Cambridge, Mass.: MIT Press.

Boyte, Harry. 2014. "Deliberative Democracy, Public Work, and Civic Agency." *Journal of Public Deliberation* 10 (1). http://www.publicdeliberation.net/jpd/vol10/iss1/art15.

Burghart, D. Brian. 2014. "What I've Learned from Two Years Collecting Data on Police Killings." *Gawker*, August 22. http://gawker.com/what-ive-learned-from-two-years-collecting-data-on-poli-1625472836.

Casper, Monica, and Lisa Jean Moore. 2009. *Missing Bodies: The Politics of Visibility*. New York: NYU Press.

Chibnall, Steve. 1975. "The Crime Reporter: A Study in the Production of Commercial Knowledge." *Sociology* 9 (1): 49–66.

Comaroff, Jean, and John L. Comaroff. 2006. "Figuring Crime: Quantifacts and the Production of the Un/Real." *Public Culture* 18 (1): 209–46.

———. 2016. *The Truth About Crime: Sovereignty, Knowledge, Social Order*. Chicago: University of Chicago Press.

Croissant, Jennifer L. 2014. "Agnotology: Ignorance and Absence or Towards a Sociology of Things That Aren't There." *Social Epistemology* 28 (1): 4–25.

Daniel, Anna, and Terry Flew. 2010. "The *Guardian* Reportage of the UK MP Expenses Scandal: A Case Study of Computational Journalism." Paper presented at the Communications Policy and Research Forum, Sydney, November 15–16.

Daston, Lorraine, and Peter Galison. 2007. *Objectivity.* Cambridge, Mass.: MIT Press.

Davis, Aaron, and Wesley Lowery. 2015. "FBI Director Calls Lack of Data on Police Shootings 'Ridiculous,' 'Embarrassing.'" *Washington Post,* October 7. http://wpo.st/aX1t0.

Ericson, Richard V., and Kevin D. Haggerty. 1997. *Policing the Risk Society.* New York: Oxford University Press.

Federal Bureau of Investigation (FBI). 2018. "Uniform Crime Reporting." FBI. Accessed April 15. https://ucr.fbi.gov/ucr.

Foucault, Michel. 1977. *History of Sexuality, Vol. 1.* New York: Vintage.

Frickel, Scott. 2014. "Absences: Methodological Note about Nothing, in Particular." *Social Epistemology* 28 (1): 86–95.

Frickel, Scott, Sahra Gibbon, Jeff Howard, Joanna Kempner, Gwen Ottinger, and David J. Hess. 2010. "Undone Science: Charting Social Movement and Civil Society Challenges to Research Agenda Setting." *Science, Technology, and Human Values* 25 (4): 444–73.

Gates, Kelly. 2016. "Professionalizing Police Media Work: Surveillance Video and the Forensic Sensibility." In *Images, Ethics, Technology,* edited by Sharrona Pearl, 41–57. New York: Routledge.

Gerbner, George. 1972. "Violence in Television Drama: Trends and Symbolic Functions." In *Television and Social Behavior,* Vol. 1, *Content and Control,* edited by George A. Comstock and Eli Rubinstein, 28–187. Washington, D.C.: U.S. Government Printing Office.

Gitelman, Lisa. 2015. "'Raw Data' Is an Oxymoron." In *New Media, Old Media: A History and Theory Reader,* 2nd ed., edited by Wendy Chun, Anna Watkins Fisher, and Thomas Keenan, 167–76. New York: Routledge.

Hess, David J. 2009. "The Potentials and Limitations of Civil Society Research: Getting Undone Science Done." *Sociological Inquiry* 79 (3): 306–27.

Klinger, David. 2012. "On the Problems and Promise of Research on Lethal Police Violence: A Research Note." *Homicide Studies* 16 (1): 78–96.

Kuchinskaya, Olga. 2014. *The Politics of Invisibility: Public Knowledge About Radiation Health Effects After Chernobyl.* Cambridge, Mass.: MIT Press.

Lanius, Candice. 2015. "Fact Check: Your Demand for Statistical Proof Is Racist." *Cyborgology,* January 12. http://thesocietypages.org/cyborgology/2015/01/12/fact-check-your-demand-for-statistical-proof-is-racist/.

Latour, Bruno. 2005. *Reassembling the Social: An Introduction to Actor-Network-Theory.* New York: Oxford University Press.

Lee, Jaeah. 2014. "Exactly How Often Do Police Shoot Unarmed Black Men?" *Mother Jones,* August 15. http://www.motherjones.com/politics/2014/08/police-shootings-michael-brown-ferguson-black-men/.

Loftin, Colin, Brian Wiersema, David McDowall, and Adam Dobrin. 2003. "Underreporting of Justifiable Homicides Committed by Police Officers in the United States, 1976–1998." *American Journal of Public Health* 93: 1117–21.

Lowery, Wesley. 2014. "How Many Police Shootings a Year? No One Knows." *Washington Post*, September 8. http://www.washingtonpost.com/news/post-nation/wp/2014/09/08/how-many-police-shootings-a-year-no-one-knows/.

Maimon, Alan. 2011. "National Data on Shootings by Police Not Collected." *Las Vegas Review-Journal*, November 28.

McCarthy, Tom. 2015. "The Uncounted." *Guardian*, March 18. https://www.theguardian.com/us-news/2015/mar/18/police-killings-government-data-count.

Mirzoeff, Nicholas. 2011. *The Right to Look: A Counterhistory of Visuality.* Durham, N.C.: Duke University Press.

Planty, Michael G., Andrea M. Burch, Duren Banks, Lance Couzens, Caroline Blanton, and Devon Cribb. 2015. "Arrest-Related Deaths Program: Data Quality Profile." U.S. Department of Justice, Office of Justice Programs, Bureau of Justice Statistics. Technical Report, NCJ 248544.

Sexton, Jared. 2011. "The Social Life of Social Death: On Afro-Pessimism and Black Optimism." *InTensions* 5 (Fall/Winter). http://www.yorku.ca/intent/issue5/articles/jaredsexton.php.

Sherman, Lawrence W., and Robert H. Langworthy. 1979. "Measuring Homicide by Police Officers." *Journal of Criminal Law and Criminology* 70 (4): 546–60.

Swaine, Jon, Oliver Laughland, and Jamiles Lartey. 2015. "Shoot to Kill: A U.S. Horror Story." *Guardian*, June 2.

Tuchman, Gaye. 1978. "Introduction: The Symbolic Annihilation of Women by the Mass Media." In *Hearth and Home: Images of Women in the Mass Media*, edited by Gaye Tuchman, Arlene Kaplan Daniels, and James Benet, 3–38. New York: Oxford University Press.

Wagner, Kyle. 2014. "We're Compiling Every Police-Involved Shooting in America. Help Us." *Deadspin*, August 20. http://regressing.deadspin.com/were-compiling-every-police-involved-shooting-in-americ-1624180387.

Weizman, Eyal. 2015. "Notes on Forensis." In *Images of Conviction: The Construction of Visual Evidence*, edited by Diane Dufour, 231–34. Paris: Le Bal.

Wilson, Christopher. 2000. *Cop Knowledge: Police Power and Cultural Narrative in Twentieth-Century America.* Chicago: University of Chicago Press.

Wines, Michael. 2014. "Race and Police Shootings: Are Blacks Targeted More?" *New York Times*, August 30. https://www.nytimes.com/2014/08/31/sunday-review/race-and-police-shootings-are-blacks-targeted-more.html.

Wolfers, Justin, David Leonhardt, and Kevin Quealy. 2015. "1.5 Million Missing Black Men." *New York Times*, April 20. http://www.nytimes.com/interactive/2015/04/20/upshot/missing-black-men.html.

CHAPTER 6

Digital Peripheries and the Politics of Expertise in Nairobi, Kenya

Lisa Poggiali

> The equipment-free aspect of reality here has become the height of artifice; the sight of immediate reality has become an orchid in the land of technology.
>
> —Walter Benjamin (1968, 233)

"We don't map those," Kyale stated emphatically, gesturing to the spigot jutting out of a makeshift mud structure from which women were collecting water in plastic jerry cans. His Global Positioning System (GPS) unit dangled from a cord wrapped around his wrist, and it swayed in step with his measured gait as we passed by the water point. A flicker of confusion must have swept across my face, and Kyale leaned over and whispered to me, "That water point is not by the government, but by the community. It's illegal, so we don't map it." It was nearing the second hour of our data collection expedition in Kyale's neighborhood, an informal settlement of Nairobi, Kenya, that I will call Muhimu. A few moments later, Kyale paused in front of a different water point—this one with a Nairobi City Water and Sewage Company (NCWSC) meter attached—and recorded its latitudinal and longitudinal coordinates with his GPS device. Later, taking respite from the heat of the day, he would retreat indoors to upload these coordinates to a computer using the software platform Java OpenStreetMap Editor (JOSM). By aggregating his data with that collected by other volunteer mappers over the span of a few months, he would help create a digital map of Muhimu; it would be the first publicly circulating map of any kind to acknowledge the settlement's existence.

Stretching across 182 acres to the east of Nairobi's central business district, Muhimu is one of Nairobi's informal settlements; its land is owned partially by the city council of Nairobi and the government of Kenya (Pamoja Trust 2012) and partially by absentee landlords, who acquired title deeds under highly ambiguous circumstances. Muhimu is considered illegally occupied, and its villages, roads, hospitals, and schools are depicted on government paper maps and, until recently, digitized Google ones as a vast swath of empty space, a large blank spot. In recent years, the neighborhood has become the headquarters of Muhimu Mapping Project (MMP), the nongovernmental organization for which Kyale was volunteering. In this chapter, I foreground settlement residents like Kyale, who make up over 50 percent of Nairobi's population (Amnesty International 2012), in order to show how "digital peripheries" are created and sustained in "Silicon Savannah," the term that Kenyans and foreigners alike use to refer to Nairobi's buzzing digital technology sector.

Silicon Savannah, as both a material space and a national imaginary, emerged from Kenya's 2007–2008 postelection violence, when politically motivated conflict led to over 1,200 deaths and 660,000 displaced citizens. In the wake of a state-initiated media blackout following the controversial 2007 presidential election results, technologically proficient Kenyans who had been living in the diaspora produced Ushahidi ("witness" or "testimony" in Kiswahili, Kenya's national language), Kenya's first digital mapping software platform (it would later become a nongovernmental organization of the same name). The platform encouraged Kenyans to text photographs, videos, and written information via SMS and the Web to a central number, where this information was plotted geospatially. In Nairobi, the platform's use was confined mostly to a small elite, but it became popular internationally, which led foreign investors and philanthropic organizations to finance the opening in 2011 of the iHub, a large space that hosted the budding group of software developers, web designers, and other technology enthusiasts who called Nairobi home. The iHub was located in the western portion of the city in the upper-middle-class neighborhood of Kilimani; initially, technologically curious Kenyans were welcome to attend free catered presentations and events there, such as a Google Mapping Party, where participants competed for prizes by adding sites to Kenya's current Google map. Outside of event times, Kenyans could use the iHub's lightning-speed wireless connection for free, and they could network with colleagues from Kenya and around the world, as it became a central meeting place for foreigners who were interested in participating in and observing the technological activity in the region. The iHub's lime-green walls, beanbag chairs, DJ booth, and floor-to-ceiling windows suggest a Google office, and the rhetoric its adherents articulate from within its walls reinforces the image of a universal digital subject who is everywhere and nowhere at the same time. As I will show below, this rhetoric paints Kenyan techies as entrepreneurial, postethnic citizens who reject both state patronage politics and governance via foreign aid, and instead aspire to design pieces of software that will catapult them into transnational circuits of capital. Techies pit Kenya's ethnically divisive history against its future modernity, fashioning "digital citizenship" as an expression of the latter (Poggiali 2017).

Much of the scholarship on Nairobi's emergent digital technology sector focuses on institutional spaces such as the iHub and the start-up cultures that they nurture (e.g., Benequista 2015; Ndemo and Weiss 2016; Gathigi and Waititu 2013); those active in such spaces are the city's upwardly mobile elite. Other academic and policy literature assesses the Kenyan state's project to build a "technology city" called Konza City on the outskirts of Nairobi (Saraswati 2014). While such elite spaces and projects appear at first blush as the bedrock of the technological activity happening in Nairobi, I posit that it is the city's informal settlements that serve as the ground on which techno-utopian claims that sustain Silicon Savannah are made, and as the site of recent sociotechnical experiments. Indeed, MMP, which I explore in detail here, is one of many techno-utopian digital mapping projects in the settlements that formed in the wake of Kenya's 2007–2008 conflict.[1]

In what follows, I draw on over two years of ethnographic research on Nairobi's emergent technology sector in order to suggest that ICT4D projects such as MMP helped to produce the urban poor as *constitutively excluded* participants of Silicon Savannah. I show how Muhimu residents navigated Nairobi's new technological terrain by attempting to make *their neighborhood visible* through digital mapping work in order to *make themselves visible* as technical experts. Making their physical location (Muhimu) known through mapping thus became a strategy to change their socioeconomic location. While I document how MMP helped to produce Nairobi's urban poor as technical experts, however, I suggest that they also undermined the mappers' ability to utilize this expertise, thus reinforcing the social and political exclusion the mappers were attempting to overcome. Throughout, I demonstrate how the mapmakers' sociopolitical status as slum dwellers colored the production and reception of the information they produced.

The Politics of Mapping in Historical Context

Mapmaking was key to the British colonial government's consolidation and assertion of its power in Kenya (cf., in other contexts, Scott 1998; Mitchell 2002; Winichakul 1994; Anderson 1991). Through acts of classification and quantification, the colonial state produced "deep social and institutional roots" as it "multiplied its size and functions" (Anderson 1991, 173). The British used maps as tools to regulate the living and working space of Africans (Cooper 1997; Elkins 2005; Zeleza 1992). In recent years, the Kenyan state has had a growing interest in geospatial technologies' potential in governance (e.g., Kenya hosted the Africa Geospatial Forum in 2012, as I discuss below), but thus far it is not clear that these new forms of visualization have led to new forms of surveillance (cf. Foucault, Burchell, and Gordon 1991; Strathern 2000; Anderson 1991). Rather, digital mapping technologies have been primarily used in citizen-led movements to counter existing versions of state record keeping. This is the case particularly in informal settlements like Muhimu.

Muhimu was one of the worst affected areas of Nairobi during Kenya's 2007–2008 postelection violence, owing to its large population of unemployed youth, its history of protracted conflicts over scant resources, and its high degree of segregated ethnic diversity. That MMP chose Muhimu to conduct its mapping work was thus not coincidental; alongside others in Kenya's growing technology sector, MMP's founders promoted digital technology, which they rhetorically cast as neutral, equalizing digital code, as a tool to foster peace and pan-ethnic cooperation in the slum (Poggiali 2017). MMP's managers—a Canadian, Sarah, and a Russian, Miroslav—believed that mapping Muhimu's infrastructure would encourage local political leaders to bring resources to the neglected area. If Muhimu's resources and needs were highlighted on digital maps, Sarah and Miroslav reasoned, the neighborhood could no longer be ignored. Bringing government attention to the settlement's well-being had recently also become a means to ensure its survival.

The citywide displacement of "informal" areas had become increasingly commonplace as Kenya attempted to fulfill its ambitious long-term economic, political, and social development plan, Vision 2030, which mandated infrastructural upgrading (Dolan 2012). This plan was eerily silent about Nairobi's settlement residents, who comprised over half of Nairobi's 3.1 million people (Amnesty International 2012). On a rainy September afternoon, I sat in a large conference room on the outskirts of Nairobi packed with digital mapping enthusiasts, cadastral experts, and state figures speaking on topics ranging from environmental conservation to economic development. This was the Africa Geospatial Forum, an annual conference celebrating the past achievements and future possibilities of geospatial technologies in areas of governance, development, and economic growth on the continent. After five years based in South Africa, the forum was meeting in Kenya for the first time, a migration that pointed to the country's growing interest in digital mapping.

"Let me begin by saying that I am very green in the area of geospatial technologies," admitted Mugo Kibati, director general of Vision 2030. Kibati was chairing a half-day panel focused on how geospatial technologies were relevant to Vision 2030, whose main goal was to transform Kenya into "a newly industrializing, middle-income country" by 2030 (Kenya Vision 2030 2014). Kibati's talk invoked familiar neoliberal economic measures—using private funds to develop a free trade port, create special economic zones, and support a strong business process outsourcing sector—which he joined with the managerial language of e-governance focused on automating and digitizing government services to "remove as much as possible the interface between public officers and citizens." He discussed technology as an "enabler" that would help the government (alongside the private sector) achieve its aims. Pointedly left out of his narrative about the nation's development were settlement residents like Kyale. Indeed, these residents were a symbol of the premodernity that Vision 2030 aimed to overcome. Miroslav, who attended the conference on MMP's behalf, raised this issue to Kibati in the question-and-answer period. How did Vision 2030 plan to contend with informal settlements, he inquired? Kibati responded brusquely: "Vision 2030's vision on informal settlements is to get rid of them. Plain and simple." But what was "plain and simple" about erasing over 50 percent of the bustling capital's residents?

Kibati's statement invoked a long history of violent state-authorized campaigns to bulldoze the settlements out of existence, acts that had left residents homeless and without financial compensation (Klopp 2008). Such evictions had become increasingly commonplace in Nairobi and Mombasa in the wake of large-scale infrastructural investment and business development that began with President Kibaki's election in 2003 and intensified amidst increasing Chinese investment in the years following. During that time, Kenya's cities slowly transformed: paved tarmac streets replaced the dirt roads on which swarms of cars had jostled for position; huge high-rises supplanted dilapidated buildings and filled empty lots. Settlement residents bore the brunt of this modernization, leading one columnist for the popular Kenyan newspaper the *Daily Nation* to conclude, "We talk of Vision 2030, a new port and improved railways, but for the poor the legacy of [the Grand Coalition[2]] is surely that of evictions" (Dolan 2012). While Kibati articulated a "people-centered, result-oriented society" whose progress could be charted through quantifying mechanisms such as forecasts, audits, and maps (cf. Foucault et al. 2009), all people, and all territories, were not envisioned as part of this society. Slum dwellers, in particular, were so abject as to lie outside of the Kenyan state's development plans.[3]

ICTs as a "New" Solution to the Problem of Development

MMP posited that maps could enhance the political legitimacy of slum dwellers and increase the concentration of government services in their neighborhoods; in so doing, it, along with many other Kenya-based organizations utilizing ICTs, aligned itself firmly with the global information and communications technologies for development (ICT4D) movement. Broadly, ICT4D is an ideological framework that presumes poverty can be mitigated by granting the poor access to technology; it is thus often posed as a solution to the so-called "digital divide" (cf. Gathigi and Waititu 2013, 206).

Social scientists have criticized ICT4D discourse for joining a functionalist argument about poverty with a political one about the failures of the state (e.g., Mazzarella 2006); epistemologically, it has much in common with modernization theory. If given unfettered access to the information economy, ICT4D presumes that individual citizens can both lift themselves up out of poverty and throw off the shackles of dictatorial regimes. Instead of tackling inequality, it produces "individualistic, market friendly, and measurable entities" (cf. Ballestero 2012, 160) and has thus been described as the ethical alibi of neoliberal governance. As William Mazzarella states, in a global context, ICT4D "was sold as a reconciliation between neoliberal capitalism and the interests of the poorest people in the world" (2010, 785).

As I will show below, Kenya's urban coders and web designers espoused this view that technologies, driven by quantifiable calculations and rapid speed, were simultaneously vectors of democracy and market efficiency, in that they could presumably bring large amounts of information to a broad scope of people instantaneously (cf. Dean 2002; Mazzarella 2010). "We are all part of a sea change in news and information flow and transparency," commented Erik Hersman (2009), cofounder of Kenyan digital mapping platform Ushahidi and founder of the iHub. "The barriers are finally so low that anyone can tell their story, and the whole world can see it. There is no stopping this change in information dynamics, there is only harnessing it in ways that add more value. . . . The more data that is collected, the less chance that bad data can have an adverse effect," he concluded.[4]

While critiques of statements such as Hersman's are helpful in exposing ICT4D as an ideology, by treating ICT4D as a smoke screen that conceals hidden machinations of power, the critiques elide the concrete cultural practices and social relations through which digital technologies—as objects with particular capacities rooted in their material specificity—actually come to matter to Kenyans. They fail to see, for example, how increased access to ICTs can also mean increased awareness of one's own exclusion, as was the case for many settlement residents. These critiques also implicitly presume that there is a fixed relationship between the purported producers of technology (e.g., NGO workers, state bureaucrats, software developers) and those who, the wool pulled over their eyes, are purportedly assumed to benefit from it (e.g., the uneducated and/or poor). The ethnographic data I present here resists such a reading by showing that slum dwellers—the so-called benefactors of ICT4D—are also invested in ICT4D discourse and strategically engage with digital technologies.

Further, in failing to point to the material specificity of ICTs, ideological critiques are therefore unable to account for the fact that although digital maps (ICTs) and drip irrigation systems (non-ICT technologies used to increase agricultural output and save water, a hallmark of agricultural development projects), for example, are both used in technology training programs aimed at poor Kenyans, and carry with them assumptions about poverty, labor, and knowledge that denigrate the expertise of the poor (Ferguson 2015, 35–36), these different technologies' effects are tied to their materiality.

For example, while many technology and infrastructure projects catalyze dreams of modernization (Larkin 2013) and have helped to imagine, produce, and maintain the nation-state as a cultural space (Philip, Irani, and Dourish 2012, 14), as communication technologies, ICTs crucially allow for continuous two-way communication across local, national, and continental borders (e.g., Brinkerhoff 2009).[5] In this way, they also differ from other communication methods, such as radio, which have historically presented limited opportunities for interaction between farmers and irrigation experts, for example, about development plans and practices (Gathigi and Waititu 2013, 209). The two-way communication allows Kenyans to reach out to so-called development experts and to make potentially lucrative international connections; the very presence of foreign NGOs such as MMP in Nairobi supports the notion that there are other foreign organizations that may bring material benefits. Further, ICTs' expansion into all domains of Kenyan life—from pleasure and entertainment to labor to communication to money transfer and bill pay, and beyond—has solidified their significance as a technology that continuously helps to construct a multiplicitous self. Unlike earlier technologies for development that were confined to designated moments of life (e.g., labor time, entertainment time, etc.), ICTs blur the boundaries of such designated time, and thus the boundaries between work and pleasure. This is even more true considering their mobile nature; they are, quite literally, always with that self.

ICTs: "Pay[ing] to Bet on the Poor"

Kenya's flirtation with digital technology began in the early 2000s, after the telecommunications sector was deregulated and the country's sole wireless provider, Safaricom, morphed from a state-owned subsidiary of Telkom Kenya into a private company. State-corporate partnerships, whose 130 million USD financed Kenya's first underwater fiber-optic cable (landing in 2009), ensured ICT would become a major political focus. Over the next few years, fiber-optic infrastructure linked Kenya to international communication networks, decreased the price of bandwidth, and drove foreign investment. With respect to the local market, Safaricom grew its customer base exponentially by offering cheap mobile phone packages and an SMS-based money-transfer system, M-Pesa. Mobile phones enabled Kenyans to circumvent the country's limited banking infrastructure and high transaction fees that barred most citizens from accessing formal savings plans. Safaricom became emblematic of ICT4D's potential, as national and international press praised the company for contributing to free-market economic growth and also helping Kenya's poor save and invest in businesses. In a particularly brazen statement of support, the *Economist* went to so far as to claim that Safaricom had probably done "more to help Kenya than decades of aid" and encouraged would-be investors that they could "pay to bet on the poor" (*Economist* 2008).

Maps are "close to that Internet thing, [which] people are crazy about right now," Njoroge, MMP's community coordinator, told me, trying to explain why mapping had become so popular in Muhimu. "For us," Njoroge said, speaking about slum dwellers like himself, "when you see a computer, you see English." We were sitting in the community center that served as the central gathering place for MMP's technical trainings and organizational meetings. The blips and bleeps of incoming instant messages in the room next door served as a fitting soundtrack for his thoughts on the symbolic significance of digital technology in the slum. While the mappers celebrated the narrative of technology-fueled success, they also had to fight continuously against the growing anxiety of being excised from it, and the persistent reality that they were not full participants in it. Shimba Technologies' Mbugua Njihia—a member of Kenya's elite technology sector—exemplified this attitude at a presentation at the DEMO fall 2011 conference in Santa Clara, California. He implored the audience to think of Kenya as an emerging market that had different characteristics from the United States. "Think long distances," he said. "Think poor infrastructure, but then again, think opportunity" (Njihia 2011). Like the sharp business minds at Safaricom, Njihia invoked the idea that the poor could drive investment to Silicon Savannah, but that they themselves were not its authors. Rather, they were stepping-stones to others' economic growth. Academics concurred, stating that "mobile telephony has completely changed the Kenyan business model by demonstrating that the low income segment is indeed profitable as a critical mass" (Gathigi and Waititu 2013, 205).

Njihia's comments invoke a double instance of fetishization: of technology as a magic-bullet solution to the problem of poverty and infrastructural lack, and also of the poor themselves as a ground on which technological experimentation could best occur; software coders and web designers constructed the poor as the constitutive outside of Kenya's technological takeoff.[6] Their views reflected a tension between what they saw as the intrinsically sociopolitically equalizing qualities of digital maps and their circulation in a milieu premised on free-market capitalism, in which ethics gave way to market calculations. In the first discourse, poverty was a problem to be solved, while in the latter it was an opportunity for foreign venture capitalists to grow their investments.

This discursive exclusion of the urban poor from the realm of technological production reflected a socioeconomic and political gap that existed between the epicenters of Silicon Savannah and the informal settlements. Aside from the technologists who worked directly on mapping projects in the impoverished sections of Nairobi, coders and web designers rarely (if ever) engaged in outreach with Nairobi's urban poor.[7] This lack of interest was reinforced by a material exclusion: Kilimani was on the other side of the city from the majority of Nairobi's slums, including Muhimu, and the approximately 1 USD public transport fee was prohibitively expensive for most residents. Indeed, only one of MMP's volunteers visited the iHub during my time in Nairobi. Despite the spirited interest in technology expressed by settlement residents, and the excellent technical skills exhibited by many of them, their access to the broader community of software coders and geospatial experts remained beyond their reach. The inclusive rhetoric of Kenya's technology sector was shadowed by its own exclusions.

"You Can't Just Sit There Because Everything Is Computerized"

Settlement residents in Muhimu (and other informal areas in Nairobi) consistently attempted to fight against their constitutive exclusion from the epicenters of Silicon Savannah by engaging with technology projects, such as MMP, in their own neighborhoods. Those who joined MMP were representative of the demographic that generally joined NGO projects in their neighborhoods: mostly male "youth" (aged eighteen to forty) with good English skills, limited domestic responsibilities, and diversified sources of income, which afforded them the ability to volunteer for indeterminate amounts of time and uncertain economic benefit. Indeed, the mappers' interest in MMP was informed by their hope that it would be a stepping-stone to potential future economic opportunities. "Nowadays people have to acquire more skills and knowledge," explained Elisa, a Muhimu resident in her early twenties, of her desire to join MMP. "Not just sit in one place. For example, say that I'm a farmer, I should [explore] other arenas such as fishing and business to add to whatever I have. . . . So I decided to join [MMP] to get knowledge for the future. You never know where your luck lies." In a socioeconomic milieu where steady, secure work was a luxury afforded to a select few, MMP was thus part of a broader employment strategy. In this respect, it was not dissimilar to other money-generating activities such as carrying a heavy load for a construction company or attending UNICEF training that promised a monetary stipend. "You cannot depend on one thing, you must have many avenues," Peter Odondo, another mapper, confirmed, echoing Elisa's comment. As a digital technology project, however, MMP was a specific kind of income-generating activity: it reflected the surge of interest in ICT4D projects more generally in Nairobi since 2008, and the sentiment expressed by young Kenyans across the class spectrum that digital technology was a pathway to a better future life.[8] "Nowadays it's a world of technology," Elisa told me. "You can't just sit there because everything is computerized . . . you can't do things manually." Doing things manually meant failing to live up to the modernist vision invoked by digitality, and the mappers, like others in Kenya, did not want to be left behind.

Indeed, in addition to slum dwellers, Kenyan and expatriate software developers, web designers, and bloggers, as well as government officials, discussed new technologies as a harbinger of Kenya's socioeconomic development. The technologies' meaning was deeply influenced by their material form, which caused their advocates to perceive them as unmediated by human action. Witness Lands Cabinet Secretary Charity Ngilu's statement regarding the Lands Ministry's decision to digitize the lands registry: "I must admit that all has not been well at the Lands Ministry because of cartels, which engage in shady deals that have defrauded Kenyans of millions of shillings. That will soon end once we digitize all records," she said (Mbaka 2013). Digitization, in this commonly articulated discourse, was understood to solve endemic bureaucratic corruption because of its perceived powers of immediation—that is, its ability to "occlude the potentialities and contingencies embedded in the mediations that comprise and enable social life" (Mazzarella 2006, 476). Muhimu's mappers echoed this discourse, expressing in more concrete terms the potential political possibilities inherent in *digitally* manufactured visibility: "Mappers can say 'this is a children's playing ground' and put it on a [digital] map," Njoroge, MMP's community coordinator, told me. "For a government to put a playground where there is a playground, it has to go through a legal process. And in the process, somebody comes in and manipulates [the situation], and grabs the land." Both Ngilu and Njoroge imagined that the speed and immediacy of digital technology would forestall the malevolent activities considered to be an everyday part of social and political life in Kenya. Immanent to the digital form, in other words, were notions of ethics, truth, and prosperity, qualities that always exceeded the technologies' seemingly banal function on the streets of Muhimu—that is, as part of a diversified economic strategy.

Producing Expertise

"This is what you need to know," Miroslav said, pointing to a sheet of paper with "NEED TO KNOW" scrawled at the top in black magic marker; he had taped it to the bright blue walls of the community center in Muhimu where MMP held regular meetings. Underneath it, he had written: "1. GPS SETUP (tracks, time, map, waypoints, units); 2. DATA TRANSFER (GPS Babel); 3. JOSM (editing; uploading, downloading)." This was day one of three days of "testing" the mappers on their knowledge of geospatial technologies. Those who passed the test would receive printed certificates attesting to their expertise and would be invited to continue volunteering for the organization. Those who failed would have to retest, and if unsuccessful, would be asked to leave. Miroslav called each of the mappers one by one to come outside the organization's headquarters; they stood abutting a large pile of trash that had been partially caked into the ground by the ravages of weather and the continual imprints of residents' footsteps. The mappers answered the questions as best they could, occasionally raising their voices over the brief snippets of reggaeton that punctured the air from passing cars. The testing ended inside, with the mappers using one of three laptops—property of MMP—to upload points using GPS Babel and plot them on a map using JOSM. Through such testing practices, MMP constructed digital mapping as an expertise-producing activity.

Months later, Miroslav and Sarah invited the mappers to an elaborately staged party at a restaurant not far from Muhimu. After noshing on *mbuzi choma* (roasted goat meat) and Tusker, the local beer, they called each of the mappers to the front of the space to receive their printed certificates, which stated that they were "proficient in GPS data collection, Basic editing with JOSM, and OpenStreetMap data entry." Crucially, these certificates also displayed the insignia of both MMP and a large health-related NGO that had sponsored the trainings. The mappers proudly displayed their certificates, and all parties paused to ensure that the multiple cameras documenting the event captured the exchange of documents, hugs, and hearty handshakes. The certificates substantiated what the day of testing had initially suggested—that the mappers were now geospatial experts. As their desire to be photographed reveals, this is a status in which the mappers reveled.

"Nowadays . . . [there are many people] teach[ing] computer lessons to students, [but] they can't award you a certificate, so you can't be recognized anywhere like you know anything about computers," Elisa said, comparing MMP's training program to others she had encountered in the area. Such comments revealed certificates to be one pathway to recognized expertise that promised the possibility of future work and a better life. Emmanuel, another mapper, concurred: "There was some NGO . . . dealing with HIV status. They wanted guys who had reached a certain level in school. But when I showed them the certs that I had, they took me for work. They said, 'Ah, this guy has been participating in many events, so let's go with him.' My level of education, they didn't see it as law, but what I've been doing to improve myself, [they saw it as] vital." Emmanuel's story suggests that the visibility of the certificate made the self visible in a new way; that is, it conferred expertise that enabled one to bypass more traditional channels to employment, such as education. Being able to show the certificate to others, to have them recognize it, was crucial for this demonstration of expertise. The mappers' preoccupation with receiving the certificates makes clear that despite the pervasive discourse that associated digitality with unmediated truth, they were aware that becoming proficient in digital mapping was not a channel unto itself; the digital maps were mediated by another document, which had been authorized by NGOs.

In his research on *campesinos*' struggle to claim land amidst sweeping political and economic changes in contemporary Paraguay, Kregg Hetherington suggests (2011, 151) that retaining control over the circulation of documents related to land titling had political consequences more profound than mining the information contained within them. Though the maps in Muhimu were consistently referred to by mappers and project managers alike as evidence to improve service provision in the slum, government officials rarely, if ever, used the maps' content in urban planning or service distribution. Yet, the maps that hung on the walls of the offices of district officers and local chiefs were the only documents displayed save tattered calendars marking the passage of time. The documents' generative effect, I suggest, was not to inspire civil servants and political figures to assume their formal duties as democratically elected representatives, as Miroslav and Sarah envisioned, but rather to signal that they understood and formed part of the world in which the maps circulated, both symbolically and materially (Larkin 2013). That the maps, pointillist conglomerations of dots and dashes, had traveled through the cavernous heart of a computer before transmogrifying into the banal tactile documents familiar to government officials everywhere only underscored the extent to which, in this case, "the medium of objectification matter[ed]" (Miller 1987, 129, quoted in Hull 2008, 504).

The digital began to serve as a shared grammar through which local government leaders and mappers could position themselves as equals in Kenya's race toward modernization. "[Mapping] made a big awareness," explained Maurice, a Muhimu mapper in his late twenties. "The mapping did a very unique thing. The DO [district officer], the chiefs . . . they are now starting to trust the youth. [We took] the first map to the DO and he asked, 'Who did this?' We said to him, 'We ourselves did this.' He said, 'You are doing a very good idea. Even those *mzees* of *kijijis* [sic; elders in the villages] who are saying you are thieves, I cannot believe it from now.' [They believe] that [the youth] can do something." When the chiefs and DOs prominently showcased the maps, they signaled their "convergence" (Mazzarella 2006) with those they are expected to govern—slum dwellers—without having to substantively engage with them, implement policies, or distribute services. Indeed, Njoroge's eyes lit up when recounting how a DO or chief had taped a printed map to his office wall, corroborating Mark's account that the maps caused local leaders to reimagine the youth of Muhimu in a positive light. Furthermore, through including the maps, technical objects associated with modern, prosperous Kenya, local government officials also sent the message that they were custodians of technical knowledge. The maps' close affiliation with the computer, which Njoroge, Ngilu, and others purported would translate human folly and malfeasance into sets of quantifiable and therefore neutral and objective standards, made them desirable. Given Muhimu's recent violent history, residents and foreigners alike contrasted cold, calculated computer knowledge with what the local press had characterized as an excess of affect that led to the 2007–2008 violence. In this way, the maps served not "as the end point, but as the site of possibility, not a store of information as a static thing but as a tool for making a political effect" (Hetherington 2011, 166).

In the settlement, the maps expunged human presence from the narrative of their creation; they signified an absence of the social relations of mundane bribery that lubricated the circulation of resources in the slum. At the same time, because Muhimu residents physically brought paper versions of the maps to the DO's and chiefs' offices, the socially mediated quality of their production could not be denied. In that powerful leaders in Muhimu chose to display the maps, these digital products transformed slum dwellers into subjects with the capacity to produce expertise, a heretofore unrealized capability. "Before, the elders just thought youths were doing drugs and hustling," Kyale told me. "Now they see; we are doing good things, too." The slum dwellers' potential credibility as experts emerged as an *effect* of the maps, simultaneously indexing digital fetishism *and* a persistent (post)colonial faith in the political authority communicated through paper documents.

By challenging state-authored cartographic depictions of Muhimu, in which the area is formally portrayed as a piece of land devoid of people and place, the mappers reconfigured existing representations of territory and authority. However, for local political authorities and the mappers themselves, the *content* of the maps—more or better information—was often overshadowed by their form—that is, the maps' material and symbolic association with digitality. In the case of Muhimu, widespread faith in the digital form, which technology enthusiasts believed would eliminate graft by removing human action from the process of monitoring, led many to claim that digital maps offered a more exact optic of place than ever before. However, while Muhimu's mappers attempted to both produce new representations (which they hoped would bring sociopolitical attention to themselves and their neighborhoods) and fulfill their aspirations to participate in Kenya's rapidly digitizing world, they first had to prove they had the authority to do so. Outside of the sociopolitical world of Muhimu, settlement residents found it difficult to leverage their expertise and make the information they produced matter.

Owing to a dearth of computers and an unreliable electricity supply in Muhimu's offices, the maps lived offline, separated from the computers that made them possible. Over the course of my time in Muhimu, their edges began to fray, and their borders slowly changed from white to yellow. Away from the radiant light of digital code, their symbolic power slowly weakened, as the maps' material fragility began to mimic the insecurity of the settlement and its residents (see also Larkin 2013). Indeed, for the residents of Muhimu, the maps embodied the duality of precarity and promise that characterized Kenya's technological takeoff. The maps were a potent metaphor for the uphill battle the mappers experienced when they attempted to shift their subject position through their engagements with digital technology. In their struggle to become socially visible, their status as technical experts—and the credibility of their digital data—was thrown into question. How could data that was so obviously *mediated* be trusted? For the mappers, the semiotic-material economy of computers, like the physical space of the iHub, proved to be just out of reach.

The Temporality of Technology

Digital maps' material capacity for speed gestured to the broader temporality of "development" itself, and Vision 2030's ambitious goals. For settlement residents, the gleaming surfaces of high-rise luxury apartments being erected all over town and the expansive highways—sturdy monuments to progress being built at breakneck speed by Chinese and Japanese contractors—signaled both the abstract promise of a grander future and the terrifying threat of impending physical eviction; racing ahead always also implied leaving something, or someone, behind.

For the mappers, digital technologies' speed often generated new fears about potentially being left behind. "It's high time we take advantage of [the fact that much of the world is not mapped]," Ronald, one of the most technically proficient mappers of the group, relayed to me, with a sense of urgency in his voice. "We are the pioneers of [digital mapping]. And we should grab that opportunity to be recognized. We should expect competition from organizations like Google. Google are coming in. If we are not creative, we will be locked out of all these things, and our idea will be stolen," he continued, gesturing to the narrow window of time they had before their own talents would be eclipsed by outsiders with more established credibility.

Ronald had reason to be worried. A few weeks after our conversation, USAID initiated a digital mapping project in Muhimu. They wanted geospatial experts to mark properties where they were planning to establish voluntary counseling and testing clinics, part of a larger project to combat HIV. USAID had previously funded MMP's technical training, but they did not approach any of Muhimu's residents about the mapping project. "If we were working in partnership with them," Njoroge lamented, "we could easily have done the mapping of the houses for them in a very professional and a very good way." The problem he identified was that despite the mappers' technical expertise and familiarity with the area, the latter of which was a huge asset in such a densely populated, difficult-to-navigate area, USAID failed to take them seriously. At its heart, digital mapping in Muhimu was a struggle over not merely *how* the neighborhood would be represented, but *who* would have the opportunity to make the neighborhood visible. In this case, the mappers' sociopolitical status as slum dwellers informed the perceived credibility, or lack thereof, of the information they produced.

Conclusion: Seeing (from) Digital Peripheries

Digital maps were materialized constellations of dreams and desires that shaped social life, subjectivity, and understandings of expertise. These technologies helped to produce differentiated sociopolitical subjects throughout the city; they were thus much more than just tools (cf. Heidegger 1977) or symbols of modernity. As a new "way of seeing" (Berger 1972), digital maps enabled Muhimu residents to produce self-representation rather than relinquish it to a negligent or oppressive state, or to foreign development workers. This speaks to the new political capacities introduced by ICTs and the institutional mediators—such as MMP—that have emerged to provide a means for slum dwellers to engage with them. Producing and tinkering with digital maps cultivated aspirational identities among the slum dwellers. By weaving a political argument about visibility, recognition, and belonging into the spaces between their strategically collected GPS coordinates, the mappers arguably used technologies to challenge the Kenyan state and elite technology sector's discursive separation of politics and technics.

Yet, the channels for sociopolitical engagement carved by these new technologies were not unobstructed. Just as submarine fiber-optic cables can be cut and rendered inoperative by vandals, sending communications networks to a grinding halt, information in Silicon Savannah, too, could be intercepted, rerouted, or impeded. In Muhimu, being able to "see" the neighborhood through the eyes of its residents was contingent not only on the mappers' relative adeptness at framing that information but also on a high degree of trust—what Rosalind Morris (2004) calls "intimacy"—between representer and observer. As the stories at the end of this piece reveal, MMP failed to carve the channels—materially or sociopolitically—for this intimacy to take shape.

Recent social scientific work has demonstrated acutely how marginalized groups have been included in and excluded from narratives of national technological progress and promise (Burrell 2012; Larkin 2008; Horst and Miller 2006; McIntosh 2010). MMP's story contributes to this dialogue, while also revealing how marginality can be reinforced through the very techno-utopian discourses to which the urban poor aspire to belong. The example I present here thus indexes not a *disjuncture* between techno-utopian ideology and the lived reality of Nairobi's urban poor, but rather a dense entanglement of the two.

While it may appear at first blush as though MMP is an example of the so-called digital divide's closure, since the organization granted Muhimu residents access to new digital technologies, I have suggested here quite the opposite. Indeed, Muhimu was actively (re)produced as a digital periphery through its very *inclusion* in the technological realm, both discursively (through the way discussion was framed at places like the iHub) and through the material engagements with technology that showed that, despite newfound visibility and expertise, Muhimu residents faced social, political, and economic barriers that prevented the translation of such expertise to spaces outside the settlement. Thus, this story demonstrates the inadequacy of understanding the "digital divide" either through the lens of access to particular technologies or as a problem that can be productively framed through the binary of "developed" and "developing," global "North" and global "South."

Instead, future scholarship on technologies in postcolonial contexts should focus not only on how new media technologies generate novel social relations or economic opportunities "at the margins" (where much scholarship has focused) but also how they produce new explanatory models that both precipitate and conceal relations of inequality. There must be more focus, in other words, on what Warwick Anderson (2002, 647) called "the translocal coproduction of technosciences and social orders" (see also Philip, Irani, and Dourish 2012; Jasanoff 2004). In order to see the inequalities (re) produced through technological imaginaries and sociotechnical engagements, we must analyze new media technologies as both potential vectors of sociopolitical recognition and battlegrounds on which the urban poor's claims to inclusion are affirmed or ignored, heeded or disregarded.

Acknowledgments

An earlier version of this chapter was published by *Cultural Anthropology* as "Seeing (from) Digital Peripheries: Technology and Transparency in Kenya's Silicon Savannah," *Cultural Anthropology* 31 (3) (2016): 387–411. The chapter draws on over two years of ethnographic research in Nairobi, Kenya, which was funded by the National Science Foundation's DIG (Award No.1023337), the Social Science Research Council's IDRF, the Wenner-Gren Foundation for Anthropological Research's Dissertation Fieldwork Grant, the Fulbright-Hays DDRA, and the Department of Anthropology at Stanford University. I thank all of these institutions, whose generous support enabled me to plant roots in Kenya that allowed me to explore my research questions deeply and broadly. I am also grateful to the Program on Democracy, Citizenship and Constitutionalism at the University of Pennsylvania—in particular, Rogers Smith, Michael X. Delli Carpini, and Greg Urban—for giving me the necessary time and space to complete this article. Audience comments at the University of Pennsylvania's Digital Media and the Future(s) of Democracy conference, where I presented parts of this piece, were instrumental to the revision process. My deepest debt is to my friends and colleagues in Kenya, who made this research possible.

Notes

1. These projects were variously organized and funded by transnational media NGOs like Internews, international development organizations like USAID and Plan International, educational institutions like Emory University, and geospatial activist groups from places as far afield as Italy and Brazil. Most mapping projects were implemented with local partners—community health workers and organizers active in the settlements.

2. The Grand Coalition was the outcome of a political power-sharing deal brokered after the 2007/2008 post-election violence. Mwai Kibaki became president, and opposition leader, Raila Odinga, became prime minister.

3. For more on abjection and subjectivity, see Judith Butler's (1999) research on politics and representation in feminist thought. She argues that the subject is shaped by the domains of political and linguistic representation through which it emerges: "Representation is extended only to what can be acknowledged as subject" (1–2). The subject, in other words, must be witnessed before it can be rendered visible.

4. The iHub created an "M-Governance project" in September 2011 with the intent to "evaluate how mobile phone technology [could] be used to improve Kenyan governance, especially in enhancing transparency through access to water information, service charters and effective communication amongst the different stakeholders" (iHub Research 2014). It hoped to replicate this project in other sectors, including education, health, and infrastructure.

5. The exception to this would be during electricity outages.

6. Of course, corporations do not hold a monopoly on fetishizing the poor. NGOs and academics have long celebrated poor peoples' creative acts of "bricolage" in the face of dire economic circumstances (cf. Koolhaas et al. 2000); this focus on the poor's alterity advances a politics that obscures the structural violence and institutional relations of power that create and sustain inequality.

7. On most digital mapping projects, digital coders and development practitioners performed different roles: the former hunkered down at the iHub to produce new software; the latter administered technical training directly to settlement residents.

8. While anthropologists have pointed out that enthusiasm for digital technology in Kenya is not universal (McIntosh 2010; Mahoney 2017), in the capital city of Nairobi, it is extremely widespread. In over two years of fieldwork between 2010 and 2013, I rarely heard anyone speak of it negatively. I attribute this in part to the fact that my research subjects—both the urban poor and elite—were involved in technology projects; however, I heard similar enthusiasm expressed colloquially by friends, taxi drivers, service workers, and civil servants.

References

Amnesty International. 2012. "Speaking Up from the Slums." April 24. https://www.amnesty.org/en/latest/news/2012/04/speaking-slums/.

Anderson, Benedict. 1991. "Census, Map, Museum." In *Imagined Communities*, 167–90. London: Verso.

Anderson, Warwick. 2002. "Introduction: Postcolonial Technoscience." *Social Studies of Science* 32 (5/6): 643–58.

Ballestero, Andrea S. 2012. "Transparency Short-Circuited: Laughter and Numbers in Costa Rican Water Politics." *PoLAR: Political and Legal Anthropology Review* 35 (2): 223–41. doi:10.1111/j.1555-2934.2012.01200.x.

Benequista, Nicholas. 2015. "Journalism from the 'Silicon Savannah': The Vexed Relationship Between Nairobi's Newsmakers and Its ICT4D Community." *Stability: International Journal of Security and Development* 4 (1). doi:10.5334/sta.fc.

Benjamin, Walter. 1968. *Illuminations*. Boston: Houghton Mifflin Harcourt.

Berger, John. 1972. *Ways of Seeing*. London: Penguin Books.

Brinkerhoff, Jennifer M. 2009. *Digital Diasporas: Identity and Transnational Engagement*. Cambridge, U.K.: Cambridge University Press.

Burrell, Jenna. 2012. *Invisible Users: Youth in the Internet Cafés of Urban Ghana*. Cambridge, Mass.: MIT Press.

Butler, Judith. 1999. *Gender Trouble: Tenth Anniversary Edition*. Taylor and Francis.

Cooper, Frederic. 1997. *From Slaves to Squatters: Plantation Labor & Agriculture in Zanzibar and Coastal Kenya, 1890–1925*. Portsmouth, N.H.: Heinemann.

Dean, Jodi. 2002. *Publicity's Secret: How Technoculture Capitalizes on Democracy.* Ithaca, N.Y.: Cornell University Press.

Dolan, Gabriel. 2012. "Evictions the Biggest Legacy of Government." *Daily Nation*, October 26. http://www.nation.co.ke/oped/Opinion/Evictions-the-biggest-legacy-of-government-/-/440808/1604262/-/154g5lhz/-/index.html.

Economist. 2008. "Africa Calling." June 5. http://www.economist.com/node/11488505.

Elkins, Caroline. 2005. *Imperial Reckoning: The Untold Story of Britain's Gulag in Kenya.* New York: Henry Holt. http://us.macmillan.com/book.aspx?name=imperialreckoning&author=CarolineElkins.

Ferguson, James. 2015. *Give a Man a Fish: Reflections on the New Politics of Distribution.* Durham, N.C.: Duke University Press.

Foucault, Michel, Graham Burchell, and Colin Gordon. 1991. *The Foucault Effect: Studies in Governmentality.* Chicago: University of Chicago Press.

Foucault, Michel, Michel Senellart, François Ewald, Alessandro Fontana, Arnold I. I. Davidson, et al. 2009. *Security, Territory, Population: Lectures at the Collège de France 1977–1978.* Translated by Graham Burchell. New York: Picador.

Gathigi, George, and Ernest Waititu. 2013. "Coding for Development in the Silicon Savannah: The Emerging Role of Digital Technology in Kenya." In *Re-Imagining Development Communication in Africa*, edited by Chuka Onwumechili and Ikechukwu Ndolo, 201–23. Lanham, Md.: Lexington Books.

Heidegger, Martin. 1977. *The Question Concerning Technology, and Other Essays.* 15th ed. New York: Harper and Row.

Hersman, Erik. 2009. "Ushahidi's Anniversary and Future." WhiteAfrican, January 8. http://whiteafrican.com/2009/01/08/ushahidis-anniversary-and-future.

Hetherington, Kregg. 2011. *Guerrilla Auditors: The Politics of Transparency in Neoliberal Paraguay.* Durham, N.C.: Duke University Press.

Horst, Heather, and Daniel Miller. 2006. *The Cell Phone: An Anthropology of Communication.* Oxford, U.K.: Berg.

Hull, Matthew S. 2008. "Ruled by Records: The Expropriation of Land and the Misappropriation of Lists in Islamabad." *American Ethnologist* 35 (4): 501–18.

iHub Research. 2014. "Spider M-Governance." iHub Nairobi. Accessed September 9. http://www.ihub.co.ke.

Jasanoff, Sheila. 2004. *States of Knowledge: The Co-Production of Science and Social Order.* London: Routledge.

Kenya Vision 2030. 2014. "The Vision." Accessed April 28. http://www.vision2030.go.ke/index.php/vision.

Klopp, Jacqueline M. 2008. "Remembering the Destruction of Muoroto: Slum Demolitions, Land and Democratisation in Kenya." *African Studies* 67 (3): 295–314. doi:10.1080/00020180802504866.

Koolhaas, Rem, Stefano Boeri, Sanford Kwnter, Nadia Tazi, and Hans Ulrich Obrist. 2000. *Mutations.* Barcelona: Actar.

Larkin, Brian. 2008. *Signal and Noise: Media, Infrastructure, and Urban Culture in Nigeria*. Durham, N.C.: Duke University Press.

———. 2013. "The Politics and Poetics of Infrastructure." *Annual Review of Anthropology* 42 (1): 327–43. doi:10.1146/annurev-anthro-092412-155522.

Mahoney, Dillon. 2017. *The Art of Connection: Risk, Mobility and the Crafting of Transparency in Coastal Kenya*. Berkeley: University of California Press.

Mazzarella, William. 2006. "Internet X-Ray: E-Governance, Transparency, and the Politics of Immediation in India." *Public Culture* 18 (3): 473–505. doi:10.1215/08992363-2006-016.

———. 2010. "Beautiful Balloon: The Digital Divide and the Charisma of New Media in India." *American Ethnologist* 37 (4): 783–804. doi:10.1111/j.1548-1425.2010.01285.x.

Mbaka, James. 2013. "Lands Ministry to Digitise Records, Says Charity Ngilu." *Standard*, September 3, sec. Kenya. http://www.standardmedia.co.ke/?articleID=2000092628&story_title=lands-ministry-to-digitise-records-says-charity-ngilu&pageNo=1.

McIntosh, Janet. 2010. "Mobile Phones and Mipoho's Prophecy: The Powers and Dangers of Flying Language." *American Ethnologist* 37 (2): 337–53.

Miller, Daniel. 1987. *Material Culture and Mass Consumption*. Cambridge, Mass.: Basil Blackwell.

Mitchell, Timothy. 2002. *Rule of Experts: Egypt, Techno-Politics, Modernity*. Berkeley: University of California Press.

Morris, Rosalind. 2004. "Intimacy and Corruption in Thailand's Age of Transparency." In *Off Stage/On Display: Intimacy and Ethnography in the Age of Public Culture*, edited by Andrew Shryock, 225–43. Stanford, Calif.: Stanford University Press.

Ndemo, Bitange, and Tim Weiss, eds. 2016. *Digital Kenya: An Entrepreneurial Revolution in the Making*. London: Palgrave Macmillan.

Njihia, Mbugua. 2011. "MedAfrica by Shimba Technologies." Presented at the DEMO Conference, Santa Clara, California, September 14. http://www.youtube.com/watch?v=Ts6Gn-KQgnk&feature=youtu.be.

Pamoja Trust. 2012. "An Inventory of the Slums in Nairobi." Accessed June 24, 2018. https://knowyourcity.info/wp-content/uploads/2015/04/Nairobi_slum_inventory_jan_09.pdf.

Philip, Kavita, Lilly Irani, and Paul Dourish. 2012. "Postcolonial Computing: A Tactical Survey." *Science, Technology, and Human Values* 37 (1): 3–29. doi:10.1177/0162243910389594.

Poggiali, Lisa. 2017. "Digital Futures and Analog Pasts?: Citizenship and Ethnicity in Techno-Utopian Kenya." *Africa* 87 (2).

Saraswati, Jyoti. 2014. "Konza City and the Kenyan Software Services Strategy: The Great Leap Backward?" *Review of African Political Economy* 41 (supl): S128–37. doi:10.1080/03056244.2014.976189.

Scott, James C. 1998. *Seeing Like a State: How Certain Schemes to Improve the Human Condition Have Failed*. New Haven, Conn.: Yale University Press.

Strathern, Marilyn. 2000. "The Tyranny of Transparency." *British Educational Research Journal* 26 (3): 309–21. doi:10.1080/713651562.

Winichakul, Thongchai. 1994. *Siam Mapped: A History of the Geo-Body of a Nation*. Honolulu: University of Hawaii Press.

Zeleza, Tiyambe. 1992. "The Colonial Labour System in Kenya." In *An Economic History of Kenya*, edited by William Robert Ochieng and Robert M. Maxon, 171–99. Nairobi, Kenya: East African Educational Publishers.

PART III

Digital Media and Public Voices

CHAPTER 7

Authoritarian Deliberation 2.0: Lurking and Discussing Politics in Chinese Social Media

Daniela Stockmann and Ting Luo

The Internet is often regarded as contributing to the democratic process by giving citizens the opportunity to engage in political talk and assess conflicting ideas. In spaces for public conversation, the Internet has been credited with creating a new public sphere of the sort envisioned by Habermas ([1962] 1990) (see, e.g., Poor 2005). Other scholars have conversely emphasized the Internet's potential to damage deliberative ideals by facilitating exposure to like-minded views, encouraging incivility, or decreasing satisfaction (see, e.g., Sunstein 2007).

In recent years, the growing importance of online political discussion in nondemocratic contexts has raised similar questions about the nature and political consequences of authoritarian deliberation. In comparison to democratic deliberation, authoritarian deliberation is more concentrated and hierarchical as the state actively shapes the boundaries of political discourse (He and Warren 2011; Jiang 2010). This research is emerging mainly out of the study of China. On the one hand, public officials actively encourage political discourse in order to receive feedback about policy making, but on the other hand, they also manage and control cyberspace in order to guide online public opinion in directions that are favorable to the state. Authoritarian deliberation also exerts pressure on public officials to respond and affects policy making (Meng, Pan, and Yang 2017; Reilly 2012).

Little is known about the citizens living under authoritarian rule who voice their views about politics. Balla's study of emails sent to the Chinese

National Development and Reform Commission regarding health reform revealed that people who sent emails tend to be male and have more specialized knowledge and work experience (Balla 2012). More active users of the Twitter-like Weibo tend to have higher levels of internal efficacy and lower levels of external efficacy (Chan et al. 2012; Zhang and Pentina 2012). We build on these findings by focusing on differences between lurkers and discussants. Studies on Internet behavior in Europe and the United States show that only a small minority posts comments online, but a large majority of "lurkers" follow the discussion without posting (see, e.g., Davis 2009). We find that Chinese discussants tend to participate because they seek social rewards, while lurkers tend to be motivated by political learning. In addition, we find that lurkers tend to be more concerned about privacy compared to discussants. As Chinese officials are receptive to online public opinion, motivations and privacy concerns among users likely lead to bias in whom public officials are responsive to (Meng, Pan, and Yang 2017; Reilly 2012).

Authoritarian Deliberation 2.0

China has built an extensive system for Internet surveillance and manipulation. This system includes configuration of Internet gateway infrastructure (Boas 2006), blocking websites and filtering (Chase and Mulvenon 2002), Internet policing (Brady 2008), regulation of Internet service providers (MacKinnon 2009, 2012), suppression of dissident use and discipline of cyber cafes (Chase and Mulvenon 2002; Qiu 2000), and employment of web commentators to shape and alter public debate (Bandurski 2008).

While much is known about what and how content is censored, people's reactions to state control remains more uncertain. In our interviews we discovered that discussants and lurkers differed in terms of how they dealt with concerns about monitoring. People who preferred to observe had strong concerns about privacy, including concerns about posts being monitored by the government. Discussants, however, split into two groups: those who were not concerned about monitoring by the state when posting messages and those who were concerned about privacy but found ways to disguise themselves online by using fake names[1] or VPNs.[2] Interestingly, monitoring by the state was not the primary reason for such actions: discussants often explained that they were much more concerned about what their family, friends, or colleagues might think about them if they found out their interests and opinions expressed in social media.[3] Especially, women stated that politics was traditionally a male domain and they thus avoided openly displaying their interest in politics.[4]

Based on our qualitative interviews in combination with insights from an online survey in China, we propose that people who are more concerned about privacy prefer to lurk, while people who are less concerned about privacy prefer to discuss (privacy hypothesis). Privacy concerns may include concerns about monitoring by the Chinese state but could also include concerns about social desirability among close social networks.

In addition to the broader political environment, the characteristics of the medium itself also determine online deliberation in China. New media allow users to connect, communicate, and interact with each other, often by posting, sharing, or coproducing information (Correa et al. 2010). Because these two functions—social interaction and information sharing—are fundamental to social media, students of social media have found that they play a key role in social media use. We propose that these two motivations can explain why some users prefer to discuss while others prefer to lurk.

Relying on the uses and gratifications model (Katz, Blumler, and Gurevitch 1973), research on social media use has demonstrated that socializing and seeking personal recognition constitute important motivations to use social media. People who socialize aim to strengthen contacts with family, friends, and the world, while people who seek personal recognition aim to strengthen credibility, confidence, stability, and status. Facebook users typically desire to meet new people, sustain offline relationships, and create a sense of community (Ellison, Steinfield, and Lampe 2007; Park, Kee, and Valenzuela 2009). Raacke and Bonds-Raacke in their study of MySpace and Facebook (2008) also found that 96.0 percent of users used social networking sites to keep in touch with old friends, 91.1 percent to maintain existing relationships, and 56.4 percent to find new friends. Seeking personal recognition is another major use by social media users. Park, Kee, and Valenzuela (2009) find that Facebook users use the platform to present themselves as cool or to develop their careers. Tufekci (2008) explains that social media plays an important role in the expression of an online identity as shown in the user's profile. Users perceive an imagined audience that they would like to be recognized by, composed of the social network within the media platform.

While it is not surprising that many users are attracted to social media out of social needs, we propose that users who have greater social needs are also more likely to post political content online. In new media, social interaction and the creation of content are fundamentally linked to each other. Users are paying for the service of social media companies by posting content, which directly translates into commercial income for the company. Social media companies have a great incentive to design the platform in a way that increases social interaction between users, because the content that is produced by social interaction between users generates profit for the company (see, e.g., Stockmann, Esarey, and Zhang 2011). Therefore, it is likely that people who are attracted by the social functions of social media are also likely to create content by posting and commenting. People who use social media to socialize and seek personal recognition are more likely to participate in political discussions by posting political content (social need hypothesis).

In addition to allowing users to connect with others, social media also can be used to strengthen information, knowledge, and understanding. Not surprisingly, information seeking constitutes another important motivation to use social media, according to studies on uses and gratifications of social media. In a study of bloggers, Sweetser and colleagues (Sweetser et al. 2008) discovered that blogs of journalists and public relations practitioners are often used as a source of credible information among Internet users. Similarly, Nov (2007) found that information seeking played a key role in motivating users to contribute to Wikipedia. In our interviews, a typical lurker used social media primarily to obtain news and information about "what happens around them."[5] We propose that people who are highly motivated to seek information are more likely to observe political discussion online by reading political content created by others (information-seeking hypothesis).

These motivations are fundamentally connected to new media technology and may make social media particularly attractive as an alternative information source in authoritarian contexts. The logic built into the design of social media creates a specific context for lurking and discussing that allows people to tap into public discourse in a controlled and information-scarce environment. For example, in China there is a lot of uncertainty about the true extent of many political, economic, and social problems because officials are appointed by the higher level in the administrative hierarchy, and lower levels therefore have incentives to underreport statistics that may point toward local problems. In such an information-scarce environment, people's ability to learn political information and observe political discussion may be of greater importance compared to other contexts. Authoritarian Deliberation

2.0 refers to lurking and discussing behavior driven by privacy concerns resulting from such an authoritarian context, in combination with motivations associated with characteristics of social media.

Data and Methods

This chapter is part of a larger study on the impact of social media on authoritarian rule in China.[6] Qualitative interviews with ninety-two Internet users inform our hypotheses and interpretation of the results. Because data from social media is created by active users, here called discussants, and misses much required data about lurkers, we conducted an online survey to observe differences between lurkers and discussants. The objective of this online survey is *not* to draw representative conclusions about Chinese users; rather, we use the online survey as an expansion of the qualitative interviews we conducted.

The Online Social Media Survey randomly sampled 1,005 Internet users from an online panel of over 2.6 million Chinese Internet users between June 30 and July 11, 2015. A comparison to a recent nationally representative survey conducted by the Research Center of Contemporary China of Peking University (RCCC) as well as the official statistics from the China Internet Network Information Center (CNNIC) for June and July 2015 reveals that our online survey is roughly comparable to these other samples in terms of gender ratio and age group, but oversampled highly educated and relatively wealthier Internet users. (The Online Appendix, available at www.daniestockmann.net, provides more details about the composition of the sample.)

Simple random sampling of an online panel is likely to oversample active Internet users, especially discussants, which will produce biased estimates of lurkers and discussants. To address this issue, we stratify our online random sample based on a national representative survey (Levy and Lemeshow 2013).[7] Based on the population distribution and sampling distribution of lurkers and discussants, we designed the poststratification weights and regress on the poststratified sample. (Please see the Online Appendix for details about the composition of strata and poststratification weights.)

The speedy implementation of the online survey also provides us with the opportunity to learn about people's reactions to specific events that are discussed on social media. Shortly before the online survey was conducted, messages regarding child trafficking circulated on social media, and we took this opportunity to add questions specific to this media event to the questionnaire.

One key concern when conducting research on deliberation and online public opinion, especially in a politically closed context like China, is the question of how to obtain truthful responses to potentially sensitive questions. This is particularly relevant to this study, as we intend to observe differences in patterns of political expression online. To cope with this challenge, we add an experimental component to the online survey: when measuring the main dependent variables, *Reading* and *Commenting*, described in detail below, one group was asked the question in a nonsensitive way, the other in a sensitive way. Differences in responses allow us to draw conclusions about differences in response bias among lurkers and discussants.

In addition, the case study of child trafficking in China provides a nonsensitive context within which we increase the likelihood that people will give honest responses in the survey. Child trafficking is a nonsensitive issue that was, to our knowledge, not censored by the Chinese state before or while the survey was conducted. The Chinese state also did not provide an official position on the issue. As a result, the survey questionnaire does not contain highly sensitive questions, and respondents will be less likely to adjust their responses to an official "politically correct" answer.

To explore differences between discussants and lurkers of political discussion in Chinese social media, we combine qualitative interviews, statistical analysis of an online survey, a case study, and an online experiment. Relying on multiple methods, this design allows us to tap into differences between lurkers and discussants.

Measuring Lurking and Discussing

Our measurements of reading information and commenting on China's cyberspace capture the breadth of social media use. Lurkers and discussants were assessed based on two questions that asked respondents which among various platforms they used (1) to seek information and (2) to post comments. To address potential response bias, respondents were randomly assigned into one of two groups. One group was asked whether they had ever sought information (*Liaojie*) and whether they had ever posted comments (*Fabiao*

Pinglun) on "hot social issues" (*Shishi Yu Shehui Redian*), which is a nonsensitive way to ask about participation in online discussion; the second group was asked exactly the same questions, but using the more sensitive term "political information and big national events" (*Zhengzhi Wenti He Guojia Dashi*). Next, respondents were asked to select all social media platforms they had used. The fourteen choices included instant messengers, BBS chat forums, microblogs, wikis, Q&A sites, video-sharing sites, social networking sites, and blogs: WeChat, QQ, Tianya, Baidu Tieba, Maopu, Sina Weibo, Tencent Weibo, Baidu Baike, Baidu Zhidao, Zhihu, Bilibili, Youku Tudou, Douban, and Sina blog. These social media platforms cover a wide range of platforms that people encounter online. To measure how widely netizens use social media for reading and commenting, we generate the dependent variables *Reading* and *Commenting* by adding the number of social media platforms respondents use to understand or comment on politics, respectively. *Reading* ranges from 0 to 14, *Commenting* from 0 and 13, whereby larger numbers indicate that the respondent uses a wide range of social media platforms. Because *Reading* and *Commenting* are not mutually exclusive behaviors, we also control for them in the empirical analysis; when used as a control variable, they are recoded to run from 0 to 1.

In the case study, the dependent variables are issue-specific to online discussion on child trafficking. In the online survey, we showed respondents a picture frequently circulated during the event (see Figure 7.1) and asked whether they had received similar pictures or messages on social media that promoted the death penalty for child traffickers. Our issue-specific hypothesis test focuses only on those respondents who reported having received such messages, which is 85 percent (855 respondents) of the sample. If people received similar messages, they were asked about their reactions to the messages. *Posting, Forwarding,* and *Reading* are dummy variables indicating whether the respondent reported having posted an original message, forwarded someone else's post including a comment, or read the message, respectively. These issue-specific dependent variables focus on people's behavioral reactions to the online discussion on child trafficking.

Measuring Response Bias

As mentioned above, we added an experiment into the survey in order to assess potential response bias among respondents. *Sensitive Question-Wording* is a dummy variable indicating whether a respondent was assigned to the sensitive question wording. Our dependent variables are self-reported behavioral measures. Self-reported behavioral measures sometimes are distorted by social desirability bias (Holbrook 2008), and thus it is likely that some respondents underreport their behaviors on social media if they are presented with the sensitive question.

Measuring Motivation

People's motivations to use social media—for socializing, seeking recognition, or seeking information—affect their preferences for various behaviors on social media. Indices for motivations were created based on Likert scales and coded 0 to 1, where higher numbers present stronger agreement with individual statements.

"Motivation to seek information" (Cronbach's $\alpha = 0.61$) was based on four items: "I use social media to understand events that are happening," "I want to know others' opinions towards issues that I am interested in," "I want to seek information on sensitive news and issues that might have been censored," and "I want to understand and know more about news that are also reported on mainstream media and their web portals."

"Motivation to socialize" (Cronbach's $\alpha = 0.72$) was based on five items: "I want to feel like I belong to a group / a community through using social media," "I want to maintain relationships that I value through using social media," "I want to meet new friends who share similar interest with me on social media," "I want to know more people on social media," and "I want to express my feeling and opinions and share my experience on social media."

"Motivation to seek recognition" (Cronbach's $\alpha = 0.60$) was based on two items: "I want to gain respect and support on social media" and "I want others to understand me better through using social media."

Measuring Concerns for Privacy

To assess concerns for privacy, we rely on self-reported attitudes and behavior. The attitudinal question asked was "Generally, when you post opinions under your real name on social media, how much do you worry about the following people's reactions or opinions regarding the content you express?" Respondents were asked to place themselves on a 7-point Likert scale regarding the following groups of people: family, friends, colleagues, strangers, criminals, web administrators, and Internet police (*Cha Shuibao De, Ru Wangluo Jingcha*). Censorship in China is largely exercised by web administrators, but in more severe cases Internet police may visit people in their homes. Concern for Censors is an index based on the items web administrators and Internet police (Cronbach's $\alpha = 0.79$). Concern for Close Social Network is an index based on the items family, friends, and colleagues (Cronbach's $\alpha = 0.81$). *Concern for Strangers* is created based on the items strangers and criminals (Cronbach's $\alpha = 0.76$). All indices were recoded to run from 0 to 1, whereby higher numbers represent stronger concern.

In addition to these attitudinal measures, we also ask about behavior that could indicate attempts to disguise one's true identity, such as using a fake account, using a VPN proxy, or not using a real picture as the profile picture on social media. All behavioral measures are dummy variables. *Using Real Profile Picture of Oneself* indicates whether respondents reported to upload real profile pictures to at least some social media accounts. "0" indicates people who report to never use a real picture of themselves (46.7 percent). *Fake User Account* indicates whether the respondents have any fake accounts (*Xiaohao*) on social media (75 percent). VPN use indicates whether respondents use or have used a VPN proxy before (36.6 percent).

Control variables include Educational Degree, Age, and Male, all coded to run from 0 to 1 to facilitate interpretation of the analysis.

Empirical Results

To explore who expresses political views we first estimate the relationship between motivations to use social media and concerns about privacy on the dependent variables *Reading* and *Commenting*.

Table 7.1 represents ordinary least squares regression equations where *Reading* or *Commenting* is regressed upon a dummy variable for each treatment condition, with the control group who had received the nonsensitive question-wording as the excluded category (reference variable). With this specification, we can directly compare the size of the effects of the sensitive

Table 7.1. OLS Regression Results of Baseline Model

Independent Variables	Dependent Variable	
	Reading Coefficient (s.e.)	*Commenting Coefficient (s.e.)*
Random Assignment of Question-Wording:		
Sensitive Question-Wording (Dummy)	−0.061	−0.286***
	(0.123)	(0.105)
Reading (Recoded 0–1)	—	7.077***
		(0.576)
Commenting (Recoded 0–1)	9.299***	—
	(0.569)	
Motivation:		
Motivation to Seek Information	1.893***	−0.067
	(0.464)	(0.386)
Motivation to Socialize	0.040	0.145
	(0.510)	(0.426)
Motivation to Seek Recognition	−0.363	0.931***
	(0.427)	(0.358)
Behavioral Measures of Privacy Concerns:		
Use Real Profile Picture of Oneself (Dummy)	−0.208	0.182*
	(0.130)	(0.109)
Fake User Account (Dummy)	−0.206	0.294**
	(0.158)	(0.118)
VPN Use (Dummy)	0.379**	0.172
	(0.162)	(0.140)
Self-Reported Privacy Concerns:		
Concern for Censors	0.767***	0.119
	(0.290)	(0.209)
Concern for Close Social Network	0.607**	−0.489**
	(0.276)	(0.232)
Concern for Strangers	−0.693***	0.195
	(0.262)	(0.216)
Control Variables:		
Educational Degree	0.208	−0.043
	(0.513)	(0.422)
Age	0.211	−0.872**
	(0.502)	(0.434)
Male (Dummy)	−0.281**	0.339***
	(0.130)	(0.108)

(continued)

Table 7.1. (continued)

	Dependent Variable	
Independent Variables	*Reading Coefficient (s.e.)*	*Commenting Coefficient (s.e.)*
Constant	0.284	0.170
	(0.588)	(0.515)
N	976	976
R-Squared	0.47	0.49

Source: Online Social Media Survey, 2015.
Notes: The coefficient obtained using survey (svy) commands in Stata and the estimates adjusted for the poststratification survey design. *** $p<0.01$; ** $p<0.05$; * $p<0.1$; standard errors, two tailed.

question-wording with the dependent variables. In addition to this first set of variables, we also include measures for motivations and concerns about privacy. The functional form of the baseline models is included in the Online Appendix.[8]

We find that sensitive question-wording has a strong and significant impact on respondents' report on commenting on politics online, but not on reading online. In the left column there is no significant effect of *Sensitive Question-Wording* (-0.061) on reading political information on social media. However, a negative relationship between *Sensitive Question-Wording* and *Commenting* is strongly present in the right column. The negative sign of *Sensitive Question-Wording* (-0.286) indicates that respondents report lower levels of commenting when the question contains the term *political issues*, and this coefficient is highly statistically significant. These results provide us with insights into the willingness of lurkers and discussants to report user behavior related to politics online: those who voice opinions online are more likely to underreport commenting on politics, while those who read are less susceptible to response bias. With those caveats about the measurement of the dependent variable in mind, we now turn to testing of our main hypotheses.

Regarding motivations, we find strong support for systematic differences between lurkers and discussants. In the left column, the strong positive coefficient (1.893) indicates that people who primarily use social media to seek information tend to use, on average, about two more social media platforms for learning about politics; social needs such as socializing or seeking recognition were unrelated to *Reading*. In the right column, we detect a strong positive and statistically significant coefficient for using social media to seek recognition (0.931) on *Commenting*. In other words, people with higher needs to be recognized tend to comment, on average, in about one social media platform more; information-seeking and socializing needs, however, were unrelated to commenting. These relationships demonstrate that lurkers and discussants differ strongly from each other: discussants like to comment because of the need for recognition; lurkers, on the other hand, are more focused on political learning. These results confirm the information-seeking hypothesis and partially the social needs hypothesis.

Finally, we turn to differences among lurkers and discussants in terms of privacy concerns. We start by discussing the relationships between self-reported privacy concerns, listed at the bottom of Table 7.1. We find that lurkers seem to be more concerned about privacy. When regressing self-reported measures on *Reading*, we detect a strong positive relationship between *Concern for Censors* (0.767) and *Concern for Close Social Network* (0.607), indicated in the left column of Table 7.1. As people report caring about censorship as well as what their immediate social network thinks about them, they tend to lurk in about one more social media platform, on average. By contrast, people who report concerns about strangers tend to read less (-0.693). This last relationship could mean that using social media to observe the online discussion requires at least some minimal levels of social trust or tolerance for people outside the immediate social network. For example, one female interviewee stated that she sticks to only the Moments of WeChat for information seeking because "I think the quality of information forwarded on Moments is the best as I can only see information posted by friends who I know and I have never added strangers to my WeChat."[9] Turning to the right column, we detect a strong negative effect of *Concern for Close Social Network* only on *Commenting* (-0.489). This indicates that people who are concerned about social desirability are less likely to comment on politics on social media. Our qualitative interviews also confirm this pattern. For example, an interviewee explains her concern about the reactions from her private social circles on WeChat Moments: "I feel like the more I express [on WeChat Moments], the more mistakes I am going to make; my teachers and leaders from the university are also my contacts on WeChat and I don't want them to judge me through what I post."[10] Interviewees explained that they were much more concerned about reactions from their close networks if they commented on political and social issues that clearly indicated their positions: "Some [political and social] issues inevitably involve taking sides . . . sometimes forwarding or commenting [on such issues] which clearly indicates one's position on WeChat Moments is not a good idea."[11]

When turning to behavioral measures of concerns for privacy, however, we find a somewhat different pattern. In the left column, using a VPN (0.379) is positively related to *Reading*. In other words, users who disguise themselves by using a VPN proxy tend to use social media more for observing the political discussion. However, discussants seem to use other means to disguise themselves online. Discussants are more willing to use real personal profile pictures of themselves on social media, as indicated by a positive coefficient (0.182) in the right column. Given their stronger motivation to express personal identities, this makes a lot of sense. Having at least one fake user account (*Xiaohao*) is also positively related to *Commenting* (0.294).

Overall, there is some evidence that lurkers tend to be more concerned about privacy compared to discussants, as shown by self-reported measures; however, discussants appear to be more likely to create online identities, perhaps in order to voice their political views online. While these results partially confirm our privacy hypothesis, results indicate that discussants may have different means than lurkers for dealing with concerns about censorship. While lurkers may not join the discussion in the first place, in part due to concerns about privacy, discussants may decide to voice their opinions but use a virtual identity to disguise themselves. With greater needs for recognition, discussants may find ways to express themselves online without identifying themselves.

The remainder of the chapter revisits these main results based on an issue-specific case study of online discussion.

Case Study: Death Penalty for Child Trafficking?

Social media discussion about child trafficking is a typical example of how Internet users experience the power of social media on a day-to-day basis: when official data and factual information are scarce, people rely on social media to learn facts and discuss how the issue should be handled. Social media is frequently used as a venue to raise public awareness about issues of public interest, on the one hand, and to place pressure on the government to take action, on the other hand. In this case, social activists celebrated a small victory in the revision of the criminal law to punish more severely the traffickers and buyers of kidnapped children.

Background

Child trafficking is a serious social problem in China. Unfortunately, simple facts about the extent of the problem are not available to the Chinese public. Recognizing the seriousness of the issue, in December 2007 the State Council issued the first national-level five-year plan, starting in 2008, aimed at combating trafficking of women and children (General Office of the State Council 2007).[12] In May 2009 the Ministry of Public Security set up an information database for missing children, the most important part of which is the DNA database containing the DNA of found missing children and parents who have reported their children missing (Anonymous 2015a). With the aid of the database, 3,745 missing children had been found and returned to their parents as of June 2015 (M. Li and Zhang 2015). Although state units release facts that show the state in a positive light, facts about how many children are reported missing remain unknown to the public.

Social activists believe that a market for child trafficking is created by migrant workers leaving their children behind in the countryside without much supervision, while a demand for children is present in mainly remote rural areas where childless people want children in order to carry on the family name and take care of them in their old age. Social activists believe that this demand for children can be reduced by more severely punishing the buyers. For example, Wei Xiong, a public intellectual and director of a civil rights institute, has spent thirteen years proposing stricter punishment of buyers of kidnapped children, submitting proposals to the National People's Congress, and lobbying national people's representatives. According to the current criminal law, if buyers of the kidnapped children cooperate with investigators and don't obstruct efforts to rescue the children, they can be exempted from punishment (National People's Congress 2011). Some activists in China have been pushing for changes in this law by submitting proposals.

In 2015, messages about child trafficking gained momentum on Weibo and also WeChat.[13] At the time, a proposal to more severely punish all criminals involved in child trafficking, including the buyers, was under consideration by the Standing Committee of the National People's Congress, China's national law-making institution. The original source of the social media messages is unknown, but perhaps social activists were inspired by the documentary *Missing Children*, broadcast on CCTV on June 15 (Li 2015). The next day, cases covered on CCTV were discussed on WeChat (S. Li and Zhang 2015); on June 17 a picture of a crying child asking for the death penalty for child traffickers went viral on WeChat and Weibo (see Figure 7.1). The text

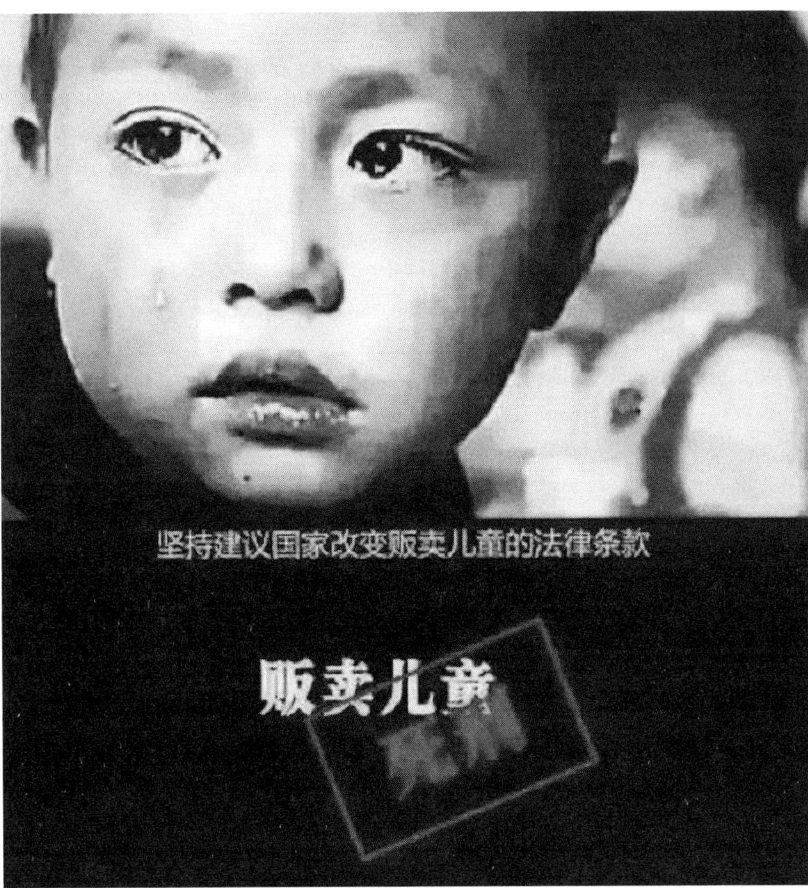

Figure 7.1. Picture supporting the death penalty for child traffickers, on WeChat
Source: http://news.sina.com.cn/c/zg/jpm/2015-06-18/20181158.html

on the picture asks users to support the death penalty for child traffickers and to forward the message rather than just "liking" it.

By June 18, 800,000 WeChat users had expressed support for the death penalty campaign by forwarding the message (Li 2015). In the meantime, some celebrities and opinion leaders expressed their support by posting and forwarding related posts and pictures on Weibo. On June 18, the death penalty campaign appeared as one of the top ten hot topics on Sina Weibo. According to Sina Weibo, 81 percent of 70,000 participants supported the death penalty for child traffickers (Anonymous 2015b).

On the same day, official accounts on Weibo and traditional media started to voice opinions regarding child trafficking. The producer of the CCTV documentary *Missing Children* published an article on XinhuaNet arguing that the issue should be tackled with a more moderate, rational solution rather than radical demands for the death penalty. This article was cited and forwarded in 197 news reports published on many mainstream media's online portals (Li 2015). *People's Daily* and CCTV news also posted comments on their official WeChat and Weibo accounts arguing that the death penalty was not a viable solution to the problem.[14] When official media became involved, discussion shifted in a moderate direction, focusing on which legal regulations would provide better solutions than the death penalty. Soon, the intense public interest started to decline.

Child trafficking falls between the boundaries of what is considered political and social in China. It certainly is not a sensitive issue, where Chinese would be hesitant to disclose political involvement. To our knowledge, the Chinese propaganda apparatus did not censor social media discussion, nor were there any restrictions imposed on traditional media. In part, this was the case because child trafficking was not a top priority to central or local officials and also because an official position was not publicized. Instead, party and state units left the issue to the regulation of courts and law-making institutions. On June 19, an official from the Supreme People's Court responded to the online campaign by stating that "the Supreme Court always sticks to the same fundamental position on the child trafficking crime—that is, all criminals involved in child trafficking shall be severely punished in accordance with law" (Ma 2015). In addition, he also released the information that the latest draft of the criminal law contained a revised article whereby buyers of kidnapped children would no longer be exempt from punishment, even when collaborating with the authorities.[15] On June 24, social activist Wei

Xiong posted on his Weibo that the proposal he and his colleagues submitted had been added to the draft criminal law.[16] Overall, online discussion played out to the satisfaction of social activists who demanded more severe punishments for buyers of children.

Empirical Results

Since our online survey was conducted shortly after this incident, we now return to our prior investigation, but this time with issue-specific questions. We limit the analysis to only those respondents in the sample who reported having received pictures or messages similar to the one in Figure 7.1 above. In the Online Social Media Survey 2015, 855 of 1,005 respondents had learned about the issue of child trafficking by receiving messages on social media; among those, about 65 percent used Sina Weibo and 89 percent used WeChat.

To further probe the relationships between motivations, concerns about privacy, and user behavior, we repeated the baseline model, this time with *Posting, Forwarding,* and *Reading* as dependent variables (see Table 7.2). Measurement of the independent and control variables are the same as before.

Regarding motivations, the issue-specific analysis replicates some but not all of our earlier results. Most importantly, there is a clear difference between lurkers and discussants regarding the death penalty against child trafficking. The coefficient for information seeking is positive and statistically significant for reading (1.057) in the left column, while seeking recognition is strongly positively related to forwarding with a comment (1.01) in the right column. We do not detect any statistically significant effect of motivations to use social media on posting an original message with regards to the issue. These results confirm the information-seeking hypothesis but only partially confirm the social need hypothesis: people forward messages out of a need for social recognition by others, but at least on the issue of child trafficking, we cannot detect the same relationship for initiating an original post.

Regarding concerns for privacy, the issue-specific analysis partially supports the privacy hypothesis. As before, people who use real pictures of themselves on at least some social media platforms are more likely to post and

Table 7.2. Estimating User Behavior Regarding Death Penalty for Child Trafficking Among Users Who Received Messages on the Issue

	Dependent Variables		
Independent Variables	*"I Read the Message or Picture" Coefficient (s.e.)*	*"I Posted an Original Message with Related Content" Coefficient (s.e.)*	*"I Forwarded the Picture or Message with a Comment" Coefficient (s.e.)*
Social Media Use:			
"I Read the Message or Picture" (Dummy)	—	−0.366** (0.179)	−0.562*** (0.146)
"I Posted a Message with Related Content" (Dummy)	0.382* (0.216)	—	0.455** (0.229)
"I Forwarded the Picture or Message with a Comment" (Dummy)	−0.533*** (0.147)	0.414** (0.183)	—
Motivation:			
Motivation to Seek Information	1.057** (0.530)	0.145 (0.727)	0.620 (0.524)
Motivation to Socialize	0.536 (0.587)	0.302 (0.774)	0.589 (0.581)
Motivation to Seek Recognition	−0.541 (0.451)	−0.015 (0.658)	1.010** (0.472)
Behavioral Measures of Privacy Concerns:			
Use of Real Profile Picture of Oneself (Dummy)	−0.071 (0.135)	0.360** (0.177)	0.396*** (0.135)
Fake User Account (Dummy)	0.064 (0.152)	−0.007 (0.198)	0.102 (0.153)
VPN Use (Dummy)	−0.047 (0.147)	0.437** (0.189)	0.084 (0.151)
Self-Reported Privacy Concerns:			
Concern for Censors	0.218 (0.286)	−0.290 (0.350)	0.309 (0.290)
Concern for Close Network	−0.138 (0.334)	0.794* (0.434)	0.022 (0.371)
Concern for Strangers	−0.338 (0.249)	0.165 (0.370)	−0.075 (0.258)

(continued)

Table 7.2. (continued)

	Dependent Variables		
Independent Variables	*"I Read the Message or Picture"* *Coefficient (s.e.)*	*"I Posted an Original Message with Related Content"* *Coefficient (s.e.)*	*"I Forwarded the Picture or Message with a Comment"* *Coefficient (s.e.)*
Educational Degree	0.006	0.105	1.205**
	(0.577)	(0.763)	(0.587)
Age	1.256**	−0.979	0.472
	(0.601)	(0.798)	(0.608)
Male (Dummy)	−0.273**	0.361**	−0.136
	(0.136)	(0.171)	(0.136)
Constant	−0.393	−2.174**	−3.275***
	(0.672)	(0.892)	(0.712)
N	830	830	830

Source: Online Social Media Survey, 2015.
Notes: The coefficient obtained using survey (svy) commands in Stata and the estimates adjusted for the poststratification survey design. *** $p<0.01$; ** $p<0.05$; * $p<0.1$; standard errors, two tailed.

comment in the discussion about the death penalty for child traffickers. In the middle and right columns, coefficients for using a real picture are positively correlated with posting (0.360) and forwarding (0.396), respectively. Those who disguise themselves by using a VPN proxy are more likely to post an original message on this issue (0.437). In stark contrast to our earlier findings, users who indicate being concerned about social desirability within their close networks are more likely to post original messages (0.794). This may be related to the issue. Concern about social desirability may on the one hand discourage users from joining an online discussion that is likely to be seen in a negative light in their close network, or it may on the other hand encourage users to participate in online discussion on a topic deemed desirable by their close network. Death penalty for child trafficking is an issue on which voicing opinion reveals potentially desirable altruistic values such as caring about children. For example, interviewees revealed that they joined discussions about death penalty against child trafficking on social media because they thought the issue was very important to their close network and because voicing opinions would make their close network aware of the seriousness or importance of the problem.[17] Given that the issue is a nonsensitive social issue in China, we do not detect any relationship between privacy concerns and people's preference to lurk. These results confirm that discussants tend to disguise themselves online, but also demonstrate that the effect of privacy concerns on people's preference to lurk depends on the issue that is discussed. As an issue becomes political, people who have higher privacy concerns are more likely to lurk, as shown in our earlier results, while on a less political issue, privacy concerns have no effect on people's tendency to lurk.

Finally, results suggest that voicing opinions on social media does not necessarily entail high levels of information. In our qualitative interviews we discovered that those who were less informed about the child trafficking issue and the law-making process in China forwarded or posted messages related to the issue on social media.[18] This pattern can also be observed in the statistical results, where there is a negative relationship between reporting to have read the message and posting and forwarding. When reading opinions posted online, it may be helpful to keep in mind that a large number of well-informed opinions held by lurkers are not expressed in the discussion.

Implications for Political Engagement

A large number of users only observe online political discourse in China. These lurkers are more concerned about privacy, not necessarily out of concern about censorship but out of concern about how their close social networks may perceive them. At the same time, lurkers follow online discourse closely as they use social media to learn about politics. Therefore, this group of people tends to be composed of people who are already engaged in politics. As they seek to satisfy cognitive needs by acquiring political knowledge online, lurkers fall into what Converse (1964) has termed "issue publics": people who are highly aware of politics and therefore tend to have more stable and logically constrained political attitudes. In U.S. politics this group of politically sophisticated citizens is often described as those persons capable of the rational, informed political decision making that is expected of citizens in liberal democracies.

The discussants, on the other hand, voice their views—not because of the information they gather from the discussion, but because of their need for recognition. People who join online political discourse enjoy being recognized online in virtual environments. There is evidence that they may not always present their views honestly, as they are more sensitive to response bias, but they are also less concerned about privacy and therefore likely to express opinions. If they have privacy concerns, discussants seem to find ways to hide in cyberspace other than lurking—for example, by using fake accounts online.

Obviously, these different profiles are not as clear-cut as we have described them here. There is a large overlap between lurkers and discussants, and people may shift between categories depending on the issue that is debated, as the case of online discussion regarding child trafficking shows. However, differences in motivations and concerns about privacy lead to tendencies among users to either join in or observe the debate.

More broadly, these findings have several important implications. First, consistent with previous studies, we find that social media contributes to political engagement; social media allows people who were otherwise likely to be excluded from public discourse to voice their opinions. We find that people who voice political views online are not primarily interested in acquiring information. Social media facilitates political discourse among people who are politically less engaged, thus fostering political engagement. This supports the view that social media contributes to political engagement by "activating" otherwise politically less engaged citizens (see, e.g., Qiu 2009).

At the same time, our findings also suggest caution about the conclusions that can be drawn from online discourse about the nature of public opinion. Social media is often used to "take the pulse" of a society. Even in societies with a lower digital divide than China, such as the United States, research has shown that social media leads to biased estimates (see, e.g., Gayo-Avello 2011; O'Connor et al. 2010), but in societies where less is known about public opinion, especially authoritarian regimes, social media is often taken as a means to tap into citizen beliefs. In China, for example, Chinese officials and journalists often use the Internet as a means to learn about citizen preferences (see, e.g., Meng, Pan, and Yang 2017; Reilly 2012; Stockmann 2013). While it is well-known that online public opinion is biased toward urban areas located in more highly developed provinces, this chapter suggests that even among the urban middle class, the most politically sophisticated remain silent. While the most politically aware are highly observant of political discourse, their sensitivity to privacy concerns suggests that they prefer personal conversations about the issues raised by social media, within their social networks rather than in online discussions. The case of online discussion regarding child trafficking suggests that lurkers motivated to learn about politics tend to abstain from online discussion, which may lead to overrepresentation of politically less informed views. As a result, social media in China is unlikely to reflect public opinion on the issues it raises. Presumably, the overrepresentation of politically less sophisticated opinions may become more pronounced as the state intervenes more directly in online discussion by actively censoring content.

One important characteristic of the political context within which online deliberation takes place in China is the lack of information about governance. This may result in greater need among citizens to use social media as an alternative source of information, and observing online discussion may have a stronger impact on people's views living in an otherwise information-scarce political environment. The case of child trafficking we included here is a typical case where citizens are unsure about the true extent of such criminal activities, due to lack of official data, but through social media, people aimed to raise public awareness about the issue, placing pressure on the government to respond.

While concerns about censorship undoubtedly also affect user behavior in China, our findings suggest that perhaps users are less concerned about political censorship and reactions by the regime compared to the reactions within their immediate social circles. When people express themselves online, they may be more concerned about normative expectations about "correct" political views within society than about potential repercussions by the Chinese state. Attempts to conform to social norms may be a more powerful mechanism leading to self-censorship among Chinese Internet users than is commonly believed. More comparative research examining the reactions to issues varying in political sensitivity, over time, and across political systems may further illuminate the specifics of who joins and who remains silent in online political discourse.

Notes

The research leading to the results on new media has received funding from the European Research Council under the European Union's Seventh Framework Programme (FP/2007–2013) / ERC Grant Agreement n. [338478]. The Hertie School of Governance and Leiden University are both beneficiaries of the grant. For more information on this project, entitled "Authoritarianism 2.0: The Internet, Political Discussion, and Authoritarian Rule in China," See www.authoritarianism.net.

1. Interview with a female student (63196), December 2014.

2. Interview with a male student (78165), February 2015.

3. Interview with a female interviewee (44937), March 2015; interview with a male student (78165), February 2015; interview with a female student (63196), December 2014.

4. Interview with a female student (63196), December 2014; interview with a female interviewee (85641), January 2016.

5. Interview with a male interviewee (89142), January 2016.

6. This research received funding from the European Research Council under the European Union's Seventh Framework Programme (FP/2007–2013) / ERC Grant Agreement n. [338478]. The Hertie School of Governance and Leiden University are both beneficiaries of the grant. For more information on this project, titled "Authoritarianism 2.0: The Internet, Political Discussion, and Authoritarian Rule in China," see www.authoritarianism.net.

7. The RCCC media survey was conducted in 2014 based on GPS random sampling. In this nationally representative survey and the online survey, we divided respondents into four strata with two degrees of frequency on lurking and discussing. For details, see Online Appendix.

8. Adding an interaction term between *Reading* and *Sensitive Wording* does not change the results; the coefficient for the interaction term was substantively and statistically insignificant and therefore excluded. Results are available on request.

9. Interview with a female interviewee (70417), March 2015.

10. Interview with 89607, December 2015.

11. Interview with 80238, December 2015.

12. For more information, see http://www.mps.gov.cn/n16/n983040/n1294479/, accessed August 23, 2015.

13. The present case is not the only social media event about child trafficking. To raise public awareness of child trafficking, Jianrong Yu, a professor at the Chinese Academy of Social Sciences, initiated a campaign in 2011. See http://baike.baidu.com/view/5184899.htm, accessed August 23, 2015. In addition, the Ministry of Public Security supported the use of Weibo and public efforts in finding the missing children; the head of its Combating Human Trafficking Office opened up a "Big V" account and asked netizens to forward photos and information about missing children (Anonymous 2013).

14. One version of a death penalty campaign picture displayed a link to a dating website, criticizing the fact that forwarding and clicking the picture promoted the dating website (Dong 2015). The dating website issued a formal apology to the public.

15. The revised article stipulated, "Those buying abducted women or children but not abusing bought children and not obstructing efforts to rescue them, may be given a light or mitigated punishment; those not obstructing bought women from returning to their original residence in accordance with their wishes, may be given a light or mitigated punishment, or be exempted from punishment." See Guo Jinchao and Ma Haiyan, *China News*, June 24, 2015, http://www.chinanews.com/gn/2015/06-24/7363467.shtml.

16. See Xiong Wei's personal Weibo: http://www.weibo.com/p/1005051927148274/home?from=page_100505&mod=TAB#place, accessed August 23, 2015.

17. Interview with 87744, November 2015; interview with 82916, January 2016.

18. Interview with a male student (89072), November 2015; interview with a female interviewee (89547), December 2015.

References

Anonymous. 2013. "Gonganbu Daguaiban Zhuren Chenshiqu Weibo Daguai Zhaohui Shangwan Beiguai Fuer" (Combating human trafficking office head Chen Shiqu uses Weibo to tackle the crime and rescue about ten thousands missing women and children). *News China*, May 18. http://news.china.com.cn/txt/2013-05/18/content_28862357.htm.

Anonymous. 2015a. "Daguai DNA Shujuku" (Combatting human trafficking DNA database). Baidu baike. http://baike.baidu.com/view/5214323.htm.

Anonymous. 2015b. "'Fanmai Ertong Yilv Sixing,' Xiangdang Bukaopu" ("Death penalty for child traffickers," Not sensible). *Xinhua Daily*, June 19. http://xh.xhby.net/mp2/html/2015-06/19/content_1267954.htm.

Balla, S. J. 2012. "Information Technology, Political Participation, and the Evolution of Chinese Policymaking." *Journal of Contemporary China* 21 (76): 655–73.

Bandurski, D. 2008. "China's Guerrilla War for the Web." *Far Eastern Economic Review* 171 (6): 41–44.

Boas, T. C. 2006. "Weaving the Authoritarian Web: The Control of Internet Use in Nondemocratic Regimes." In *How Revolutionary Was the Digital Revolution? National Responses, Market Transitions, and Global Technology*, edited by John Zysman and Abraham Newman, 361–78. Stanford, Calif.: Stanford Business Books.

Brady, A.-M. 2008. *Marketing Dictatorship: Propaganda and Thought Work in Contemporary China*. Lanham, Md.: Rowman & Littlefield.

Chan, M., X. Wu, Y. Hao, R. Xi, and T. Jin., T. 2012. "Microblogging, Online Expression, and Political Efficacy among Young Chinese Citizens: The Moderating Role of Information and Entertainment Needs in the Use of Weibo." *Cyberpsychology, Behavior, and Social Networking* 15 (7): 345–49.

Chase, M., and J. Mulvenon. 2002. *You've got Dissent! Chinese Dissident Use of the Internet and Beijing's Counter-Strategies*. Santa Monica, Calif.: Rand.

Converse, P. E. 1964. "The Nature of Belief in Mass Publics." In *Ideology and Discontent*, edited by D. Apter, 206–61. New York: Free Press.

Correa, T., A. W. Hinsley, and H. G. de Zúñiga. 2010. "Who Interacts on the Web? The Intersection of Users' Personality and Social Media Use." *Computers And Human Behavior* 26 (2): 247–53. doi:10.1016/j.chb.2009.09.003.

Davis, R. 2009. *Typing Politics: The Role of Blogs in American Politics*. New York: Oxford University Press.

Dong, J. 2015. "Pengyouquan Turan Bei 'Fanmai Funv Ertong Yilv Pan Sixing' Shuaping Jiujing Zahuishi?" (Why was the death penalty campaign for woman and child trafficking suddenly spread on Moments?). Guanchazhe, June 18. http://www.guancha.cn/FaZhi/2015_06_18_323776.shtml.

Ellison, N. B., C. Steinfield, and C. Lampe, C. 2007. "The Benefits of Facebook 'Friends': Social Capital and College Students' Use of Online Social Network Sites." *Journal of Computer-Mediated Communication* 12 (4): 1143–68. doi:10.1111/j.1083-6101.2007.00367.x.

Gayo-Avello, D. 2011. "Don't Turn Social Media into Another 'Literary Digest' Poll." *Communications of the ACM* 54 (10): 121–28. doi:10.1145/2001269.2001297.

General Office of the State Council. 2007. *Guowuyuan Bangongting Guanyu YInfa Zhongguo Fandui Guaimai Funv Ertong Xingdong Jihua (2008–2012 Nian) De Tongzhi* (Issue of China's action plan 2008–2012 combating trafficking in women and children by the General Office of the State Council). Beijing: Author. http://www.gov.cn/zwgk/2007-12/20/content_839479.htm.

Habermas, J. (1962) 1990. *Strukturwandel der Oeffentlichkeit: Untersuchungen zu einer Kategorie der buergerlichen Gesellschaft*. Frankfurt am Main: Suhrkamp.

He, B., and M. E. Warren. 2011. "Authoritarian Deliberation: The Deliberative Turn in Chinese Political Development." *Perspectives on Politics* 9 (2): 269–89.

Holbrook, A. 2008. "Self-Reported Measure." In *Encyclopedia of Survey Research Methods*, edited by P. J. Lavrakas, 805–7. Thousand Oaks, Calif.: Sage.

Jiang, M. 2010. "Authoritarian Deliberation on Chinese Internet." *Electronic Journal of Communication* 20 (3–4).

Katz, E., J. G. Blumler, and M. Gurevitch. 1973. "Uses and Gratifications Research." *Public Opinion Quarterly* 37 (4): 509–23. doi:10.1086/268109.

Levy, P. S., and S. Lemeshow. 2013. *Sampling of Populations: Methods and Applications*. Hoboken, N.J.: Wiley.

Li, B. 2015. "'Manpingsha'! 'Fanmai Ertong Pan Sixing' Yuqing Fenxi" (An analysis of the public attention cycle of the death penalty campaign for child traffickers). Geren Tushuguan, June 18. http://www.360doc.com/content/15/0618/22/7872436_479088182.shtml.

Li, M., and L. Zhang. 2015. "Daguai Liqi DNA Shujuku 3745 Ming Beiguai Ertong Zhaodaole Huijialu" (The DNA database is a strong weapon, 3745 missing children were rescued and found their parents). *Yangchen Evening*, June 1. http://www.gd.xinhuanet.com/newscenter/2015-06/01/c_1115465564.htm.

Li, S., and Y. Zhang. 2015. "'Guaimai Ertong Pan Sixing' Shuabao Pengyouquan, Huanlian Wangzhan Dache Zuo Yingxiao Zaoqianze" (The death penalty campaign widely spread on Moments, dating website criticized for using the opportunity for advertisement). *Xiandai Kuaibao*, June 19. http://news.sohu.com/20150619/n415299549.shtml.

Ma, X. 2015. "Zuigaofa Huiying 'Fanmai Ertong Yingpan Sixing': Shizhong Jianchi Yifa Yancheng" (Response from the Supreme People's Court to "death penalty to child traffickers": child trafficking crime should be severely punished in accordance with law). *China News*, June 19. http://www.chinanews.com/sh/2015/06-19/7356103.shtml.

MacKinnon, R. 2009. "China's Censorship 2.0: How Companies Censor Bloggers." *First Monday* 14 (2). doi:10.5210/fm.v14i2.2378.

———. 2012. *Consent of the Networked: The Worldwide Struggle for Internet Freedom.* New York: Basic Books.

Meng, T., J. Pan, and P. Yang. 2017. "Conditional Receptivity to Citizen Participation: Evidence from a Survey Experiment in China." *Comparative Political Studies* 50 (4): 399–433.

Nov, O. 2007. "What Motivates Wikipedians?" *Communications of the ACM* 50 (11): 60–64. doi:10.1145/1297797.1297798.

O'Connor, B., R. Balasubramanyan, B. R. Routledge, and N. A. Smith. 2010. "From Tweets to Polls: Linking Text Sentiment to Public Opinion Time Series." *Proceedings of the Fourth International AAAI Conference on Weblogs and Social Media.* https://www.aaai.org/ocs/index.php/ICWSM/ICWSM10/paper/viewFile/1536/1842.

Park, N., K. F. Kee, and S. Valenzuela, S. 2009. "Being Immersed in Social Networking Environment: Facebook Groups, Uses and Gratifications, and Social Outcomes." *CyberPsychology and Behavior* 12 (6): 729–33. doi:10.1089/cpb.2009.0003.

Poor, N. 2005. "Mechanisms of an Online Public Sphere: The Website Slashdot." *Journal of Computer-Mediated Communication* 10 (2). http://jcmc.indiana.edu/vol10/issue2/poor.html.

Qiu, J. L. 2000. "Virtual Censorship in China: Keeping the Gate Between the Cyberspaces." *International Journal of Communications Law and Policy* 4: 1–25.

———. 2009. *Working-Class Network Society: Communication Technology and the Information Have-Less in Urban China.* Cambridge, Mass.: MIT Press.

Raacke, J., and J. Bonds-Raacke. 2008. "MySpace and Facebook: Applying the Uses and Gratifications Theory to Exploring Friend-Networking Sites." *CyberPsychology and Behavior* 11 (2): 169–74. doi:10.1089/cpb.2007.0056.

Reilly, J. 2012. *Strong Society, Smart State: The Rise of Public Opinion in China's Japan Policy.* New York: Columbia University Press.

Stockmann, D. 2013. *Media Commercialization and Authoritarian Rule in China.* New York: Cambridge University Press.

Stockmann, D., A. Esarey, and J. Zhang. 2011. "Advertising Chinese Politics: How Public Service Advertising Prime and Alter Political Trust in China." Paper presented at the Annual Meeting of the American Political Science Association, Seattle, September.

Sunstein, C. 2007. *Republic.com 2.0.* Princeton, N.J.: Princeton University Press.

Sweetser, K. D., L. V. Porter, D. S. Chung, and E. Kim. 2008. "Credibility and the Use of Blogs Among Professionals in the Communication Industry." *Journalism and Mass Communication Quarterly* 85 (1): 169–85. doi:10.1177/107769900808500111.

Tufekci, Z. 2008. "Grooming, Gossip, Facebook and Myspace." *Information, Communication and Society* 11 (4): 544–64. doi:10.1080/13691180801999050.

Zhang, L., and I. Pentina. 2012. "Motivations and Usage Patterns of Weibo." *Cyberpsychology, Behavior, and Social Networking* 15 (6): 312–17.

CHAPTER 8

How the Market for Social Media Shapes Strategies of Internet Censorship

Jennifer Pan

Introduction

Authoritarian regimes have gone to great lengths to impose control over traditional media—newspapers, television, radio—through government ownership of media outlets as well as methods ranging from bribes to intimidation (Djankov et al. 2001; Egorov, Guriev, and Sonin 2009; Enikolopov, Petrova, and Zhuravskaya 2010; Lipman 2005; McMillan and Zoido 2004; Zuckerman et al. 2010). These efforts to control traditional media have been largely successful, even in a context of increased media commercialization (Stockmann 2013; Zhao 1998). However, there is ongoing debate over the ability of authoritarian regimes to control the creation and dissemination of information on the Internet and social media platforms. One side of the debate argues that new media—in particular, social media—disrupt the ability of authoritarian regimes to censor, and ultimately, to maintain political power, because every individual can act as a broadcaster, and the generation of information becomes too diffuse to control (Ferdinand 2000; Earl and Kimport 2011; Howard et al. 2011; Lotan et al. 2011). Indeed, the difficulty of controlling social media has led to speculation about how social media can improve coordination in collective action against authoritarian regimes and increase the reliability of information, especially information that is not accommodating toward the regime (Edmond 2013).[1] The other side of the debate casts doubt over this outlook by arguing that most authoritarian regimes where Internet penetration has increased use technology and more traditional forms of repression, such as arrests, to counter the dangers posed by social media (Kalathil and Boas 2010; Pariser 2011; MacKinnon 2012; Morozov 2012).

In this debate, the Chinese regime is often described as successful in controlling the dangers posed by the Internet (Kalathil and Boas 2010; MacKinnon 2012).[2] However, we know little about whether the Chinese regime's success in censorship is an outlier or foreshadows what other authoritarian regimes will also achieve. Research has not focused on whether the Chinese government's censorship activities can be replicated in other authoritarian regimes, or even in democratic regimes wanting to impose control over online content. This chapter moves a step forward in filling this gap by focusing on whether technical strategies of censoring social media employed by China are likely to be replicated by other countries.

Using a variety of quantitative and qualitative analyses, this chapter shows that China's success in social media censorship is inexorably tied to the dominance of domestic companies such as Tencent, Sina, and Alibaba in China's market for social media. This market dynamic allows the Chinese government to engage in censorship through content removal that quickly and reliably eliminates content deemed to be inappropriate, which in turn decreases the coordination potential of social media and covertly diminishes the reliability of information. In contrast, for most other countries, the market for social media content is dominated by multinational firms (e.g., Facebook, YouTube, Twitter), which prevents these regimes from engaging effectively in censorship through content removal. Instead, these regimes rely on content blocking, which, though powerful, is less effective than content removal in reducing the potential of social media for coordination and in diminishing the reliability of information. With content blocking, content can still be accessed using circumvention technology.

This chapter also examines the development of China's social media market and shows that government protectionism in the form of long-term content blocking of U.S. social media sites is not sufficient to explain the success or failure of domestic social media firms. For most countries that engage in long-term content blocking, U.S. social media firms are still dominant. In the Chinese case, where long-term blocking of U.S. social media coincides with the dominance of domestic social media firms, the success of Chinese firms against U.S. competitors often predated the imposition of content blocking.

The chapter proceeds in four main sections. The first section contrasts China's market for social media with those of other regimes by using data on website traffic. The second section demonstrates the difficulty for both autocratic and democratic regimes to engage in content removal on these U.S. social media platforms. The subsequent section examines the relationship between long-term content blocking (de facto protectionism) and the rise of several Chinese Internet companies. The final section concludes by discussing the implications of the results.

Dominance of Domestic Social Media in China

To compare China's market for social media to those of other regimes, I use website traffic data from Alexa, a company that gathers information on visitors to more than thirty million websites. Using data from ninety-six countries, the social media landscape of each country is assessed through the number of social media firms among the twenty-five most trafficked sites for each country and the ownership of each social media firm. (For details on how traffic rankings were determined and discussion of the data, see Pan 2017.) Of the countries in the data set, twenty-five are authoritarian regimes and seventy-one are democratic.[3]

Among the ninety-six countries, the twenty-five top trafficked sites yielded 1,146 unique domain names, which represent 948 unique domains if the top-level domain or second-level domain is removed. For example, google .co.cr and google.co.kr are two unique domain names found among the 1,112, but once the second-level domains (co.cr and co.kr) are removed, they represent the same domain: Google. Each of the 948 unique domains was visited to determine whether it is a social media site. Social media sites are defined as platforms where anyone can produce and share content, including text, images, and videos. Example sites include social networking sites, blogs, microblogs, forums, bulletin boards, group messaging platforms, and Q&A sites. As shown in Table 8.1, among the 1,146 unique domain names, 76 are social media sites, and among the 948 unique domains, 66 (7 percent) are social media sites.

Each of the seventy-six unique social media domain names was analyzed to determine the origin of the firm with ownership over the site by examining the registrar of the site and the country of origin for the registrar (for additional details, see Pan 2017). This analysis generates a list of top social

Table 8.1. Most Trafficked Sites by Category

Type	*Unique domain names*	*Unique domains*	*Proportion of unique domains*
News	459	443	46.7%
E-commerce	194	138	14.6%
Search	108	12	1.3%
Company	87	81	8.5%
Social media	76	66	7.0%
Entertainment	55	55	5.8%
Portal	54	51	5.4%
Information	38	33	3.5%
Other	28	24	2.5%
Ads	25	24	2.5%
Unknown	22	21	2.2%
Total	1,146	948	

media sites by country, as well as the ownership country of each social media site. The seventy-six unique social media domain names appear 559 times among the top twenty-five most trafficked sites for the ninety-six countries in the data set. Ten social media sites (Facebook.com, YouTube.com, Twitter.com, Blogspot.com, LinkedIn.com, Instagram.com, Wordpress.com, Vk.com, Ok.ru, and Reddit.com) represent 477 (85 percent) of these 559 social media appearances.

If a top social media site is owned by a company from that country, then the social media site is considered to be domestic. For example, Reddit.com is the top social media site in the United States and it also has U.S. ownership, so we say for the United States that Reddit.com is a domestic social media firm. However, Reddit.com is also among the top social media sites in Sweden, and for Sweden, Reddit.com is considered a foreign social media site. Among the seventy-six unique social media domain names, Table 8.2 shows that twenty-four (31 percent) are owned by U.S. companies, six by Iranian companies (8 percent), five (7 percent) by Russian companies, five (6 percent) by Japanese firms, and four (5 percent) by Chinese firms.

The left panel of Figure 8.1 shows, for each country, the proportion of social media sites that are owned by domestic firms. Black denotes authoritarian regimes, while light gray denotes democratic regimes. This figure shows that the United States and China are distinct from all the other countries in that all of their top social media firms are domestic. Excluding China and

Table 8.2. Social Media Site Ownership

Country of ownership	*Number of social media sites in country*	*Total appearances among top sites*
United States	24	483
Russia	5	27
Iran	6	6
Japan	5	5
China	4	5
Georgia	2	2
Hungary	2	2
Poland	2	2
South Korea	2	2
Turkey	2	2

Note: The following 22 countries each have one social media firm, and all of these firms only appear one time among the top social media sites: Australia, Bulgaria, Canada, Croatia, France, Germany, Indonesia, Ireland, Italy, Kazakhstan, Korea, Kyrgyzstan, Latvia, Malaysia, Netherlands, Nigeria, Oman, Romania, Saudi Arabia, Sri Lanka, Thailand, Vietnam.

the United States, on average, only 7 percent of social media firms are domestic across countries. The key distinction between the United States and China is that while U.S. social media firms are dominant across many countries, Chinese social media firms are popular primarily in China. The only Chinese social media site that appears among the top twenty-five most trafficked sites for another country is qq.com, found within the top twenty-five most trafficked sites in South Korea. However, because Internet users in China represent over 20 percent of the world's share of Internet users (over six hundred million as of July 2014),[4] the top social media sites confined to the Chinese market still emerge as major global players in terms of the size of their user base.

The right panel of Figure 8.1 shows the proportion of social media platforms among the twenty-five most trafficked sites that are owned by U.S. firms. Here, China and Iran differ from all other countries in that none of their top social media firms are U.S.-owned. Among authoritarian regimes other than China and Iran, 83 percent of social media firms are American. For many authoritarian regimes, including Venezuela, Singapore, Yemen, and Kuwait, all social media sites in the country are owned by U.S. firms.

Figure 8.1 shows the country that most resembles China in its market for social media is Iran. In Iran, 75 percent of social media sites are owned by

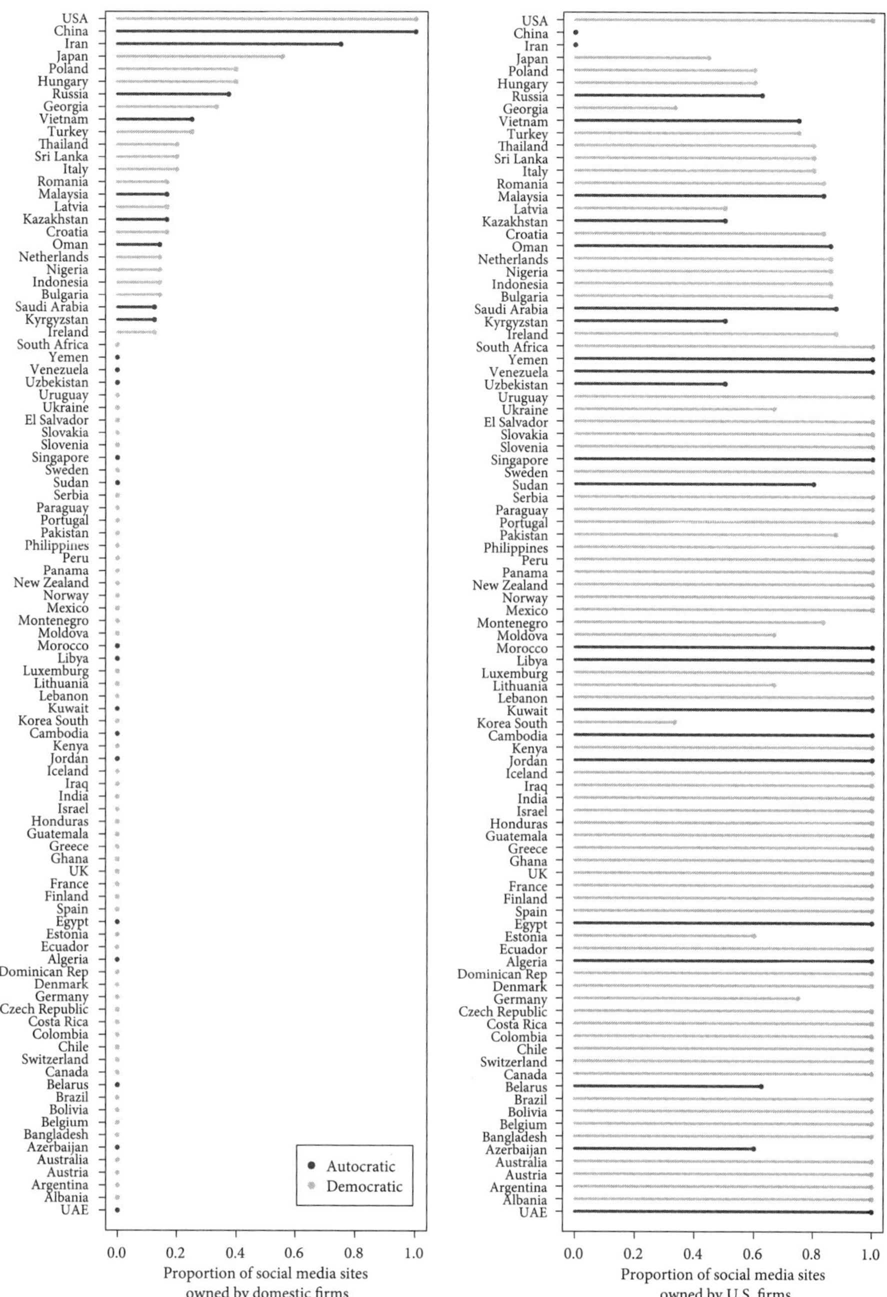

Figure 8.1. Proportion of social media sites by ownership type for democratic and autocratic countries

domestic firms, and none of the most trafficked sites are U.S. social media platforms. However, while neither country's top social media sites are owned by U.S. firms, all of the top social media sites in China are Chinese companies, but this is not the case in Iran. The most trafficked social media site among Iranians is blogfa.com, a blog service targeting Persian speakers. While blogfa.com has close ties to Iran, it is wholly owned by Ravand Cybertech, a company headquartered in Toronto, Canada.[5] In addition to blogfa.com, another Persian-language social media platform popular in Iran, Persianblog.ir, is also registered to a company located outside of Iran.

Altogether, website traffic data shows that the landscape for social media differs between China and most other authoritarian regimes. These patterns based on traffic data are corroborated by user data, specifically the number of Chinese users registered on Chinese versus U.S. social media platforms. Chinese social media platforms such as QQ and Weibo, where over 97 percent of visitors come from mainland China, have hundreds of millions of users.[6] As of the first half of 2014, there were 829 million active QQ accounts, and a peak of 176 million concurrent users;[7] as of the end of 2014, Weibo had 176 million monthly active users and 81 million daily active users.[8] In stark contrast, Ethan Zuckerman, director of the MIT Center for Civic Media, estimated in 2011 that the number of Twitter users in China was 1 percent of those who use domestic microblogging sites.[9] More recent estimates of the number of U.S. social media users in China as a share of those who use domestic social media are even smaller. Estimates put mainland Chinese Twitter users at between ten thousand and one hundred thousand and Facebook users around six hundred thousand.[10]

Content Removal Between Domestic and Foreign Social Media Firms

Putting aside methods of censorship such as physical repression, there remains a variety of technical methods for controlling online media. The best-known is content blocking, often called website blocking or Internet filtering. Content blocking prevents individuals in a certain geographic location from accessing specified websites and other resources on the Internet. Content blocking can be achieved through a variety of technical means that differ in terms of resources required and degree of reliability.[11]

Other forms of Internet controls include keyword blocking, which prevents certain terms from being included in online content; search filtering, where search engines filter results to prevent or make it very difficult for users to find certain content; and content removal, which is the deletion of content that has already appeared online. While keyword blocking prevents the production of certain types of information, content blocking, search filtering, and content removal prevent the dissemination of existing information.

Content removal is more difficult to detect and a more reliable method of preventing the spread of information compared to content blocking and search filtering, because offending content is erased. In the case of content blocking, the information remains in existence and can be accessed using circumvention technology such as VPNs, Tor, or Psiphon (Feamster et al. 2002; Dingledine 2011).[12] For search filtering, changing the search engine can uncover the hidden content.

Although content removal is more effective, many authoritarian regimes engage in content blocking because it can be implemented directly by the government as long as the government has the relevant technical expertise. Of the eighteen authoritarian regimes that had Internet penetration of over 40 percent as of 2014, all but four countries engage in content blocking related to political and/or religious topics.[13] As the results demonstrate below, the feasibility of implementing content removal depends not on a regime's technical expertise but on whether it can garner the cooperation of Internet content providers where content resides.

Domestic Social Media and Content Removal

China's widespread content removal efforts are heavily dependent on the compliance of Chinese social media and other Internet companies to act in accordance with the wishes of the regime. In China, failure to comply with censorship directives can result in punishments ranging from fines to being shut down (MacKinnon 2008). Sina Weibo, which is listed on NASDAQ, describes in its 2014 SEC filings that failure to adequately comply with government regulations on censorship "may subject us to liabilities and penalties and may even result in the temporary blockage or complete shutdown of our online operations."[14] Chinese social media firms comply with censorship requirements and have numerous employees who are focused on conducting censorship (King, Pan, and Roberts 2013, 2014). Censorship generates direct costs and can also entail indirect costs by adversely affecting users. Weibo reports in its SEC filings that

> although our active user base has increased over the past several years, regulation and censorship of information disseminated over the internet in China may adversely affect our user experience and reduce users' engagement and activities on our platform as well as adversely affect our ability to attract new users to our platform. Any and all of these adverse impacts may ultimately materially and adversely affect our business and results of operations.

These costs are accepted because they allow Internet companies to compete in the Chinese market, where most of their revenue is derived. This is not to say that large Chinese social media firms always blindly follow the directives of the central regime; they push the boundaries of what is acceptable (Yang 2009).[15] However, censorship is widely tolerated by domestic firms as part and parcel of being in the Internet business in China.

Analyses of censorship in China show that content removal occurs very quickly, usually within a few hours and almost always within a day (Zhu et al. 2013). Content removal in China has also been shown to be pervasive and systematic. King, Pan, and Roberts (2013, 2014) show through a large-scale observation study as well as randomized experiments that content removal is focused on suppressing discussion of events with collective action potential, while allowing content critical of the regime. When collective action events such as protest occur, all discussion of this event, whether critical or supportive of the regime, is permanently removed. King, Pan, and Roberts (2014) also show through participant observation that responsibility for content removal is devolved to the content provider, echoing prior experiments (MacKinnon 2009).

China's strategy of content removal, focused on suppressing all discussion of collective action, by definition decreases the coordination potential of social media. Namely, if individuals do not know that protests are occurring, they have no opportunity to join. China's method of content removal also covertly diminishes the reliability of information because a great deal of public discourse remains online, presenting a mirage of openness. In

China, 45 percent of Internet users believe that the Internet is a safe place to express their opinions, which is much higher than in places like Russia (28 percent of Russians believe the Internet to be safe) where social desirability bias is a similar concern.[16] Furthermore, the method of content removal practiced by the Chinese regime is the opposite strategy to sudden and ubiquitous interruption of Internet access, which has been shown to facilitate social mobilization (Hassanpour 2014).

After China, Iran and Russia have the largest number of domestic social media firms. Although the content removal strategy employed by China has not been systematically documented in the other two regimes, anecdotal evidence suggests that domestic social media firms also play a role in content removal in Iran and Russia, and these regimes exert pressure on domestic firms to engage in content removal even when firms are reluctant to do so.

There have been reports of collaboration between China and Iran on online censorship efforts. In the beginning of 2014, Iran's Ministry of Communications and Information Technology announced that China would assist the country in implementing a "clean Internet." The Iranian spokesperson expressed a desire to learn from China's experience in managing online content (Eades 2014). There are a growing number of Iranian Internet start-ups, and these domestic companies conform to the boundaries set by the regime (Azali 2015; Faucon and Jones 2015).

In the case of Russia, increasing limits on new media in many ways reflect the country's move from a transitional democracy back to authoritarianism (Becker 2004). In contrast to China, where compliance with content removal is primarily motivated by financial incentives, Russia seems to employ more strong-arm tactics to ensure the compliance of domestic Internet firms. This is the plight of vk.com, a successful domestic social media company that lost the fight against the regime on censorship with the ouster of its founder, Pavel Durov, in 2014 (Johnston 2015).

U.S. Social Media and Content Removal

Examples from Iran and Russia suggest that even if domestic companies are not systematically engaged in widespread content removal, as they are in China, authoritarian regimes can impose a great deal of control over domestic social media companies. This section turns to examining the outcomes of government requests for content removal on foreign social media companies, using data from Twitter and YouTube.

Twitter: Low Rates of Content Removal

Twitter publishes on a biannual basis data on government requests to remove content from Twitter.[17] Data available from 2012 to 2014 show for each six-month period the number of removal requests based on court orders, the number of removal requests from any government agency, the number of accounts specified in removal requests, the percentage where some content was removed or withheld from view in certain geographic locations, the accounts affected, and the number of tweets affected by country. This publicly available data is used in this chapter to measure the level of compliance of U.S. social media companies with removal requests from foreign governments. Although this data may be incomplete, the data that is available reveals that compliance with removal requests is incomplete and slow to take place.

Government requests for Twitter to remove content have increased over time. Table 8.3 shows that in the second half of 2012 there were eighty-four requests, but by the second half of 2014 there were 1,592 requests. Over this entire time period, the largest number of removal requests came from Turkey (678 requests total), France (456 requests), and Russia (154 requests).

Figure 8.2 shows that Twitter does not comply with most government content removal requests. Overall from 2012 to 2014, Twitter complied with 10 percent of removal requests, taking actions that include removal as well as withholding content from specific countries. The latter case is more similar to content blocking than content removal since circumvention technologies can be used to access geographically restricted content. As a result, the

Table 8.3. Government Removal Requests for Twitter by Period

Period	*Total requests*	*Country with greatest number of requests*	*Share of total requests*
Jul.–Dec. 2012	84	Brazil	19%
Jan.–Jun. 2013	120	Russia	23%
Jul.–Dec. 2013	754	France	41%
Jan.–Jun. 2014	864	Turkey	22%
Jul.–Dec. 2014	1,592	Turkey	30%

10 percent compliance rate with removal requests represents a ceiling on the proportion of content removed. The highest compliance rate for requests is 68 percent for the Netherlands; however, the Netherlands submitted only 19 requests in this period. The second highest compliance rate for censorship was 53 percent for Russia, which submitted 154 requests, followed by France at 48 percent (with 456 submitted requests), Japan at 39 percent (with 32 submitted requests), Germany at 32 percent (with 53 submitted requests), and Brazil at 17 percent (with 73 submitted requests).

YouTube: Content Blocking, Not Removal

Google also makes public on a biannual basis court orders and requests from government agencies to remove content. Google provides the number of requests and the relevant product for each country during each six-month period.[18] In the second half of 2013, Google revealed, of the 2,199 government requests to remove content from YouTube, 973 (44 percent) resulted in restriction or removal. However, Google does not release the outcome of every government request for content removal, only the outcomes for a selected sample, and it does not specify how this sample of outcomes is selected; thus, this data is used primarily to give insight into how Google deals with content removal requests. What these results show is that although compliance rates appear higher for YouTube than for Twitter, compliance largely entails restricting videos from view in specified geographies, not removing them from the platform altogether.

The sample of government requests for which there is data on outcomes contains seventy separate requests from governments for content removal between 2010 and 2013. The scope of each request varies greatly—a request could pertain to the removal of a single YouTube video or could ask that hundreds of videos be removed. Of these seventy requests, twenty relate to the video "Innocence of Muslims" and were made in second half of 2012 (see left panel of Figure 8.3). When this data is examined by country, the right panel of Figure 8.3 shows that the majority of content removal requests resulted in no content being removed or restricted (in light gray) for requests coming from both democratic and authoritarian regimes, and very few requests receive full compliance (in black). Since the requests related to "Innocence of Muslims" constitute a burst of activity that deviates from the norm, excluding these twenty requests, 66 percent of requests to remove or limit access to YouTube content were completely denied, 26 percent of requests resulted in

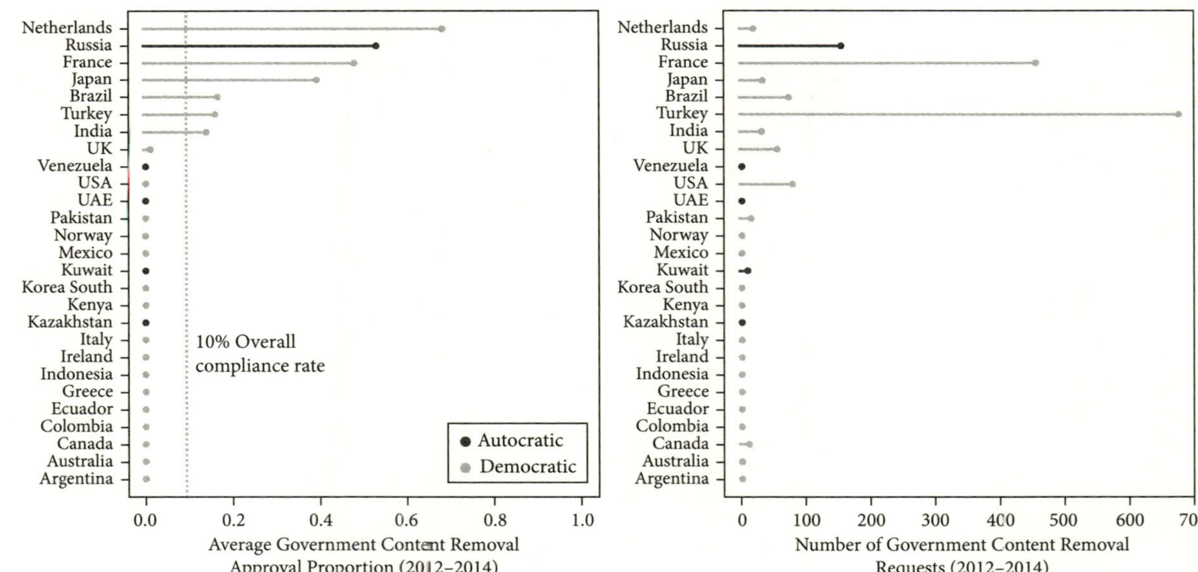

Figure 8.2. Twitter does not approve most government content removal requests

some geographic restriction or partial removal of content, and only 8 percent of requests received complete compliance.

Looking at the details of how Google deals with government requests to remove content from YouTube, we see that Google removes content only when it clearly violates YouTube's community guidelines, and restricts content from countries where the content violates local laws. In other words, unless content violates YouTube's community guidelines, Google does not engage in content removal but instead uses content blocking, which allows content to be retrieved with circumvention technology. The YouTube community guidelines prohibit pornography and sexual content, copyright infringement, "harmful or dangerous" content, "violent or graphic content," "hateful" content, and threats. Anyone can report content they believe violates these rules, and reports are evaluated by YouTube staff.[19]

As described above, twenty removal requests related to the video "Innocence of Muslims," which YouTube ultimately restricted from view in eleven countries where the content violated local laws. Among the requests unrelated to "Innocence of Muslims," forty were related to politics, pertaining to individuals such as government officials or to political actions such as opposition protest. Content critical of or unflattering to government leaders is almost never removed. For example, a request from an Armenian politician to remove three YouTube videos that used profane language in reference to him was denied, and a request from the government of Pakistan's Ministry of Information Technology to remove videos that satirized the Pakistan Army and senior politicians was denied.

Refusals to remove videos with unflattering political content are not limited to requests from authoritarian regimes. Requests from democratic regimes are similarly rejected. When government officials from Mexico requested that content accusing them of corruption be removed because of defamation, Google denied the request. When the Indonesian consul general requested that six videos be removed, Google refused and stated that the videos appeared critical of the consulate. When Indian law enforcement agencies requested the removal of videos criticizing chief ministers and senior officials, Google denied the request. Requests to remove content pertaining to political opposition are also denied. The sample of data includes a request from the Turkish government to remove a YouTube video containing a survey of protesters that asked questions about the protesters' political aims and reasons for protesting, as well as a request from a local ministry in Kazakhstan to remove a YouTube channel supportive of the opposition. Both requests were denied.

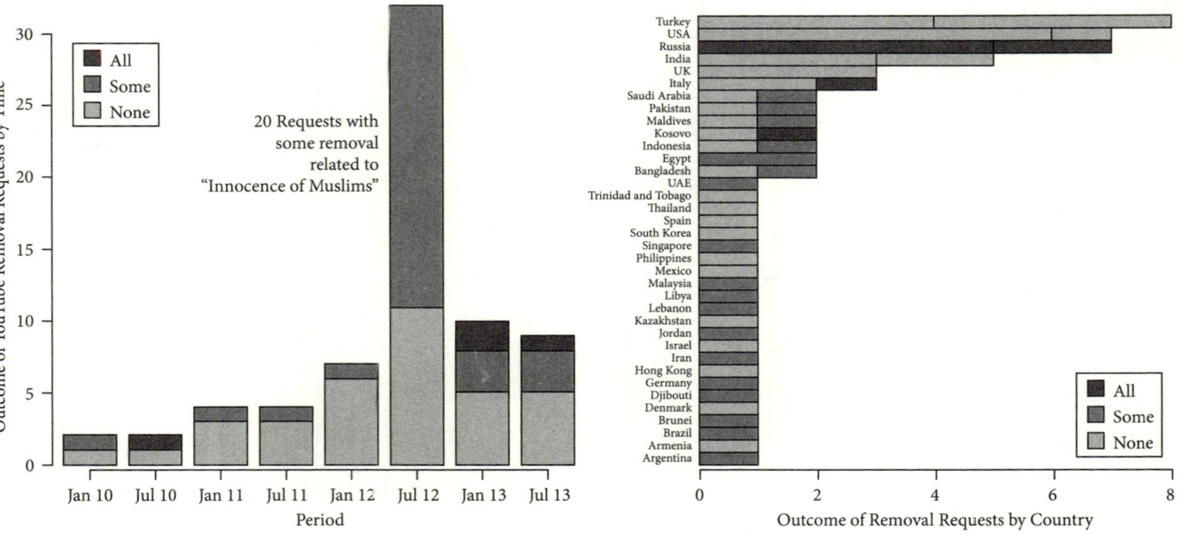

Figure 8.3. YouTube has limited approval of government content removal requests

In the YouTube data, removal requests related to political content result in removal only when they violate YouTube's community guidelines. When local laws prohibit certain forms of content, YouTube restricts the video from view in the geography where the law is in effect but does not remove the content entirely. The right panel of Figure 8.3 shows that in Russia, about two-thirds of requests result in some removal or restriction (dark gray segment in the right panel of Figure 8.3) and one-third of requests result in complete removal or restriction (black segment in the right panel of Figure 8.3). This high level of censorship, and especially geographic restriction, with respect to Russian content is crucially related to amendments to Russia's administrative code and laws protecting children from harmful content as well as laws counteracting extremist activity enacted in the past few years. For example, in the second half of 2013, Google received a request from Russia's Federal Service for Supervision in the Sphere of Telecom, Information Technologies, and Mass Communications to remove a YouTube video related to the self-immolation of a Buddhist monk. Google restricted the video from Russia because Russia's law to protect children from harmful content prohibited content that encouraged suicide.

These examples come from a sample of data made public by Google, and we do not know if they are representative of the overall outcomes of content removal requests. However, even if this sample of requests is not representative, it provides examples of how Google decides to comply with or reject government requests for content removal. Together, data from Twitter and Google show that U.S. social media firms generally reject government requests for content removal. If any action is taken, it is typically to restrict or block content from certain geographies where local laws apply. As a result, it is extremely difficult for regimes to engage in content removal on U.S. social media platforms, and China's strategy of content removal, where domestic social media firms quickly remove all content related to real-world collective action events as they are happening, is practically impossible for governments to replicate on U.S. social media platforms.

Replicating China's Censorship Strategy

Given the difficulty of implementing China's strategy of content removal on U.S. social media platforms, are there other ways for countries to replicate China's strategy of censorship? Two potential courses of action are examined here: (1) protectionism to facilitate the development of domestic social media platforms, and (2) importing Chinese social media platforms to conduct content removal. The success of Chinese social media companies is often attributed to the first approach: China's content blocking through the so-called Great Firewall, which prevents users in mainland China from accessing international websites such as Twitter and Facebook, is often thought to be the reason Chinese firms have flourished (Zhang and Pentina 2012).[20] This section takes a closer look at this claim by examining the relationship between the share of domestic social media and long-term blocking of U.S. websites across authoritarian regimes, and then examining the rise of Chinese Internet companies through several case studies. A second potential path to replicating China's censorship strategy is for countries to import Chinese social media companies. The assumptions underlying this approach are discussed.

Protectionism and Domestic Social Media

Blocking access to U.S. social media platforms occurs frequently across authoritarian and democratic regimes.[21] The dominant rationale for preventing users from accessing U.S. social media sites is to prevent access to content, not to protect domestic social media firms from U.S. competitors. Even if protectionism were the motivation, it is unlikely that a short-term blocking would be helpful to domestic companies. Only when content blocking is persistent over time can content blocking potentially serve as a form of de facto protectionism, to create conditions more amenable for the success of local companies.

Examining countries that have blocked U.S. social media sites for more than one year (365 days) as an indicator of de facto protectionism, Table 8.4 shows for each of these countries which U.S. social media sites were blocked, the timing of the block, and the country's share of domestic social media firms as of 2015.[22] The number of countries that have engaged in long-term content blocking is very small, so conclusions should be taken with a grain of salt; however, there does not appear to be any relationship between the strength of domestic social media and content blocking, either in terms of the duration of blocks or the number of sites blocked. Table 8.4 shows that China, Iran, and Vietnam have all been blocking U.S. sites since 2009, but the strength of domestic firms in these countries greatly varies. In China, 100 percent of social media firms are owned by domestic firms, but in Viet-

Table 8.4. Long-Term Content Blocking by Country and Platform

Country	*U.S. Social media sites blocked*	*Share of social media sites owned by domestic firms*
China	Blogspot (2009–) Facebook (2009–) Twitter (2009–) YouTube (2009–) Instagram (2014–)	100%
Iran	Facebook (2009–) YouTube (2009–) Twitter (2009–)	75%
Vietnam	Facebook (2009–) YouTube* (2009–) Twitter* (2009–)	25%
Kazakhstan	Blogger (2010–2012)	17%
Libya	YouTube (2010–2011)	0
Pakistan	YouTube (2012–)	0

* YouTube and Twitter are intermittently unavailable in Vietnam but not systematically banned.

nam only 25 percent are. Likewise, the number of blocked U.S. sites does not appear to be related to the strength of domestic social media. Kazakhstan, Libya, and Pakistan all block one U.S. site, but in Kazakhstan only one social media site is domestic (representing 17 percent of all social media sites), while the other two countries have no domestic social media presence. Iran and Vietnam both block the same three platforms, but the domestic share of social media in Iran is 75 percent and only 25 percent in Vietnam. Altogether, protectionism coincides with the dominance of domestic firms in China but not in other countries.

Rise of Chinese Internet Firms

This section uses case studies of Chinese social media firms and Internet companies to show that content blocking is not a sufficient explanation for the success of Chinese social media companies, and to shed light on other factors both within and outside of the regime's control that contributed to the success of these firms. Together, the evidence suggests that recreating China's market of domestic social media sites will be challenging for most regimes, both authoritarian and democratic.

Tencent QQ

Tencent was founded in 1998 by Ma Huateng and Zhang Zhidong. Early the next year, Tencent released its first product, then called OICQ, based closely on ICQ, an instant-messaging program developed by an Israeli company in 1996 and purchased by AOL in 1998. Due to the threat of trademark infringement litigation by ICQ, Tencent changed the name of its messaging product to QQ. Within two months of the product's launch, two hundred thousand users had registered QQ accounts; registered users exceeded one million by November 1999, and by early 2002, QQ exceed one hundred million registered users (Wu and Frantz 2011). Tencent was listed on the Stock Exchange of Hong Kong in June 2004, and a decade later, in 2014, Tencent had revenues of 78.9 billion RMB (12.7 billion USD) and gross profits of 48.1 billion RMB (6.7 billion USD).[23] Tencent's meteoric rise may seem inevitable in hindsight, but in the late 1990s, its success was far from guaranteed. Facing competitive pressure from Microsoft's MSN as well as state-run China Mobile, Tencent's success depended on its ability to access capital and its products and business model innovations, as well as China's large market of Internet users.

Within sixteen months of its founding, Tencent had raised 2.2 million USD in capital from IDG capital partners, a venture fund originally based in San Francisco, and from PCCW, a Hong Kong–based information communications technology company, giving each of these investors a 20 percent ownership stake. With this initial funding, Tencent launched mobile and telecom value-added services in August 2000 and Internet value-added services in June 2001 to expand its sources of revenue beyond advertising. In 2001, Myriad International Holdings (MIH), the offshore investment arm and holding company of the Naspers Group, bought PCCW's 20 percent share as well as 13 percent of IDG's shares. By the time of Tencent's IPO on the Hong Kong stock exchange, MIH held 37.5 percent of Tencent's shares, the two initial cofounders 30.74 percent of shares, other founders 6.77 percent of shares, and public shareholders 25 percent of shares. These infusions of capital from foreign investors were critical in Tencent's early years, but depended on complex legal and contractual structures that sidestepped Chinese law prohibiting foreign ownership of Internet and telecommunications companies.

In order to gain access to foreign capital, Tencent initially consisted of an investment holding company incorporated in the British Virgin Islands and later transferred to the Cayman Islands by Ma Huateng and Zhang Zhidong, a limited liability company (Tencent Computer) established in mainland China and legally owned by the Chinese founders, and a subsidiary of the investment holding company incorporated in mainland China as a wholly foreign-owned enterprise (Tencent Technology). Among these three entities, Tencent Computer is the only one authorized to run an Internet and telecommunications company, but foreign funders could not take a stake in Tencent Computer. Instead, foreign financing was provided to Tencent Computer via Tencent Technology, so that foreign investors had no direct stake in the Chinese company. Only through contractual agreements was it stipulated that decision-making rights, operations, and financial activities of Tencent Computer are ultimately controlled by the company and its subsidiary Tencent Technology. Most importantly, contracts stipulated that all the operating profits residual benefits and intellectual property of Tencent Computer belong to the investment holding company.[24]

This complex structure, commonly referred to as a variable interest entity (VIE), is the primary method through which Chinese Internet companies including Sina, Baidu, and Alibaba were able to obtain foreign capital to support their early activities. For decades, this structure was neither blessed nor condemned by key Chinese regulators.[25] What is notable is that many of the most successful Chinese Internet companies did not receive Chinese government funding at their inception but rather competed for foreign venture capital funding, and firms that obtained foreign funding did so through a complex financial arrangement that in essence circumvented or at least stretched limits set by the Chinese regime on the influx of foreign investment.

In its early days, Tencent faced competition from Microsoft's MSN as well as China Mobile. MSN, an instant-messaging platform owned by Microsoft, also launched in China in 1999. At the time, MSN had a better brand reputation than QQ and was the platform preferred by white-collar workers. In the early years, many believed that MSN would beat QQ in the China market; however, MSN quickly lost market share, and by 2003, QQ had 74 percent of China's market share for instant messaging and MSN only 11 percent (Lu 2011). Individuals familiar with China's technology market whom I interviewed attributed MSN's loss to its stagnant product, which was not tailored to the Chinese market, while QQ was designed and evolved to meet the needs of Chinese consumers. As to which specific features differentiated QQ from MSN, Meng and Zuo (2008) argue that QQ's key product differentiation from MSN was allowing for interactions among strangers (e.g., any user could find any other users by searching for location, online status, and nickname) and complementing this feature with stronger tools to block existing contacts. Others cite QQ's ability to resume interrupted downloads (Clarke 2009) or its addition of new features such as message boards, virtual items that could be purchased using virtual currency, and gaming (Bethune and Viard 2012). Regardless of the exact features that led QQ to greater user adoption, by 2012 MSN had less than 5 percent of China's instant-messaging market, and by 2014 it had shut down its services in China.

QQ competed against MSN and won against MSN on the basis of its product, not because of government protectionism. In reality, in its early years, Tencent came under pressure from the state and state-owned enterprises. Prior to 2004, a substantial part of Tencent's revenues (45 percent) came from its partnership with China Mobile. In this partnership, Tencent created mobile QQ that China Mobile, which held a monopoly over 3G and 4G technology, sold to users for 5 RMB (0.60 USD based on 2000 exchange rates), with Tencent keeping 20 percent of these revenues. By the end of 2004, China Mobile had ended this fee-sharing agreement with Tencent and moved to a fixed monthly maintenance fee agreement that decreased Tencent revenues by millions of RMB. In 2006, China Mobile announced its own mobile-messaging product and banned the use of QQ and MSN on its phones. During this time, QQ market share declined from 79 percent in 2005 to 69 percent in 2006,[26] and MSN tried to take advantage of Tencent's weakness by entering into a joint venture backed by Shanghai's state-owned Assets Supervision and Administration Commission. Neither China Mobile nor MSN was successful in its efforts to develop a competitive product, while the competitive pressure motivated Tencent to shift to new sources of revenue, specifically gaming combined with the sale of virtual goods and premium services (together called value-added services). Because of China's large Internet and mobile user base, and Tencent's ability to attract users, value-added services generated a large amount of revenue for the company, even though they represent relatively small financial outlays on a per user or per transaction basis. For example, in 2014 these services were 80 percent (63.3 billion CNY) of Tencent's revenues, far ahead of advertising revenues, and represented approximately 80 RMB of annual spending per user. On the basis of this business model, Tencent is estimated to have had the highest shareholder total return of any large firm globally from 2008 to 2012, ahead of Amazon and Apple, and with much greater revenues and profit margins than social media competitors such as Facebook.[27]

Alibaba and Taobao

Tencent's rise to market dominance despite foreign and government competitive pressures is echoed in the story of Alibaba's Taobao. Founded in 1999 by Jack Ma, Alibaba was initially a business-to-business portal that connected Chinese manufacturers to overseas buyers. Like Tencent, Alibaba was funded by foreign capital—initially, investors like Goldman Sachs and Fidelity Capital, and later on, investors such as AIG Global Investment, Taiwanese billionaire Terry Gou, and Yahoo.[28] In 2003, eBay entered China by buying EachNet, China's leading consumer auction site at the time, for 150 million USD.[29] Ma was concerned that eBay would move into business-to-business transactions, so as a defensive strategy he launched Taobao, a consumer-to-consumer auction site, to prevent eBay from taking away Alibaba's customers. At the time, industry experts were skeptical of Taobao's financial sustainability because Taobao allowed sellers to make listings for free, unlike eBay, which charged sellers to list products. However, this approach, combined with better terms for customers and extra services such as communications between buyers and sellers, paid off, and Taobao quickly gained users over eBay. By March 2006, Taobao had 67 percent of user market share, while eBay's share fell to 29 percent, and by the end of 2006, eBay exited China.

Baidu and Google

Unlike the cases of QQ and Taobao, Baidu's success over Google is more controversial. There are many who argue that Baidu's success is a result of government intervention that prevented Google from being able to succeed in the Chinese market. However, what the data shows is that Google lagged behind Baidu in the market even before Google's relationship with the Chinese regime became antagonistic.

Baidu was founded in 2000 by Robin Li, who had developed a new search algorithm while working as a developer for IDD Information Services in the United States in 1996, along with Eric Xu. Li and Xu raised 1.2 million USD from Integrity Partners and Peninsula Capital, two U.S. venture capital firms, as seed capital to launch Baidu. Later in 2000, they raised another 10 million USD from two other U.S. venture capital firms, Draper Fisher Jurvetson and IDG Technology Venture. Initially offering search services to other Chinese sites, Baidu created its own site, baidu.com, in September 2001. Baidu raised a third round of financing in 2004, and Google was one of the investors, contributing 5 million USD. When Baidu filed to go public in 2005, Google offered a bid of 1.6 billion USD to acquire Baidu, but ultimately the Baidu board voted to go public instead. Individuals involved in that decision speculate Google could have acquired Baidu at that time had it made a higher offer, but instead Google launched google.cn that same year.

Prior to 2005, Chinese Internet users could use google.com or baidu.com. In 2003, google.com and baidu.com had very similar market shares in China—35 percent and 31 percent, respectively (Lu 2011). However, by the time google.cn launched, Baidu's market share had already increased to 57 percent while Google's had stagnated at 33 percent (Lu 2011). In other words, even before Google entered the Chinese market and faced decisions on whether to engage in censorship, it already trailed Baidu in market share. Baidu's gain in market share between 2003 and 2005 is often attributed to Baidu's MP3 search, which allowed Chinese Internet users to search for and download music for free, regardless of copyright restrictions. By the end of 2004, Baidu estimated that nearly 50 percent of China's Internet users searched for music.[30] When pressed about intellectual property protection, Li said, "If [users] are looking for certain type of content that is publicly available, we cannot say, in order to make sure record companies are happy, let's completely block out this type of service. We choose not to do that" (Stone and Einhorn 2010). Google could not do the same because it faced strong constraints from the U.S. music industry and U.S. regulators. During this period, Baidu's popularity among young people, individuals in western and central China, and less highly educated individuals soared. Google's share of China's market for Internet search continued to decline, falling to 23 percent by 2009, while Baidu's share continued to grow, reaching 72 percent by the same year (Lu 2011).

From 2005 forward, the antagonistic relationship between the Chinese government and Google may well have prevented Google from succeeding in the Chinese market, but what is clear from this timeline is that Baidu surpassed Google in the China market before government interventions in google.cn began. Moreover, Baidu also faced pressures from the government.

For example, in late 2008, the government-controlled China Central Television (CCTV) aired investigations into Baidu's business practices on Robin Li's fortieth birthday, likely as a warning to the company. Baidu's spokesperson Kaiser Kuo said of Baidu's relationship with the government, "We get smacked as hard as anyone" (Stone and Einhorn 2010).

Microblogging in China

Sina Weibo is a leading microblogging site in China today. Its success is often attributed to the Chinese government's ban on Twitter (Zhang and Pentina 2012) because of the timing of Sina Weibo's launch: content blocking of Twitter began in June 2009 and Sina Weibo was launched in August 2009. However, prior to June 2009, when Twitter was universally accessible in China, Twitter faced stiff competition from a number of Chinese microblogging sites and lagged behind Chinese competitors in share of users. Twitter was blocked in June 2009 as part of a wide-ranging government clampdown on microblogging platforms that resulted in blockages of Chinese microblogging platforms as well. Although Sina Weibo benefited from the Chinese government clampdown on microblogs in 2009, it is unclear whether the Chinese government ban of Twitter was beneficial or detrimental to domestic microblogging firms overall.

Twitter was launched in July 2006, and by 2007 a number of domestic microblogging sites had emerged in China, including Taotao, Fanfou, Digu, Jiwai.de, Zuosa, kommo.cn, and SBTalk. Many of these sites were almost identical replicas of Twitter (Kotowski 2009), but others incorporated features such as embedded video and images then unavailable on Twitter (Li and Rao 2010). A breakthrough moment for microblogging in China occurred in May 2008 when news of the 2008 Sichuan earthquake first broke on Twitter and was widely discussed on Twitter and Chinese microblogs (Moore 2008).

Before Twitter was blocked, it competed with both foreign and Chinese microblogs for market share in China, and what evidence is available suggests that Twitter did not dominate the Chinese market. In 2008, Twitter likely had only a few thousand users in China. In February 2008, the Twitter Blog released data on Twitter traffic from around the world that showed that 60 percent of Twitter traffic came from outside the United States.[31] In the graphic—a pie chart—released by Twitter, none of the international traffic came from China. Around the same time, a search of Twitter users by self-declared location revealed 2,754 users located in mainland China.[32] In early 2008, Twitter had one million users overall; if we round up and assume Twitter had three thousand users in China, China accounted for only 0.5 percent of international Twitter users (0.3 percent of all Twitter users). By July 2009, according to leaked internal Twitter documents, Twitter had grown to over thirty-seven million users globally, of which seventeen million (46 percent) came from outside the United States.[33] These documents revealed that adoption was particularly weak in China and South Korea, where Twitter faced competition from domestic social media services (Hedencrona 2009). Assuming that Twitter's share of users in China did not decrease from the 2008 estimate of 0.5 percent of international users, then by 2009 there were eighty-five thousand Twitter users in China. By contrast, the local microblogging site Fanfou had one million users by 2009 (Li and Rao 2010).

In June 2009, before the twentieth anniversary of the Tiananmen Square incident, Twitter and its Chinese competitors, including Fanfou, Digu, and Jiawai.de, were blocked in China. After this clampdown, Sina launched Weibo with assurances to the Chinese regime that content would be tightly controlled. Sina Weibo copied Twitter's 140-character limit, but added functionality such as direct comments and comment threading to appeal to Chinese users (Sullivan 2012). Sina Weibo quickly outpaced other domestic microblogging competitors that emerged after the June 2009 clampdown, and dominated China's microblogging market until Tencent launched its microblogging product, Tencent QQ Weibo, in 2010. Since 2010, Sina Weibo and Tencent Weibo have held onto China's microblogging market in a virtual tie.

In sum, domestic microblogging companies in China dominated Twitter in market share before the government crackdown on Twitter and Chinese microblogs in mid-2009. Without the 2009 clampdown, Chinese microblogs such as Fanfou might very well have outcompeted Twitter. Although the rise of Sina Weibo is no doubt related to government crackdown on microblogs, even without the 2009 clampdown and banning of Twitter, Chinese firms might have become the leaders of China's microblogging market.

De facto protectionism resulting from content blocking is insufficient to explain the success of Chinese Internet firms. The cases described above paint a picture of the rise of domestic Chinese firms despite government limits on access to capital, burdensome stipulations related to censorship, and competitive pressures from state-owned companies. Chinese firms led U.S. competitors in market share before U.S. platforms were blocked from China. These cases suggest that the success of Chinese firms in gaining users more quickly than their U.S. counterparts during the initial stages of competition was rooted in a better understanding of the Chinese market and their ability to innovate based on this knowledge. Examples of these innovations from the cases discussed above include QQ's features allowing strangers to connect and chat, Alibaba's free seller listing, Baidu's MP3 search, and Chinese microblogs' embedded videos and image features. While a thorough examination of what accounts for the success of Chinese firms in product design goes beyond the purview of this chapter, relevant factors may include the availability of entrepreneurial and technological talent in China and their ability to access funding from U.S. financial firms as well as structural factors such as China's large consumer market for Internet products and ambiguous intellectual property protections.

Importing Chinese Social Media

The development of domestic social media firms obedient to the censorship demands of the government is one path to mimicking China's "success" in Internet censorship. The above sections reveal that developing domestic players is not as straightforward as imposing government protection against foreign social media companies. Another path to copying China's censorship strategy of content removal is to import Chinese social media platforms. Indeed, Iran seemed to hint at this path when its Ministry of Communications and Information Technology expressed a desire for Chinese Internet companies to increase their presence in Iran (Eades 2014). However, in order for regimes to replicate China's model of content removal by importing Chinese social media platforms, two critical assumptions must hold.

The first assumption relates to market competition. In order for other countries to replicate China's content removal by importing Chinese social media firms, users in those countries have to adopt Chinese social media platforms instead of the U.S. platforms they are currently using. There is a large literature on market competition that shows how established platforms are difficult to displace in sectors like social media, where users' interactions are subject to network effects (Economides 1996; Evans, Hagiu, and Schmalensee 2008; Katz and Shapiro 1985; Rochet and Tirole 2003). There is a cost for switching to different platforms, and thus the success of Chinese firms is far from guaranteed.

The second assumption is that Chinese social media companies would comply with content removal requests of the local regime. Chinese social media firms comply with content removal requests from China, and they incur costs to do so. As previously discussed, costs of content removal include the direct cost of employing in-house censors, as well as indirect costs of losing users because of censorship. Chinese firms willingly incur these costs in China because being able to operate in the Chinese market, where there are more than six hundred million Internet users (over 20 percent of the world's share of Internet users), is economically attractive. It cannot be taken for granted that Chinese firms would be willing to incur these costs in every market, unless the potential revenues to be gained in those markets could offset these costs. Potential revenues may depend on the size of the market and existing competitors for the market.

Both of the approaches countries could take to replicate China's strategy of content removal depend heavily on conditions outside of the regime's control. Regimes could enact protectionism through long-term content blocking, but that does not guarantee the development and success of domestic firms. Regimes could bring in Chinese social media companies, but there is no guarantee that local users would adopt Chinese platforms or that Chinese firms would agree to censor. Existing research on sectors subject to network effect suggests that until there are revolutionary products or services, new entrants are unlikely to displace current market leaders (Bresnahan and Greenstein 1999; Henderson and Clark 1990). This means that even with protectionism and/or the importation of Chinese social media companies willing to censor, domestic and Chinese platforms are unlikely to displace U.S. platforms in markets where U.S. social media firms already dominate. Likewise, even without protectionism, it is unlikely that U.S. platforms would have surpassed Chinese competitors after they had already fallen behind in the early days of competition.

Conclusion

This chapter shows that China's social media landscape, which is dominated by domestic social media platforms, differs greatly from that of other authoritarian regimes where U.S. firms tend to dominate. China's domestic firms comply with China's censorship requirements, allowing the Chinese regime to engage in content censorship that quickly removes online content pertaining to collective action while retaining a great deal of other information, including criticisms of the government. In contrast, content removal is incredibly difficult for authoritarian regimes to achieve on U.S. social media platforms, making it practically impossible for regimes where U.S. social media firms dominate to engage in the type of social media censorship found in China.

Given the futility of pursuing content removal on U.S. platforms, other countries could try to replicate China's censorship model by developing domestic social media firms or by importing Chinese social media platforms that engage in content removal. However, the success of these approaches does not rest entirely within a regime's control. For the first path, development of domestic social media does not appear to be endogenous to government blocking of U.S. social media platforms. De facto protectionism through long-term content blocking rarely coincides with strong domestic social media presence. In China, where de facto protectionism coincides with a dominant domestic social media sector, the rise of China's social media companies suggests that success in these efforts requires much more than government protectionism against foreign competitors. For the second path, the ability of authoritarian regimes to replicate China's content removal efforts by attracting Chinese social media companies rests on the assumption that Chinese firms would agree to engage in content censorship outside of China and that Chinese firms could displace entrenched U.S. platforms.

Finally, two points deserve emphasis. The first is that this research does not address the motivations of authoritarian regimes to censor or adopt specific methods of censorship, but simply whether one of the censorship strategies successfully employed by China is available to other authoritarian regimes. This means that even if another country could replicate China's market dynamics, it may choose to use other strategies, such as real-world repression, to impose control over social media. Russia may fall into this camp. Russia has strong domestic social media companies, which the regime can control; however, existing evidence suggests that Russia relies more heavily on technical methods such as distributed denial of service (DDoS) attacks, bots, and trolls to control media.[34] The second point is that while China's content removal efforts may be a success in the eyes of the regime from the perspective of media control, they may negatively affect the country's economic potential by constraining the success of Chinese companies. Most directly, content removal depresses the profits of Chinese social media firms and hurts the prospects of these firms for expanding beyond China. If Chinese social media firms stopped content removal today, their profits would increase because they no longer would have to bear the cost of employing censors and complying with government stipulations. Furthermore, because Chinese Internet companies are known to engage in pervasive censorship, they are often perceived negatively by U.S. and European consumers, which hurts their prospects for expanding into lucrative markets.

Notes

This is an edited version of an article published by Taylor & Francis as "How Market Dynamics of Domestic and Foreign Social Media Firms Shape Strategies of Internet Censorship," in *Problems of Post-Communism* 64 (3–4) (2017): 167–88. Permission granted by Taylor & Francis.

1. There has been a great deal of discussion and debate about the role of social media platforms such as Facebook, Twitter, and YouTube in the Arab Spring and anti-regime demonstrations from Iran to Russia (Axford 2011; Stepanova 2011; Van Niekerk, Pillay, and Maharaj 2011; Weber 2011; Wilson and Dunn 2011; Aday et al. 2012; Bellin 2012; Hassanpour 2014).

2. Although research focused on the early days of the Internet in China argued that new technologies would lend power to dissidents and the population at large vis-à-vis the regime (Chase and Mulvenon 2002; Yang 2006; Esarey and Qiang 2008; Lindtner and Szablewicz 2011), more recent analyses have focused on the high degree of control the Chinese regime exerts over online content (MacKinnon 2008; Stockmann and Gallagher 2011; King, Pan, and Roberts 2013, 2014).

3. Regime type based on Geddes, Wright, and Frantz (2014).

4. See details at http://www.internetlivestats.com/internet-users-by-country/, accessed June 1, 2015, based on data from International Telecommunication Union, United Nations Population Division, Internet and Mobile Association of India, and the World Bank.

5. See http://www.blogfa.com/en/about.htm and http://www.ravand.com/aboutus.cfm. Note that because blogfa serves Persian-speaking users, the Iranian regime may have more control over the company than, say, a large multinational firm less dependent on accessing Iran's user base.

6. Visitor traffic statistics based on Alexa data.

7. See Tencent investor report at http://tencent.com/en-us/ir/news/2014.shtml, accessed June 3, 2015.

8. See http://bit.ly/1IUEiqm, accessed June 3, 2015.

9. For details, see http://www.ted.com/talks/ethan_zuckerman.html.

10. See http://bit.ly/1hgCcVE, http://bitly.com/1pH7Isr, and http://bit.ly/1Dm85Gv (accessed June 20, 2015), which uses information such as the language of posts, time

zone of the users, and self-described location of users to refute the widely reported claim that there were thirty-five million Twitter users and sixty-four million Facebook users in China in 2013. Along similar lines, research has found that Chinese is not among the most commonly used languages on Twitter, even though that is what we would see given the global share of Internet users from China if circumvention technology were widely used by Chinese speakers to access Twitter (Hong, Convertino, and Chi 2011).

11. For the purposes of this chapter, content blocking includes TCP/IP header filtering, TCP/IP content filtering, DNS tampering, HTTP proxy filtering, and hybrid TCP/IP and HTTP proxy methods (Murdoch and Anderson 2008).

12. For more information on Tor, see http://www.torproject.org/, and for Psiphon, see https://psiphon.ca/.

13. These eighteen countries are Armenia, Azerbaijan, Belarus, China, Jordan, Kazakhstan, Kuwait, Madagascar, Malaysia, Morocco, Oman, Russia, Saudi Arabia, Singapore, United Arab Emirates, Uzbekistan, Venezuela, and Vietnam, based on the 2014 Freedom House report on Internet controls (Kelly et al. 2014). Among these countries, there has been no evidence of Internet filtering in the past five years in Morocco, Singapore, and Venezuela, although both Singapore and Venezuela have the legal and technical infrastructure in place to conduct Internet filtering. No data is available for Madagascar.

14. http://1.usa.gov/1fzstAZ.

15. Later discussion provides more details of the pressures Chinese social media firms have faced from the regime.

16. Based on a survey from December 2013 to February 2014 of 1,000 respondents in urban China and 1,021 respondents in Russia. For details, see http://bit.ly/1K22TnJ, accessed July 15, 2015.

17. Data found at https://transparency.twitter.com/, accessed June 3, 2015.

18. For example, in the second half of 2013, Turkey issued 172 court orders and 723 government requests to Google to remove content for reasons ranging from copyright infringement to government criticism, pertaining to eleven Google products. Products affected include Blog Search, Blogger, Gmail, Google Docs, Google Images, Google Maps, Google Play Apps, Google+, Web Search, and YouTube.

19. For additional details, see http://www.youtube.com/yt/policyandsafety/communityguidelines.html, accessed June 3, 2015.

20. News reports of China's social media market often begin with this premise. For examples, see http://bit.ly/1E6DeIC and http://bit.ly/1T12Rl5, accessed June 3, 2015.

21. Google reports that users in more than thirty countries have been unable to access its products and services at some point in time. These countries range from democratic regimes such as Australia to authoritarian regimes such as Syria.

22. Data from Google Transparency Report, http://bit.ly/1UuHEE3, and news reporting of site blockages.

23. Based on Tencent investor and annual reports; see http://bit.ly/1SKiMt9, http://bit.ly/1hikxwP, accessed June 3, 2015.

24. See Tencent 2004 Annual Report at http://bit.ly/1KPgc0K, accessed June 3, 2015.

25. In early 2015, the Chinese Ministry of Commerce publicized draft legislation that would regulate foreign investment based not on ownership but on control. This legislation would threaten current VIE structures, but its outcome has yet to be determined.

26. See http://en.people.cn/200607/07/eng20060707281020. html, accessed June 1, 2015.

27. See http://econ.st/1DoHZme, accessed June 3, 2015.

28. Alibaba press release, May 2001, http://bit.ly/1JL4wKJ.

29. eBay financial release, July 2003, http://bit.ly/1JL4X7S.

30. Baidu IPO prospectus, http://1.usa.gov/1KPqTQN, accessed June 3, 2015.

31. See https://blog.twitter.com/2008/twitter-web-traffic-around-theworld, accessed June 3, 2015.

32. See http://theory.isthereason.com/p=2163, accessed June 3, 2015.

33. See http://tcrn.ch/1TGtZch, http://tcrn.ch/1LMAiVk, accessed June 3, 2015.

34. See http://bit.ly/1g9P2nM and Zuckerman et al. (2010), accessed June 3, 2015.

References

Aday, Sean, Henry Farrell, Marc Lynch, John Sides, and Deen Freelon. 2012. "Blogs and Bullets II: New Media and Conflict after the Arab Spring." United States Institute of Peace, July 10. https://www.usip.org/publications/2012/07/blogs-and-bullets-ii-new-media-and-conflict-after-arab-spring.

Axford, Barrie. 2011. "Talk About a Revolution: Social Media and the MENA Uprisings." *Globalizations* 8 (5): 681–86.

Azali, Mohammadreza. 2015. "Iran: Censorship and Opportunities Afterwards." *Techrasa*, June 24. http://techrasa.com/2015/06/24/iran-censorship-and-opportunities-afterwards/.

Becker, Jonathan. 2004. "Lessons from Russia: A Neo-Authoritarian Media System." *European Journal of Communication* 19 (2): 139–63.

Bellin, Eva. 2012. "Reconsidering the Robustness of Authoritarianism in the Middle East: Lessons from the Arab Spring." *Comparative Politics* 44 (2): 127–49.

Bethune, Richard, and V. Brian Viard. 2012. *When Monopolies Collide: Winning Mobile IM in China*. Beijing: Cheung Kong Case Center. http://cn.ckgsb.com/userfiles/doc/2012-09-1-243-2e.pdf.

Bresnahan, Timothy F., and Shane Greenstein. 1999. "Technological Competition and the Structure of the Computer Industry." *Journal of Industrial Economics* 47 (1): 1–40.

Chase, Michael S., and James C. Mulvenon. 2002. *You've Got Dissent! Chinese Dissident Use of the Internet and Beijing's Counter-Strategies*. Santa Monica, Calif.: Rand Corporation.

Clarke, Tom. 2009. "QQ: The MSN Killer That's Made in China." Softonic, November 6. https://en.softonic.com/articles/qq-the-msn-killer-thats-made-in-china.

Dingledine, Roger. 2011. "Tor and Circumvention: Lessons Learned." In *Advances in Cryptology-CRYPTO 2011*, edited by Phillip Rogaway, 485–86. Berlin: Springer.

Djankov, Simeon, Caralee McLiesh, Tatiana Nenova, and Andrei Shleifer. 2001. *Who Owns the Media?* World Bank Policy Research Working Paper No. 2620. Washington, D.C.: World Bank.

Eades, Mark C. 2014. "China's Newest Export: Internet Censorship." *US News and World Report*, January 30.

Earl, Jennifer, and Katrina Kimport. 2011. *Digitally Enabled Social Change: Activism in the Internet Age*. Cambridge, Mass.: MIT Press.

Economides, Nicholas. 1996. "The Economics of Networks." *International Journal of Industrial Organization* 14 (6): 673–99.

Edmond, Chris. 2013. "Information Manipulation, Coordination, and Regime Change." *Review of Economic Studies* 80 (4): 1422–58.

Egorov, Georgy, Sergei Guriev, and Konstantin Sonin. 2009. "Why Resource-Poor Dictators Allow Freer Media: A Theory and Evidence from Panel Data." *American Political Science Review* 103 (4): 645–68.

Enikolopov, Ruben, Maria Petrova, and Ekaterina Zhuravskaya. 2010. "Media and Political Persuasion: Evidence from Russia." *American Economic Review* 101: 3253–85.

Esarey, Ashley, and Xiao Qiang. 2008. "Political Expression in the Chinese Blogosphere Below the Radar." *Asian Survey* 48 (5): 752–72.

Evans, David S., Andrei Hagiu, and Richard Schmalensee. 2008. *Invisible Engines: How Software Platforms Drive Innovation and Transform Industries*. Cambridge, Mass.: MIT Press.

Faucon, Benoît, and Rory Jones. 2015. "Technology Startups Take Root in Tehran: Iranian Versions of Amazon, Google Play, Groupon Fill the Void Left by Censorship and Sanctions." *Wall Street Journal*, February 25.

Feamster, Nick, Magdalena Balazinska, Greg Harfst, Hari Balakrishnan, and David R. Karger. 2002. "Infranet: Circumventing Web Censorship and Surveillance." In *Proceedings of the 11th USENIX Security Symposium*, 247–62. Berkeley, Calif.: USENIX.

Ferdinand, Peter. 2000. "The Internet, Democracy and Democratization." *Democratization* 7 (1): 1–17.

Geddes, Barbara, Joseph Wright, and Erica Frantz. 2014. "Autocratic Breakdown and Regime Transitions: A New Data Set." *Perspectives on Politics* 12 (2): 313–31.

Hassanpour, Navid. 2014. "Media Disruption and Revolutionary Unrest: Evidence from Mubarak's Quasi-Experiment." *Political Communication* 31 (1): 1–24.

Hedencrona, Sebastian. 2009. "Twitter—to the Billion?" Global Web Index, August 18. https://blog.globalwebindex.com/chart-of-the-day/twitter-to-the-billion/.

Henderson, Rebecca M., and Kim B. Clark. 1990. "Architectural Innovation: The Reconfiguration of Existing Product Technologies and the Failure of Established Firms." *Administrative Science Quarterly* 35 (1): 9–30.

Hong, Lichan, Gregorio Convertino, and Ed H. Chi. 2011. "Language Matters in Twitter: A Large Scale Study." In *Proceedings of the Fifth International AAAI Conference on Weblogs and Social Media*. Menlo Park, Calif.: AAAI Press.

Howard, Philip N., Aiden Duffy, Deen Freelon, Muzammil M. Hussain, Will Mari, and Marwa Maziad. 2011. *Opening Closed Regimes: What Was the Role of Social Media During the Arab Spring?* Seattle: PITPI.

Johnston, Casey. 2015. "Crime, Punishment, and Russia's Original Social Network." *Motherboard*, February 12. https://motherboard.vice.com/en_us/article/vvbq73/v-for-vkontakte.

Kalathil, Shanthi, and Taylor C. Boas. 2010. *Open Networks, Closed Regimes: The Impact of the Internet on Authoritarian Rule*. Washington, D.C.: Carnegie Endowment for International Peace.

Katz, Michael L., and Carl Shapiro. 1985. "Network Externalities, Competition, and Compatibility." *American Economic Review* 75 (3): 424–40.

Kelly, Sanja, Madeline Earp, Laura Reed, Adrian Shahbaz, and Mai Truong. 2014. "Tightening the Net: Governments Expand Online Controls." Freedom House. https://freedomhouse.org/report/freedom-net/2014/tightening-net-governments.

King, Gary, Jennifer Pan, and Margaret E. Roberts. 2013. "How Censorship in China Allows Government Criticism but Silences Collective Expression." *American Political Science Review* 107 (2): 1–18.

———. 2014. "Reverse-Engineering Censorship in China: Randomized Experimentation and Participant Observation." *Science* 345 (6199): 1–10.

Kotowski, Timo. 2009. "Twitter-Alternativen: Zwitscher-Küken aus aller Welt." Spiegel Online, May 22. https://bit.ly/2L73zkX.

Li, Jessica, and H. R. Rao. 2010. "Twitter as a Rapid Response News Service: An Exploration in the Context of the 2008 China Earthquake." *Electronic Journal of Information Systems in Developing Countries* 42: 1–22.

Lindtner, Silvia, and Marcella Szablewicz. 2011. "China's Many Internets: Participation and Digital Game Play Across a Changing Technology Landscape." In *Online Society in China: Creating, Celebrating, and Instrumentalising the Online Carnival*, edited by David Herold and Peter Marolt, 89–105. New York: Routledge.

Lipman, Maria. 2005. "Constrained or Irrelevant: The Media in Putin's Russia." *Current History* 104 (684): 319–24.

Lotan, Gilad, Erhardt Graeff, Mike Ananny, Devin Gaffney, Ian Pearce, and danah boyd. 2011. "The Revolutions Were Tweeted: Information Flows During the

2011 Tunisian and Egyptian Revolutions." *International Journal of Communication* 5 (31): 1375–405.

Lu, Jia. 2011. "American Internet Companies' Predicament in China: Google, eBay, and MSN Messenger." *Javnost/The Public* 18 (1): 75–91.

MacKinnon, Rebecca. 2008. "Flatter World and Thicker Walls? Blogs, Censorship and Civic Discourse in China." *Public Choice* 134 (1–2): 31–46.

———. 2009. "China's Censorship 2.0: How Companies Censor Bloggers." *First Monday* 14 (2).

———. 2012. *Consent of the Networked: The Worldwide Struggle for Internet Freedom.* New York: Basic Books.

McMillan, John, and Pablo Zoido. 2004. "How to Subvert Democracy: Montesinos in Peru." *Journal of Economic Perspectives* 18 (4): 69–92.

Meng, Zhaoli, and Meiyun Zuo. 2008. "Why MSN Lost to QQ in China Market? Different Privacy Protection Design." *International Journal of Security and Its Applications* 2 (4): 81–87.

Moore, Malcolm. 2008. "China Earthquake Brings Out Citizen Journalists." *Telegraph*, May 12. https://www.telegraph.co.uk/news/worldnews/asia/china/1950212/China-earthquake-brings-out-citizen-journalists.html.

Morozov, Evgeny. 2012. *The Net Delusion: The Dark Side of Internet Freedom.* New York: Public Affairs.

Murdoch, Steven J., and Ross Anderson. 2008. "Tools and Technology of Internet Filtering." In *Access Denied: The Practice and Policy of Global Internet Filtering*, edited by Ronald Deibert, John Palfrey, Rafal Rohozinski, and Jonathan Zittrain, 57–72. Cambridge, Mass.: MIT Press.

Pan, Jennifer. 2017. "How Market Dynamics of Domestic and Foreign Social Media Firms Shape Strategies of Internet Censorship." *Problems of Post-Communism* 64 (3–4): 167–88.

Pariser, Eli. 2011. *The Filter Bubble: What the Internet Is Hiding from You.* London: Penguin.

Rochet, Jean-Charles, and Jean Tirole. 2003. "Platform Competition in Two-Sided Markets." *Journal of the European Economic Association* 1 (4): 990–1029.

Stepanova, Ekaterina. 2011. "The Role of Information Communication Technologies in the 'Arab Spring.'" *Ponars Eurasia* 15: 1–6.

Stockmann, Daniela. 2013. *Media Commercialization and Authoritarian Rule in China.* New York: Cambridge University Press.

Stockmann, Daniela, and Mary E. Gallagher. 2011. "Remote Control: How the Media Sustain Authoritarian Rule in China." *Comparative Political Studies* 44 (4): 436–67.

Stone, Brad, and Bruce Einhorn. 2010. "How Baidu Won China." *Bloomberg Businessweek*, November 11. https://www.bloomberg.com/news/articles/2010-11-11/how-baidu-won-china.

Sullivan, Jonathan. 2012. "A Tale of Two Microblogs in China." *Media, Culture and Society* 34 (6): 773–83.

Van Niekerk, Brett, Kiru Pillay, and Manoj Maharaj. 2011. "Analyzing the Role of ICTs in the Tunisian and Egyptian Unrest from an Information Warfare Perspective." *International Journal of Communication* 5 (11): 1406–16.

Weber, Rolf H. 2011. "Politics Through Social Networks and Politics by Government Blocking: Do We Need New Rules?" *International Journal of Communication* 5 (9): 1186–94.

Wilson, Christopher, and Alexandra Dunn. 2011. "Digital Media in the Egyptian Revolution: Descriptive Analysis from the Tahrir Data Set." *International Journal of Communication* 5 (25): 1248–72.

Wu, Jane Peihusn, and Terrill L. Frantz. 2011. "Largest IM Platform in China—Tencent's QQ." *Journal of Business Case Studies* 8 (1): 95–102.

Yang, Guobin. 2006. "Activists Beyond Virtual Borders: Internet-Mediated Networks and Informational Politics in China." *First Monday* 7. http://firstmonday.org/ojs/index.php/fm/article/view/1609.

———. 2009. *The Power of the Internet in China*. New York: Columbia University Press.

Zhang, Lixuan, and Iryna Pentina. 2012. "Motivations and Usage Patterns of Weibo." *Cyberpsychology, Behavior, and Social Networking* 15 (6): 312–17.

Zhao, Yuezhi. 1998. *Media, Market, and Democracy in China: Between the Party Line and the Bottom Line*. Champaign: University of Illinois Press.

Zhu, Tao, David Phipps, Adam Pridgen, Jedidiah R. Crandall, and Dan S. Wallach. 2013. "The Velocity of Censorship: High-Fidelity Detection of Microblog Post Deletions." In *Proceedings of the 22nd USENIX Conference on Security*, 227–240. Berkeley, Calif.: USENIX.

Zuckerman, Ethan, Hal Roberts, Ryan McGrady, Jillian York, and John Palfrey. 2010. *Distributed Denial of Service Attacks Against Independent Media and Human Rights Sites*. Cambridge, Mass.: Berkman Center for Internet and Society.

CHAPTER 9

The Measure of a Movement: Quantifying Black Lives Matter's Social Media Power

Deen Freelon

Social media has become an essential tool for twenty-first-century social movements as they pursue their various causes. From Cairo to Ferguson and seemingly everywhere in between, online traces of movement activity are ubiquitous. Social movement uses of digital tools is a thriving research area, with studies applying both qualitative and quantitative methods to understand the nature and magnitude of this phenomenon. Most researchers in this area seem to agree that social media can be consequential in at least some contexts, though there is less agreement on exactly how (Bennett and Segerberg 2012; Howard et al. 2011; Shirky 2011).

Much of this research is case-based, focusing on one or a small number of social movements or protest episodes. The present study, which examines the Black Lives Matter movement, is no exception in this regard. However, many case-based studies primarily or solely analyze the movement and its various digital pursuits as opposed to the broader set of actors that interact with one another on the issue. Most popular social media platforms are open enough that movement actors cannot isolate themselves from commentary and criticism from individuals outside the movement. Such outside actors and interests can provide insight into a social movement's capacity to achieve its goals. This capacity is an important type of power, as I will argue below. Yet, while the literature has certainly not ignored questions of power, its ability to measure it empirically online has been limited.

This chapter represents a step toward that scholarly goal. It defines several forms of social media power that are particularly relevant to social movements and proposes accompanying techniques to measure them. Critically, other nonmovement parties to the conversation may also wield these forms of power. In digital conversation spaces where movement-allied, -opposed, and -unaligned interests all jockey for attention, the ability to measure their respective potentials to effect change and control the narrative is important. The conception of power I rely on here draws heavily on Charles Tilly's concept of WUNC (worthiness, unity, numbers, commitment) (Tilly 1999; Tilly and Wood 2013), the components of which he cites as indicators of movement power. Using tweets about police shootings of unarmed black people in 2014 and 2015, I demonstrate that the digital manifestations of three of WUNC's four elements can be measured quantitatively, and argue that these measures constitute consequential forms of social media power.

Power in Social Movements

By definition, every social movement's overarching goal is to effect some sort of social change, be it in individual attitudes, cultural conventions, or institutional policies. Between the decision to begin pressing for a particular change and its ultimate fulfillment lie many proximate goals, the achievement of which increases the likelihood of the desired change. For example, after the principals of the civil rights movement decided to agitate for legislation banning segregation, they and their followers engaged in protests, sit-ins, and other tactics that emphasized the urgency of that change. The success of these tactics—specifically their participation rates, persistence, and perceived legitimacy—contributed to the achievement of the policy goal.

In the social sciences, *power* is an "elementary concept" (Giddens 1987, 7) laden with an abundance of overlapping and incommensurable meanings. A comprehensive review of those meanings is beyond the scope of this chapter, but I will use the term here to refer generally to the ability to spread and control a given message or perspective. This is consistent with Giddens's conception of power as "the capability to intervene in a given set of events so as in some way to alter them" (1987, 7) as well as with Castells's view that power operates "by the construction of meaning on the basis of discourses" (2013, 10). The assumption that shifts in discourse may eventually lead to broader social changes is ingrained in every social movement's communication efforts. Movement-led discussions of (for example) police brutality on social media do not constitute an end in and of itself, but rather one of multiple means of addressing a bigger problem.

Power is also closely associated with perceptions of legitimacy, in that movements perceived as legitimate will generally be in a stronger position to achieve their goals. The communicative components of activism cannot succeed through sheer numbers alone: activists must also argue that their goals and methods deserve the broader public's sympathy and support. For movements that have forsworn violence, persuasion is essential. And when attempts to induce change are directed at public policy, institutional policy, or social attitudes, legitimacy often makes the difference between whether a movement's claims are considered seriously or dismissed outright. The importance of legitimacy to social movements is so paramount it is often simply assumed without further discussion (e.g., in McCarthy and Zald 1977; Williams 1995).

To measure social movements' power in social media, a theoretically informed conceptualization of the sort of power most useful for social movements would be helpful. Charles Tilly's concept of WUNC provides just such a conceptualization (Tilly 1999; Tilly and Wood 2013). WUNC is an acronym whose letters signify *worthiness, unity, numbers,* and *commitment,* all essential elements for social movements to wield adeptly. Tilly describes WUNC as both a defining characteristic of social movements and as a source or index of social movement power. He associates the concept with movement "strength" and notes that its elements "increase the plausibility of the implied threat that the claimant will use its weight to enter, realign, or disrupt the existing polity" (Tilly 1999, 262; see also Vliegenthart and Walgrave 2012). Thus, it is no major conceptual leap to consider WUNC as a form of power in Giddens's and Castells's senses.

Tilly conceives of WUNC as a measurable set of properties. He writes of "high" and "low" values of its four components, which clearly implies possibilities for quantification (Tilly 1999). Yet most empirical applications of the concept seem to be qualitative, with authors describing how the various characteristics of specific social movements fit the WUNC framework (e.g., Agbaria and Mustafa 2012; Bennett and Segerberg 2012; Reese 2009). For example, in developing their theory of connective action, Bennett and Segerberg note that "digitally mediated action networks often seem to be accorded higher levels of WUNC than their more conventional social movement counterparts" (2012, 742). Again, we see a clear suggestion that WUNC can be measured—and in digital contexts, no less—but it is followed by no methodological suggestions as to how.

Digital WUNC: Measuring Contestation Online

Social movements do not communicate in a vacuum: those fortunate enough to attract substantial public attention online will in the process attract allies, opponents, journalists, curious onlookers, would-be entertainers seeking to capitalize on the latest trend, and others. In other words, social movements that use social media inevitably share those spaces with others interested in having their say on the issue in question. Every party to a conversation within a social media space is involved in power negotiations, whether they are aware of it or not. The simple act of sharing one party's message rather than another's contributes to this process. The narratives and perspectives that spread farthest stand the greatest chance of persuading the unconverted, being broadcast through mass media channels, and reaching elites with the power to implement the desired changes.

This in turn suggests that when researchers seek to measure social movements' power online, they should not focus solely on the movement itself. Instead, they should look to the broader set of actors and interests involved in the conversation and measure each one's power. In some cases, the social movement may emerge as the most powerful constituency; in others, movement opponents may gain dominance; and in still others, "neutral" mass media narratives may overwhelm all others. And of course, these arrangements seem likely to change with time. The point is that where social movements are engaged online, the researcher should consider the broader conversations in which they are embedded as systems of power relations with multiple interactants, each of which requires independent measurement.

The concept of *digital WUNC* is an apt one for this task, as it makes explicit the proposition that WUNC takes on specific, measurable forms online. Critical to this proposition is the argument that WUNC can be fruitfully applied to constituencies that are not social movements. With the exception of worthiness, which is not applicable to all non–social movements, I contend that this is both possible and worthwhile. Measuring WUNC's digital manifestations in multiple parties to online conversations involving social movements enables power comparisons between them. Of course, these may or may not reflect analogous power relations between the parties beyond the particular digital platform being studied.

In the following paragraphs I discuss the components of digital WUNC through the example of the Black Lives Matter movement. This requires that I first briefly introduce the movement.

Black Lives Matter

Black Lives Matter (BLM) is a loosely coordinated, nationwide movement dedicated to ending police brutality, which rose to prominence in late 2014. It takes its name from a hashtag started by three black feminist activists—Patrisse Cullors, Alicia Garza, and Opal Tometi—but the movement and the hashtag are not synonymous. BLM has achieved national prominence through their online and offline organizing, obtaining extensive news media coverage and glowing references in music and entertainment television. Participants have cited the importance of social media in helping them pursue their goals, and recent research has supported this claim (Freelon, McIlwain, and Clark 2016; Jackson and Welles 2016; Stephen 2015).

Worthiness

Placing BLM's digital presence into the digital WUNC framework helps us understand how both the movement and the concept operate. I begin with worthiness, perhaps the most difficult of WUNC's components to quantify. Tilly and Wood offer the following offline examples of worthiness: "sober demeanor; neat clothing; presence of clergy, dignitaries, and mothers with children" (2013, 5). Aside from the fact that most BLM participants would likely dismiss these features as the contemptible "politics of respectability" (Higginbotham 1994), digital environments offer few opportunities for demonstrating worthiness in the way Tilly describes it. Aspects of demeanor and dress could be coded in profile pictures and protest photos, but doing so would assume an accurate correspondence between online and offline self-presentation. Many people's profile photos present static self-impressions that cannot be considered indicators of worthiness in a social movement context. Activists may display some aspects of Tilly's worthiness in photos of street protests, but at best, these are merely online displays of offline actions—there is nothing distinctly digital about them.

Given this, it makes more sense to briefly analyze BLM's implementation of worthiness qualitatively. Having self-consciously rejected respectability politics, participants insist through their movement's name that the worthiness of black lives is, quite literally, axiomatic. In other words, no further explanation or proof is required to substantiate the claim, and requests for such proof are inherently antiblack because no comparable requests are made of whites. For BLM, the signs of worthiness cited by Tilly are laborious and ultimately futile attempts to prove a truth that some will never believe. This is one reason BLM protests appear so much less orderly and respectful than the popular image of the civil rights movement, with its well-dressed protesters marching solemnly alongside religious leaders. BLM's most basic assumption is that no amount of unruly conduct can ever diminish the fundamental humanity of the perpetrators, and it is on this belief that the movement's claim to worthiness rests (Harris 2015).

Unity

As a theoretical construct, unity makes a much smoother transition to online contexts than worthiness. Tilly cites the "wearing or bearing of common symbols [and] direct affirmation of a common program or identity" (1999, 261) as key signifiers of unity, among others. In social media contexts in general, and for BLM's online presence in particular, few common symbols are as emblematic as the movement's major hashtags. #Blacklivesmatter is only the best-known among many hashtags that bespeak movement interest and involvement. Creating hashtags based on victims' names after police killings is a common practice, so much so that participants sometimes speak of their fear of "becoming a hashtag" (Moodie-Mills 2015). Participants have also cited hashtags as important sources of information about police killings and the resulting protests (Freelon, McIlwain, and Clark 2016).

Empirically, unity can be expressed through social media as a tendency for a given community to use a small number of hashtags disproportionately more often than others. This indicates that participants are conveying a unified message, particularly when the hashtag in question expresses a normative claim (e.g., #Blacklivesmatter). A lack of consensus in hashtag use suggests, at a minimum, a corresponding lack of unity in messaging, and perhaps also in deeper philosophical or tactical viewpoints. Inequality in hashtag use is a metric that is likely to differ between distinct parties to a conversation, so that they may be compared quantitatively. Qualitative inspection of each community's top hashtags can offer impressions of the kinds of discourses being carried aloft by the power of unity.

Numbers

Of WUNC's four elements, numbers is probably the most straightforward to conceptualize and measure in social media. Counting the participants who post a particular hashtag or keyword is one of the most basic descriptive analyses a social media researcher can conduct. But our task is not quite so simple: while the total number of users in a given data set is certainly worth knowing, what is more interesting for our purposes are the numbers of users associated with each party to the conversation. Until now I have been fairly vague about what I mean by "party," but the time has come to elaborate. A party or a community within a social media conversation is a collection of individuals who share one or more key identity characteristics and regularly discuss the topic at hand (which for us is police brutality). Communities are almost always "led" by high-profile participants with large audiences whose messages are seen much more often than everyone else's. A network analysis technique known as community detection offers an effective means of identifying such communities (see "Data and Methods" below). I use communities as the main unit of analysis throughout this chapter because their structure closely resembles the loose, meso-level associations that make up most social movements.

Once a set of communities has been identified and labeled, the participants in each can be counted just as easily as for the entire data set. It is perhaps self-evident that, barring purchased followers, "bots," and other obfuscatory shenanigans, larger communities generally wield more power.

Commitment

Tilly defines commitment as, among other things, "declarations of readiness to persevere" (1999, 261). Social media allow us to improve on this operational definition and observe perseverance itself directly. This capability relies on the fundamentally longitudinal nature of social media data. Having first disaggregated a social media conversation into multiple communities, and then reconstituted those communities at sequential points in time, it becomes possible to measure how committed each community's participants are. I suggest a simple method of doing so: computing the proportion of participants in a given community at one time period who appear at least once in the following time period. Note that a given participant does not need to appear in the same community in time period 2 as in time period 1—she simply needs to send at least one relevant message in time period 2.

Comparing what we might call the "repeat participation rate" between communities allows us to determine which are most and least committed. High proportions indicate that many participants from a given community are returning to continue promulgating its point of view. Low proportions, in contrast, indicate a high turnover rate and therefore a less committed and less stable community. Commitment expressed in this way sends the message that movements and their interactants will not disperse (digitally speaking) when the next trending topic emerges. No less than for the past century's offline movements, more commitment means more power.

Research Questions

The prospect of measuring digital WUNC within both a social movement and its interactants is, to my knowledge, novel. Therefore, there is little theoretical basis for predicting how various communities of interactants are likely to differ from one another on each individual metric. The data set I describe in the following section offers three communities, each of which fits its own abstract category. There is one social movement (BLM), one countermovement (Political Conservatives, or PC), and one community that does not consistently support or oppose the movement or countermovement (Mainstream News, or MN). If we consider social movements as issue publics strongly interested in their defining issue (Krosnick 1990), we might conjecture that they would exercise the most power in conversations on that issue. However, strong interest does not guarantee strength—if movement opponents have greater access to public attention, for example, they may be able to overwhelm even highly enthusiastic activists. It is also conceivable that mainstream news outlets could draw large numbers of united onlookers at times when major stories break. The phrasing of the following research questions reflects this conceptual uncertainty:

- RQ1: How will the communities compare on the *unity* metric, and how will these comparisons change over time?
- RQ2: How will the communities compare on the *numbers* metric, and how will these comparisons change over time?
- RQ3: How will the communities compare on the *commitment* metric, and how will these comparisons change over time?

Data and Methods

This study analyzes Twitter data pertaining to BLM's main topic of concern, police brutality. I purchased directly from Twitter all public tweets posted during the yearlong period between June 1, 2014 and May 31, 2015 containing at least one of forty-five keywords related to BLM and police killings of black people under questionable circumstances (see Table 9.1). The keywords consist mostly of the full and hashtagged names of twenty black individuals killed by police in 2014 and 2015. I counted a tweet as including a particular name if it contained either the case-insensitive full name or hashtagged name as written below. The resulting data set contains 40,815,975 tweets contributed by 4,435,217 unique users.

The keywords in Table 9.1 were collated from two sources: a series of tweets posted by the NAACP Legal Defense Fund's Twitter account (@naacp_ldf) on December 3, 2014 containing the names of unarmed black people killed by police between 1999 and 2014; and a May 1, 2015 BuzzFeed article listing a number of unarmed black males killed by police in 2014 and 2015 (Quah and Davis 2015).[1] Neither of these lists is necessarily complete, but they were the most comprehensive I could find. From the NAACP list I pulled all of the 2014 names, and from the BuzzFeed list I pulled all names except two, which resulted in a combined total of twenty names.[2] To these I added the hashtags #blacklivesmatter and #ferguson and the phrase "black lives matter" due to their significance to the movement.

I analyzed the tweet data using software I wrote myself in Python.[3] First I separated the authors and full text of all tweets into nine time periods of varying lengths. The boundaries of these time periods were set based on the

Table 9.1. Twitter Keywords and Relevant Metadata

Keyword(s)	*Date Killed*	*Location*	*N of Tweets*
#ferguson	N/A	N/A	21,626,901
"michael brown"/"mike brown"/ #michaelbrown/#mikebrown	8/9/2014	Ferguson, MO	9,360,239
#Blacklivesmatter	N/A	N/A	4,312,599
"eric garner"/#ericgarner	7/17/2014	Staten Island, NY	4,286,350
"freddie gray"/#freddiegray	4/19/2015	Baltimore, MD	2,559,316
"walter scott"/#walterscott	4/4/2015	North Charleston, SC	1,083,316
"tamir rice"/#tamirrice	11/22/2014	Cleveland, OH	1,001,971
"black lives matter"	N/A	N/A	445,514
"john crawford"/#johncrawford	8/5/2014	Beavercreek, OH	331,793
"tony robinson"/#tonyrobinson	3/6/2015	Madison, WI	245,020
"eric harris"/#ericharris	4/2/2015	Tulsa, OK	200,641
"ezell ford"/#ezellford	8/11/2014	Los Angeles, CA	184,141
"akai gurley"/#akaigurley	11/20/2014	Brooklyn, NY	150,966
"kajieme powell"/#kajiemepowell	8/19/2014	St. Louis, MO	102,524
"tanisha anderson"/#tanishaanderson	11/13/2014	Cleveland, OH	27,130
"victor white"/#victorwhite	3/3/2014	New Iberia, LA	27,048
"jordan baker"/#jordanbaker	1/16/2014	Houston, TX	21,565
"jerame reid"/#jeramereid	12/30/2014	Bridgeton, NJ	14,651
"yvette smith"/#yvettesmith	2/16/2014	Bastrop County, TX	13,266
"phillip white"/#philipwhite	3/31/2015	Vineland, NJ	6,756
"dante parker"/#danteparker	8/12/2014	Victorville, CA	5,713
"mckenzie cochran"/#mckenziecochran	1/28/2014	Southfield, MI	1,931
"tyree woodson"/#tyreewoodson	8/5/2014	Baltimore, MD	1,914

ebbs and flows of tweet volume over the data collection period. Table 9.2 lists the nine periods and the events that distinguish them. (For more detailed descriptions and analysis of these periods, see Freelon, McIlwain, and Clark 2016.)

After defining the periods, I created a network edge list for each that connected usernames (nodes) to one another on the basis of retweets or mentions (edges), so that each period was represented by its own network. This was an effective means of analyzing this data, given that well over 80 percent of the tweets consisted of retweets and mentions. Mentions of multiple users within a single tweet were counted as distinct edges. I then generated a set of network communities within each period's edge list using an algorithm called

Table 9.2. Nine Periods of Tweets About Police Brutality

Period	*Date Range*	*Defining Event(s)*
1	6/1/14–7/16/14	None
2	7/17/14–8/8/14	Eric Garner
3	8/9/14–8/31/14	Michael Brown
4	9/1/14–11/23/14	Post-Ferguson protests
5	11/24/14–12/2/14	Darren Wilson nonindictment
6	12/3/14–12/10/14	Daniel Pantaleo nonindictment
7	12/11/14–4/3/15	Various BLM protests
8	4/4/15–4/18/15	Walter Scott
9	4/19/15–5/31/15	Freddie Gray

the Louvain method (Blondel et al. 2008). The Louvain method creates communities by maximizing edge density within communities and minimizing it between communities. For very large networks like these, Louvain creates small numbers of very large communities and large numbers of very small communities (many of which consist of a single user retweeting or mentioning another once). In each period, I analyzed only the ten largest communities, which in most cases accounted for well over half of all users involved in retweets or mentions. A more in-depth justification of this methodological choice is available in Freelon, Lynch, and Aday (2015).

Communities initially emerge from the Louvain algorithm with numerical labels. I qualitatively inspected the usernames, profiles, and tweets of each community's hubs (i.e., its most prominent users) to give it a descriptive label. This process involved a fair degree of subjectivity, and some may have chosen labels other than the ones I chose. However, labeling communities in this way is a well-established practice in network analysis (Bode et al. 2015; Etling et al. 2010; Freelon, Lynch, and Aday 2015).

This process generated a total of ninety network communities (nine time periods x ten communities per period). Using a procedure developed by Freelon, Lynch, and Aday (2015), I ran a Python script that attempted to aggregate these distinct communities into *persistent communities.* A persistent community is a chronological sequence of communities in different periods whose memberships overlap substantially. Each member of a persistent community sequence represents that community's identity at that particular point in time.

The procedure to identify persistent communities operates as follows. In the first step, a Jaccard coefficient weighted by the network in-degree of the top 1 percent of each community is computed between every community from time period 1 and every community from the immediately subsequent time period 2. The Jaccards are weighted by in-degree to account for the fact that participants with high in-degrees contribute proportionately to community cohesion. The procedure finds a match between two communities (one in period 1 and one in period 2) based on two criteria: (1) the weighted Jaccard between them must be higher than all others, and (2) it must exceed 0.25, a threshold chosen based on the interpretability of its results. If both of these criteria are not satisfied, no match is identified. This technique is performed for all possible community pairs between periods 1 and 2 and then continues iteratively with each pair of adjacent periods until it reaches the end.

The persistent communities with the most members represent the most committed parties to the conversation. The procedure described above detected three communities that persisted across seven periods (periods 3 through 9), the maximum number found. These are BLM, Political Conservatives, and Mainstream News.

Black Lives Matter (BLM)

Many of BLM's hubs identified with the Black Lives Matter movement by name. They typically framed police brutality as an oppressive social scourge, emphasizing its disproportionate impact on black people and the urgency of systemic change. BLM was a haven for prominent left-wing activists of color, including DeRay Mckesson (@deray), Johnetta Elzie (@nettaaaaaaaa), Shaun King (@shaunking), Daniel Jose Older (@djolder), Bassem Masri (@bassem_masri), Hands Up United (@handsupunited_), Kayla Reed (@re_invent_ed), @brownblaze, @awkward_duck, and many others.

Political Conservatives (PC)

Beginning during the initial Ferguson protests, a persistent community of politically conservative Twitter users began discussing police brutality issues. Most of the time they vigorously opposed the protesters and their goals, with two major exceptions which are discussed further below. This community was the only one to mount a sustained, high-profile oppositional narrative against the movement—most other communities were either predominantly supportive or unaligned. Some of the top voices here belonged to media personalities Larry Elder (@larryelder), Wayne Dupree (@waynedupreeshow), Pat Dollard (@patdollard), and Sean Hannity (@seanhannity); popular Twitter conservatives Crystal Wright (@gopblackchick) and Amy Mek (@amymek); and conservative media outlets Fox News (@foxnews), the *Washington Times* (@washtimes), and TheBlaze (@theblaze).

Mainstream News (MN)

Followers of this persistent community received their information about police killings, protests, and related events primarily from corporate news outlets like CNN, the *New York Times*, the Associated Press, the *LA Times*, CBS News, and Reuters. Digital-first media outlets such as Mashable, BuzzFeed, the Daily Beast, and the Huffington Post were also sometimes included here, even though they occasionally voiced explicit support for the movement. Most of the hubs in these communities are institutional accounts; although a few individual reporters are present, more are scattered throughout other communities.

Results

RQ1 posits a test of the unity metric, which analyzes the extent to which intracommunity hashtag usage is dominated by a small number of hashtags. To investigate this, I apply the Gini coefficient, which is often used to measure inequality in distributions of national wealth but works equally well for hashtags. Ginis for the unique hashtag counts of the three communities across the seven periods are plotted in Figure 9.1.

Figure 9.1's y-axis shows that the three communities' Ginis all remain quite high throughout the seven periods. Still, BLM's Ginis remain higher than the other two communities', without exception. PC's exceed MN's in all time periods except 8, when the trend is reversed. Overall, these results indicate slight differences in unity between the communities, with the greatest consistent difference between BLM and MN.

Basic descriptive statistics can help us summarize the power comparisons between these three communities across all seven periods. Table 9.3 shows the medians and variances of all hashtag Ginis for each community. The

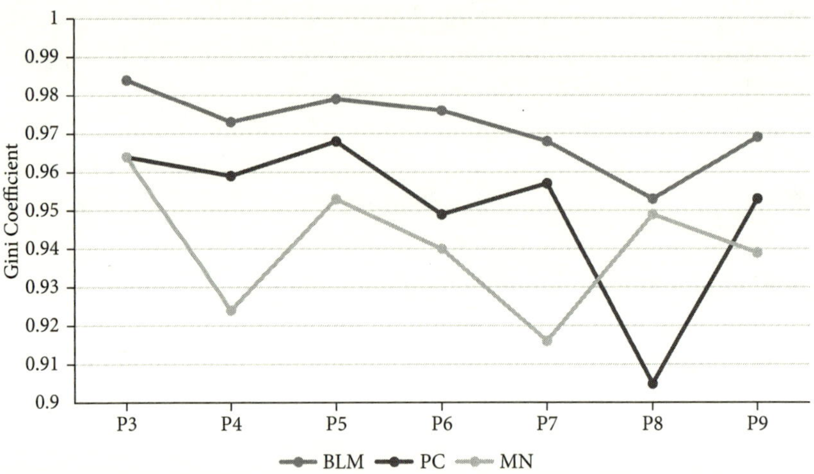

Figure 9.1. Gini coefficients for hashtag inequality for three persistent communities over time

Table 9.3. Medians and Variances of Hashtag Gini Coefficients

Community	*Median*	*Variance*
BLM	0.973	0.000085061
PC	0.957	0.000383061
MN	0.94	0.000236490

medians reveal that overall, BLM was the most unified community, followed by PC, with MN as least unified. These differences are close but consistent. BLM also shows the lowest variance among the three, which, combined with its top-ranked median, indicates a strong capacity to remain on-message. PC's variance was the highest, suggesting that its unity levels may be more strongly influenced by external factors.

RQ2 addresses differences in population numbers between the communities over time. To answer it, I simply plotted each community's sizes (in users) across the same x-axis as Figure 9.1 (see Figure 9.2). Community sizes are determined by the Louvain algorithm.

Intercommunity differences are clearly more pronounced for the numbers metric than for unity. In spite of the low number of data points, it is clear that the population counts for all three communities are strongly correlated.

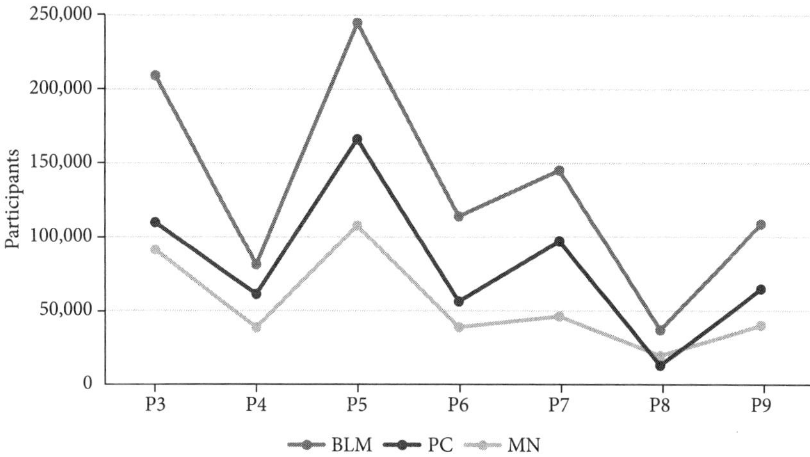

Figure 9.2. Population sizes for three persistent communities over time

Table 9.4. Medians and Variances of Population Counts

Community	*Median*	*Variance*
BLM	114102	4464035145
PC	64728	2027413516
MN	40004	880228944

BLM consistently surpasses the other two communities in size across all periods, although the magnitude of the disparity differs between periods. PC definitively exceeds MN in all periods except 8, during which their sizes are very similar.

Turning to the descriptive statistics (Table 9.4), we see that BLM's median community size is the largest by nearly double, with PC at second and MN third. Given its generally larger audiences, BLM is in a position to circulate its narratives and perspectives much more widely than PC or MN. But BLM's numbers also exhibit a much higher variance than the other two communities, suggesting that this dimension of power is quite fickle for the movement's online component.

RQ3 proposes to compare levels of commitment between the three communities. To do so, I plotted over time each community's repeat participation rate (Figure 9.3), which gives the proportion of community participants in the first of two sequential periods that posted at least once in the latter

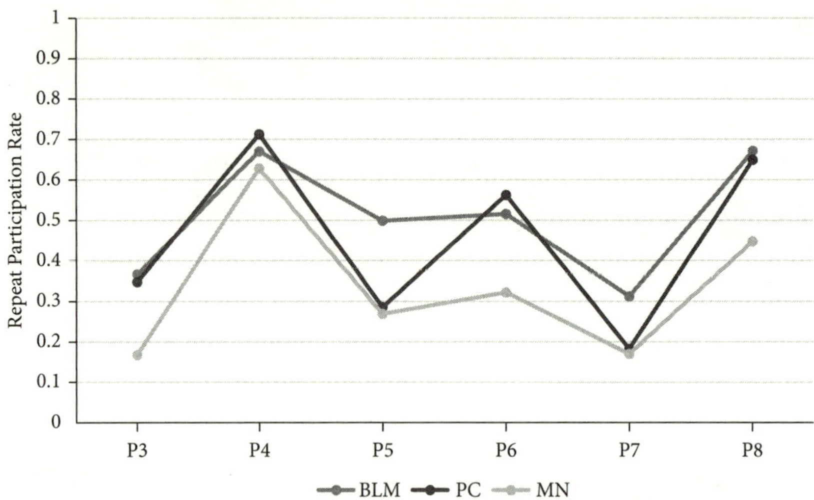

Figure 9.3. Repeat participation rates for three persistent communities over time

Table 9.5. Medians and Variances of Repeat Participation Rates

Community	*Median*	*Variance*
BLM	0.507547	0.015932
PC	0.455221	0.032938
MN	0.29489	0.02286

period. Data points are labeled on the x-axis based on the earlier period in each pair, so that Figure 9.3 contains only six x-axis data points instead of seven (period 9 is omitted).

The results here reveal an interesting pattern. As with previous metrics, BLM participants consistently outperform MN in terms of repeat participation, but PC behaves differently. During some periods, such as 4, 6, and 8, PC's repeat participation rate is very close to or in one case even higher than BLM's. But in periods 5 and 7, PC's rates drop precipitously below BLM's. Neither community consistently outperforms the other in terms of commitment; rather, commitment levels fluctuate in response to external events and the passage of time.

Table 9.5 reveals BLM's median rate to be only slightly higher than PC's, but that MN's is much lower than the other two. Both the movement and its chief opponents appear to be similarly committed, but the news audience experiences very high participant turnover. BLM is also highly consistent in its commitment with the lowest variance of the three, while PC has the highest. This raises the possibility that certain events may be prompting substantial turnover among conservatives, which I discuss below.

Discussion

In this chapter I have proposed and demonstrated several techniques of measuring power in movement-relevant social media conversations. My results contribute to a theoretical understanding of how power circulates in such conversations, such that future research will be able to discern which power metrics are most closely associated with which communities. But even at this preliminary stage, several theoretically relevant conclusions are apparent. First, at least in this case, the party that qualifies as the issue public (which in most cases will be the social movement) bears the highest overall levels of all three metrics. This implies that it wields the most power online. BLM's success in inserting its perspectives into mainstream news accounts and eliciting elite responses is consistent with this finding (Freelon, McIlwain, and Clark 2016).

However, BLM's dominance is not consistent in magnitude across metrics or across time. While it is invariably the most numerous community, it runs very close to or falls below one of the other metrics on at least one occasion. The general trend toward decreasing hashtag unity may indicate the movement's widening focus on multiple victims, as opposed to the overwhelming focus on Michael Brown and Eric Garner that dominated the earlier periods (Freelon, McIlwain, and Clark 2016). On the other hand, this metric varies within an extremely narrow range, so some of these vicissitudes could be random. This is less likely with the comparatively steep drops in PC's unity from period 5 to period 6 and from period 7 to period 8. These may have something to do with the fact that conservatives were split on how to interpret the nonindictment of Eric Garner's killer, which occurred during period 6, and the Walter Scott shooting, which occurred during period 8. Some conservatives condemned the police's actions in these cases while others continued to castigate the movement (Freelon, McIlwain, and Clark 2016). In any case, it seems reasonable to conclude that the dynamics of online power may change quickly in response to major events.

Indeed, some of the communities analyzed here appear more sensitive to the passage of time and outside events than others. On the unity and commitment metrics, BLM is less sensitive than PC and MN, but on numbers, it features the highest variance. Ideally, a social movement would want to rank highly on all metrics and deviate as little as possible to project a sustained impression of online power. Of course, this may not be possible given all the external factors that could potentially influence online unity, numbers, and commitment. On the other hand, nonmovement participants may have less incentive to engage consistently, being motivated instead by intense media attention. The evidence is mixed on this possibility—more research will help to clarify the situation.

As we build toward a more comprehensive theory of social media power for social movements, we must consider these metrics not only as dependent variables, but also as independent variables. Not only should we search for factors like external events and the community's relationship to the issue that could influence the metrics, we should also investigate the extent to which these metrics actually behave as power indicators should. For example, if unity, numbers, and commitment as I have operationalized them here denote power in any meaningful sense, they ought to be correlated with results such as media coverage, public perceptions of issue importance, issue mentions by politicians, and (over the long term) policy changes in the desired direction. Otherwise, they amount to little more than slacktivism (Christensen 2011), and movements would be well advised to use social media differently or abandon it altogether.

The suggestion that indicators of online power be evaluated in part by their association with desired results may ultimately move this research enterprise away from its roots in WUNC. WUNC is an attractive starting point for the quantitative measurement of online social movement power because of its theoretical pedigree and its conceptual fit with readily accessible digital traces. Yet, if digital WUNC as defined here cannot be empirically associated with desired results, several paths forward present themselves. Researchers may attempt to operationalize the components of WUNC in new ways, choose to work with alternative frameworks, or work backward from social movement desiderata to try to inductively discover online traces that are consistently associated with them. These possibilities remind us to keep our measures of power as closely tied to our foundational definitions thereof as possible.

The analysis presented above highlights key challenges for researchers interested in contributing to this research area. The low number of data points precludes the application of appropriately powered statistical models that might help elucidate the dynamics of social media power. Unfortunately, the qualitative work involved in labeling network communities is painstaking, and it usually must be performed by a subject matter expert. For most social media platforms, it requires recognizing the shared identities of each community's top members and accurately interpreting what they say. The amount of effort required to do this on a scale large enough to create statistically viable data sets is daunting, to say the least.

At the same time, my findings suggest that much interesting work can be conducted without elaborate statistical modeling. Simple longitudinal charts can reveal how distributions of power change over time, which in turn feeds theories of whose discourses predominate and under what conditions. An in-depth understanding of the event timeline can help explain how and why a movement's power rose or fell at particular times. Analysis of the extent to which the metrics point in the same direction or diverge can offer a degree of clarity and confidence in the conclusions. Ultimately, these metrics may lend themselves more to a mixed-methods approach in which quantitative data is closely interpreted in light of deep subject matter expertise and existing theory.

The true measure of any social research endeavor is whether it reveals anything of value about the world. The general pursuit of measuring power in digital media spaces should interest any research community that cares about power as a social phenomenon. The suggestions I propose here are intended to contribute to that pursuit; however, there are certainly other methods of measuring online power, and the current ones may need to be adapted for platforms other than Twitter. But their origins in WUNC—an established theoretical framework in the social movement literature—make the current metrics especially attractive for researchers studying online movement activity.

Notes

1. The first tweet in this series is here: https://twitter.com/naacp_ldf/status/540250644658278401.

2. Dontre Hamilton and Rumain Brisbon's names did not make it onto our final list due to a clerical error.

3. Most of this software is available through the Python module TSM, which can be found here: http://github.com/dfreelon/tsm.

References

Agbaria, A. K., and M. Mustafa. 2012. "Two States for Three Peoples: The 'Palestinian-Israeli' in the Future Vision Documents of the Palestinians in Israel." *Ethnic and Racial Studies* 35 (4): 718–36. http://doi.org/10.1080/01419870.2011.598234.

Bennett, W. L., and A. Segerberg. 2012. "The Logic of Connective Action: Digital Media and the Personalization of Contentious Politics." *Information, Communication and Society* 15 (5): 739–68. http://doi.org/10.1080/1369118X.2012.670661.

Blondel, V. D., J.-L. Guillaume, R., Lambiotte, and E. Lefebvre. 2008. "Fast Unfolding of Communities in Large Networks." *Journal of Statistical Mechanics: Theory and Experiment* 2008 (10): 10008.

Bode, L., A. Hanna, J. Yang, and D. V. Shah. 2015. "Candidate Networks, Citizen Clusters, and Political Expression: Strategic Hashtag Use in the 2010 Midterms." *ANNALS of the American Academy of Political and Social Science* 659 (1): 149–65. http://doi.org/10.1177/0002716214563923.

Castells, M. 2013. *Communication Power*. New York: Oxford University Press.

Christensen, H. S. 2011. "Political Activities on the Internet: Slacktivism or Political Participation by Other Means?" *First Monday* 16 (2). http://doi.org/10.5210/fm.v16i2.3336.

Etling, B., J. Kelly, R. Faris, and J. Palfrey. 2010. "Mapping the Arabic Blogosphere: Politics and Dissent Online." *New Media and Society* 12 (8): 1225–43. http://doi.org/10.1177/1461444810385096.

Freelon, D., M. Lynch, and S. Aday. 2015. "Online Fragmentation in Wartime: A Longitudinal Analysis of Tweets About Syria, 2011–2013." *ANNALS of the American Academy of Political and Social Science* 659 (1): 166–79. http://doi.org/10.1177/0002716214563921.

Freelon, D., C. McIlwain, and M. D. Clark. 2016. *Beyond the Hashtags: #Ferguson, #Blacklivesmatter, and the Online Struggle for Offline Justice*. Washington, D.C.: Center for Media and Social Impact, American University. http://cmsimpact.org/blmreport.

Giddens, A. 1987. *A Contemporary Critique of Historical Materialism: The Nation-State and Violence*. Berkeley: University of California Press.

Harris, Fredrick C. 2015. "The Next Civil Rights Movement?" *Dissent*, Summer. https://www.dissentmagazine.org/article/black-lives-matter-new-civil-rights-movement-fredrick-harris.

Higginbotham, E. B. 1994. *Righteous Discontent: The Women's Movement in the Black Baptist Church, 1880–1920*. Cambridge, Mass.: Harvard University Press.

Howard, P. N., A. Duffy, D. Freelon, M. Hussain, W. Mari, and M. Maziad. 2011. *Opening Closed Regimes: What Was the Role of Social Media During the Arab Spring?* Project on Information Technology and Political Islam. http://pitpi.org/wp-content/uploads/2013/02/2011_Howard-Duffy-Freelon-Hussain-Mari-Mazaid_pITPI.pdf.

Jackson, S. J., and B. F. Welles. 2016. "#Ferguson Is Everywhere: Initiators in Emerging Counterpublic Networks." *Information, Communication and Society* 19 (3): 397–418. http://doi.org/10.1080/1369118X.2015.1106571.

Krosnick, J. A. 1990. "Government Policy and Citizen Passion: A Study of Issue Publics in Contemporary America." *Political Behavior* 12 (1): 59–92. http://doi.org/10.1007/BF00992332.

McCarthy, J. D., and M. N. Zald. 1977. "Resource Mobilization and Social Movements: A Partial Theory." *American Journal of Sociology* 82 (6): 1212–41.

Moodie-Mills, D. 2015. "OpEd: Are We All Just One Bullet Away from Becoming a Hashtag?" NBC News, April 8. http://www.nbcnews.com/storyline/walter-scott-shooting/oped-are-we-all-just-one-bullet-away-becoming-hashtag-n338111.

Quah, N., and L. E. Davis. 2015. "Here's a Timeline of Unarmed Black People Killed by Police over Past Year." BuzzFeed, May 1. http://www.buzzfeed.com/nicholasquah/heres-a-timeline-of-unarmed-black-men-killed-by-police-over.

Reese, A. 2009. "Framing April 6: Discursive Dominance in the Egyptian Print Media." *Arab Media & Society*, May 6. https://www.arabmediasociety.com/framing-april-6-discursive-dominance-in-the-egyptian-print-media/.

Shirky, C. 2011. "The Political Power of Social Media: Technology, the Public Sphere, and Political Change." *Foreign Affairs* 90: 28.

Stephen, B. 2015. "Social Media Helps Black Lives Matter Fight the Power." *WIRED*, October 21. http://www.wired.com/2015/10/how-black-lives-matter-uses-social-media-to-fight-the-power/.

Tilly, C. 1999. "Conclusion: From Interactions to Outcomes in Social Movements." In *How Social Movements Matter*, edited by M. Giugni, D. McAdam, and C. Tilly, 253–70. Minneapolis: University of Minnesota Press.

Tilly, C., and L. J. Wood. 2013. *Social Movements 1768–2012*. New York: Routledge.

Vliegenthart, R., and S. Walgrave. 2012. "The Interdependency of Mass Media and Social Movements." In *The Sage Handbook of Political Communication*, edited by H. Semetko and M. Scammell, 387–98. Thousand Oaks, Calif.: Sage.

Williams, R. H. 1995. "Constructing the Public Good: Social Movements and Cultural Resources." *Social Problems* 42 (1): 124–44. http://doi.org/10.2307/3097008.

PART IV

Regulating Digital Democracies

CHAPTER 10

Must Privacy Give Way to Use Regulation?

Helen Nissenbaum

Prologue

In "Big Data's End Run Around Anonymity and Consent,"[1] Solon Barocas and I demonstrated that two mainstays of privacy regulation were fatally challenged by technical capabilities of data science. It was not that consent and anonymity no longer performed any useful function, but no longer could we count on them for the critical functions they had previously performed—consent as privacy's gatekeeper, anonymity as a boundary for privacy's remit. Although we warned against confusing the *means* of protecting privacy, namely, consent and anonymity, with privacy *itself*, understood as appropriate flow, we realized that our article could lend force to a position steadily gathering momentum in the academy, information industries, and public policy. The position is that since privacy, insofar as it restricts information collection, is untenable, attention should focus instead on how information is used. The present chapter dissects this position—what it means and whether its worldview is inevitable in light of data science—and ultimately finds it flawed.

Privacy Skeptics

In January 1999 Scott McNealy, then CEO of Sun Microsystems, brashly threw down the gauntlet, saying, "You have zero privacy anyway. Get over it!"[2] Repeated countless times since then, the statement hardly bore serious consideration, partly because the conception of privacy McNealy presumed was muddled and partly because while threatened, privacy is far from dead, and continues to inspire defenders. Nevertheless, there was no denying the popular appeal of this "bad-boy" stance, which has resurfaced in various guises and versions. David Brin's popular book *The Transparent Society* (1998),[3] another instance, asserts that privacy, in light of technological advancement, is no longer feasible, and is also no longer desirable. Instead, he supports total transparency, arguing that this would advance the cause of weaker parties, those captured in the webs of surveillance. With transparency, the weaker can turn the tables on the stronger by holding them accountable for their actions. Big data and data science has yielded its own bad-boy stance: forget about restricting information collection; focus on restricting its uses instead.[4]

I would have liked to dismiss these pronouncements either as fringe provocations or as venal ploys of the information sector, including obvious beneficiaries such as Google, Facebook, Amazon, and Twitter, and less publicly visible actors such as Acxiom, IMS Health, and LexisNexis. Other commercial actors, though not information product providers, telecommunications companies, financial companies, insurance companies, media and publishing companies, and, increasingly, retail merchants,[5] also stand to benefit from reduced constraints on collection. Outside the commercial realm, too, many actors eagerly collect, record, and hold on to data without restraint, including governmental agencies, utilities companies, healthcare organizations, educational institutions, and a range of not-for-profit public interest organizations. Unlike previous bad-boy stances, the contemporary position has captured mainstream interest. A technological infrastructure designed to capture data, the imperative of data-driven institutional bureaucracies, and a "horses out the barn" stance all point to the futility of resistance.

This chapter argues that the push to deregulate collection is problematic and possibly even dangerous. Before establishing this conclusion, however, the first step is to expose deep conceptual ambiguities in the position statement and to establish terminological consistency.

Introducing Big Data Exceptionalism (BDE)

It is a shame one cannot rest an argument on anecdotal observations, because it would then be possible to refer to the countless conference panels and presentations at which speakers, with a wave of a hand, relegate collection restrictions to the zone of the impossible and characterize privacy as hopelessly passé. The term I have coined for the claim that the regulation of collection—no longer tenable in light of big data—must be ceded to the regulation of use is *big data exceptionalism*, or BDE. More a convenient label than a precise definition, BDE refers to a class of generally similar claims, further explicated throughout the rest of the chapter. Although written accounts are less numerous than the anecdotal, those that exist provide a window into the position and its variations.

One such account can be found in the report of the President's Council of Advisors on Science and Technology (PCAST), *Big Data and Privacy: A Technological Perspective*, which asserts that

> policy attention should focus more on the actual uses of big data and less on its collection and analysis. By actual uses, we mean the specific events where something happens that can cause an adverse consequence or harm to an individual or class of individuals. In the context of big data, these events ("uses") are almost always actions of a computer program or app interacting either with the raw data or with the fruits of analysis of those data. In this formulation, it is not the data themselves that cause the harm nor the program itself (absent any data), but the confluence of the two. These "use" events (in commerce, by government, or by individuals) embody the necessary specificity to be the subject of regulation. By contrast, PCAST judges that policies focused on the regulation of data collection, storage, retention, a priori limitations on applications, and analysis (absent identifiable actual uses of the data or products of analysis) are unlikely to yield effective strategies for improving privacy. Such policies would be unlikely to scale over time, or be enforceable by other than severe and economically damaging measures.[6]

In another account, Michael Seemann offers a different rationale: "So instead of trying to defend privacy against surveillance, we should be fighting institutionalized punishment. Authoritarian border controls, racist police cohorts, homophobic social structures, inequality in health and welfare systems, and institutional discrimination are the true danger zones in terms of surveillance. Above all, the state itself, with its monopoly on force and its sweeping claims to regulatory authority, is the source of most of the threat scenarios that *do* jeopardize freedom by way of surveillance."[7] He agrees with Jane Yakowitz that privacy is selfish as "open data is a major source of social welfare."[8] According to Seemann, new capabilities call for a new orientation toward data regulation: "In the Old Game, it was often purposeful to enforce data control in order to limit existing powers. . . . Privacy was intended to shield civilians from the control exerted by institutions. In the New Game, however, this approach no longer works, and in fact, it may produce exactly the opposite effects. . . . Data protection requirements give platforms reason to shut themselves off, limiting their interoperability, and reinforcing lock-in effects."[9] He continues, "So instead of demanding more privacy, we should convince platform operators to open up their data. Because the more open the data becomes, and the more queries can be applied to it, the easier it will be to fence in the power of platforms."[10]

One of the clearest expressions is found in an essay by Craig Mundie, senior advisor to the CEO and former chief research and strategy officer of Microsoft:

> Today, the widespread and perpetual collection and storage of personal data have become practically inevitable. Every day, people knowingly provide enormous amounts of data to a wide array of organizations, including government agencies, Internet service providers, telecommunications companies, and financial firms. Such organizations—and many other kinds, as well—also obtain massive quantities of data through "passive" collection, when people provide data in the act of doing something else: for example, by simply moving from one place to another while carrying a GPS-enabled cell phone. Indeed, there is hardly any part of one's life that does not emit some sort of "data exhaust" as a byproduct. And it has become virtually impossible for someone to know exactly how much of his data is out there or where it is stored. Meanwhile, ever more powerful processors and servers have made it possible to analyze all this data and to generate new insights and inferences about individual preferences and behavior.
>
> This is the reality of the era of "big data," which has rendered obsolete the current approach to protecting individual privacy and civil liberties. Today's laws and regulations focus largely on controlling the collection and retention of personal data, an approach that is becoming impractical for individuals, while also potentially cutting

> off future uses of data that could benefit society. The time has come for a new approach: shifting the focus from limiting the collection and retention of data to controlling data at the most important point—the moment when it is used.[11]

Bert-Jaap Koops, an eminent EU legal scholar, addressing the question "How can data protection meet the challenge of decisions increasingly being taken on the basis of large-scale, complex, and multi-purpose processes of matching and mining enormous amounts of data?," answers that "the focus in data protection should shift from ex ante regulation of data processing to ex post regulation of decision-making," supporting "an alternative approach, one that focuses less on data minimisation, user control, and procedural accountability, but instead directs its arrows at the outcome of computation-based decision making: the decision itself."[12]

Reporting on a series of international, regional discussions about privacy and big data, Viktor Mayer-Schonberger and Fred Cate observe that "one of the most widely discussed alternatives was focusing more attention on the 'use' of personal information rather than on its 'collection,' given the increasingly pervasive nature of data collection and surveillance, inexpensive data storage and sharing, and the development of valuable new uses for personal data."[13] Although constraints on collection may be necessary in exceptional cases, the focus should be on clarifying what "use" covers, and what outcomes should be considered when analyzing the associated costs and benefits.

Finally, in "Big Data for All: Privacy and User Control in the Age of Analytics," Omer Tene and Jules Polonetsky call for a retrenchment of data minimization, a pillar of privacy regulation that restricts collection and retention of data based on expressed purposes. They observe, "The big data business model is antithetical to data minimization. It incentivizes collection of more data for longer periods of time. It is aimed precisely at those unanticipated secondary uses, the 'crown jewels' of big data. After all, who could have anticipated that Bing search queries would be used to unearth harmful drug interactions?" They continue, "Legal rules collide with technological and business realities. Organizations today collect and retain personal data through multiple channels including the Internet, mobile, biological and industrial sensors, video, e-mail, and social networking tools. Modern organizations amass data collected directly from individuals or third parties, and they harvest private, semi-public (e.g., Facebook), or public (e.g., the electoral roll) sources. Data minimization is simply no longer the market norm."[14]

The common thread running through each of these statements seems to be that regulatory effort should attend to data use rather than data collection, in light of big data. What they *really* mean, however, is impossible to establish before unraveling terminological ambiguities and incompatible supporting arguments.

Ambiguities: Privacy

One source of ambiguity is the conception of privacy underlying different accounts of BDE. In Michael Seemann's "big data world order," for instance, privacy, taken to mean the suppression of data, does not empower individuals but entrenches the powers of overbearing government and commercial actors. Pitting big data's benefits against privacy, Seemann implies that we can have big data or privacy but not both; we must have big data, ergo, no privacy. In contrast, other proponents of BDE see no direct conflict with privacy. They seem ready to say, "If we really want to protect privacy, we must protect against harmful uses of information (not against collection)." These accounts do not join the chorus—either privacy or big data, but not both—but urge changes in how we think about privacy protection in light of big data.

These proponents of big data exceptionalism often identify privacy protection with compliance with Fair Information Practices (FIPs) in the influential OECD Privacy Principles, including Collection Limitation, Data Quality, Purpose Specification, Use Limitation, Safeguards, Openness, Individual Participation, and Accountability. Like international experts, such as Bert-Jaap Koops, who are troubled by the incongruity of big data practices with traditional FIPs principles,[15] some have suggested revised formulations of FIPs. These revised formulations would qualify or relax one or more of the principles, such as those requiring advance specification of purpose and fine-grained informed consent, for any departures from specified purpose. Relaxing traditional formulations so as not to obstruct machinations of big data, they suggest filling the gaps with strategic cost-benefit analyses to justify noncompliant uses. In sections that follow, I challenge this approach.

In my own view, when considering the triad—privacy, FIPs, big data—I will say only that "something's gotta give," and that "something" is FIPs. As an alternative, the theory of contextual integrity (CI) offers a less brittle conception of privacy in the face of challenges from big data.[16] According to it, privacy is about the appropriate flow of personal information, not, as other theories assert, control or secrecy. Flow is appropriate when it complies with expectations, that is, with social, informational norms specific to contexts (e.g., education, healthcare, political citizenship, home life, etc.). Contextual informational norms (also called privacy norms) prescribe flows of certain types of information from senders to recipients, about data subjects (acting in context-defined capacities), under certain constraints, called "transmission principles." Thus, when a patient shares health information with his or her physician *in confidence*, the transmission principle is confidentiality, and when police seek incriminating evidence in a suspect's home *with a warrant*, with-a-warrant is the transmission principle. Whereas FIPs-based accounts typically hold informed choice to be necessary and sufficient for privacy (except, arguably, in the few areas covered by statutory protections), CI considers it to be merely one among countless transmission principles.[17] Unlike conceptions of privacy grounded in FIPs, CI need not always require ex ante consent from the data subject, but instead may impose substantive constraints on illegitimate information flows.

Contextual integrity is upheld when information practices comply with informational norms. Norm transgressions are not necessarily condemned but instead are flagged for further analysis. This applies to countless disruptions resulting from deployments of computational and digital systems that shift what information is disseminated to which recipients under what constraints. A presumption favoring norm compliance inevitably triggers questions about why entrenched practices deserve to be favored in this way, whether through law or any other regulatory modality.[18] To this, CI answers that entrenched practices are likely to reflect a settled accommodation of interests and unlikely to infringe on conspicuously ethical and political values (e.g., autonomy, fairness, social justice, security), and may be well calibrated with contextual ends and purposes. If, however, disruptive flows improve on entrenched flows in these ways, they may legitimately replace them.

Taking *privacy* to mean contextual integrity, *collection* refers to the class of flows of information emanating from data subjects into the hands of collecting agents, or *recipients*. Ascertaining whether collection respects privacy means assessing its compliance with preexisting informational norms, or, where not, evaluating its impact on relevant interests, ethical and political values, and contextual purposes and values. As such, privacy as contextual integrity rejects BDE's blanket assertion that this particular class of flows does not warrant regulation, irrespective of the values of parameters—subject, sender, recipient, information type, and transmission principle. In return, BDE proponents reject CI's assertion that collection itself can be assessed as acceptable or unacceptable, holding that carefully regulating data usage is sufficient. Whether the BDE challenge holds up to scrutiny is the crux of this chapter; the first obstacle to characterizing the substantive meaning of BDE, however, is locating a coherent conceptual line between collection and use. As shown below, this goal is virtually unattainable.

What Is Collection? What Is Use?

A clear understanding of use and collection is critical; otherwise, the fundamental thesis—that only use and not collection should be regulated—eludes comprehension, let alone evaluation. Despite confidently urging differential treatment, proponents have remained silent on the precise meanings of these central concepts, and we are left to surmise them from common usage and intuition.

You may be thinking that not much rides on sharp lines. After all, countless distinctions drawn with natural language concepts have supported ethical, political, and practical deliberations, despite their fuzzy borders. These cases work, it seems, because typical instances are clear, while rare or exceptional cases falling at the border need not undercut the utility of the distinctions. Theoretical jargon may offer greater precision, but rich concepts drawn from natural language can spike imagination and have a broader appeal. It may appear that the case of collection and use fits this model because intuition is strong in certain instances, such as online merchants *collecting* information from consumers when they complete online order forms and *using* information about consumers' purchases when recommending items of interest to them or delivering goods to consumers' addresses. Unlike other politically sensitive distinctions, however, the fuzzy boundary between use and collection ensnares not just a mere handful of exceptional and rare cases, which may be handled on a case-by-case, ad hoc basis.

Collection and use may once have fit the model of other politically useful if fuzzy dichotomies with "use" implying consequential action, causation, and agency and "collection" implying passivity, reaction, and a mere garnering of material lying about. The cultural implication of collection is one of innocuous, often beneficial and legitimate "cleaning up" (e.g., garbage collection, church collection). Use tends to be ambiguous because it could imply the harmful as readily as the beneficial. As such, collection can be left alone while use is deserving of guidance and oversight.[19] With the emergence of big data technologies, the borderline has become less defined, now capturing a broad swath of vexing challenges, including practices that mark radical departures from the familiar.

The story of big data told by enthusiastic academics, policy makers, activists, and pundits centers on data science and technology and their unprecedented deployment.[20] They point to the confluence of mathematical discovery and computational insights with feats of engineering, the existence of global digital networks that connect fixed and mobile devices, and a layered software infrastructure with prodigious capacities to collect, amass, store, and distribute data. Sheer bulk is but one factor; another is the diversity of input and data capture modalities. Increasingly sensitive and sophisticated sensing apparatus renders digital what its sensors detect and capture, thereby making it available for quantitative and statistical analysis and networked distribution. These novel data sources supply existing stockpiles drawn from traditional data sources as well as from Internet mediated activity, mobile phones, wearables, self-tracking devices (the so-called Internet of Things)—generally, the ephemera of everyday life, which, through device and platform conduits, are permanently imprinted as data. Dimensions of experience and expression, affect, sound, text, image, video, type and strength of relationships (social network graphs), biological characteristics ("biometrics"), even "brain waves" indicative of thought patterns and sensations, to name a few things that are grist for the data mill—are *datafied*, a term invented to label the transformation of phenomena into collectable and usable data.[21]

Techniques for creating databases, preparing data, extracting knowledge and utility from data (even unstructured data), seeing complex patterns, and rendering models through statistical analysis and machine learning are coalescing in the disciplinary field of data science. Its quest to make sense of data, to draw insight and meaning, to produce new data from data already at hand, reveals a codependency between data analytics and data accrual. This point, which may be obvious to experts, is revelatory for nonexperts (such as myself) and worth emphasizing. Enhanced capacities to create, capture, and collect data mean not only that we have more data with which to work, but also that accrual can transform insignificant data, already at-hand, into data that counts, that informs and provides insight. With increased scale, density, and diversity, previously sparse data on, say, rare diseases, meet statistically significant thresholds. The click or motion of a mouse takes on meaning when set against other data fields or combined with clicks and motions from dense population data sets. Against the noisy backdrop of normal communication, we may discern a dangerous plot; against learning patterns of whole populations, we may identify those more and less efficacious. In short, extracting meaning from data is not additive; or, according to a well-worn saying, accrual makes the whole more than the sum of parts.

Even if no one can single out a radical discontinuity, quantum leap, or scientific revolution,[22] the convergence of factors seems to have spawned an epistemological paradigm shift that construes data as knowledge itself.[23] Whether the data supports our hunches, hypotheses, and theories or surprises and vexes us with results that are counterintuitive and unanticipated, it has, for many, become the primary reference point of knowledge.[24]

In the sections that follow, we see how the paradigm of big data expands the fuzzy boundary between use and collection, yielding troubling ambiguity in the very meaning of BDE.

Minimalist, Maximalist, and In Between

A minimalist notion of collection covers only the initial capture by a collecting agent (e.g., data processor, data controller, data recipient, first party, etc.) of data[25] as it leaves its impression on a given medium; any processing beyond the moment of uptake counts as use. The simplicity of this definition is misleading, however, and not only because of conceptual perils lurking within it. Rather, it is undone when considering how to apply it, presumably, to quite clear cases, such as information registered in an online form, mouse-click records, images captured on surveillance cameras, and even the digital exhaust (sometimes called "metadata") such as temporal data, geolocation, and more, to which Craig Mundie refers.

Recent critical scholarship on big data[26] rightly resists the idea of data as a raw resource lying about awaiting collection. Unlike a raw resource, data does not preexist our collection of it, a shapeless thing until hewn into something useful for humanity.[27] Instead, the act of collecting, whether registering, logging, recording, acquiring, observing, sensing, or documenting, involves more. A foot leaves an impression in damp beach sand, but we would hardly say that the sand "collects" the footprint. Wishing to dispel this myth of data being merely collected, critical scholars have sought to replace the notion of data gathered as a raw resource with data *constructed* or *created* from the signals of countless technical devices and systems (cameras, sensors, receivers, servers, networks, etc.). For the impression in sand to be interesting and worth fighting for, it must be conceived *as* a footprint, perhaps even a human footprint, a male footprint; and in so conceiving, the data is created. Similarly, data is interesting and worth fighting for once it has acquired meaning, whether this meaning comes from context of collection, assignment of labels, categorization, interpretation, scientific discovery (e.g., geospatial coordinates), or merely how it is conceived in natural language.[28]

It is plain to see, in the cases mentioned earlier, differences between mere impressions and data: a mouse click is a digital pulse, but as data it could be the placement of a shoe order, an acknowledgment of terms of service, a place marker in a document, or expressed interest in a particular online ad. Similarly, a pattern of pixels is an image of a suspect on video surveillance footage; a word or phrase is a web search term or an element in a letter, email, or novel; a timed series of location coordinates recorded by a GPS device is the route driven from home to work. To fully capture the layered complexity of data interpretation and classification, a single paragraph is clearly insufficient. Nevertheless, to sustain momentum with the central argument, we must leave this task undone, merely acknowledging the considerable interpretive labor that goes into assigning meaning to pixels, clusters of pixels, and their assemblage before finally, for example, identifying it as the image of a human face—and even more so when this image is recognized as the face of a particular, identified individual.

If a minimalist definition of collection assumes no more than that data collected is interpreted or labeled, questions remain about how to characterize the holding of data—that is, storing it, either in the long or short term—and about processing that may be necessary to make this happen. If storage is classified not as a type of collection but a type of use, it will be snagged in a net of regulation. Although the collection minimalist might be willing to bite the bullet, there surely are BDE proponents who would balk at liberating collected data from regulation only to see these freedoms dissipate as they are granted only to fleeting ephemera with no staying power. They would prefer to see data storage remain within the realms of unregulated collection, (obviously) along with practices required for the creation and management of databases (relational or nonrelational). Moreover, as anyone with overstuffed, untidy closets knows, it is no use storing data unless it is organized, tagged, labeled, structured, and available for systematic querying. Finally, who is to say where one database ends and another begins? With storage included within the scope of collection, it seems inevitable that concatenation of databases, whether real or virtual (as the ability to query across distributed databases), would come along for the ride. This inclusive conception of collection is compatible with the definition proffered by Joris van Hoboken. In his insightful comparative analysis of U.S. and EU perspectives on the collection-use distinction, van Hoboken suggests that proponents of collection deregulation mean to cover all activities that provide "access to or control over (personal) data for any potential use."[29]

Beyond data storage, two further access practices bear consideration. One is analysis; the other, flow. Although the former, "data analytics," may appear to be a new phenomenon, in fact, it is a descendent of a 1980s practice known as "computer matching"—the ability to triangulate records across multiple databases.[30] Almost quaint when compared with the sophisticated present-day techniques of data mining, predictive analytics, and machine learning conducted over vast repositories of aggregated data and distributed databases, computer matching was sufficiently worrying that it provoked the passage of the 1988 Computer Matching and Privacy Protection Act. Setting aside ethical and political questions about matching and analytics, we mark as an open question whether inferring new information from data previously collected counts as collection or use. Here, too, the answer—not obvious—would have ramifications for the scope and power of BDE.

Information *flow*, or dissemination, raises similar questions. Beyond the dyad, collector, and subject, flow involves other parties—intermediaries—beyond the initial collecting agent. It is no secret that data flows prodigiously; it is disclosed, distributed, shared, and disseminated. It flows under a host of transmission principles—sold, bought, freely given, exchanged, required by law, or, one supposes, even stolen. The information landscape is teaming with parties to this flow—first, second, third parties and so on—including information service providers, ad networks, analytics companies, public health authorities, insurance companies, data brokers, government agencies, and many more. Should flow of data from one party to another be understood as collection or use? Although a collection *minimalist* would surely say flow is use, there is a coherent, contrasting collection *maximalism* that would incorporate flow into collection, as well as all the other steps discussed above.

Drawing the Line

Drawing a line between collection and use is important because it defines the scope of BDE. Although some fuzziness at the border is inevitable, the distance between intuitively clear cases of collection on the one hand and use on the other leaves BDE indeterminate in a broad spectrum of contemporary data practices, including many of the most important and controversial. As noted previously, these range from initial impression (or uptake), creation (or interpretation, conceptualization), assembly, storage in databases (or repositories), structuring (or organization), indexing, and query access, to analysis (or so-called data analytics) and flow, to parties beyond the first. I characterized collection minimalism as a position that categorized only the first two as collection, and collection maximalism as covering them all. The balance, in respective cases, would count as use. For the maximalist, this is reserved for intuitive cases, such as delivering a package to a given address or denying a loan because of an applicant's unemployment status.[31]

No written accounts of BDE that I have encountered, except the PCAST report, have clarified, let alone defined, the key terms *collection* and *use*. The PCAST report belongs in the minimalist camp, as it considers everything from storage onward as use, and consequently, subject to regulation. For purposes of this chapter, however, instead of preemptively declaring a line and proceeding with an evaluation of BDE, I have devised two criteria for assessing where a line might be drawn in the hierarchy from impression to analytics and flow, how the placement of the line affects what BDE is, and the extent to which BDE disrupts normative expectations. One criterion is whether a given placement achieves a sufficient departure from business-as-usual to explain the earnest efforts of BDE proponents on its behalf. A corollary is that the greater the extent to which a definition of collection satisfies this criterion, the more likely is BDE to vex privacy efforts. The second criterion is coherence. By this I mean whether a line that categorizes certain practices as collection and others as use is internally consistent and nonarbitrary. As we move through the practices identified in the hierarchy we consider how they affect the scope of BDE, and its challenges, according to the two criteria.

Arguably, the least controversial disruptive version of BDE is one that assumes collection to include only the initial uptake when data is captured as an impression on a variety of media. Until such impressions are given meaning, conceptualized in accordance with a given ontology, understood against a background context allowing, for example, the association of a digital blip with a particular person, they are unlikely to excite proponents of BDE. Although the placement of meaning-giving, interpretive activity, labeling, and classification outside the concept of *collection* would raise fewer privacy concerns (perhaps none), it would yield a barely interesting BDE. I will assume, therefore, that even those BDE proponents we have called minimalists, who give narrow berth to collection, would include in collection the processing of digital input that results in the ascription of meaning to it.

But what is collection without storage? Extinguishing restrictions that could staunch the lifeblood of big data, as do ex-ante commitments to explicit purposes and consent,[32] is a small victory for BDE without the ability to record and store data for future access; and what is mere storage unless it involves order, organization, classification, and a means of finding, extracting, querying? Some might think this is a good place to draw the boundary between collection and use. Once data is organized to allow for access and query, however, analytics—processing, extraction, inference, the generation of new information—is but a small conceptual step away. If we allow collection to include processing for storage and access, then there seems to be no independent basis for deciding that analytics is data use, and subject to regulation. On grounds of the second, the coherence criterion, it falls within the scope of BDE.

If, finally, we suggest that a natural place to draw a line between collection and use is at this point, including analytics but excluding flow, it may be that we will have taken one step too far down the slippery slope and run afoul of the coherence criterion. Why? Processes covered under the label of analytics include discovery of new information from information at hand. Said another way, this involves collection of data not directly from data subjects themselves (either from them or generated by them through their activities). From the data collector's perspective, receiving data from a third party is similar to inference because, likewise, it constitutes collection not directly from data subjects. The coherence criterion would impel us to treat the two alike. But if we are to bless analytics and flow with deregulation, the slippery slope transports us to data brokers, whose practices of gathering and supplying data from and to others (governments and commercial first-party collectors alike) would, accordingly, earn freedom from regulation. This conclusion, that data broker practices elude regulation under BDE, might stir queasiness among even the most enthusiastic proponents.

The mistake, in my view, originates with setting too much store by the question of whether data is collected directly from a subject or not. Consider, for example, an exchange of email over Google's Gmail. When someone sends me information via email, we may describe this transaction as one in which I have collected this information. The fact that the transmission is mediated via network nodes and ultimately a Gmail server before landing in my account does not make me a third party to it. Something about the intention of the originator, the sender of the email, is more relevant to who is the first party collector than the service intermediary, which happens to relay the information. For similar reasons, I would argue, the common practice of large information corporations gobbling smaller ones, and each other (e.g., Google and Waze, Facebook and Instagram, Microsoft and LinkedIn, and countless others), ought not, by itself, allow for deregulation of flow that prior to acquisition was subject to regulation.[33]

Finally, since BDE proponents tout the promise of vast caches of data, such as health-related data from primary (i.e., data subjects) and secondary sources, it would not make sense to invite regulation for the former but not the latter. Van Hoboken's definition of collection, focusing on the capacity to access data for processing, likewise does not distinguish between collection from subject and from other sources. Although it may be worth considering asymmetric regulation for outward flow (i.e., dissemination) versus inward flow (i.e., collection), this idea will not be further developed here.

To summarize: we have demonstrated how the definitions of *collection* and *use* markedly affect the scope of BDE, and by implication, determine how radical its departure from present-day practices is. A minimalist account of collection marks a minimal departure, leaving a critical range of practices within the purview of regulation; this conservatism offers solace to some, but gives little leeway to proponents of BDE. The maximalist, by opening the door wide to the full range of data practices typically associated with big data, does not hold any of the parties to account for any of these practices, except at the moment when lives are directly affected—the individual is or is not stopped at the border, does or does not get the job offer, the mortgage, medical insurance, or ads for a high-paying job.[34] No limits placed on what, how, or how much data is collected, or how long it is stored, how it is stored, and where it travels may make BDE proponents happy, but it raises grave privacy concerns.

Where one draws the use-collection line, similarly, is significant for most conceptions of privacy; understood as contextual integrity, it challenges the expectations of appropriate flow. More paths of flow escaping regulation means fewer paths subject to normative constraints, and a radical weakening of privacy. The remainder of this chapter will argue that even if BDE reveals consent to be a flawed gatekeeper, it does not justify wholesale surrender of accountability or answerability for all collection.

In order to proceed with evaluation, it is necessary to specify meanings of *use* and *collection* without the benefit of validation by BDE proponents but in ways that stay true to their key thesis. Collection will cover uptake and classification; that is, the *creation* of data. It will extend to assembly of data into organized, systematically accessible repositories, or databases, and also cover retention and processing; that is, analysis and inference. Although I see no way to draw a nonarbitrary line between these and flow, I will not press for a defense of these practices from defenders of BDE.

Big Data Exceptionalism: Descriptive or Normative

Clearing the definitional hurdle still leaves open questions about BDE itself, whether it stands as a factual (i.e., descriptive) assertion or a normative prescription. According to the first, it is impossible to apply privacy regulation to collection; according to the second, it is undesirable or wrong. Although they are not mutually exclusive—Craig Mundie, for example, defends both—they warrant separate consideration because they rely on different arguments and call for different responses.

Descriptive BDE: Impossibility

When proponents say, "Forget about regulating collection; it is impossible!," we may rightly wonder what they mean by collection, regulation, and impossible. We have already seen that plausible variation in the meaning of collection significantly affects the scope of BDE. But it is worthwhile probing the meanings of regulation and impossibility, too.

Regarding regulation, there is some irony: it seems the stronger one's commitment to the synonymy of FIPs with privacy, the more natural the slide to BDE. As already noted, the burgeoning array of data sources integrated into big data machinations presents a dilemma: embrace the promise of these technologies and practices knowing that core FIPs principles such as use limitation and informed consent must be compromised, or insist on fair information practice principles (FIPPs) and forgo the technologies. Even before the passion for big data took hold, online tracking—arguably, a precursor—revealed fault lines in FIPPs-based regulation, which has been operationalized, ubiquitously, with so-called privacy notices, requiring ostensible consent. Researchers, academics, regulators, and even nonexpert users are well aware of the inefficacy, even failure, of this approach.[35] In short, FIPPs are incompatible with big data because the potential insights from data cannot be anticipated until after enough of the data has been collected—chicken and egg. In response, proponents of BDE have embraced the first horn of the dilemma.

The dilemma, however, could be an artifact of FIPPs-based collection regulation and regulation generally.[36] Following contextual integrity, the substantive regulation of data flow (including collection as one form of flow) offers an alternative that does not demand specification of purpose to data subjects as a condition of each instance of data collection.[37] Contextual integrity is not completely immune from the requirement of teleological justification, specifically, in terms of stakeholder interests, ethical and political rights and values, and contextual ends and purposes, but these deliberations occur as a matter of societal policy and not in a pairwise transaction relegated to data subjects. This still holds collectors to account and thus will not satisfy those who insist on no restriction on collection whatsoever.

Regarding impossibility, what could BDE proponents mean when they say collection cannot be regulated in either of the senses of regulation? Three plausible alternatives come to mind, which, for the sake of convenience, I have labeled technical, institutional, and prior rights, with the caveat that they are not fully independent of one another.

Technical Impossibility: "It Cannot Be Helped!"

Digital impressions are created in the very functioning of the broad class of technologies that provide computational power, communications networks, and information services. Naïve intuition might conceive of digital technologies as mere conduits for messages sent, calculations performed, information provided, transactions enabled, and the myriad other activities mediated by information technologies, but instead these occur by the transmission of copies and imprints. This means that all activity leaves behind inexorable traces; it is simply how the technology works. Data is collected because it must be collected. For the swath of actors (many commercial) generally called data intermediaries or information service providers, including Web, email, social networks, content (text, video, etc.) usage leaves digital marked trails. A tweet creates content and a shocking trail of metadata far in excess of this.[38] The capture of these trails as data is a technological imperative; it is irresistible.

If BDE is allowed only these observations about irresistible collection, its minimal scope is unlikely to excite proponents, per our discussion in the previous section. Higher value collecting, including interpretation, storage, and analysis, requires the development of complex systems comprising hardware and software, whose architecture and design is far from inevitable. Capture, transformation, channeling, and pooling of data impressions engages creativity, savvy, and scientific doggedness, resulting in familiar contemporary systems; the Internet is a prime example, Google's search engine is another. Each could have been different, could have yielded different data flows and repositories. A case in point is the protocol regulating Web cookies: contentious at the time, the "winning" protocol allowed third parties to make an end run around restrictions on websites being able to harvest cookies from other sites. Had alternative protocols prevailed, we might have been spared the great privacy disaster of cross-site tracking.

It may be that once system features are established, data creation and flow is inevitable, as when a canal bed is dug, the direction of water flow is inevitable. Those who claim their services cannot but collect data because they have adopted a centralized architecture that affords capture and aggregation of information flows across multiple users and services are hiding the contingency of their system design.[39] Even after they have been settled, technical properties are often malleable and reversible or, as in the case of contemporary digital networks, allow intermediating layers that correct and refine the actions of layers above and below.[40] Such adjustments may allow systems to hide or expose certain data, or to carefully channel its flow according to fine-grained distinctions among recipients, attributes, and purposes. Facebook may claim that it cannot but collect the metadata of its WhatsApp service, but the design choices Signal has made enable not only encrypted messaging but a backend that maintains minimal metadata.[41] Denying such contingencies belies the carefully calibrated distinctions that manage targeted advertising, meticulously channeling data streams to the myriad enabling parties, pushing content, recording clicks, performing analysis, running real-time auctions, defining which parties are entitled to what data, and so forth. There is nothing inevitable in this, and policy makers and academics with limited technical savvy who may be unable to imagine alternatives are mistaking unwillingness for impossibility.

Institutional Impossibility

To conclude that BDE is the only logical course given immutable technical properties reflects a limited grasp of design contingencies and a readiness to take as given what, in fact, can be questioned. In the struggle over property rights in digitized content, for example, when supposedly inherent capabilities of digital systems threatened commercial interests, stakeholders redoubled their efforts on both technical and regulatory fronts.[42] In a similar manner, the information industry may readily accept technology determined data flows inward, but resists them for outward flow. In the institutional ecology that has sprung up around information and communications services, companies that have realized the value of data about individuals—consumers, customers, users—have emerged as global powers. Incumbents have resisted efforts to alter the technological rubric in unfavorable ways at the same time they have sought to secure the political economy, nationally and globally, that fostered their emergence and sustains their entrenchment and growth.

Attempts to curtail data practices through privacy regulation, which would significantly raise the cost of doing business and dampen potential profit margins, have been rebuffed, and the struggle of incumbents to resist regulation has been costly on regulators who are frequently poorer in both resources and technological savvy. In a political economy that accords companies enormous power over their assets and that views data, even data about individuals, as a company's asset, the amalgamation of data holdings may motivate mergers, purchases, and takeovers.[43] One could view these as standard instances of vertical integration of essential services.[44] Yet, these moves allow companies to acquire personal data through strategic purchases that may have been disallowed by privacy rules where the companies in question are separate entities. A rigorous account of these imbroglios involving global information corporations, national governments, and public interest organizations lies outside the purview of this chapter. Nevertheless, even an outsider's view reveals a bleak picture of what political representatives and regulatory bodies have been able to achieve in the name of their citizens' privacy interests. When considering the national and global influence of corporate forces arrayed in opposition, it is no surprise that commentators see collection regulation as impossible, not as a hard fact of metaphysics but as a consequence of institutional inertia—that is, intransigent key actors creating institutional barriers resistant to regulatory efforts.

Institutional barriers, like technical ones, are surmountable when there is a rationale and a collective will to do so. Mere difficulty is not necessarily a reason to halt attempts; for example, we have not ceased in our quest to staunch the flow of narcotics in the United States, and financial markets require relentless vigilance and oversight, which is costly to all members of society, and yet we persist. Furthermore, in times past, we have successfully regulated data intermediaries, imposing limits on what telecommunications providers ("common carriers") can record and share with third parties. Data may want to be free and, like low-hanging fruit, may entice collection, but the National Security Agency (NSA), the Internal Revenue Service (IRS), Google, Facebook, Diebold, and others—even with the integrity of national elections at stake—have utilized technology and regulation to enclose data they consider theirs.

Conflicting Rights and Values

According to this argument, constraints on collection conflict with ethical values and political rights to which liberal democracies are committed as matters of Constitutional principle, explicit law, or both. Citing national security, intellectual property, free speech, and associated intellectual freedoms,[45] this theme has recurred in public debates and significant milestones involving privacy, such as the 1890s landmark article by Warren and Brandeis,[46] the 1960s proposal for a federal data center,[47] the 2000s rise of social media, and the 2010s Snowden revelations. Digital rights management systems (DRMs) and technological protection measures (TPMs) have monitored users in the name of intellectual property; governments have surveilled populations in the name of safety and security;[48] data brokers have aggregated data and performed analytics in the name of First Amendment rights.[49]

Finally, overlapping with concerns raised above, having acquired data, organizations claiming property rights over it may cite their right to use it at their discretion, including to analyze and sell the products of this analysis.

But If Collection Cannot Be Regulated, Can Use Be?

In David Brin's fantastical world, not unlike Michael Seemann's postapocalyptic state, citizens "get over" the death of privacy and cleverly opt for full transparency to keep tabs on powerful governmental and commercial actors. These visions contrast with the present situation in which we foolishly demand secrecy, which not only fails to protect us against these overbearing actors who are able to obtain this information anyway but also allows these actors to operate in obscurity. Assuming we share with these visions the belief that public and commercial incumbents will not forgo the lifeblood of their wealth and power, and resign ourselves to the impossibility of meaningfully regulating data collection, it is unclear that faith in the corollary is justified. If the powers we wish to check are able to resist efforts to constrain their data collection, surely they will resist with equal vigor and determination equivalent efforts to constrain their uses of data, should these, too, prove to be equally profitable, equal in serving will-to-power, and equally surreptitious. In other words, there is little to support the wishful thinking of those holding bad-boy views, or proponents of BDE, that use will be susceptible to regulation if collection is not.

Craig Mundie's pragmatic vision for holding these actors accountable is to enfold or tag data in metadata and construct systems of verifiable identities that will allow use restrictions to be expressed and monitored. I daresay, with such mechanisms in place, the task of regulating collection, too, would be greatly eased. Further, since such approaches impose costs and rely on the cooperation of the very class of actors who have worked determinedly to shake off meaningful restraints on collection (and thus far have succeeded), anything short of direct regulation points away from success. Those whose collection activities defy close monitoring and regulation are unlikely to offer an easier target for use regulation. Here I do not refer primarily to, for example, Russian mobsters seeking to evade discovery when setting up botnets, but to mainstream actors seeking immunity from watchdog organizations and public interest vigilantes. Using technological means such as obfuscation, as well as legal means such as nondisclosure clauses, these mainstream actors have managed to obscure problematic information flows. (Nowhere is this more evident than in the mobile domain.)

In sum, if the reason for giving up on collection restrictions is that the barn door is open, the cat is out of the bag, then there is little reason to believe that regulation of use is likely to succeed.

Normative BDE: Foreclosure of Benefits

From what we learned in the prior section, if metaphysics, architecture, and institutional obduracy make it impossible to regulate collection, then just as surely, they will impede the regulation of use. Although this calls into question key premises of a descriptive account of BDE, it still leaves open a normative account, which asserts that it is undesirable, even wrong, to regulate collection. The case does not rest on the inability to regulate data collection but on the legitimacy of so doing. Normative BDE's underlying rationale, embodied in statements cited earlier, for example, is utilitarian: the potential of big data to deliver benefits to individuals and societies is so great that we dare not staunch its lifeblood. Imposing constraints on data collection would foreclose the benefits of this promising enterprise, particularly since we cannot tell, in advance of collecting, what these might be. Harms that may follow certain big data practices should be minimized by identifying and regulating problematic uses.

As with descriptive BDE, the strength of supporting arguments depends on both premises, namely, (1) that benefits will be foreclosed through regulation of collection, and (2) that harms can effectively be addressed through the regulation of use. In this section I elaborate on these two premises; in the following section I then evaluate them, concluding that at times, BDE proponents have misidentified and overvalued the global benefit of unregulated collection for big data systems and have missed and undervalued its costs.

The Benefits

On what grounds have big data champions asserted its unprecedented promise? To answer, they point to some already realized in multiple applications and domains as evidence of more to come. Yet, if we are to take seriously one of the core ideas behind BDE, namely, that one cannot say in advance of collection what the likely findings will be, then the claims must, of necessity, be general ones. A quick survey of the popular literature on big data and data science reveals some of its dazzling feats: Web search patterns that reveal unanticipated drug interactions[50] and flu trends (later discredited);[51] the ability to detect fraud automatically from subtle credit card usage patterns; findings on the impact of sentiment manipulation in Facebook news feeds on the sentiment of ensuing user commentary;[52] personalized advertising; a winning Major League Baseball team;[53] and Target figuring out which customers were pregnant.[54] There are laudable efforts in health, such as National Institutes of Health (NIH) researchers turning to big data techniques to learn about HIV infection and treatment efficacy;[55] in public utilities companies spurring energy conservation through smarter energy grids; in IBM's Watson amassing health and lifestyle data to reveal actionable correlations; and in educational institutions employing virtual learning platforms (including massive open online courses, or MOOCs) to draw insight about learning styles.[56] These less dazzling but arguably more important advances have been seen, and are foreseen, across the spectrum of social life, in finance; public health; public safety; medicine; national security; commerce; marketing; romantic love; employment; law; cultural creation; personalized, automated information services; and more reliable recommendation and ranking systems.[57]

A recent wave of interest in machine learning and artificial intelligence (AI)[58] has publicized mind-boggling achievements accomplished by cleverly exploiting vast data repositories—in machine translation, robotics, and complex games, such as Go and chess. Although this chapter's focus is on data about people, the repositories yielding these important insights are drawn from a wide range of sources and information types.

Ethics of Use

Generally, supporters acknowledge that this is a significant departure from existing privacy regimes. Unlike earlier "bad-boy" privacy skeptics, BDE proponents, generally, do not deny the important role strong privacy regulation can and has served in addressing a host of privacy or informational harms. While acknowledging that BDE constitutes a significant departure, they hold that directly focusing on harms resulting from *uses* of information can supplant privacy regulation of collection, broadly construed, without foreclosing the benefits. With an awareness of the vulnerabilities exposed by stripping the protective shield of privacy (as constraints on flow), the burden of concern falls on justifying uses of information. Whereas previously, privacy may have dictated that a cost-benefit analysis support a given intention to collect information, BDE shifts a cost-benefit assessment to the point of use,[59] allowing such uses only if the assessment supports it.[60]

In support of this thinking, an emerging field of data ethics has attracted interest not necessarily supporting BDE, but compatible with the idea that data use be the linchpin.[61] Although many issues discussed in an already burgeoning literature are echoes of those aired in privacy scholarship, in the context of big data and AI, their reprise has new urgency and sometimes a new twist. Social justice, to date, has been the most preoccupying: as decisions affecting quality of life and even life itself in all social domains—including workplace and employment, advertising and marketing, finance and healthcare, education and politics—are increasingly informed by big data analytics, commentators point to error, unfair discrimination, historical prejudice, and inequitable allotment of resources and opportunities as potential consequences of automated, algorithmic prediction and decision making.[62] Whether persons are stopped at the border; whether they are offered employment, acceptance at a prestigious university, an apartment, or favorable rates for health and life insurance or a mortgage; what prices they are charged for merchandise and what ads and offers they receive all comes down to the results of automated decision systems, which may be biased. Calls for accountability apply not only to data mining and analytics algorithms but even to the selection data, which cannot be assumed to be objective and impartial.[63]

Threats to autonomy due to manipulation and exploitation constitute another class of issues that have attracted attention. Since any information that increases accuracy in clustering and prediction may be attractive to data holders, processors, and decision makers, people may have little clue about the bases on which they are being judged. Thus, our fates may be sealed by processes that are opaque (to us and even to the processors themselves) and according to information we may deem irrelevant.[64] Models that emerge from statistical learning may map well onto the training data and offer statistically respectable predictions, but they may defy human sense-making and consequently, human explanation.[65] Decisions affecting your prospects and well-being, accordingly, may seem as arbitrary as the toss of a coin. Raising questions about due process,[66] critics have urged transparency in the key operations of automation, from an account of the data and algorithms to thresholds and criteria affecting the transition from findings to practical decision making. Fairness is certainly a factor, but autonomy is challenged when seemingly arbitrary decisions interfere with our capacity to achieve important life goals. Veering to the sinister, practices that critics such as Frank Pasquale[67] have called attention to involve ferreting out information from which particular vulnerabilities are inferred. Preying on these vulnerabilities, which individuals may themselves be seeking to overcome, third parties manipulate those individuals through behavioral advertising, targeted marketing, and disadvantageous offers to which they are likely to accede, thereby diminishing their autonomy.[68] More directly, data ethicists anticipate oppressive working conditions in which employees' performance and work schedules are optimized for maximum business efficiency.[69]

Other harms from data uses include chilling effects—on speech and association—as people grow aware that the friends we keep online, the opinions that we and they post, and the searches we conduct may earmark us as people of this or that type.[70] Critics warn of threats to democracy from political messages finely targeted down to particular individuals and households.[71] They warn of the filter bubbles engineered by recommender systems and personalized ranking algorithms.[72]

The question to which we turn in the next section is whether we can afford to forgo restrictions on collection, confidently assuming that use regulation, guided by data ethics, subject to cost-benefit scrutiny, will protect against privacy and other harms.

Reality Check

Undoubtedly, there are new and good reasons, in light of big data, to recalibrate contextual informational norms and forge new approaches to privacy regulation. Contextual integrity allows for such reassessment, permitting challengers to entrenched practices to replace them if they meet the normative criteria at least as well, or ideally, better—justly serving interests, promoting ethical and political values, and fostering contextual ends and purposes. But BDE goes further. It wants to situate collection entirely outside the remit of political accountability; it recommends a blanket lifting of constraints on data collection (as defined above) with the expressed *faith* that we will be better off if we do and will suffer an opportunity cost if we do not, and that we will be able to address ills by addressing ethical use.

I am skeptical. In my view, this path will leave data subjects vulnerable to privacy harms and hard-fought political values vulnerable to erosion, with no clear path to compensatory benefits. The evaluation I provide in this section does not challenge the logic of BDE; rather, it is informed by what I would call "a dose of realism." I say realism, not pragmatism, because while pragmatists might agree that collection deregulation is wrong, they may believe that resistance is futile and half-measures (i.e., use restrictions) are all we can achieve. By contrast, I argue that deeply engrained realities of the information and data landscape belie the well-meaning beliefs and assumptions making up the justification for BDE. In *this* reality, it simply is not rational to expect that unconstrained data collection will optimally serve societal needs and values. Thus, even if one optimistically holds that we can regulate data use reasonably well, the additional risks to data subjects of removing the cushion of collection constraints are not justified. Finally, I will argue that even if data use could effectively be regulated to minimize informational harms, there are risks and harms inherent to collection itself that must be directly addressed.

Who Is "We"?

BDE asserts that ex ante restrictions on collection are likely to inhibit the tremendous benefits that big data promises to individuals and societies. Because results of algorithmic learning are not knowable in advance (particularly with unsupervised learning) and may not even map easily onto concepts that are natural or meaningful to humans, we cannot perform cost-benefit analyses or require purposes to be specified *before* data is collected. We need the data first in order to extract knowledge from it and be guided in actions and decisions. So, as we have seen, goes the argument.

It is surprising that the logic of this argument has not been more aggressively challenged, most glaringly for the shift in meaning of the crucial term *we* in "*We* should not restrict, otherwise *we* have much to lose."[73] Whereas some of the cases we have cited, such as NIH researchers incorporating big data in their studies of HIV infection and treatment[74] and public utilities companies spurring energy conservation through smarter energy grids, a sprinkling of reality dust reveals that all is not as it is claimed to be.

To begin, the sources of the data deluge and the costliness and even futility of regulation are not predominantly patient health records and student records, or records from innumerable government databases, which in the 1960s had aroused great privacy fears. Yes, these traditional data stores contribute to the deluge, but the sources that have excited BDE proponents are the emanations of technology-mediated behaviors, including intentional activity (online purchases, searches, comments, ratings, etc.) and the data exhaust created and captured alongside it, including social networks, communications metadata, interest profiles, and so on. The "we" surely refers to all of us, the data subjects. What of the "we" whose benefits ought not be foreclosed?

It is worth noting that the bulk of this data is concentrated in the hands of a few private, global, commercial entities. These include the familiar ones with which we interact directly, such as Google, Apple, Twitter, LinkedIn, Amazon, Netflix, and Facebook, and indirectly, in their capacities as platforms, operating systems, and intermediaries.[75] Vast repositories are also assembled by those with whom we have not been aware of contact, such as analytics companies and data brokers like Acxiom. Others about whom we think only rarely, including traditional telecommunications providers such as Sprint and AT&T, Internet service providers such as Verizon, medical and other insurance companies such as Medical Information Bureau and Aetna, and financial institutions (such as banks and credit card providers), accumulate vast data stores, sometimes because it is necessary for conducting business, sometimes because data retention regulation requires it, and mostly because in their functioning as platforms and intermediaries, data falls into their possession and nothing prevents them from staking claims to it.[76]

In this reality, *we* the beneficiaries are not one and the same as *we* the people, the data subjects and those who represent our interests, exhorted to accept deregulated collection. In reality, there are no assurances that opening the floodgates and relieving these dominant data collectors of accountability will result in celebrated knowledge gains and decisional integrity in service of the individual's or, for that matter, the common good. It is not that it will *not* serve them at all, only that it is unlikely to be the primary motivation. In saying so, I impute no ill will or evildoing on the part of these companies; on the contrary, many of them have contributed greatly to quality of life. It is merely that they are, understandably, driven by different imperatives—business and profit—and the data they record and the questions they ask of it are related (arguably, must be related) to these imperatives. The unthinkably large trove of Web use data is optimized for effective targeted advertising; for the massive accumulation of medical data accruing to medical insurance companies for assessing premiums;[77] for studies Facebook underwrites with its vast stock of networked data shaped by company interests such as attracting advertising dollars and preventing defection to other services.[78] To be sure, individuals have also benefited and societal needs have been served, but collaterally, not systematically.[79]

These are best-case scenarios: legitimate, competent, largely well-meaning companies producing useful services, sometimes contributing to knowledge and underwriting decisions that happen to be important to the quality of individual lives and societal well-being. Although interests might align at least partially, and benefits flow, there is nothing to compel this. Utilitarian thinkers, including economists, should also be asking about opportunity costs—that is, not only whether there is benefit from unregulated collection but also whether the set-up is optimal. The question to ask is whether greater benefits might accrue from a different arrangement of entitlements if *we* were allowed to frame the questions, where the "we" in question could range over government representatives with citizens' interest in mind, independent academic researchers, and public interest organizations.[80] When the referent of "we" slips from one party to others, the distribution of winners and losers may change, no matter what happens to overall gains and losses. As it stands, not only is much of this data outside the grasp of many who might want to put it to use for the public good, but the view into what data there is and what the collectors do with it is utterly blocked to all but a rarefied few,[81] and even they see only a highly circumscribed, measured slice.[82] Trade secrecy and competitive business advantage routinely trump public interest.[83]

In circumstances where interests of *we* the data collectors and *we* the data subjects are more obviously misaligned, it is particularly important to scrutinize the rhetoric of benefits foreclosed. Online behavioral advertising, which has depended on what is, effectively, unregulated online tracking, is a case in point. Those endorsing it claim that we are all better off when ads match our interests. Although persuasive to lawmakers and regulators who have offered little resistance to data collection, online and off, within and across platforms,[84] these claims are inconsistent with surveys that repeatedly show strong opposition to online surveillance and targeting from those who are its subjects.[85] Undoubtedly there are beneficiaries of the practice, but there is little published evidence that the benefits are fairly distributed. Although this is not the place for a full-blown discussion of online, targeted advertising, the case clearly illustrates how the interests of *we* the subjects of deregulated collection diverge from *we* whose benefits would be foreclosed were deregulation resisted.

To hold moral sway, it is insufficient to demonstrate that one set of stakeholders benefits from deregulating collection; we must show common, nonprejudicial benefit. One promising candidate is risk reduction. If a free hand collecting data from and about people can convincingly be linked to reduced risk and increased security for all against, for example, a terrorist attack, the two "we" groups seem to be aligned. Rigorously evaluating this claim requires strong empirical evidence, but equally importantly, the scope and logic of the argument should be sound. Contextual integrity would require that an analysis specify all relevant parameters. Thus, whereas for some parties freedom to collect certain types of information, under certain constraints, might be justified, the same may not hold for other collecting parties. In the case of the commercial actors we have been discussing, the evidence for overall risk reduction from deregulated collection is simply not present. In fact, one should remain astute to mere shifting of risk from one party to others, at times, even in a zero-sum configuration—I reduce my risk by increasing yours—masquerading as reductions in overall risk. Massive data breaches often reveal such shifting as companies collect and accrue data with an eye to extracting forward value and reducing their own costs, while in the process exposing individuals to greater risks.[86] One of the most spectacular of these instances, announced in September 2016, was a massive breach that had occurred two years earlier of databases held by Yahoo!, which compromised records of an estimated five hundred million customers containing user names, log-in credentials, birth dates, and zip codes.[87] To date, there appears to be no recourse in the law for exposure to risk for victims of such breaches.[88]

Another type of risk shifting occurs when companies relying on the results of data analysis and profiling are able to identify consumers from whom to extract higher prices for their goods and services—thus lowering their risk and increasing it for buyers.[89] Free reign on collection and analysis may place individuals in adversarial relationships not only with companies (or government agencies) but also with one another, as differentiation among individuals, which is advantageous to companies, may unfairly disadvantage some individuals over others. One person's personalization and reduction of risk may be another's discrimination and exaggeration of risk, particularly in competitive situations where resources are limited, such as admission to a prestigious college, discriminatory pricing, and apartment rentals in desirable urban neighborhoods. Probabilistic modeling inevitably means that some people will be misclassified, not so much in error but as an inherent property of such modeling.[90] Here, too, this may mitigate risk for the data collector but increase risk of wrongful treatment for the individual. Depending on where thresholds are set for false negatives and positives, data processors may shift the risk of erroneous classification toward or away from themselves. The selection of data fields, too, can affect which individuals are blessed with a positive outcome and which a negative.[91] Cost-benefit analyses on use alone will not successfully root out risk shifting unless this world—not our world—includes political mechanisms to ensure impartial access to data sets and democratic guidance on what questions are posed to data and how emergent models are exploited.

To conclude this section, let us consider one of big data's risk-reduction success stories: credit card fraud detection. The story told is that over time, dogged collection of data has enabled credit card companies to detect anomalous card usage based on patterns of normal usage. Fortuitously, everyone (both "we" groups) is happy (except the fraudsters, to be sure). Why highlight this case? Although it is true that machine learning over vast data sets is the proximal agent of mutual benefit, the confluence of interests was due in large measure to strategic legal regulation and the establishment of industry standards[92] that assigned liability for losses due to fraud to credit card issuers, not to individuals or merchants. In service of realism, it is critical to recognize the role of legislation in aligning the interests of consumers and credit card companies. In hindsight, this allocation of liability was even more brilliant given that transaction data naturally accrues to these companies, placing them in the best position to perform these analyses.

The case of credit card fraud is instructive because it steers away from simple connections between unrestricted collection and mutual benefits. Even in this success story of big data, the win-win outcome is as much a product of smart regulation. Data breach notification laws strive to a similar achievement by tying the fate of data holders to data subjects. To date, the sting of notification seems not to be painful enough to moderate the accumulation of data, which in turn creates honeypots for destructive hackers, mobsters, fraudsters, and their ilk, with ultimate risk shifted to individual data subjects.[93] This should give pause to those who believe that regulating use and misuse alone will or can be effective in mitigating harm to data subjects.

In the contemporary landscape, fair information practice principles may not protect privacy, but one of the fundamental purposes behind them, leveling the playing field for data holders and data subjects, remains as vital now as it was in the 1960s and 1970s.[94] Strategically imposing constraints on data flows seeks to address enormous disparities of power and wealth and to sustain differentiated societal roles and positions that are important for societal integrity. We may not care to level the playing field for everyone—criminals, for example—but for others, the modulated collection and use of information provides security for legitimate ends.

In sum, the key aim of this section is to challenge an implicit assumption behind the normative version of BDE that warns against ex ante limits on collection and the risk of foreclosing unanticipated discoveries based on machine learning and other forms of data analytics over large, aggregated data sets. The assumption is that we individuals should support unrestricted collection in order for us collectively to reap the benefits. But scrutiny reveals that the beneficiaries are not the same as the contributors; moreover, those controlling and processing big data, in reality, are not obliged to serve the collective good, nor are they restrained in uses that may even cause undeserved harm. In the present-day political economy of data and digital technology, ordinary people—the data subjects—or those representing our interests will never achieve insight and transparency into what data owners and processors are doing. Aside from gross and obvious instances, it will be impossible to regulate use for the variety of subtle harms against which privacy norms, over thousands of years of social life, have evolved to guard.

We the NSA

A reader may agree with the findings in the previous section but chalk up the problem to misuse, not to deregulated collection. After all, the worrying cases of risk shifting, unbalanced distribution of costs and benefits, and suboptimal extraction of value from data are due to wrongful uses and, except for the case of data breaches, are only indirectly due to unfettered collection. Such readers misunderstand the argument, which is to reverse the burden of proof. If you assert that I have a social obligation to allow unfettered collection, despite its infringement of privacy norms, you must demonstrate the overwhelming social value of so doing. I have shown the opposite: in the present-day political economy and legal landscape there are few, if any, assurances that general social welfare will guide the extraction of value from this data, or mitigate potential costs to data subjects. These observations undermine the BDE supporter's opportunity-cost worries. Admitting that the likely across-the-board benefits may be exaggerated undermines the BDE supporters' opportunity-cost worries. More importantly, it raises the bar for efficacious use regulation, because with less clear benefits, we need greater assurances of minimal harm; this, given the existing landscape of practice and policy, is impossible to provide.

Here, however, I want to go further. Even, hypothetically, allowing that efficacious regulation of misuse were possible, I want to suggest that collection itself deserves scrutiny and restraint. To explore this proposition, let us consider an equivalent configuration of means and ends where collection is regulated, independently of whether the ultimate target is restraints on use. I refer to one of the constitutional pillars of political democracy in the United States, the Fourth Amendment of the Bill of Rights.[95] Now, let us proceed with a thought experiment: imagine that Fourth Amendment critics are advocating for its repeal on grounds that it unnecessarily obstructs law enforcement and national security. Leaving aside whether such arguments could have held sway in 1791, consider their strength in the present climate. First, the rising incidence of domestic and international terror means there are more reasons to be fearful; and second, improvements in technologies of surveillance—to monitor communications and geolocation, to capture and log visual images and commercial transactions, to aggregate the above data, and to extract useful insight—means the potential fruits of dragnet surveillance are assuredly plentiful.

Advocates of repeal could calm us with assurances that full attention will be given to preventing misuse (assuming agreement on what counts as such) and holding perpetrators to account. Requiring antecedent specification of particularized purpose, as required by the Fourth Amendment, severely handicaps efforts to catch criminals and expose dangerous plots and other serious threats, because we cannot always predict what patterns the data reveals and whether they will be useful.[96] Requiring probable cause undermines the efficacy of big data analytics because a backdrop of normal patterns of communications, activity on social networks, and transactional configurations is crucial to detecting the suspicious, the abnormal, the worthy of note. This is particularly relevant in applications of unsupervised machine learning, where patterns must be discovered in *all* the data, not merely a focused subset.

Respondents insist, however, that a liberal democracy must retain some version of the Fourth Amendment. They warn against dragnets and remind us of the invasive and demeaning character of random or universal "stop and frisk," mandatory drug testing, and house-to-house searches. They spell out the important work of the Fourth and other amendments, such as the First, in forestalling totalitarianism by restricting the *scope* of government's intrusions into citizens' private endeavors and maintaining certain spheres—home, religion, political association—as off limits. In the clearly demarcated instances where administrative functions allow government agencies into certain areas of private life—for example, to process Medicare reimbursements, long-form tax filings to the IRS, the decennial census surveys, and welfare benefits—data holdings generated through these interactions have been rigorously siloed.[97] The fact of mass monitoring is bad enough, respondents may say, but equally so is the mere *feeling* of it, chilling activities crucial to quality of life and civil society, including, but not limited to, free association and speech.

The repeal advocate smiles indulgently. Present-day dragnets may be cast with enormous discretion, via hidden cameras, unobtrusive motion sensors, concealed listening devices, passive capture of signals from mobile devices, black box recorders attached to broadband cables, government-installed network malware, third-party data aggregators, and so forth. Citizens will neither *feel* invaded nor will they even know. "If you have nothing to hide, you have nothing to fear" is their final reassurance; the innocent should not worry because although collection will be unfettered, harmful uses will be curtailed. My guess is that few readers of this chapter will feel reassured, though they may differ on the grounds for their unease. For some, it is the special relation of government to private citizen that calls for special attention, a need that is evident to lawmakers and even privacy skeptics. The furor over what Edward Snowden revealed about NSA practices speaks clearly to this concern.[98]

But what are the reasons for fencing in government power[99] despite obstacles it may create for its administrative function, guardianship of national security, and protection against crime? Why have we refused to open the floodgates? In addressing these questions, an account of republicanism offered by the political philosopher Philip Pettit provides insight.[100] According to it, to achieve political liberty we must do more than thwart repressive governmental actions; we also must contain government domination, meaning the *power* of government to interfere arbitrarily in our lives. The point is worth emphasizing: concern does not stop with arbitrary interference enacted but extends to the *power*, or potential, of arbitrary interference.[101] Adapting this principle to data, the inappropriate collection of information about private individuals and mass collection about populations provides government with inordinate *powers to* interfere. With the phrase "knowledge is power," the qualification "when you use it" is unnecessary because the mere having of knowledge *is* a form of power in itself. Because the gathering and holding of information are empowering to government, the Bill of Rights and other legislative acts that strengthen informational privacy through procedural barriers and prohibitions[102] are critical measures to protect individuals and populations against government domination.

In the 2016 case *Birchfield v. North Dakota*, which decided whether doctrine permits police officers to conduct warrantless breath tests, the U.S. Supreme Court concluded that while breathalyzer blood alcohol content (BAC) readings do not require a warrant, blood tests do, first because they are invasive (i.e., pricking the skin) and second because they generate a lasting sample: "A blood test, unlike a breath test, places in the hands of law enforcement authorities a sample that can be preserved and from which it is possible to extract information beyond a simple BAC reading. Even if the law enforcement agency is precluded from testing the blood for any purpose other than to measure BAC, the potential remains and may result in anxiety for the person tested."[103] This brief snippet recognizes the mere potential of use as warranting a higher standard—in particular, the requirement of an ex ante rationale for collection of this type of nonephemeral product. Data collection has equivalent properties, as it generates "a sample that can be preserved and from which it is possible to extract information beyond."

Appreciating the Fourth Amendment as a meticulously crafted trade-off, we may, nevertheless, find persuasive the enthusiasm of government agencies—from the NSA to law enforcement to the NIH[104]—for the positive potential of big data. The scales may tip against its barriers and prohibitions on a credible showing that mass collection of communication and transactional data, augmented with vast data commercial holdings, would enable more effective mining of suspicious activity and criminal or terrorist networks, or that enhancing traditional medical records with broad swaths of lifestyle records could afford great cross-over understanding in both spheres.[105] It may be time to recalibrate the balance. But if the benefits of vast data repositories have soared, so have its distinctive threats. Big data (including analytics) produces unpredictable insights, and individuals rightly may worry about what could trigger special interest and scrutiny of them—

ordinary things, features of their tax returns, persons with whom they socialize, where they travel, and how they pay. If the machinations of big data cause greater worry to the terrorist bringing a bomb aboard a plane, their unconstrained application also raises concerns for which past precedent does not readily prepare us.

In her concurring opinion in *United States v. Jones*, Justice Sotomayor highlights distinctive threats associated with GPS-enabled tracking, rightly pointing out that the creation of a "precise, comprehensive record of a person's public movements" exceeds the scope of allowable, "plain view" surveillance by a police officer.[106] Similar concerns have engaged the scholarly literature that seeks to characterize the distinctive, incremental threats from amassing data continuously over time or aggregating data across a myriad of sources.[107] These works locate the potential to destabilize the tenuous balance of power between government and other data holders not merely in the additive powers of expanded data sets, but also in the multiplicative powers of analysis and inference. Although these concerns focus on the capture and accrual of information about individuals, one at a time, the power of big data is once more multiplied by capture and accrual across populations. Traditionally, in the context of governance, population or mass surveillance and "dragnet," or bulk collection are reviled, and typically associated with authoritarian and totalitarian regimes and a disregard for civil liberties and due process. By contrast, big data boosters extol the capacity it offers to acquire and analyze data from whole populations, not mere samples.[108] Machine learning can perform its magic ever more dramatically over ever more data; the larger the population, the greater the number of features that can be integrated in its scope. Intelligence gleaned from wide-ranging features (properties, attributes, or types of data) across large populations may include emergent associations, networks, and relationships and predictive accuracy in areas of life in which government has no legitimate business. Individuals must worry not only about what data they may have produced or information about them that may arouse suspicion, but also about others with whom they associate—not an unprecedented concern—and whom they happen to resemble.[109] Whether such resemblances track natural attributes or those concatenated from the mysterious workings of machine learning algorithms, these processes undermine the discretion ordinary individuals have in defining their relationship with government and, further, increase uncertainty over what might be exposed and exploited in this relationship. These, precisely, are the powers to interfere, arbitrarily, that characterize government domination and understandably provoke the anxiety anticipated by the Court in *Birchfield*.

A favorite taunt of privacy skeptics is that we have more privacy today than in bygone days when everyone in the village knew everyone else's secrets. But even these skeptics draw the line at government, and not only because of how much it knows. Knowledge may give power to your nosey neighbor, but the government has a lot more of it to wield—it can deprive you of liberty and life. When it comes to powers of the state, therefore, even those generally skeptical of privacy-based constraints on big data are measured in what they support. The harsh realities are sobering. Many of us may trust in the restraint and integrity of today's executive branch, the NSA, and our local police to apply their practices of noninvasive, dragnet surveillance to the singular purposes of societal safety and security and efficient administration. But centuries of recorded history featuring rulers who have exploited and tyrannized their subjects, and governments that have oppressed their citizens time and time again, reaffirms the wisdom of protective barriers. In the age of information and big data, insurance against abuses means selectively diminishing access to data, not merely circumscribing certain uses of it.

Is Government an Exception to Big Data Exceptionalism? Another Reality Check

Viewing government as a special case has been justified by the historical record. The public outcry following Snowden's revelations shows no inclination to surrender civil liberties and concede to government's wish to amass and hold information on all citizens willy-nilly. Indeed, over the past five decades, as difficult as it has been to hammer out privacy regulation for the private, commercial sector (with a few exceptions), we have clung to limits on prying, surveillance, intrusions, and invasions provided by a combination of the Bill of Rights and legislation, notably the Privacy Act of 1974 and various wiretap statutes. Proponents of BDE could follow the lead of privacy skeptics who have made an exception of government even as they have resisted legal restraints on commercial actors, citing efficiency, free speech (of these actors), free "stuff," innovation, and the fact that people really do not care. Outlawing harmful uses would suffice as a safety net.

Let us view this familiar position through the reality filter. In the previous section, we cited threats to political liberty from government domination as reason to see collection as a contributing factor in its own right. There is compelling reason to extend this scrutiny to private, commercial organizations, which in a relatively short period of time not only have accrued and enclosed vast data holdings about individuals within discrete nations but also have amassed vast powers, globally, to shape national and international policy.[110] They may not have armies at their direct disposal, but they do have the ability to affect the lives of individuals in basic ways—shelter, security, employment—and to exploit the reliance on them for data that governments cannot obtain by dint of either regulation or incapacity.[111] Whereas, for the most part, national borders circumscribe governments' exercise of direct power, such borders have been notoriously porous where global information companies are concerned. No doubt, as global corporations across different industries have found ways to evade national laws in one country by selectively situating questionable practices where they anticipate least resistance, those in the information services and data industries have an advantage from their command of global digital networks and their direct grip on popular engagement.[112]

Even without the mortal powers wielded by governmental actors, corporate actors armed with the power of data can affect the attainment of a decent life—shelter, employment, nourishment, family, friends, health, education, and security. Tyranny and domination come not from the power merely to interfere with people's actions and choices, but to interfere arbitrarily. Celebrating the promise of big data, its boosters have cited predictive capacities that exceed the capacity to explain systematically. Thus, companies may maximize their utility function in various areas—hiring practices, marketing, operational decisions—on the basis of data alone. Yet, what may be expedient for a decision maker might be a decisive blow to the subjects of such decisions whose prospects are stymied in vital spheres of life, particularly those in the margins of actuarial error, without rhyme or reason. Already much discussed, the opacity of decision systems based on machine learning algorithms, compounded by lack of access to data held in private hands, creates a fortress against public inspection. Where a demand for explanation and justification goes unanswered, it is impossible to know whether life-critical decisions are fair or unfair, relevant or irrelevant, and to those affected, they might as well be arbitrary. By any name, this is domination. In a free society, cumbersome as it may be for private, commercial actors, the burden of accountability falls on them for their collection practices, just as it does on governments.

Summation

In a departure from received principles of privacy regulation, the thesis I have called big data exceptionalism (BDE) supports the deregulation of data collection. Its key assertions are that (1) characteristics inherent to digital technologies make collection inevitable and unavoidable; (2) inherent characteristics of big data make it impossible to anticipate in advance what knowledge may be extracted and what purposes are served by large data aggregations; (3) not exploiting the promise of big data to its fullest will be costly to society; and (4) to address harms and risks typically associated with threats to privacy the regulation of data *use* is sufficient.

This chapter disputes BDE on conceptual, normative, and descriptive grounds. To begin with, ambiguity in the key terms *use* and *collection* challenges the coherence of the distinction. Take collection. As an inevitable byproduct of functioning digital technologies, it resembles the imprint of a foot in wet sand. If that were all collection entailed, BDE would not amount to much, but if collection entails more, how much more? At minimum, one would expect the digital imprint to mean something—that is, be conceptualized and classified—and beyond this, for collection to allow a degree of permanence and recovery, hence storage in an indexed or searchable database, allowing for later access. An ability to organize, amass, aggregate, and curate seems also inevitably to follow. Data flow from a first-party collector and a third party might appear to be a use instance, but third parties could argue that they are "collecting" data, albeit not from data subjects directly. And while something may seem wrong with placing data brokers, in their data gathering mode, outside the remit of regulation, it is consistent with the industry practice of acquiring data through mergers and acquisitions.

Although proponents rarely acknowledge these ambiguities, where one draws the line can change what BDE means and poses a dilemma: an attenuated definition of collection that keeps more activities within the scope of regulation is more palatable to privacy advocates but reduces the scope of allowable practices; more activities outside the scope means greater freedom for big data processors and is farther from traditional privacy needs. This chapter has assumed a more inclusive definition of collection.

In support of deregulating collection, proponents cite grandiose forecasts—progress on the world's direst problems of economy, health, and security—and offer a handful of dramatic applications that have given cause for optimism. My chapter counters this logic. Data available for public and public interest research is a small fraction of data held in private, commercial hands—for that matter, concentrated in the hands of a few dominant actors. These actors effectively hoard the data, obligated neither to pursue beneficial and progressive applications nor to open their troves to third parties to do so, or even to allow access for inspection and scrutiny of their internal practices. Such powers of use and exclusion, sustained and enforced through a combination of property rights, commercial freedom, contracts, and technologies, will not be dislodged without a concentrated effort on several fronts, including regulation. Without it, the illusion cannot be sustained that these holders will ask questions about their data and address problems to serve the common good. Similarly, risks to data subjects will be addressed only to the extent that this aligns with the interests of data holders. (Such an alignment was ingeniously achieved in the case of credit card fraud liability.)

The BDE proposition comprises two interdependent halves: lifting restrictions on collection, counterbalanced by restrictions on use. I have concluded that collection without accountability is not currently justified. Furthermore, past failures to harness and guide information use in ethically legitimate directions, or even to audit data holdings as a precursor to prevention, cast into serious doubt the grounds for faith in use restrictions.[113] The greatest challenge yet to the positive promise of use restrictions is (and will be) contestation over what uses should be allowed and what should be restricted.[114] Controversial use regulation will be no less subject to stakeholder manipulation in all the data practices that concern us—from holding data processers responsible for breaches and preventing insurance companies from incorporating preexisting medical conditions to using proxies to reveal union sympathizers and inferring pregnancy to determine marketing strategies.

Finally, I have challenged the notion that collection itself is innocuous. On the contrary, the mere holding of data by powerful parties bolsters their domination over the subjects of this data; a metaphorical sword dangles overhead, but we know neither the nature of the weapon nor what will trigger its plunge. Such threats, for centuries understood in the relation of government to citizens, increasingly characterize the relation of individuals to powerful corporate actors.

A paragraph of recommendations is inadequate to address the issues presented in this chapter. In broad brushstrokes, one clear candidate is that we sustain and strengthen efforts to regulate both collection and use. Another is that we regulate collection and use along contextual lines, not lines of data ownership. This means resisting the common practice of companies accruing data through acquisition, which might have raised eyebrows if achieved through the sharing of the same data across company lines. It also means regulating the willy-nilly merging of data sets accumulated from different domains already within a single company. It means meaningfully holding data proprietors responsible for data breaches. It means insisting that whereas there can be flexibility in how data may be used, we can still insist that all data holders commit to broad purposes and that, depending on the nature of the purposes, we will regulate. Finally, with the accumulation of vast data holdings comes the responsibility to allow this data to serve the public interest, not merely at the discretion of the data holder (i.e., not as "data philanthropy") but at the determination of the people's will.

Notes

1. Solon Barocas and Helen Nissenbaum, "Big Data's End Run Around Anonymity and Consent," in *Privacy, Big Data and the Public Good: Frameworks for Engagement*, ed. Julia Lane et al. (Cambridge: Cambridge University Press, 2015), 44–75.

2. Polly Sprenger, "Sun on Privacy: 'Get Over It,'" *WIRED*, January 26, 1999, http://archive.wired.com/politics/law/news/1999/01/17538.

3. David Brin, *Transparent Society: Will Technology Force Us to Choose Between Privacy and Freedom?* (Cambridge, Mass.: Perseus Books, 1998).

4. See also Christian Heller, *Post-Privacy: Prima leben ohne Privatsphäre* (Munich: C. H. Beck, 2011).

5. See Joseph Turow, *The Daily You: How the New Advertising Industry Is Defining Your Identity and Your Worth* (New Haven, Conn.: Yale University Press, 2011).

6. Recommendation 1 in President's Council of Advisors on Science and Technology (PCAST), *Big Data and Privacy: A Technological Perspective*, (North Charleston, S.C.: CreateSpace, 2014), 49.

7. Michael Seemann, *Digital Tailspin: Ten Rules for the Internet After Snowden* (Amsterdam: Institute of Network Cultures, 2015), 22.

8. Seemann, *Digital Tailspin*, 28, quoting Jane Yakowitz, "Tragedy of the Data Commons," *Harvard Journal of Law and Technology* 25, no. 1 (Fall 2011): 1–67.

9. Seemann, *Digital Tailspin*, 49.

10. Seemann, *Digital Tailspin*, 55.

11. Craig Mundie, "Privacy Pragmatism: Focus on Data Use, Not Data Collection," *Foreign Affairs*, March/April 2014, https://www.foreignaffairs.com/articles/2014-02-12/privacy-pragmatism.

12. Bert-Jaap Koops, "On Decision Transparency, or How to Enhance Privacy After the Computational Turn," in *Privacy, Due Process and the Computational Turn: The Philosophy of Law Meets the Philosophy of Technology*, ed. Mireille Hildebrandt and Katja De Vries (New York: Routledge, 2013), 197.

13. Fred H. Cate and Viktor Mayer-Schönberger, "Notice and Consent in a World of Big Data," *International Data Privacy Law* 3, no. 2 (2013), 69.

14. Omer Tene and Jules Polonetsky, "Big Data for All: Privacy and User Control in the Age of Analytics," *Northwestern Journal of Technology and Intellectual Property* 11, no. 5 (2013): 259–60.

15. See Fred H. Cate, Peter Cullen, and Viktor Mayer-Schönberger, "Data Protection Principles for the 21st Century: Revising the 1980 OECD Guidelines," Oxford Internet Institute, March 2014, http://www.oii.ox.ac.uk/publications/Data_Protection_Principles_for_the_21st_Century.pdf; Ira Rubinstein, "Big Data: The End of Privacy or a New Beginning?" *International Data Privacy Law* 3, no. 2 (2013): 74–87; Tene and Polonetsky, "Big Data for All."

16. For a detailed account of contextual integrity, see, e.g., Helen Nissenbaum, *Privacy in Context: Technology, Policy, and the Integrity of Social Life* (Palo Alto, Calif.: Stanford University Press, 2010); Nissenbaum, "Respect for Context as a Benchmark for Privacy Online: What It Is and Isn't," in *Social Dimensions of Privacy: Interdisciplinary Perspectives*, ed. Beate Roessler and Dorota Mokrosinska (Cambridge: Cambridge University Press, 2015), 278–302.

17. Nissenbaum, *Privacy in Context*.

18. See Lawrence Lessig, "The Law of the Horse: What Cyberlaw Might Teach," *Harvard Law Review* 113, no. 2 (1999): 501–49.

19. I owe thanks to Jason Schultz for drawing these cultural meanings to my attention.

20. See, e.g., Kenneth Neil Cukier and Viktor Mayer-Schönberger, "The Rise of Big Data: How It's Changing the Way We Think About the World," *Foreign Affairs* 92, no. 3 (May/June 2013): 28–40; Mundie, "Privacy Pragmatism"; PCAST, *Big Data and Privacy*; Tene and Polonetsky, "Big Data for All"; Yakowitz, "Tragedy of the Data Commons"; Executive Office of the President, *Big Data: Seizing Opportunities, Preserving Values* (North Charleston, S.C.: CreateSpace, 2014); and a host of newly minted trade books.

21. See, e.g., Katherine J. Strandburg, "Monitoring, Datafication, and Consent: Legal Approaches to Privacy in the Big Data Context," in *Privacy, Big Data and the Public Good: Frameworks for Engagement*, ed. Julia Lane et al. (Cambridge: Cambridge

University Press, 2015), 5–43; Viktor Mayer-Schönberger and Kenneth Cukier, *Big Data: A Revolution That Will Transform How We Live, Work, and Think* (New York: Houghton, Mifflin, Harcourt, 2013).

22. See, e.g., Thomas S. Kuhn, *The Structure of Scientific Revolutions*, 3rd ed. (Chicago: University of Chicago Press, 1996), and Paul Feyerabend, *Against Method*, 4th ed. (New York: Verso, 2010).

23. Some have gone so far as declaring the end of theory. See Chris Anderson, "The End of Theory: The Data Deluge Makes the Scientific Method Obsolete," *Wired*, June 23, 2008, https://www.wired.com/2008/06/pb-theory/.

24. See, e.g., Charles Duhigg, "How Companies Learn Your Secrets," *New York Times*, February 16, 2012, http://www.nytimes.com/2012/02/19/magazine/shopping-habits.html; Mara Hvistendahl, "Can Predictive Policing Prevent Crime Before It Happens?" *Science*, September 28, 2016, http://www.sciencemag.org/news/2016/09/can-predictive-policing-prevent-crime-it-happens. Nate Silver, *The Signal and the Noise: Why So Many Predictions Fail—But Some Don't* (New York: Penguin Books, 2012).

25. I have not been persuaded by efforts to define and distinguish the terms *data* and *information*, and since a rigorous distinction is not necessary for the overall argument of this chapter, I have used the terms interchangeably.

26. See Lisa Gitelman, ed., *"Raw Data" Is an Oxymoron* (Cambridge, Mass.: MIT Press, 2013); Geoffrey C. Bowker, *Memory Practices in the Sciences* (Cambridge, Mass.: MIT Press, 2005), 184 (suggesting that "Raw data is both an oxymoron and a bad idea; to the contrary, data should be cooked with care"); Geoffrey C. Bowker and Susan Leigh Star, eds., *Sorting Things Out: Classification and Its Consequences* (Cambridge, Mass.: MIT Press, 1999); Rob Kitchin, *The Data Revolution: Big Data, Open Data, Data Infrastructures and Their Consequences* (London: Sage, 2014).

27. Ahead of his time, in 2011 Ken Farrall was the first person I heard making this argument, though unfortunately he did not publish it.

28. Katherine Strandburg has dubbed this as "datafication," that is, "the recording, aggregation, and organization of information into a form that can be used for data mining" ("Monitoring, Datafication," 5).

29. Joris van Hoboken, "From Collection to Use in Privacy Regulation? A Forward-Looking Comparison of European and US Frameworks for Personal Data Processing," in *Exploring the Boundaries of Big Data*, ed. Bart van der Sloot, Dennis Broeders, and Erik Schrijvers (Amsterdam: Amsterdam University Press, 2016), 233.

30. See, e.g., Richard P. Kusserow, "The Government Needs Computer Matching to Root Out Waste and Fraud," *Communications of the ACM* 27, no. 6 (June 1984): 542–45, and John Shattuck, "Computer Matching Is a Serious Threat to Individual Rights," *Communications of the ACM* 27, no. 6 (June 1984): 538–41.

31. I include impacts on people which are derived from algorithmic models generated from information that is not necessarily drawn from them, as discussed in Barocas and Nissenbaum, "Big Data's End Run."

32. See van Hoboken, "From Collection to Use," for a clear discussion of collection deregulation in relation to FIPs.

33. For instance, in 2013 Google faced lawsuits from six different European countries over the unification of its privacy policies across platforms. See Charles Arthur, "Google Facing Legal Threat from Six European Countries over Privacy," *Guardian*, April 2, 2013, https://www.theguardian.com/technology/2013/apr/02/google-privacy-policy-legal-threat-europe. For a related discussion of the disjuncture of privacy norms and political economy, see Helen Nissenbaum, "Respecting Context to Protect Privacy: Why Meaning Matters," *Science and Engineering Ethics*, July 12, 2015, http://link.springer.com/article/10.1007%2Fs11948-015-9674-9.

34. See, e.g., Amit Datta, Michael Carl Tschantz, and Anupam Datta, "Automated Experiments on Ad Privacy Settings," *Proceedings on Privacy Enhancing Technologies 2015* 1 (2015): 92–112.

35. See Kirsten Martin, "Privacy Notices as Tabula Rasa: An Empirical Investigation into How Complying with a Privacy Notice Is Related to Meeting Privacy Expectations Online," *Journal of Public Policy and Marketing* 34, no. 2 (Fall 2015): 210–27. See also Aleecia McDonald and Lorrie Faith Cranor, "The Cost of Reading Privacy Policies," *I/S: A Journal of Law and Policy for the Information Society* 4, no. 3 (2008): 540–65. See also Joel R. Reidenberg and Lorrie Faith Cranor, "Can User Agents Accurately Represent Privacy Policies?," Discussion Draft 1.0, August 30, 2002, http://papers.ssrn.com/sol3/papers.cfm?abstractid=328860.

36. Notwithstanding admirable work seeking to improve notice and consent by privacy scholars such as M. Ryan Calo, "Against Notice Skepticism in Privacy (and Elsewhere)," *Notre Dame Law Review* 87, no. 3 (2013): 1027–72; Joel R. Reidenberg et al., "Privacy Harms and the Effectiveness of the Notice and Choice Framework," Fordham Law Legal Studies Research Paper No. 2418247, March 29, 2014, http://papers.ssrn.com/sol3/papers.cfm?abstract_id=2418247.

37. See Helen Nissenbaum, "A Contextual Approach to Privacy Online," *Daedalus* 140, no. 4 (Fall 2011): 32–48; Barocas and Nissenbaum, "Big Data's End Run."

38. See, e.g., Brendan Meeder, Jennifer Tam, Patrick G. Kelley, and Lorrie F. Cranor, "RT @IWantPrivacy: Widespread Violation of Privacy Settings in the Twitter Social Network," *Proceedings of Web 2.0 Security and Privacy (W2SP 2010)*, Oakland, Calif., 2010.

39. See Vincent Toubiana et al., "Adnostic: Privacy Preserving Targeted Advertising," paper presented at the 17th Annual Network and Distributed System Security Symposium, San Diego, March 2010.

40. Great Firewall of China, http://www.greatfirewallofchina.org/.

41. Signal demonstrates that one can choose not to collect data about users—that data collection is a choice rather than a technological requirement. All websites make certain choices, including Wikipedia, which can provide editors with a certain amount of anonymity but will deny access to Wikipedia to an editor using Tor unless the user requests special permission and reveals personal information to the Wikimedia Foundation while making her case. See "Advice to Users Using Tor," Wikipedia,

December 17, 2016, https://en.wikipedia.org/wiki/Wikipedia:Advice_to_users_using_Tor.

42. "Unintended Consequences: Fifteen Years under the DMCA," *Electronic Frontier Foundation*, https://www.eff.org/pages/unintended-consequences-fifteen-years-under-dmca.

43. For example, LiveRamp's purchase of several publisher databases to track consumers across devices. See Kate Kaye, "Acxiom's LiveRamp Buys Two Publisher Data Firms in Race to I.D. Consumers Across Devices," *AdAge*, November 17, 2016, http://adage.com/article/datadriven-marketing/acxiom-s-liveramp-buys-publisher-data-firms/306831/. See also Microsoft's acquisition of LinkedIn; Nick Wingfield, "With LinkedIn, Microsoft Looks to Avoid Past Acquisition Busts," December 8, 2016, https://www.nytimes.com/2016/12/08/technology/with-linkedin-microsoft-looks-to-avoid-past-acquisition-busts.html.

44. Thomas P. Hughes, *Networks of Power* (Baltimore: Johns Hopkins University Press, 1983), 6.

45. See, e.g., Eugene Volokh, "Freedom of Speech, Information Privacy, and the Troubling Implications of a Right to Stop People from Speaking About You," *Stanford Law Review* 52, no. 5 (2000): 1049–124.

46. Samuel D. Warren and Louis D. Brandeis, "The Right to Privacy," *Harvard Law Review* 4, no. 5 (1890): 193–220.

47. Proposed in 1965 by the Social Science Research Council (SSRC) of the American Economic Association after a three-year study revealing that neither scholars nor other agencies were able to make use of public data because of decentralization. *Report of the Committee on the Preservation and Use of Economic Data*, Social Science Research Council (April 1965). The SSRC urged the creation of a federal data center to make basic statistical data from all federal agencies available to nongovernmental users and other federal agencies.

48. For an overview, see, e.g., Nissenbaum, *Privacy in Context*, especially part 2.

49. See, e.g., *Sorrell v. IMS Health*, 564 U.S. 552 (2011). See also Julie E. Cohen, "The Zombie First Amendment," *William and Mary Law Review* 56, no. 3 (2015): 1119–58.

50. See Ryen W. White et al., "Web-Scale Pharmacovigilance: Listening to Signals from the Crowd," *Journal of the American Medical Informatics Association* 20, no. 3 (2013): 404–8.

51. But which failed to be replicated; see David Lazar et al., "The Parable of Google Flu: Traps in Big Data Analysis," *Science* 343, no. 6176 (2014): 1203–5.

52. See Gregory S. McNeal, "Facebook Manipulated User News Feeds to Create Emotional Responses," *Forbes*, June 28, 2014, http://www.forbes.com/sites/gregorymcneal/2014/06/28/facebook-manipulated-user-news-feeds-to-create-emotional-contagion/#2715e4857a0b11dcc1245fd8.

53. See Michael Lewis, *Moneyball: The Art of Winning an Unfair Game* (New York: W. W. Norton, 2004).

54. See Duhigg, "How Companies Learn Your Secrets."

55. This was recently discussed at the Harnessing "Big Data" to Stop HIV conference cohosted by the NIAID Division of AIDS, NIMH Division of AIDS Research, NIH Big Data to Knowledge, and the Bill and Melinda Gates Foundation. See "Harnessing Big Data to Stop HIV," National Institutes of Health, accessed June 13, 2018, https://www.datascience.nih.gov/node/249.

56. See, e.g., "IBM Watson Health," IBM Think, http://www.ibm.com/smarterplanet/us/en/think/watson-health/; Tene and Polonetsky, "Big Data for All," 248; Marie Bienkowski et al., *Enhancing Teaching and Learning Through Educational Data Mining and Learning Analytics: An Issue Brief* (Washington, D.C.: U.S. Department of Education, 2012), https://tech.ed.gov/wp-content/uploads/2014/03/edm-la-brief.pdf.

57. See, e.g., "IBM Watson Health"; Rachel Willcox, "Big-Data Analytics: The Power of Prediction," *Public Finance*, January 27, 2016, http://www.publicfinance.co.uk/feature/2016/01/big-data-analytics-power-prediction; Paul Wormeli, "The Promise of Big Data in Public Safety and Justice: Making Data Easier to Digest for More Law Enforcement Users," *Government Technology*, September 10, 2012, http://www.govtech.com/public-safety/The-Promise-of-Big-Data-in-Public-Safety-and-Justice.html; Kalorama Information, "Evidence-Based Medicine: Bringing Big Data to Healthcare Consumers," *Scientific Computing*, November 26, 2014, http://www.scientificcomputing.com/news/2014/11/evidence-based-medicine-bringing-big-data-healthcare-consumers; Babak Akhgar et al., *Application of Big Data for National Security: A Practitioner's Guide to Emerging Technologies* (Oxford: Elsevier, 2015); Greg Satell, "The Future of Marketing Combines Big Data with Human Intuition," *Forbes*, October 12, 2014, http://www.forbes.com/sites/gregsatell/2014/10/12/the-future-of-marketing-combines-big-data-with-human-intuition/#2715e4857a0b7fd34974331d; Paul Rubens, "Is Big Data Dating the Key to Long-Lasting Romance?" *BBC*, March 25, 2014, http://www.bbc.com/news/business-26613909; Erik Brynjolfsson and Andrew McAfee, *The Second Machine Age: Work, Progress, and Prosperity in a Time of Brilliant Technologies* (New York: W. W. Norton, 2014).

58. Executive Office of the President National Science and Technology Council Committee on Technology, "Preparing for the Future of Artificial Intelligence," *Office of Science and Technology Policy*, October 2016, https://www.whitehouse.gov/sites/default/files/whitehouse_files/microsites/ostp/NSTC/preparing_for_the_future_of_ai.pdf.

59. See, e.g., Tene and Polonetsky, "Big Data for All"; Executive Office of the President, *Big Data*.

60. This move is reminiscent of public debate in the 1980s over computer matching of federal databases to extract useful knowledge, resulting in the 1986 Computer Matching and Privacy Protection Act, which placed restraints on the matching of disparate databases. The details do not matter; what matters is that the path taken was to put protocols in place that required an articulation of benefits while allowing stakeholders (or their representatives) to identify potential harms.

61. See, e.g., danah boyd and Kate Crawford, "Critical Questions for Big Data: Provocations for a Cultural, Technological and Scholarly Phenomenon," *Information,*

Communication and Society 15, no. 5 (2012): 662–79; Neil M. Richards and Jonathan H. King, "Big Data Ethics," *Wake Forest Law Review* 49, no. 2 (Summer 2014): 393–432.

62. See, e.g., Frank Pasquale, *The Black Box Society: The Secret Algorithms That Control Money and Information* (Boston: Harvard University Press, 2015); Solon Barocas and Andrew D. Selbst, "Big Data's Disparate Impact," *California Law Review* 104, no. 3 (2016): 671–732.

63. See boyd and Crawford, "Critical Questions for Big Data."

64. See Tad Friend, "Sam Altman's Manifest Destiny," *New Yorker*, October 10, 2016, http://www.newyorker.com/magazine/2016/10/10/sam-altmans-manifest-destiny. "Y Combinator has even begun using an A.I. bot, Hal9000, to help it sift admission applications: the bot's neural net trains itself by assessing previous applications and those companies' outcomes. 'What's it looking for?' [Tad Friend] asked Altman. 'I have no idea,' he replied. 'That's the unsettling thing about neural networks—you have no idea what they're doing, and they can't tell you.'" My thanks to Ira Rubenstein for drawing this to my attention.

65. See Jenna Burrell, "How the Machine 'Thinks': Understanding Opacity in Machine Learning Algorithms," *Big Data and Society*, January 5, 2016.

66. See Kate Crawford and Jason Schultz, "Big Data and Due Process: Toward a Framework to Redress Predictive Privacy Harms," *Boston College Law Review* 55 (2014): 93–128; Danielle K. Citron and Frank Pasquale, "The Scored Society: Due Process for Automated Predictions," *Washington Law Review* 89, no. 1 (2014): 1–34.

67. See Pasquale, *Black Box Society.*

68. See Pasquale, *Black Box Society.* See also Cathy O'Neil, *Weapons of Math Destruction: How Big Data Increases Inequality and Threatens Democracy* (New York: Crown, 2016).

69. See, e.g., Karen Levy, "The Future of Work: What Isn't Counted Counts," *Pacific Standard*, August 3, 2015, http://www.psmag.com/business-economics/the-future-of-work-what-isnt-counted-counts; Jodi Kantor, "Working Anything but 9 to 5," *New York Times*, August 13, 2014, http://www.nytimes.com/interactive/2014/08/13/us/starbucks-workers-scheduling-hours.html.

70. An (albeit extreme) example of how this information may be used is the "social credit system" that China wishes to roll out nationwide by 2020. See Josh Chin and Gillian Wong, "China's New Tool for Social Control: A Credit Rating for Everything," *Wall Street Journal*, November 28, 2016, http://www.wsj.com/articles/chinas-new-tool-for-social-control-a-credit-rating-for-everything-1480351590.

71. See, e.g., William A. Gorton, "Manipulating Citizens: How Political Campaigns' Use of Behavioral Social Science Harms Democracy," *New Political Science* 38, no. 1 (2016); "Cross-Device Offers Political Advertisers Great Promise—and Significant Challenges," *AdExchanger*, January 12, 2016, https://adexchanger.com/politics/cross-device-offers-political-advertisers-great-promise-and-significant-challenges/.

72. See, e.g., Ira Rubinstein et al., "Data Mining and Internet Profiling: Emerging Regulatory and Technological Approaches," *University of Chicago Law Review* 75, no. 1 (2008): 261–85.

73. One exception is Rachel Schutt and Cathy O'Neil, *Doing Data Science: Straight Talk from the Frontline* (Sebastopol, Calif.: O'Reilly Media, 2014), 6.

74. See https://www.niaid.nih.gov/about/organization/daids/Pages/big-data.aspx.

75. See Bernard Marr, "The 7 Most Data-Rich Companies in the World," *Data Science Central*, April 18, 2015, http://www.datasciencecentral.com/profiles/blogs/the-7-most-data-rich-companies-in-the-world; see also Lev Manovich, "Trending: The Promises and the Challenges of Big Social Data," April 28, 2011, http://manovich.net/content/04-projects/067-trending-the-promises-and-the-challenges-of-big-social-data/64-article-2011.pdf, quoted in boyd and Crawford, "Critical Questions for Big Data," 673.

76. See, e.g., boyd and Crawford, "Critical Questions for Big Data"; Tene and Polonetsky, "Big Data for All." Mandatory data retention differs from country to country; see https://www.eff.org/issues/mandatory-data-retention/us.

77. See Craig Konnoth, "Health Information Equity," *Penn Law Review* 165, no. 6 (2017): 1317–76.

78. To understand how serious this motivation is, consider Facebook's confrontation with ad blockers; see Josh Constine, "Facebook Rolls Out Code to Nullify AdBlock Plus' Workaround Again," *Tech Crunch*, August 11, 2016, https://techcrunch.com/2016/08/11/friendblock/.

79. Compare Google's monitoring of Gmail inboxes for child pornography. With the practice of scanning emails for advertising keywords, "Google's creepy data practices have helped police catch who they think is an even bigger creep." Kevin Roose, "Google Detected a User Sending Child Porn from His Gmail Account and Alerted the Police," *New York Magazine*, August 4, 2014, http://nymag.com/daily/intelligencer/2014/08/google-scans-users-email-finds-child-porn.html. See also Samuel Gibbs, "Gmail Does Scan All Emails, New Google Terms Clarify," *Guardian*, April 15, 2014, https://www.theguardian.com/technology/2014/apr/15/gmail-scans-all-emails-new-google-terms-clarify.

80. Experts seem to be unanimous in worrying about the egregious wealth disparities in the United States and around the world. Perhaps data disparities are at the root of the issue. This seems to be an important issue worth studying.

81. "Increasingly, it has begun to seem as though there is one set of rules for the ordinary consumer and institutional investors serving that consumer and a very different set for the financial cognoscenti." Julie E. Cohen, "The Regulatory State in the Information Age," *Theoretical Inquiries in Law* 17, no. 2 (2016): 387.

82. See Adam D. I. Kramer, Jamie E. Guillory, and Jeffrey T. Hancock, "Experimental Evidence of Massive-Scale Emotional Contagion Through Social Networks," *Proceedings of the National Academy of Sciences* 111, no. 24 (2014): 8788–90; Adam Tanner, "How Data Brokers Make Money Off Your Medical Records," *Scientific*

American, February 1, 2016, https://www.scientificamerican.com/article/how-data-brokers-make-money-off-your-medical-records/; Erin Digitale, "On the Records: Tapping into Stanford's Mother Lode of Clinical Information," *Stanford Medicine* (Summer 2012), http://sm.stanford.edu/archive/stanmed/2012summer/article5.html.

83. See, e.g., Bev Harris et al., *Black Box Voting: Ballot Tampering in the 21st Century* (High Point, N.C.: Plan Nine, 2003).

84. See Executive Office of the President, *Big Data*, 40–43.

85. See Joseph Turow et al., "Americans Reject Tailored Advertising and Three Activities That Enable It," University of Pennsylvania Departmental Papers of the Annenberg School for Communication, September 2009, http://repository.upenn.edu/cgi/viewcontent.cgi?article=1138&context=asc_papers.

86. See Privacy Rights Clearing House, "Data Breaches," accessed October 7, 2016, https://www.privacyrights.org/data-breaches.

87. Nicole Perlroth, "Yahoo Says Hackers Stole Data on 500 Million Users in 2014," *New York Times*, September 22, 2016, http://www.nytimes.com/2016/09/23/technology/yahoo-hackers.html?_r=0. BBC, "Yahoo 'State' Hackers Stole Data from 500 Million Users," September 23, 2016, http://www.bbc.com/news/world-us-canada-37447016. Harriet Taylor, "Yahoo CEO Mayer Knew About Data Breach in July: Report." CNBC, September 23, 2016. http://www.cnbc.com/2016/09/23/yahoo-ceo-mayer-knew-about-data-breach-in-july-report.html. Jeff John Roberts. "Yahoo Has Been Hacked: What You Need to Know." *Fortune*, September 22, 2016, http://fortune.com/2016/09/22/yahoo-hack-qa/.

88. Courts have difficulty dealing with litigation involving data breaches, as a central component of standing (a required element for judicial review) is an articulation of harm or injury. For an in-depth explanation of this difficulty in the courts, see Daniel J. Solove and Danielle Keats Citron, "Risk and Anxiety: A Theory of Data-Breach Harms," December 14, 2016, https://ssrn.com/abstract=2885638.

89. See Pasquale, *Black Box Society*, 149.

90. See, e.g., Federal Trade Commission, "Big Data: A Tool for Inclusion or Exclusion? Understanding the Issues," FTC Report, January 2016, https://www.ftc.gov/system/files/documents/reports/big-data-tool-inclusion-or-exclusion-understanding-issues/160106big-data-rpt.pdf.

91. See David Robinson et al., "Civil Rights, Big Data and Our Algorithmic Future," *Upturn*, September 2014, https://bigdata.fairness.io/.

92. See, e.g., the 1974 Fair Credit Billing Act. I am indebted to Finn Brunton for pointing out these connections.

93. For an overview of state legislation regarding security breach notifications, see "Security Breach Notification Laws," *National Conference of State Legislatures*, March 29, 2018, http://www.ncsl.org/research/telecommunications-and-information-technology/security-breach-notification-laws.aspx. For two recent high-profile hacking cases, see David E. Sanger et al., "Attack Gave Chinese Hackers Privileged Access to U.S. Systems," *New York Times*, June 20, 2015, http://www.nytimes.com/2015/06/21/us/attack-gave-chinese-hackers-privileged-access-to-us-systems.html, and Jessica

Silver-Greenberg et al., "JPMorgan Chase Hacking Affects 76 Million Households," *New York Times*, October 2, 2014, http://dealbook.nytimes.com/2014/10/02/jpmorgan-discovers-further-cyber-security-issues/.

94. See U.S. Department of Health, Education and Welfare, *Records, Computers, and the Rights of Citizens: Report of the Secretary's Advisory Committee on Automated Personal Data Systems* (Washington, D.C.: Author, 1973), http://www.justice.gov/opcl/docs/rec-com-rights.pdf.

95. This, of course, is not unique to the United States. Equivalent principles exist in other liberal democracies; see, e.g., Article 8 of the Canadian Charter of Rights and Freedoms (stipulating that "Everyone has the right to be secure against unreasonable search or seizure").

96. For a discussion of predictive policing, see Sarah Brayne et al., "Predictive Policing," *Data and Civil Rights*, October 27, 2015, http://www.datacivilrights.org/pubs/2015-1027/Predictive_Policing.pdf, and Cynthia Rudin, "Predictive Policing: Using Machine Learning to Detect Patterns of Crime," *WIRED*, August 2013, http://www.wired.com/insights/2013/08/predictive-policing-using-machine-learning-to-detect-patterns-of-crime/.

97. The 1974 Privacy Act was one effort to maintain separation among the databases accrued by disparate government agencies.

98. For a comprehensive overview of the revelations, see *Guardian*, "The NSA Files," accessed October 7, 2016, https://www.theguardian.com/us-news/the-nsa-files.

99. Compare the concept of *gezeihra* as a "fence around the Torah" in Jewish law; see "Halakhah: Jewish Law," *Judaism 101*, accessed February 9, 2016, http://www.jewfaq.org/halakhah.htm.

100. Philip Pettit, *Republicanism: A Theory of Freedom and Government*, (Oxford: Oxford University Press, 1997), cited in Finn Brunton and Helen Nissenbaum, *Obfuscation: A User's Guide for Privacy and Protest* (Cambridge, Mass.: MIT Press, 2015), 79–80.

101. Finn Brunton and I have argued that information yields power to the holder, which is particularly dangerous when that holder is already powerful. See Brunton and Nissenbaum, *Obfuscation*.

102. E.g., the 1968 Omnibus Crime Control and Safe Streets Act, 1974 Privacy Act, 1988 Computer Matching and Privacy Protection Act, 1996 Health Insurance Portability and Accountability Act, 1999 Financial Services Modernization (Gramm-Leach-Bliley) Act, etc.

103. See *Birchfield v. North Dakota*, 136 S. Ct. 2160, 2178 (2016). Thanks to Kiel Brennan-Marquez for drawing my attention to this case. For further discussion on anxiety as an articulation of injury sufficient to satisfy standing requirements, see Solove and Citron, "Risk and Anxiety."

104. "The ability to harvest the wealth of information contained in biomedical Big Data will advance our understanding of human health and disease." "Big Data to Knowledge," National Institutes of Health, accessed January 19, 2017, https://datascience.nih.gov/bd2k.

105. See Federal Trade Commission, "Data Brokers: A Call for Transparency and Accountability," May 2014, https://www.ftc.gov/system/files/documents/reports/data-brokers-call-transparency-accountability-report-federal-trade-commission-may-2014/140527databrokerreport.pdf. See also Katherine J. Strandburg, "Home, Home on the Web and Other Fourth Amendment Implications of Technosocial Change," *Maryland Law Review* 70, no. 3 (2011): 614–80.

106. *United States v. Jones*, 565 U.S. 400, 415 (2012) (Sotomayor, J., concurring).

107. See David C. Gray and Danielle Keats Citron, "The Right to Quantitative Privacy," *Minnesota Law Review* 98 (2013): 62–144; see also Helen Nissenbaum, "Toward an Approach to Privacy in Public: Challenges of Information Technology," *Ethics and Behavior* 7, no. 3 (1997): 207–19; Daniel Solove, *The Digital Person: Technology and Privacy in the Information Age* (New York: NYU Press, 2004), chap. 8.

108. See Mayer-Schönberger and Cukier, *Big Data*.

109. See discussion of this and related points in Barocas and Nissenbaum, "Big Data's End Run," and also Katherine J. Strandburg, "Freedom of Association in a Networked World: First Amendment Regulation of Relational Surveillance," *Boston College Law Review* 49 (2008): 741–821.

110. For a discussion of how this played out in the Volkswagen scandal, see generally Cohen, "Regulatory State."

111. See Philip N. Howard, *Pax Technica: How the Internet of Things May Set Us Free or Lock Us Up* (New Haven, Conn.: Yale University Press, 2015). See also Michael D. Birnhack and Niva Elkin-Koren, "The Invisible Handshake: The Reemergence of the State in the Digital Environment," *Virginia Journal of Law and Technology* 8, no. 2 (Summer 2003): 1–57; Kiel Brennan-Marquez, "Private Searches in an Age of Big Data," July 12, 2016, http://papers.ssrn.com/sol3/papers.cfm?abstract_id=2808829.

112. See Tech 2, "EU Says Firms Like Google and Facebook Must Meet Privacy Laws," Firstpost, June 7, 2014, http://tech.firstpost.com/news-analysis/eu-says-firms-like-google-facebook-must-meet-privacy-rules-225348.html.

113. For a non–big data example of this problem, see David E. Sanger, "Prospect of Self-Inspections by Iran Feeds Opposition to Nuclear Deal," *New York Times*, August 21, 2015, http://www.nytimes.com/2015/08/22/world/middleeast/prospect-of-self-inspections-by-iran-feeds-opposition-to-nuclear-deal.html.

114. Inspired by this argument, there has been growth in research focusing on issues of fairness, due process for decision making, and so forth.

References

Akhgar, Babak, Gregor Saathoff, Hamid R. Arabnia, Richard Hill, Andrew Staniforth, and Petra Saskia Bayerl. *Application of Big Data for National Security: A Practitioner's Guide to Emerging Technologies*. Oxford: Elsevier, 2015.

Anderson, Chris. "The End of Theory: The Data Deluge Makes the Scientific Method Obsolete." *Wired*, June 23, 2008. https://www.wired.com/2008/06/pb-theory/.

Arthur, Charles. "Google Facing Legal Threat from Six European Countries over Privacy." *Guardian*, April 2, 2013. https://www.theguardian.com/technology/2013/apr/02/google-privacy-policy-legal-threat-europe.

Barocas, Solon, and Helen Nissenbaum. "Big Data's End Run Around Anonymity and Consent." In *Privacy, Big Data and the Public Good: Frameworks for Engagement*, edited by Julia Lane, Victoria Stodden, Stefan Bender, and Helen Nissenbaum, 44–75. Cambridge: Cambridge University Press, 2015.

Barocas, Solon, and Andrew D. Selbst. "Big Data's Disparate Impact." *California Law Review* 104, no. 3 (2016): 671–732.

BBC. "Yahoo 'State' Hackers Stole Data from 500 Million Users." September 23, 2016. http://www.bbc.com/news/world-us-canada-37447016.

Bienkowski, Marie, Mingyu Feng, and Barbara Means. *Enhancing Teaching and Learning Through Educational Data Mining and Learning Analytics: An Issue Brief.* Washington, D.C.: U.S. Department of Education, 2012. https://tech.ed.gov/wp-content/uploads/2014/03/edm-la-brief.pdf.

Birnhack, Michael D., and Niva Elkin-Koren. "The Invisible Handshake: The Reemergence of the State in the Digital Environment." *Virginia Journal of Law and Technology* 8, no. 2 (Summer 2003): 1–57.

boyd, danah, and Kate Crawford. "Critical Questions for Big Data: Provocations for a Cultural, Technological and Scholarly Phenomenon." *Information, Communication and Society* 15, no. 5 (2012): 662–79.

Bowker, Geoffrey C. *Memory Practices in the Sciences.* Cambridge, Mass.: MIT Press, 2005.

Bowker, Geoffrey C., and Susan Leigh Star, eds. *Sorting Things Out: Classification and Its Consequences.* Cambridge, Mass.: MIT Press, 1999.

Brayne, Sarah, Alex Rosenblat, and danah boyd. "Predictive Policing." *Data and Civil Rights*, October 27, 2015. http://www.datacivilrights.org/pubs/2015-1027/Predictive_Policing.pdf.

Brennan-Marquez, Kiel. "Fourth Amendment Fiduciaries." *Fordham Law Review* 84, no. 2 (2015): 611–59.

———. "Private Searches in an Age of Big Data." July 12, 2016. http://papers.ssrn.com/sol3/papers.cfm?abstract_id=2808829.

Brin, David. *The Transparent Society: Will Technology Force Us to Choose Between Privacy and Freedom?* Cambridge, Mass.: Perseus Books, 1998.

Brunton, Finn, and Helen Nissenbaum. *Obfuscation: A User's Guide for Privacy and Protest.* Cambridge, Mass.: MIT Press, 2015.

Brynjolfsson, Erik, and Andrew McAfee. *The Second Machine Age: Work, Progress, and Prosperity in a Time of Brilliant Technologies.* New York: W. W. Norton, 2014.

Burrell, Jenna. "How the Machine 'Thinks': Understanding Opacity in Machine Learning Algorithms." *Big Data and Society*, January 5, 2016.

Calo, M. Ryan "Against Notice Skepticism in Privacy (and Elsewhere)." *Notre Dame Law Review* 87, no. 3 (2013): 1027–72.

Cate, Fred H. "The Failure of Fair Information Practice Principles." In *Consumer Protection in the Age of the Information Economy*, edited by Jane K. Winn, 341–78. Burlington, Vt.: Ashgate, 2006.

Cate, Fred H., Peter Cullen, and Viktor Mayer-Schönberger. "Data Protection Principles for the 21st Century: Revising the 1980 OECD Guidelines." Oxford Internet Institute, March 2014. http://www.oii.ox.ac.uk/publications/Data_Protection_Principles_for_the_21st_Century.pdf.

Cate, Fred H., and Viktor Mayer-Schönberger. "Notice and Consent in a World of Big Data." *International Data Privacy Law* 3, no. 2 (2013), 67–73.

Citron, Danielle K., and Frank Pasquale. "The Scored Society: Due Process for Automated Predictions." *Washington Law Review* 89, no. 1 (2014): 1–34.

Cohen, Julie E. "The Zombie First Amendment." *William and Mary Law Review* 56, no. 3 (2015): 1119–58.

Constine, Josh. "Facebook Rolls Out Code to Nullify AdBlock Plus' Workaround Again." *Tech Crunch*, August 11, 2016. https://techcrunch.com/2016/08/11/friendblock/.

Crawford, Kate, and Jason Schultz. "Big Data and Due Process: Toward a Framework to Redress Predictive Privacy Harms." *Boston College Law Review* 55 (2014): 93–128.

Cukier, Kenneth Neil, and Viktor Mayer-Schönberger. "The Rise of Big Data: How It's Changing the Way We Think About the World." *Foreign Affairs* 92, no. 3 (May/June 2013): 28–40.

Datta, Amit, Michael Carl Tschantz, and Anupam Datta. "Automated Experiments on Ad Privacy Settings." *Proceedings on Privacy Enhancing Technologies 2015* 1 (2015): 92–112.

Digitale, Erin. "On the Records: Tapping into Stanford's Mother Lode of Clinical Information." *Stanford Medicine* (Summer 2012). http://sm.stanford.edu/archive/stanmed/2012summer/article5.html.

Duhigg, Charles. "How Companies Learn Your Secrets." *New York Times*, February 16, 2012. http://www.nytimes.com/2012/02/19/magazine/shopping-habits.html.

Executive Office of the President. *Big Data: Seizing Opportunities, Preserving Values*. North Charleston, S.C.: CreateSpace, 2014.

Federal Trade Commission. "Big Data: A Tool for Inclusion or Exclusion? Understanding the Issues." FTC Report, January 2016. https://www.ftc.gov/system/files/documents/reports/big-data-tool-inclusion-or-exclusion-understanding-issues/160106big-data-rpt.pdf.

———. "Data Brokers: A Call for Transparency and Accountability." FTC Report, May 2014. https://www.ftc.gov/system/files/documents/reports/data-brokers-call-transparency-accountability-report-federal-trade-commission-may-2014/140527databrokerreport.pdf.

Feyerabend, Paul. *Against Method*. 4th ed.. New York: Verso, 2010.

Gitelman, Lisa, ed. *"Raw Data" Is an Oxymoron*. Cambridge, Mass.: MIT Press, 2013.

Gray, David C., and Danielle Keats Citron. "The Right to Quantitative Privacy." *Minnesota Law Review* 98 (2013): 62–144.

Guardian. "The NSA Files." Accessed October 7, 2016. https://www.theguardian.com/us-news/the-nsa-files.

"Halakhah: Jewish Law." *Judaism 101*. Accessed February 9, 2016. http://www.jewfaq.org/halakhah.htm.

Heller, Christian. *Post-Privacy: Prima leben ohne Privatsphäre*. Munich: C. H. Beck, 2011.

Howard, Philip N. *Pax Technica: How the Internet of Things May Set Us Free or Lock Us Up*. New Haven, Conn.: Yale University Press, 2015.

Hvistendahl, Mara. "Can Predictive Policing Prevent Crime Before It Happens?" *Science*, September 28, 2016. http://www.sciencemag.org/news/2016/09/can-predictive-policing-prevent-crime-it-happens.

"IBM Watson Health." IBM Think. Accessed February 9, 2016. http://www.ibm.com/smarterplanet/us/en/think/watson-health/.

Kalorama Information. "Evidence-Based Medicine: Bringing Big Data to Healthcare Consumers." *Scientific Computing*, November 26, 2014. http://www.scientificcomputing.com/news/2014/11/evidence-based-medicine-bringing-big-data-healthcare-consumers.

Kantor, Jodi. "Working Anything but 9 to 5." *New York Times*, August 13, 2014. http://www.nytimes.com/interactive/2014/08/13/us/starbucks-workers-scheduling-hours.html.

Kitchin, Rob. *The Data Revolution: Big Data, Open Data, Data Infrastructures and Their Consequences*. London: Sage, 2014.

Konnoth, Craig. "Health Information Equity." *University of Pennsylvania Law Review* 165, no. 6 (2017): 1317–76.

Koops, Bert-Jaap. "On Decision Transparency, or How to Enhance Privacy After the Computational Turn." In *Privacy, Due Process and the Computational Turn: The Philosophy of Law Meets the Philosophy of Technology*, edited by Mireille Hildebrandt and Katja De Vries, 196–220. New York: Routledge, 2013.

Kramer, Adam D. I., Jamie E. Guillory, and Jeffrey T. Hancock. "Experimental Evidence of Massive-Scale Emotional Contagion Through Social Networks." *Proceedings of the National Academy of Sciences* 111, no. 24 (2014): 8788–90.

Kuhn, Thomas S. *The Structure of Scientific Revolutions*. 3rd ed. Chicago: University of Chicago Press, 1996.

Kusserow, Richard P. "The Government Needs Computer Matching to Root Out Waste and Fraud." *Communications of the ACM* 27, no. 6 (June 1984): 542–45.

Lazar, David, Ryan Kennedy, Gary King, and Alessandro Vespignani. "The Parable of Google Flu: Traps in Big Data Analysis." *Science* 343, no. 6176 (2014): 1203–5.

Lessig, Lawrence. "The Law of the Horse: What Cyberlaw Might Teach." *Harvard Law Review* 113, no. 2 (1999): 501–49.

Levy, Karen. "The Future of Work: What Isn't Counted Counts." *Pacific Standard*, August 3, 2015. http://www.psmag.com/business-economics/the-future-of-work-what-isnt-counted-counts.

Lewis, Michael. *Moneyball: The Art of Winning an Unfair Game*. New York: W. W. Norton, 2004.

Manovich, Lev. "Trending: The Promises and the Challenges of Big Social Data." Manovich [blog], April 28, 2011. http://manovich.net/content/04-projects/067-trending-the-promises-and-the-challenges-of-big-social-data/64-article-2011.pdf.

Marr, Bernard. "The 7 Most Data-Rich Companies in the World." *Data Science Central*, April 18, 2015. http://www.datasciencecentral.com/profiles/blogs/the-7-most-data-rich-companies-in-the-world.

Martin, Kirsten. "Privacy Notices as Tabula Rasa: An Empirical Investigation into How Complying with a Privacy Notice Is Related to Meeting Privacy Expectations Online." *Journal of Public Policy and Marketing* 34, no. 2 (Fall 2015): 210–27.

Mayer-Schönberger, Viktor, and Kenneth Cukier. *Big Data: A Revolution That Will Transform How We Live, Work, and Think*. New York: Houghton, Mifflin, Harcourt, 2013.

McDonald, Aleecia, and Lorrie Faith Cranor. "The Cost of Reading Privacy Policies." *I/S: A Journal of Law and Policy for the Information Society* 4, no. 3 (2008): 540–65.

McNeal, Gregory S. "Facebook Manipulated User News Feeds to Create Emotional Responses." *Forbes*, June 28, 2014. http://www.forbes.com/sites/gregorymcneal/2014/06/28/facebook-manipulated-user-news-feeds-to-create-emotional-contagion/#2715e4857a0b11dcc1245fd8.

Meeder, Brendan, Jennifer Tam, Patrick G. Kelley, and Lorrie F. Cranor. "RT @IWantPrivacy: Widespread Violation of Privacy Settings in the Twitter Social Network." *Proceedings of Web 2.0 Security and Privacy (W2SP 2010)*. Oakland, Calif., 2010.

Mundie, Craig. "Privacy Pragmatism: Focus on Data Use, Not Data Collection." *Foreign Affairs*, March/April 2014. https://www.foreignaffairs.com/articles/2014-02-12/privacy-pragmatism.

Nissenbaum, Helen. "A Contextual Approach to Privacy Online." *Daedalus* 140, no. 4 (Fall 2011): 32–48.

———. *Privacy in Context: Technology, Policy, and the Integrity of Social Life*. Palo Alto, Calif.: Stanford University Press, 2010.

———. "Respect for Context as a Benchmark for Privacy Online: What It Is and Isn't." In *Social Dimensions of Privacy: Interdisciplinary Perspectives*, edited by Beate Roessler and Dorota Mokrosinska, 278–302. Cambridge: Cambridge University Press, 2015.

———. "Respecting Context to Protect Privacy: Why Meaning Matters." *Science and Engineering Ethics*, July 12, 2015. http://link.springer.com/article/10.1007%2Fs11948-015-9674-9.

———. "Toward an Approach to Privacy in Public: Challenges of Information Technology." *Ethics and Behavior* 7, no. 3 (1997): 207–19.

O'Neil, Cathy. *Weapons of Math Destruction: How Big Data Increases Inequality and Threatens Democracy*. New York: Crown, 2016.

Pasquale, Frank. *The Black Box Society: The Secret Algorithms That Control Money and Information*. Boston: Harvard University Press, 2015.

Perlroth, Nicole. "Yahoo Says Hackers Stole Data on 500 Million Users in 2014." *New York Times*, September 22, 2016. http://www.nytimes.com/2016/09/23/technology/yahoo-hackers.html?_r=0.

Pettit, Philip. *Republicanism: A Theory of Freedom and Government*. Oxford: Oxford University Press, 1997.

President's Council of Advisors on Science and Technology (PCAST). *Big Data and Privacy: A Technological Perspective*. North Charleston, S.C.: CreateSpace, 2014.

Privacy Rights Clearing House. "Data Breaches." Accessed October 7, 2016. https://www.privacyrights.org/data-breaches.

Reidenberg, Joel R., and Lorrie Faith Cranor, "Can User Agents Accurately Represent Privacy Policies?" Discussion Draft 1.0. August 30, 2002. http://papers.ssrn.com/sol3/papers.cfm?abstract_id=328860.

Reidenberg, Joel R., N. Cameron Russell, Alexander J. Callen, Sophia Qasir, and Thomas B. Norton. "Privacy Harms and the Effectiveness of the Notice and Choice Framework." Fordham Law Legal Studies Research Paper No. 2418247. March 29, 2014. http://papers.ssrn.com/sol3/papers.cfm?abstract_id=2418247.

Richards, Neil M., and Jonathan H. King. "Big Data Ethics." *Wake Forest Law Review* 49, no. 2 (Summer 2014): 393–432.

Roberts, Jeff John. "Yahoo Has Been Hacked: What You Need to Know." *Fortune*, September 22, 2016. http://fortune.com/2016/09/22/yahoo-hack-qa/.

Robinson, David, Harlan Yu, and Aaron Rieke. "Civil Rights, Big Data and Our Algorithmic Future." *Upturn*, September 2014. https://bigdata.fairness.io/.

Rubens, Paul. "Is Big Data Dating the Key to Long-Lasting Romance?" BBC, March 25, 2014. http://www.bbc.com/news/business-26613909.

Rubinstein, Ira. "Big Data: The End of Privacy or a New Beginning?" *International Data Privacy Law* 3, no. 2 (2013): 74–87.

Rubinstein, Ira, Ronald D. Lee, and Paul M. Schwartz. "Data Mining and Internet Profiling: Emerging Regulatory and Technological Approaches." *University of Chicago Law Review* 75, no. 1 (2008): 261–85.

Rudin, Cynthia. "Predictive Policing: Using Machine Learning to Detect Patterns of Crime." *WIRED*, August 2013. http://www.wired.com/insights/2013/08/predictive-policing-using-machine-learning-to-detect-patterns-of-crime/.

Sanger, David E. "Prospect of Self-Inspections by Iran Feeds Opposition to Nuclear Deal." *New York Times*, August 21, 2015. http://www.nytimes.com/2015/08/22/world/middleeast/prospect-of-self-inspections-by-iran-feeds-opposition-to-nuclear-deal.html.

Sanger, David E., Nicole Perlroth, and Michael D. Shear. "Attack Gave Chinese Hackers Privileged Access to U.S. Systems." *New York Times*, June 20, 2015. http://www

.nytimes.com/2015/06/21/us/attack-gave-chinese-hackers-privileged-access-to-us-systems.html.

Satell, Greg. "The Future of Marketing Combines Big Data with Human Intuition." *Forbes*, October 12, 2014. http://www.forbes.com/sites/gregsatell/2014/10/12/the-future-of-marketing-combines-big-data-with-human-intuition/#2715e4857a0b7fd34974331d.

Schutt, Rachel, and Cathy O'Neil. *Doing Data Science: Straight Talk from the Frontline.* Sebastopol, Calif.: O'Reilly Media, 2014.

"Security Breach Notification Laws." National Conference of State Legislatures, March 29, 2018. http://www.ncsl.org/research/telecommunications-and-information-technology/security-breach-notification-laws.aspx.

Seemann, Michael. *Digital Tailspin: Ten Rules for the Internet After Snowden.* Amsterdam: Institute of Network Cultures, 2015.

Shattuck, John. "Computer Matching Is a Serious Threat to Individual Rights." *Communications of the ACM* 27, no. 6 (June 1984): 538–41.

Silver, Nate. *The Signal and the Noise: Why So Many Predictions Fail—But Some Don't.* New York: Penguin Books, 2012.

Silver-Greenberg, Jessica, Matthew Goldstein, and Nicole Perlroth. "JPMorgan Chase Hacking Affects 76 Million Households." *New York Times*, October 2, 2014. http://dealbook.nytimes.com/2014/10/02/jpmorgan-discovers-further-cyber-security-issues/.

Sprenger, Polly. "Sun on Privacy: 'Get Over It.'" *WIRED*, January 26, 1999. http://archive.wired.com/politics/law/news/1999/01/17538.

Strandburg, Katherine J. "Freedom of Association in a Networked World: First Amendment Regulation of Relational Surveillance." *Boston College Law Review* 49 (2008): 741–821.

———. "Home, Home on the Web and Other Fourth Amendment Implications of Technosocial Change." *Maryland Law Review* 70, no. 3 (2011): 614–80.

———. "Monitoring, Datafication, and Consent: Legal Approaches to Privacy in the Big Data Context." In *Privacy, Big Data and the Public Good: Frameworks for Engagement*, edited by Julia Lane, Victoria Stodden, Stefan Bender, and Helen Nissenbaum, 5–43. Cambridge: Cambridge University Press, 2015.

Tanner, Adam. "How Data Brokers Make Money Off Your Medical Records." *Scientific American*, February 1, 2016. https://www.scientificamerican.com/article/how-data-brokers-make-money-off-your-medical-records/.

Taylor, Harriet. "Yahoo CEO Mayer Knew About Data Breach in July: Report." CNBC, September 23, 2016. http://www.cnbc.com/2016/09/23/yahoo-ceo-mayer-knew-about-data-breach-in-july-report.html.

Tech 2. "EU Says Firms Like Google and Facebook Must Meet Privacy Laws." Firstpost, June 7, 2014. http://tech.firstpost.com/news-analysis/eu-says-firms-like-google-facebook-must-meet-privacy-rules-225348.html.

Tene, Omer, and Jules Polonetsky. "Big Data for All: Privacy and User Control in the Age of Analytics." *Northwestern Journal of Technology and Intellectual Property* 11, no. 5 (2013): 239–73.

Toubiana, Vincent, Arvind Narayanan, Dan Boneh, Helen Nissenbaum, and Solon Barocas. "Adnostic: Privacy Preserving Targeted Advertising." Paper presented at the 17th Annual Network and Distributed System Security Symposium, San Diego, March 2010.

Turow, Joseph. *The Daily You: How the New Advertising Industry Is Defining Your Identity and Your Worth*. New Haven, Conn.: Yale University Press, 2011.

Turow, Joseph, Jennifer King, Chris Jay Hoofnagle, Amy Bleakley, and Michael Hennessey. "Americans Reject Tailored Advertising and Three Activities That Enable It." University of Pennsylvania Departmental Papers of the Annenberg School for Communication, September 2009. http://repository.upenn.edu/cgi/viewcontent.cgi?article=1138&context=asc_papers.

U.S. Department of Health, Education, and Welfare. *Records, Computers, and the Rights of Citizens: Report of the Secretary's Advisory Committee on Automated Personal Data Systems*. Washington, D.C.: Author, 1973. http://www.justice.gov/opcl/docs/rec-com-rights.pdf.

Van Hoboken, Joris. "From Collection to Use in Privacy Regulation? A Forward-Looking Comparison of European and US Frameworks for Personal Data Processing." In *Exploring the Boundaries of Big Data*, edited by Bart van der Sloot, Dennis Broeders, and Erik Schrijvers, 231–59. Amsterdam: Amsterdam University Press, 2016.

Volokh, Eugene. "Freedom of Speech, Information Privacy, and the Troubling Implications of a Right to Stop People from Speaking About You." *Stanford Law Review* 52, no. 5 (2000): 1049–124.

Warren, Samuel D., and Louis D. Brandeis. "The Right to Privacy," *Harvard Law Review* 4, no. 5 (1890): 193–220.

White, Ryen W., Nicholas P. Tatonetti, Nigam H. Shah, Russ B. Altman, and Eric Horvitz. "Web-Scale Pharmacovigilance: Listening to Signals from the Crowd." *Journal of the American Medical Informatics Association* 20, no. 3 (2013): 404–8.

Willcox, Rachel. "Big-Data Analytics: The Power of Prediction." *Public Finance*, January 27, 2016. http://www.publicfinance.co.uk/feature/2016/01/big-data-analytics-power-prediction.

Wormeli, Paul. "The Promise of Big Data in Public Safety and Justice: Making Data Easier to Digest for More Law Enforcement Users." *Government Technology*, September 10, 2012. http://www.govtech.com/public-safety/The-Promise-of-Big-Data-in-Public-Safety-and-Justice.html.

Yakowitz, Jane. "Tragedy of the Data Commons." *Harvard Journal of Law and Technology* 25, no. 1 (Fall 2011): 1–67.

CHAPTER 11

Democratic Futures and the Internet of Things: How Information Infrastructure Will Become a Political Constitution

Philip N. Howard

Constitutions are collections of codified traditions and conventions that provide structure for political life. Good constitutions enunciate a governance system and define the relationships between and among citizens and political actors. In the years ahead, the Internet of Things (IoT), made up of billions of devices with small sensors, will encapsulate our political lives, communicate our political values, and constitute our political identities. These device networks will generate perfect behavioral data without giving citizens the right to opt out of data collection. The algorithms, terms of service, and interoperability protocols should not be of interest only to the engineers trying to build more consumer electronics; the scripts that make the IoT operate will have immense implications for governments and governance. Citizens will have their civic engagement shaped and constrained by the software and hardware of the IoT.

It is widely accepted that the Internet and social media have become a key component of modern civic engagement around the world, but the Internet of personal computers and mobile phones is transforming into a global network of devices. This next Internet is going to be very different, and constituted by billions of everyday objects with embedded batteries, sensors, and an address on the Internet. We will not notice or control most of the device networks that collect and share data on our behavior, but it will be a massive information infrastructure that could be put to the public good. There should be little doubt that the IoT will fully formalize how citizens express preferences and that it will be the means by which public policy is developed and enforced (Howard 2015b).

While lobbyists and campaign managers are playing with these rich and voluminous records of our lives, government agencies are tapping them, too. Tax agencies use complex fraud detection programs that look for suspicious Internet addresses and metadata. Ten years ago, New York state identified and stopped fifty thousand fraudulent tax returns; last year, its new analysis techniques caught 250,000 (Verhulst 2015). In Los Angeles, the city government's data-sharing program with a Google-owned navigation service is expected to turn smartphones into traffic sensors that will route participating drivers, and help reduce congestion and make the city more navigable (Bradley 2015). Such programs have their critics, but many government offices in the United States are now openly seeking help in analyzing the plethora of data at their disposal.

It is also important to realize that governance systems involve not just governments; they appear whenever a powerful actor can set rules and restrictions on people's behavior. For example, Uber has ordered its drivers to stay away from protests in China. To enforce the order, it will use drivers' cell phones to track car location and cancel the contracts of violators (Murphy 2015). Although Uber's policy is a business decision, this rule has the political implication of cutting off a transportation option for Chinese citizens who want to help reform their government. The ever-expanding IoT has emerged through an array of consumer electronics and industrial applications, but the scripts that operate it should be a public concern. Terms of service agreements, interoperability protocols, and the algorithms used for predictive behavioral targeting will all have immense implications for political participation and civic engagement in modern democracies.

There has never been anything like the constant and intimate feedback loop that the IoT is creating between citizens and whoever is on the other end of their data. Public policy makers, technology firms, and lobbyists are already seeking and using political information, so it is crucial to identify some ways of preserving a role for citizens and civil society groups in a political system fully constituted by its information infrastructure. If constitutions are collections of codified traditions and conventions that establish rules for governance systems and define levels of involvement between and among citizens and political actors, now is a good time to ask how the IoT might rival a constitution as the primary structure of political life. More important is thinking through the ways in which the IoT could be constructively built to support democratic values and civic engagement, rather than just commercial advertising and police surveillance.

Growing Scale, Deeper Collection

The "things" in IoT refer to a rapidly growing number of objects consumers use every day—such as eyeglasses, cars, thermostats—that have become "smart" with embedded power supplies, sensors, and Internet addresses that relay information about user behavior and device status across information networks. Most of these networked devices are everyday household items that are sending and receiving data about their status and our behavior. Unlike mobile phones and computers, devices on these networks are not designed for deliberate social interaction, content creation, or cultural consumption. The bulk of these networked devices simply communicate with other devices: coffee makers with coffee suppliers, car parts with service centers, clothes with designers, and on and on. The IoT will not be experienced through a browser. Indeed, as technology develops, many of us will be barely aware that so many objects around us have power, sensors, and the ability to send and receive data on their location, status, and how they are being used.

Industry estimates on the size of the IoT are often bullish (Howard 2015a), but it is safe to say that by 2020 there will be around eight billion people on the planet, and up to four times as many connected devices. Engineers expect so many of these connected devices that they have reconfigured the addressing system to allow for 2 to the 128th power addresses—which would allow for each atom on the face of the earth to have one hundred Internet addresses. So we can already give everything we produce an address, we have enough bandwidth to allow device-to-device communications, and we have the capacity to store all the data those exchanges create. One industry analyst estimates that the IoT will have an installed base of twenty-six billion devices by 2020, only a billion of which will be personal computers, tablets, and smartphones.

The IoT will be deeply embedded in our homes, and it will form a sensory network above our communities. The Organization for Economic Cooperation and Development estimates that a family of four will go from having an average of twenty-five devices connected to the Internet in 2017 to fifty devices by 2022. In the next five years, more than a thousand networked nanosatellites, which operate in formation and have low transition power, will be launched into space. Drone production, whether for the military or hobbyists, is difficult to track. But government security services have drones, and so do activists and humanitarian organizations. Every drone will have sensors and a radio that can broadcast information about the time, the device's location, its status, and how it has been used.

Politically Valuable Data, from Our Devices

Just how much do our smartphones, watches, and wearable technologies represent us to the wider world? Most cell phones sold in 2018 have the ability to take one location point per second. If you give an application on your phone permission to use location information, it will send information to a server at the rate the developer chooses and battery life allows. If you use a crowdsourcing application for traffic data, your phone is sending data about your commute. If you use an application to keep track of your jogging, your phone is generating geotagged data about your movements relative to other people. As a citizen in the United States, every time you take a picture, check in with your favorite social networking application, or track your health, data is sent from your phone to a cell phone tower or router and over a vast network of digital switches (Neff and Nafus 2016). The current objective for geolocation engineers is to design chips that require so little power that they can be left on all day. This would mean being able to generate one location point per second, all day long. Of course, as the price of making chips declines, even more wireless sensors can be put into devices other than your cell phone.

More important for political life, the data flows through many different kinds of organizations: the companies that maintain your digital networks, the start-ups that build the apps, and the third-party advertising agencies that have licensed access to this information. Companies such as Google, Facebook, and Microsoft can also retrieve this data at several points in the information flow. The national security services of several countries also have access to the data that flows over global device networks.

Unfortunately, freedom and privacy may not be the only political norms we sacrifice to have the consumer conveniences of networked devices. We are launching a political communication system coordinated by network devices that citizens and politicians are exploiting with varying degrees of sophistication. When the IoT is fully embedded in our polities, the unambiguous categories of democracy and dictatorship may no longer apply. In political science we treat governments as representative systems; however, we must also evaluate them as sociotechnical systems. We look at the informal and formal ways that citizens express their preferences, and the means by which public policy is developed and enforced. Instead, it may be more revealing to characterize a government on the basis of its policies and practices regarding network devices and information infrastructure. "Big data" can be usefully defined as large amounts of information, collected about many people, from many kinds of devices. Clearly, this next generation of the Internet is going to make big data truly gargantuan, with real consequences for our political lives. We are accustomed to defining politics as a process by which a few people represent the interests of many, either through some democratic process or by fiat. But political communication is less and less about a dialogue between and among citizens and politicians, because the IoT is increasingly reporting on our actual behavior, generating politically valuable data, and reflecting our habits, tastes, and beliefs.

Public opinion polling will no longer be small survey samples with noticeable error margins and carefully worded questions. Device networks will generate precise details on what we purchase and under which circumstances. The end result will not be a stream of data—it will be a tsunami of information about our real-world behavior, movements, and habits, not just our attitudes and aspirations. Political campaign managers have already adapted their political analysis and communication tools to be able to interpret and manipulate the public sphere through device networks. Polls, registration rolls, and credit-card data help campaign managers efficiently target the citizens most likely to give donations and show up on voting day (Nickerson and Rogers 2014; Howard 2005). And access to big data has allowed party strategists to focus on the coveted mid-spectrum of politics: undecided or ideologically "soft" voters who can be purposefully shown the personalities, policies, and content that will attract and appeal to them (Hersh 2015).

Scenarios for Behavioral Data and Political Participation

A very plausible scenario, however, is that the IoT evolves as a network of barely interoperable devices and networks locked down by a kind of digital-rights-management-for-the-material-world. The data collected over such devices may not be particularly controlled by us, and will be bought and sold by political campaign managers and industry lobbyists who seek to keep our participation bounded. To help think this through, it is useful to imagine how a consumer product like a coffee maker will evolve in the coming years.

Several manufacturers of pod coffee machines are already talking about ways to put wireless sensors into coffee machines and the coffee pods themselves. This would allow a company like Keurig to lock customers into their coffee supply chain. You may have a favorite Haitian fair-trade bean that is not available from the supplier—the coffee you really want to try might be "out of network." If you, as a consumer, try to slip in unlicensed coffee beans, the machine might refuse to produce coffee; in this scenario, your attempted hack might lock up the device. In addition, all of a user's attempts to play with the coffee machine will generate data for the manufacturer of the device, the supplier of pods, other devices in the household that belong to the same family, the coffee company's political action committee, and the industry association working on digital rights management for household devices.

The first attempt at controlling entire product coffee streams involved hidden ink and infrared scanners, the predecessor to IoT product stream control. The specific collaboration between Green Mountain Coffee Roasters and Keurig over single-serving coffee machines was beneficial for both firms (Howard 2014; Losey and Meinrath 2016). The coffee roasting company eventually bought up the coffee machine company, as sales grew from 1.2 billion USD in 2010 to 4 billion USD by 2014. To combat unlicensed coffee pods, the newly amalgamated firm attempted to introduce digital rights management (DRM) to the coffee pods, through machines that would scan pods for special ink markings. Without the digital rights to insert a particular pod into a particular machine, the machines would fail to brew. Unfortunately, the system was not backwards compatible, meaning that users of new machines could not use older pods (which conceptually had been licensed under a previous license). Even in the face of declining sales, the company's response was to allow a broader range of pods to be used, though still through a DRM licensing agreement (McGinn 2011; Dzieza 2014). Since IoT technologies will allow cheaper wireless sensors to be put into almost everything that is human made, the expansion of DRM to material goods will likely go hand in hand with the diffusion of the technology.

What will all this mean for democracy? Studies of Internet use in advanced democracies have found positive, though modest, causal effects on social capital and political participation (Gibson, Howard, and Ward 2000;

Norris 2000). If political participation and voluntary civic engagement is to be meaningfully democratic, we have to imagine ways that would allow you to commit valuable data about your coffee needs to the groups you want to support. In a few years, it may simply not be possible to buy a coffee machine that is not equipped with sensors and an address on the Internet. It may not be possible to buy this device and ask it to stop sending data to industry lobbyists. But it may be possible to require that the industry produce interoperable devices, so that you can put other pods in the machine and be politically active as a consumer. And it may be possible to tell the device to share your data with a fair-trade alliance and even the Haitian collective that is producing your favorite roast.

However the IoT evolves, it is safe to say that in a few years, the theories we have for understanding democratic processes will be tested and strained in ways we cannot anticipate. If the sensors on your coffee machine are sharing information over a network, and generating information that is useful on some political issues, has your coffee maker become media? If your coffee maker is intelligent enough to be tasked with sharing your data with the political groups you support, will it help you participate in civics? How many people will actually be able—with informed consent—to encode their devices with their political values?

The basis of a democracy is voluntary civic engagement: a person's participation in setting government policy should be intentional and a matter of choice. In democracies, citizens express their preferences through activism and voting.

The IoT could be the most effective mass surveillance infrastructure we have ever conceived and built, and the most detailed constitutional structure for our political interaction. As more of the objects we manufacture are powered and networked, more of our devices will communicate with other devices and with their original manufacturer, the information services we subscribe to, national security agencies, contractors, cloud computing services, and anyone else in the data stream. It is certain that the politics of the future will be guided by a new power paradigm: whoever controls the largest device networks will get the most sensor data and thus manage the largest number of connections between and among people and devices. Working with the behavioral data they have assembled from the IoT, they will use algorithms—the constitutive scripts for our political institutions—to mete out capacities and constraints on our political lives.

Historically, governments and politicians eager to interpret (and manipulate) citizen intent also relied on opinion polls, conversations with civic groups, social science research, and huge record-keeping projects like the census. Politicians have long tried to interpret citizen intent and manipulate it through rhetoric and campaign tricks. But pervasive device networks will change the rules. Civic engagement will increasingly become involuntary. None of us will have the opportunity to opt out of the behavioral data collection that generates public policy. Voluntary conversations among elected officials, political parties, lobbyists, and civic groups will be *less* important. Activism and petition-signing will be overshadowed by volumes of behavioral information—extracted from the IoT and of incalculable value because it will inform firms of consumer habits, enlighten policy makers as to the needs of citizens, and reveal the whims of voters to politicians.

Political lobbying is not a new sport, yet the IoT is going to be a game-changing resource for lobbyists. The more a lobbyist knows about the behavior of voters and donors, the easier it is to activate and organize those people on clients' behalf. Furthermore, the prohibitive cost of smart data mining will place it out of the reach of many civic groups, scientists, and journalists. If we are not careful, civil society groups will not have access to check on what big political players are doing with the IoT.

Scenarios for Special Interests and the IoT

Vast amounts of bandwidth are now used by devices communicating about their status and our behavior. Experts estimate that there will be over sixty billion devices in the IoT by 2020. That means almost a million new devices are being connected to the Internet each hour—and that the time to craft public policy is now.

These device networks will have an impact on our lives both as citizens and consumers. In 2015 the global car manufacturer Volkswagen (VW) was caught designing software for cheating on federal pollution tests (Hulac 2015). In this case, the cars were programmed to deceive the emission testing equipment, a large dynamometer or "rolling road" that measures pollutants as the car drives on a large treadmill-type platform. The scandal caused immense damage to VW's global brand; it was not simply about misleading consumers, but about undermining civic virtue as well. There are good reasons for pollution regulation—we need government to help us achieve a civic goal of polluting less. People who bought VW cars were misled as consumers, and drivers of those cars are implicated as bad citizens. VW was a bad corporate citizen for contributing to more photochemical smog in our cities.

With billions of sensors to learn from, there is no reason governments should not use them to make better public policy. And firms should be allowed to do in-depth market research on the behavior of their customers and use smart devices to run their businesses efficiently. It is very likely that citizens and consumers will benefit from IoT innovations, but policy makers have to let go of the idea that the Internet is made up of cell phones and laptops. First and foremost, they must provide ways to ensure that people are presented with choices about who gets to use their individual data for politics. And they have to treat device networks as common carriers for the public good.

Conclusion: Politics, Constituted by the IoT

If the IoT is going to be politically constitutive, could we craft its precepts and clauses in advance? The real value of the IoT is going to be in the data it collects from us. Like the feudal kings of centuries ago, technology firms and government agencies are used to expropriating that data in return for services and security (through questionable legal means and convoluted terms of service agreements). The IoT will greatly increase the value and volume of our data. And many of the device networks that make up the infrastructure will be always on, collecting behavioral data about both people and devices. In terms of timing, this is the moment to begin thinking about how such device networks can and should be used for political purposes. If we wish to maintain transparency in our democratic institutions, this is also the moment to demand more say in how our data—and data about us—gets used.

Constitutionally, we currently have a governance system that (among other things) sets the rules by which we elect people to represent our political interests. In the years ahead, much of that representative work will be done by devices—the everyday objects that render behavioral data when built with sensors and linked to a network. When we purchase a smart lightbulb and our home is suitably networked, the device will yield information about our consumption of goods, services, and energy that may inform wise public policy. This will influence how retailers and governments serve our communities, long after we have bought a lightbulb and regardless of whether we cast a vote.

It is obvious that regulating the IoT to protect personal privacy and political freedom will be challenging, but there is still time for citizens to step up and have a voice in how it is constructed and operated. To help shape the IoT responsibly and wisely, citizens must be made aware of the importance of cultivating its highest purpose as an information infrastructure for public life. The next Internet will be the material structure of our political constitution, reporting on our civic engagement, generating data for policy makers, and providing insight for lobbyists. So we must change our thinking—now—about what the IoT is and what it means for our political culture. Along with dreaming of consumer electronics and modern conveniences, we need to treat the IoT concretely as public information infrastructure.

We need a new pact between those who extract value from the IoT and those of us who generate the value. We should learn from recent surveillance and manipulation revelations but also set our eyes on the greater prize: a code of design and use for an IoT that serves the public good. A new constitution, one written for the public life and information infrastructure we are developing, should spell out the rights and responsibilities of the parties creating and using the IoT. It would provide a role for civil society actors—not just government and technology firms—in setting technology standards and sharing in the flow of data. Indeed, the "checks and balances" in this new constitution of infrastructure and information will need to refer to the ability of government agencies, civic groups, and private firms to both play with data and track each other's activities.

The new constitution would have to balance business interests with civic ones, and simultaneously supervise how spy agencies use networked devices. This next IoT will generate huge amounts of socially valuable information—especially if device networks are open and interoperable—for civic groups, health professionals, and scientific endeavors. Indeed, the IoT will be the primary means by which we reorganize social institutions and track public behavior. Citizens, the source of value for the IoT, need concrete assurances against abuse, and civic groups need a codified role in technology governance. The next Internet will be the greatest surveillance network ever established. Assembling it is the opportunity to settle on some basic forms of representation for the coming world of networked devices.

Good constitutions offer the terms under which we citizens agree to submit to an authority that is legitimate and not abusive. We need to consent to the IoT, because we will be surrendering our privacy for good. We will be submitting ourselves to data mining and behavioral analysis orders of magnitude more invasive, comprehensive, and valuable than we live with now. If we surrender our privacy to the IoT, we should get some protections and rights in exchange. Thus, if data is valuable and the primary value of the IoT, we need a social contract that turns on the notion that if we give up data, it must generate some public good. Data that flows from the IoT must concurrently generate value for innovative entrepreneurs and support civic values.

If we pledge our data to the IoT, the data should be turned into a public good at the source, by giving us the choice to share data with the civic groups we deem relevant. Realistically, it will be impossible to cut out governments and firms and fully guarantee our privacy. Our data will never be an exclusive resource. We will probably never win full control of our data. We probably will never get micropayments, as Jaron Lanier advocates, for the use of our data (Lanier 2013). Moreover, some citizens may prefer having the opportunity to express themselves politically through the data they generate rather than simply monetizing such a resource. The best we can hope for is the right to concurrently share our data with civic groups we want to support.

One founding principle should be that individuals have the right and ability to track where personally identifiable records end up. This is, of course, easier said than done. Even at this early stage of the IoT, it would be difficult for the manufacturer or operator of a device to list all the third-party vendors, market analysts, and government agencies that have access to the data the device has collected. Various privacy policies now give us choices to opt out of data sharing, but most privacy policies do not give users much privacy and do not actively reveal what third parties are making use of personally identifiable records. Down the road, we may have little choice about where our data ends up. Standards to determine access to data are now being set behind closed doors, defined by industry engineers arguing for secrecy and proprietary systems. There are already rival technology standards for different industry groups and governments (Clark 2015; Geiger and Preuschat 2015). If these arguments are successful, the next Internet will be even more personally intrusive, publicly unaccountable, and susceptible to unsupervised surveillance than the current one.

A basic step we can take toward preventing such abuses would be passing legislation that requires any connected device to be capable of disclosing a list of entities who benefit from its sensor data. Critics may argue this will be impossible. They will say that terms of service always get modified, ownership structures change over time, and the number of third parties paying for access to our data will lengthen over time. But the sheer complexity of the IoT will mean there are no functional limits to data collection or sharing. If the smart lightbulb we buy is able to relay some data up the network to other organizations, it should also be able to pull down a list of the corporate, government, and civic entities using that data. Subsequently, we need to make sure the IoT is designed for civic engagement, not simply government policy making and industry marketing. These days, it is customary for civil society groups to have an Internet strategy and a social media strategy, and a foundational part of such a strategy will be transparent records on what organizations are getting what data.

The protocols and algorithms that power the IoT will be a constitutional script for our political lives. For democracies, the IoT will transform how we as voters affect and interact with government—and how government touches and monitors our lives. Authoritarian governments will have their own uses for the IoT, and have already found ways to use this information to bolster their regimes. Many of the worst-case scenarios presented here are unavoidable, but if we act now, taking care with the standards set around the IoT, we can craft both technology and a functional policy that will serve us well at a constitutional level. The basis of a democracy is voluntary civic engagement. Before us is a final chance to integrate new devices into institutional arrangements we might all like. Indeed, such active civic engagement with the rollout of the IoT represents the last best chance for an open society.

Acknowledgments

I am grateful to have had the opportunity to present these ideas to the University of Pennsylvania Program on Democracy, Citizenship and Constitutionalism on September 17, 2015 and the Sociology of Culture, Organizations, Politics and Economics Seminar at the University of Washington on October 23, 2015. I gratefully acknowledge the support of the National Science Foundation ("EAGER CNS: Computational Propaganda and the Production/Detection of Bots," BIGDATA-1450193, 2014–16) and the support of the European Research Council ("Computational Propaganda: Investigating the Impact of Algorithms and Bots on Political Discourse in Europe," #648311, 2015–2020). Any opinions, findings, and conclusions or recommendations expressed in this material are those of the author and do not necessarily reflect the views of the National Science Foundation or European Research Council.

References

Bradley, Ryan. 2015. "Waze and the Traffic Panopticon." *New Yorker*, June 2. http://www.newyorker.com/business/currency/waze-and-the-traffic-panopticon.

Clark, Don. 2015. "Internet of Things Spurs Rival Consortia." *Wall Street Journal*, January 15. http://blogs.wsj.com/digits/2015/01/15/internet-of-things-spurs-rival-consortia/.

Dzieza, Josh. 2014. "Inside Keurig's Plan to Stop You from Buying Knockoff K-Cups." The Verge, June 30. http://www.theverge.com/2014/6/30/5857030/keurig-digital-rights-management-coffee-pod-pirates.

Geiger, Friedrich, and Archibald Preuschat. 2015. "Germany Moves Away From U.S.-Dominated IoT Standards Groups." *Wall Street Journal*, March 18.

Gibson, Rachel K., Philip E. N. Howard, and Stephen Ward. 2000. "Social Capital, Internet Connectedness and Political Participation: A Four-Country Study." Paper presented at the 18th World Congress of the International Political Science Association, Québec, Canada, August. http://citeseerx.ist.psu.edu/viewdoc/download?doi=10.1.1.11.8677&rep=rep1&type=pdf.

Hersh, Eitan. 2015. *Hacking the Electorate*. New Haven, Conn.: Yale University Press. http://www.cambridge.org/us/academic/subjects/politics-international-relations/american-government-politics-and-policy/hacking-electorate-how-campaigns-perceive-voters.

Howard, Philip N. 2005. *New Media Campaigns and the Managed Citizen*. New York: Cambridge University Press.

———. 2014. "Participation, Civics and Your Next Coffee Maker." *Policy and Internet* 6 (2): 199–201. doi:10.1002/1944-2866.POI356.

———. 2015a. *How Big Is the Internet of Things and How Big Will It Get?* Washington, D.C.: Brookings Institution. http://www.brookings.edu/blogs/techtank/posts/2015/06/8-future-of-iot-part-1.

———. 2015b. *Pax Technica: How the Internet of Things May Set Us Free or Lock Us Up*. New Haven, Conn.: Yale University Press.

Hulac, Benjamin. 2015. "Volkswagen Uses Software to Fool EPA Pollution Tests." *Scientific American*, September 15. http://www.scientificamerican.com/article/volkswagen-uses-software-to-fool-epa-pollution-tests/.

Lanier, Jaron. 2013. *Who Owns the Future?* New York: Simon and Schuster.

Losey, James, and Sascha Meinrath. 2016. "In Defense of the Digital Craftsperson." *Journal of Peer Production*, no. 9. http://peerproduction.net/issues/issue-9-alternative-internets/peer-reviewed-papers/in-defense-of-the-digital-craftsperson/.

McGinn, Daniel. 2011. "The Buzz Machine." Boston.com, August 7. http://archive.boston.com/business/articles/2011/08/07/the_inside_story_of_keurigs_rise_to_a_billion_dollar_coffee_empire/?page=6.

Murphy, Colum. 2015. "Uber Orders Drivers in China to Steer Clear of Taxi Protests." *Wall Street Journal*, June 13, sec. Business. http://www.wsj.com/articles/uber-orders-drivers-in-china-to-steer-clear-of-taxi-protests-1434181092.

Neff, Gina, and Dawn Nafus. 2016. *Self-Tracking*. Cambridge, Mass.: MIT Press.

Nickerson, David, and Todd Rogers. 2014. "Political Campaigns and Big Data." *Journal of Economic Perspectives* 28 (2): 51–74.

Norris, Pippa. 2000. *A Virtuous Circle: Political Communications in Postindustrial Societies*. Cambridge: Cambridge University Press. http://www.loc.gov/catdir/description/cam021/00023673.html http://www.loc.gov/catdir/toc/cam026/00023673.html.

Verhulst, Stefaan. 2015. "States Use Big Data to Nab Tax Fraudsters." Governance Lab @ NYU, March 5. http://thegovlab.org/states-use-big-data-to-nab-tax-fraudsters/.

CONTRIBUTORS

Rena Bivens (rena.bivens@carleton.ca) is an assistant professor of communication in the School of Journalism and Communication at Carleton University. Her research interrogates normative design practices that become embedded within media technologies, including social media software, mobile phone apps, and technologies associated with television news production. She is author of *Digital Currents: How Technology and the Public Are Shaping TV News* (University of Toronto Press, 2014).

Michael X. Delli Carpini (mxd@asc.upenn.edu) is dean of the Annenberg School for Communication. His research explores the role of the citizen in American politics, with particular emphasis on the impact of the mass media on public opinion, political knowledge, and political participation. He is coauthor of *After Broadcast News: Media Regimes, Democracy, and the New Information Environment* (Cambridge University Press, 2011).

Jennifer Earl (jenniferearl@email.arizona.edu) is a professor of sociology and (by courtesy) government and public policy at the University of Arizona. Her research focuses on social movements and the sociology of law, with emphases on the Internet and social movements, social movement repression, and legal change. She is coauthor of *Digitally Enabled Social Change* (MIT Press, 2011).

Thomas Elliott (telliott@fastmail.com) is a data scientist at GitHub. He has a PhD in sociology from the University of California, Irvine, where he studied the cultural consequences of social movements, especially as they relate to cultural attitudes about sexuality. He is coauthor of "Recipes for Attention: Policy Reforms, Crises, Organizational Characteristics and Newspaper Coverage of the LGBT Movement, 1969–2010" (*Sociological Forum*, 2016).

Deen Freelon (freelon@email.unc.edu) is an associate professor in the School of Media and Journalism at the University of North Carolina, Chapel Hill. His research covers two major areas of scholarship: political expression through digital media and data science and computational methods for analyzing large digital datasets. His work has appeared in *New Media & Society*; *Information, Communication & Society*; and the *International Journal of Communication*, among other publications.

Kelly Gates (kagates@ucsd.edu) is an associate professor in communication and science studies in the Department of Communication at the University of California, San Diego. Her research focuses on the critical analysis of digital media technologies, with a main emphasis on the politics and social implications of computerization, and particularly the automation of surveillance in the United States from the mid-twentieth century to the present. She is author of *Our Biometric Future: Facial Recognition Technology and the Culture of Surveillance* (NYU Press, 2011).

Philip N. Howard (philip.howard@oii.ox.ac.uk) is a professor of Internet studies and director of the Oxford Internet Institute at University of Oxford. His research investigates how new information technologies are used in both civic engagement and social control in countries around the world, with a focus on digital activism, information access, and modern governance in both democracies and authoritarian regimes. He is author of *Pax Technica: How the Internet of Things May Set Us Free or Lock Us Up* (Yale University Press, 2015).

Daniel Kreiss (dkreiss@email.unc.edu) is an associate professor in the School of Media and Journalism at the University of North Carolina, Chapel Hill. His research explores the impact of technological change on the public sphere and political practice. He is author of *Prototype Politics: Technology-Intensive Campaigning and the Data of Democracy* (Oxford University Press, 2016) and *Taking Our Country Back: The Crafting of Networked Politics from Howard Dean to Barack Obama* (Oxford University Press, 2012).

Ting Luo (t.luo@fsw.leidenuniv.nl) is a postdoctoral fellow at the Institute of Political Science at Leiden University. Her current research explores the impact of digital politics in authoritarian regimes by focusing on the role of digital media in political expression and participation. Her work has appeared in peer-reviewed journals such as *Problems of Post-Communism*, *Democratization*, and *International Journal of Communication*.

Helen Nissenbaum (helen.nissenbaum@cornell.edu) is professor of information science at Cornell Tech, where she is founding director of the Digital Life Initiative. Her research takes ethical and policy perspectives on science and engineering, relating to information technology, computing, digital media, and data science; topics have included privacy, trust, accountability, cybersecurity, and values in technology design. Her books include *Obfuscation: A User's Guide for Privacy and Protest* (with Finn Bruton, MIT Press, 2015) and *Privacy in Context: Technology, Policy, and the Integrity of Social Life* (Stanford University Press, 2010).

Beth Simone Noveck (noveck@thegovlab.org) is a professor in technology, culture, and society at New York University's Tandon School of Engineering, and director of the Governance Lab (The GovLab) and its MacArthur Research Network on Opening Governance. Her current research focuses on "people-led innovation," or the ability of communities and institutions to work together to solve problems more effectively and legitimately. She is author of *Smart Citizens, Smarter State: The Technologies of Expertise and the Future of Governing* (Harvard University Press, 2015) and *Wiki Government: How Technology Can Make Government Better, Democracy Stronger, and Citizens More Powerful* (Brookings Institution Press, 2009).

Jennifer Pan (jp1@stanford.edu) is an assistant professor of communication and an assistant professor, by courtesy, of political science and sociology at Stanford University. She works at the intersection of political communication and computational social science, focusing on questions of media censorship and surveillance in authoritarian regimes. Her work has appeared in peer-reviewed publications such as the *American Political Science Review*, *American Journal of Political Science*, *Comparative Political Studies*, *Journal of Politics*, and *Science*.

Lisa Poggiali (lpoggialipenn@gmail.com) is an anthropologist and postdoctoral fellow at the Price Lab for Digital Humanities at the University of Pennsylvania. Her research interests concern political and social life in colonial and postcolonial East Africa, especially with regard to urban development, migration, and technologies. Her work has been published in *Cultural*

Anthropology and *Africa*, and her research has been supported by Facebook, the National Science Foundation, the Social Science Research Council, and other institutions. She is currently working on a research project that explores how urban refugees in Nairobi, Kenya, navigate their online and offline worlds in an increasingly securitized city.

Daniela Stockmann (ds@daniestockmann.net) is professor of digital politics and media at the Hertie School of Governance. Her current research focuses on the impact of digitalization and its challenges for policy makers and citizens. Her most recent research project, funded by a Starting Grant of the European Research Council, explores the impact of the technological design of social media platforms on user behavior regarding politics. She is author of *Media Commercialization and Authoritarian Rule in China* (Cambridge University Press, 2013).

INDEX

ACKNOWLEDGMENTS

The chapters in this volume emerged from a series of projects dedicated to the theme of digital media and the future(s) of democracy. Thanks are owed to the founding director of the Andrea Mitchell Center (formerly the University of Pennsylvania's Center for Democracy, Citizenship, and Constitutionalism), Rogers Smith, its current director, Jeffrey Green, and administrator, Matthew Roth, as well as its faculty advisory board: Sigal Ben-Porath, Serena Mayeri, Eric Orts, Emilio Parrado, Sophia Rosenfeld, and Greg Urban. Thanks as well to David Grazian and Sandra González-Bailón for their helpful suggestions on possible contributors to this volume. Thanks are also owed to the chapter contributors themselves, as well as those who provided valuable feedback on the original versions of these chapters, including Jacques deLisle, Chloé Bakalar, Sandra González-Bailón, Nancy Hirschmann, Michael Horowitz, Marwan Kraidy, John MacDonald, Victor Pickard, and Lisa Poggiali. We also benefited from the comments of two anonymous University of Pennsylvania Press reviewers and the support of the press's editor-in-chief Peter Agree, acquisitions assistant Elizabeth Hallgren, managing editor Noreen O'Connor-Abel, and production editor Brian Ostrander. Finally, thanks to all who influenced our collective understanding of the interplay between digital media and democratic practice.